Traditionally, when the human sciences consider foundational issues such as epistemology and method, they do so by *theorising* them. Ethnomethodology, however, attempts to make such foundational matters a focus of attention, through direct *enquiry*. This book reappraises the significance of ethnomethodology in sociology in particular, and in the human sciences in general. It demonstrates how, through its empirical enquiries into the ordered properties of social action, ethnomethodology provides a radical respecification of the foundations of the human sciences, an achievement that has often been misunderstood. The chapters, by leading scholars, take up the specification of action and order in theorising, logic, epistemology, measurement, evidence, inference, the social actor, cognition, language and culture, and moral judgement, and underscore the ramifications for the human sciences of the ethnomethodologist's approach.

This is a systematic and coherent collection which explicitly addresses fundamental conceptual issues. The clear exposition of the central tenets of ethnomethodology is especially welcome.

Ethnomethodology and the human sciences

Ethnomethodology and the human sciences

Edited by

GRAHAM BUTTON

Principal Lecturer, Department of Applied Social Science,
Polytechnic South West, Plymouth

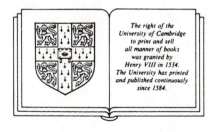

The right of the
University of Cambridge
to print and sell
all manner of books
was granted by
Henry VIII in 1534.
The University has printed
and published continuously
since 1584.

CAMBRIDGE UNIVERSITY PRESS
Cambridge
New York   Port Chester
Melbourne   Sydney

Published by the Press Syndicate of the University of Cambridge
The Pitt Building, Trumpington Street, Cambridge CB2 1RP
40 West 20th Street, New York, NY 10011, USA
10 Stamford Road, Oakleigh, Melbourne 3166, Australia

First published 1991

Printed in Great Britain at the University Press, Cambridge

British Library cataloguing in publication data

Ethnomethodology and the human sciences
1. Ethnomethodology
I. Button, Graham
305.80072

Library of Congress cataloguing in publication data

Ethnomethodology and the human sciences / edited by
Graham Button.
     p.   cm.
Includes bibliographical references and index.
ISBN 0 521 38048 0. – ISBN 0 521 38952 6 (paperback).
1. Ethnomethodology. I. Button, Graham.
HM24.E83 1991
305.8'001–dc 20   90–45310

ISBN 0 521 38048 0 hardback
ISBN 0 521 38952 6 paperback

WD

Contents

Contents

Contributors

BOB ANDERSON, Director, Rank Xerox, EuroPARC, Cambridge

DOUGLAS BENSON, Senior Lecturer in Sociology, Department of Applied Social Science, Polytechnic South West, Plymouth

GRAHAM BUTTON, Principal Lecturer in Sociology, Department of Applied Social Science, Polytechnic South West, Plymouth

JEFF COULTER, Professor and Chair of Sociology, Department of Sociology, Boston University, Massachusetts

HAROLD GARFINKEL, Professor of Sociology, Department of Sociology, University of California, Los Angeles, California

JOHN HUGHES, Professor of Sociology, Department of Sociology, University of Lancaster, Lancaster

LENA JAYYUSI, Chair of Communication Studies, Department of Communications, Cedar Crest College, Pennsylvania

JOHN LEE, Lecturer in Sociology, Department of Sociology, University of Manchester, Manchester

MIKE LYNCH, Associate Professor of Sociology, Department of Sociology, Boston University, Massachusetts

WES SHARROCK, Reader in Sociology, Department of Sociology, University of Manchester, Manchester

Preface

This book has its origins in discussions I had with Jeff Coulter and Lena Jayyusi whilst I was on fellowship leave at Boston University. Aspects of the turbulent relationship between ethnomethodology and sociology (and as we came to argue, the human sciences) perplexed us. The first was that despite the fact that ethnomethodology has, during thirty or more years of ethnomethodological studies, provided a respecification of foundational matters for sociology, in the main, the discipline blithely carries on as usual. For example, the indifference that is shown to the radicalising respecification of sociological method is astounding for a subject that, above others in the human sciences, attempts to ensure that its students are methodologically trained.

The second aspect concerns the fact that although ethnomethodology is, in part, the product of Garfinkel's problem of operationalising Parson's theory of social action in situated circumstances of action, and is thus firmly rooted and located within sociology, his problem leaks into the other human sciences. This is because, although the disciplines propose separate and sometimes exclusive topics of enquiry, they have conceptual, methodological, epistemological, theoretical, and other foundations in common. In many respects, however, the human sciences at large are unaware of the foundational respecification that is proposed by ethnomethodology and the significance, or at least the implication, this respecification has for them.

The third feature was that within sociology, yet also within other departments of the human sciences that have engaged some ethnomethodological studies (often those in conversation analysis), there persists an obstinate, at times almost wilfully malicious misunderstanding of an ethnomethodological study policy. As a consequence, ethnomethodology is either marginalised or is made to jump through analytic hoops that confound ethnomethodologists just as much as other onlookers.

This book addresses these matters with various degrees of emphasis. Its starting point is that ethnomethodological studies have provided a radical respecification of foundational matters across the human sciences, but that within sociology, in particular, and the human sciences in general, what this respecification can amount to has been too often either overlooked, ignored, or misunderstood. One reason for this may reside in the nature of ethnomethodological studies. They are unremittingly empirical, and the respecification of the foundations of the human sciences is embedded in their enquiries, and within their descriptions of detailed, embodied, situated action and interaction. Further, ethnomethodological studies do not resemble empirical studies as they are traditionally understood. On both counts the respecification may have been lost to the human sciences: first, foundational issues are not normally thought through via enquiry and the empirical inspection of the social world, they are normally theorised about; second, the form of enquiry may appear to be so strange that it is easier to assign it the role of a specialist hobby within the main stream of sociology than it is to come to grips with its elusive character.

It thus seems that the radical respecification of foundational matters for the human sciences needs to be cogently spelt out by ethnomethodologists if ethnomethodology's very serious intentions are to have the lasting impact on the human sciences that ethnomethodologists have envisaged. Ethnomethodology is not just another paradigm, another perspective, another theory, another method, a once cherished now discarded plaything, a new toy, a tarnished argument, a club to beat people with, or whatever other characterisation that comes to mind when considering other initiatives in the human sciences. Ethnomethodology breaks the mould of enquiry and topic, for unlike other ventures in the human sciences it takes foundational matters in the human sciences to be matters for enquiry as opposed to matters to be theorised.

The aim of this book is not, however, to overwhelm entrenched positions. It is simply to draw the lessons of ethnomethodological studies for foundational issues in the human sciences. There are a number of aspects to this, though. First, that when the human sciences address their foundations they cannot be excused if they fail to invoke an ethnomethodological respecification. Second, that researchers in sociology and the human sciences at large, who are encountering problems that originate in the articulation of their enquiries with reference to the specified foundations of the human sciences, may find in an ethnomethodological respecification a way through their problems. Third, that those who are marshalling for embarkation on their careers in the human sciences and hence, as yet, or hopefully as yet, have nothing to lose by breaking the fetters of specified thought, may pull on the chains to test their strength. Fourth, that the idea that rigorous enquiry into the social world may be constrained by the details of action found in that world, rather than by the specifications of that world in social science, may be advocated and advanced in the strongest, and most articulate ways possible.

I want to thank Jeff Coulter and Lena Jayyusi. Without our discussions and their generous hospitality this book would not have been started. Jeff Coulter also decisively started the ball rolling with his initial contribution. Wes Sharrock and Bob Anderson proffered crucial ideas at crucial junctures. Their advice and encouragement have been very important. Wes Sharrock also generously and courageously waded in during a very sticky moment in the compilation of the book. The editors at Cambridge University Press have been very supportive. In the beginning Sue Allen-Mills, then Penny Carter, and latterly Marion Smith and Judith Ayling: they asked the right questions, pointed out the problems and in so doing they helped to forge the appropriate solutions. Gillian Maude, as copy-editor, coaxed many a recalcitrant sentence to make sense.

In conclusion I also want to thank the authors, for they worked under unusual circumstances. In the main they were furnished with a topic and a brief which they had to vigorously prosecute within very tightly circumscribed parameters. It is the quality of their advocacy which provides the ethno-methodological respecification of their concerns.

GRAHAM BUTTON

1

Introduction: ethnomethodology and the foundational respecification of the human sciences

Graham Button

The vogue for fashionable ideas in sociology is fickle. Sociologists eagerly latch onto what appear to be new bodies of thought; they toy with them for awhile (organising symposium to discuss their significance for the discipline, giving over special editions of the discipline's journals to them, and proliferating texts that debate their merits), but then, often as not, sociology moves on. Giddens and Turner's (1987) *Social Theory Today*, is, in some respects, a partial history of fashionable thought in sociology. Many of the 'theories' they include once held the attention of the whole discipline, but now, by and large, whilst they still have their adherents, sociology is not as keenly focussed upon the distinctive issues they raise as it once was. The bloom of the 'new moment' fades, and it becomes part of the humus of 'social theory today' which generally nourishes the discipline.

The way in which sociology generates, and then accommodates, the advent of a 'new moment', tells us something about the business of sociology. Both the merchandisers and consumers of 'new moves' work that business in their testimony to what they constitute, even in their seeming mercurial character, as 'the stable properties of the discipline's foundations'. This means that despite the radical claims that often accompany the development of a 'new body of thought'[1] there is just as often a comforting conceptual, epistemological, and methodological familiarity to the arguments.

A reaction to what is considered to be a very radical and perhaps even foundational challenge in sociology, the vogue for 'feminist social theory', illustrates this. Goldthorpe (1983) addresses an argument (amongst others) which arises in 'feminist social theory': that the location of married women's class position through male heads of families is intellectual sexism. Goldthorpe attempts to accommodate this argument in a vigorous defence of what he calls 'the conventional view'. Although, the feminist argument was not as prominent as it is now when he conducted his original social stratification researches, he is, however (in his 1983 paper and later, Goldthorpe (1984), in a response to a critic of his defence of the 'conventional view', Stanworth (1984)) able to accommodate the main points of the feminist argument into

1

the existing conventional wisdom of sociology on social stratification theory which his own studies have, in part, been responsible for developing. Goldthorpe's achievement may have something to do with the fact that although the body of thought that grounds, for example, Stanworth's indictment against him and his ilk represents a 'new turn' in sociology, the charges are nevertheless, in great part, articulated in terms that are not all that 'new': as Goldthorpe had done before her, Stanworth provides theoretically generated constructs which stand proxy for people, and which engage in statistically represented action which stands proxy for embodied activity.

The debate about social stratification theory and research that I am referring to, enlivened the British Sociological Association's journal *Sociology* for three issues.[2] Despite appearances it was not, however, in one very important respect, really about a radical departure in sociology, nor, in the same respect, was it really the clash of alternatives. Rather, it was an argument over how to cut up the data. Although on the face of it, it seemed that the old blood of stratification theory and research was being replaced with new blood from the alternative body of feminist thought, it turned out that the protagonists had the same methodological orientation to gender as a sociological phenomenon: they took gender to be a non-problematically given possession of persons that can be non-problematically counted, and they thus all overtly oriented to the social world as a mathematically construable phenomenon. They were arguing over who should be counted, never questioning what they were doing in counting; never questioning what counting was doing for their findings or arguments. The mutual intractability of their arguments notwithstanding, they all stood on very familiar methodological territory. In this respect, although Stanworth challenges Goldthorpe's political integrity, his survey design and his findings, the epistemological and methodological foundations upon which the survey and findings were based are attested to in the epistemology and methodology of the challenge. The business of sociology was being transacted in the coinage of 'the stable properties of the discipline's foundations'.

Even the epistemology of 'feminist social theory' is very familiar. Indeed, 'that happy coinage' (Littlewood 1983), 'malestream sociology', although newly minted has a familiar ring to it. The claim is that malestream sociology generates and reproduces 'male knowledge' (sic) that legitimates the exploiting relationships between men and women and denies women knowledge of their real position within the social structure. The shock that such an argument could cause is, though, blunted by the prior claim made by Marxist sociologists that 'bourgeois sociology' reproduces 'bourgeois knowledge' that legitimises the exploiting relationships between the bourgeoisie and the proletariate and denies the proletariate knowledge of their real position within the social structure. The idea of 'malestream sociology' may be a new idea but the order of argument, and the order of knowledge about social arrangements that is claimed, is not.

Ethnomethodologists are familiar with having their arguments misunderstood. When they voice this objection it is commonly said that it is because they do not make themselves clear. Thus, I will anticipate a misunderstanding and try to be clear and stress that I am not criticising 'feminist social theory' here. I am acknowledging that feminist social theory is considered by some to be a 'new' and important turn[3] in sociology that provides a new and radical insight into the structural arrangements of society. This is the very reason I am using it to illustrate the point I am making. However, if we consider the way in which 'feminist social theory' articulates its insights which, it is argued, have important consequences for the way in which sociology generates its knowledge of society, and the way in which sociological knowledge of society should be oriented to,[4] we can see that despite the challenge, it is done *as* the business of sociology: it *theorises* the matter.

This is aptly illustrated with respect to the issue of 'patriarchy'. For example, Walby (1989a and 1989b) 'theorists patriarchy' in both an argument that underscores the importance of patriarchy for feminist thought, and (in Walby 1989a) in order to obviate the criticism that patriarchy cannot deal with historical and cross-cultural variation. Through *theorising*, it is argued that the problem can be attended to. In the process of theorising, other concepts that are often used to transact sociological business are used: 'power', 'domination', 'oppression', 'exploitation', 'marginalisation', and 'control'. Although some sociologists might dissent from the feminist argument, it is, thus, nevertheless, intelligible within the *mutually understood and mutually ratified* business of sociology. In theorising the structural arrangements of society as patriarchal, 'feminist social theory' testifies to 'the stable properties of the discipline's foundations', even in its challenge to the patriarchal nature of the generation of the discipline's knowledge of social structure.

To avoid the accusation of something I do not intend, because I have used 'feminist social theory' to illustrate the point, I will also illustrate it with reference to another 'new moment' in sociology: sociological concerns with 'post-modernism'. Post-modernism has recently become a popular matter in sociology. The 1990 British Sociological Association's Annual Conference organised a 'Key Questions Panel' on the question: 'Are advanced societies moving from a modernist towards a post-modernist culture?'[5] I am not going to address that question here, I just want to make the simple point that although a 'new' issue, with 'new' arguments for sociology, the question also trades in the very coinage of sociology. Not only does sociology continually pose the question of cultural transformation, but sociologists attempt to embody and accommodate the 'new' ideas within that tradition. For example, to the great relief of Marxists (Callinicos, 1990) the argument that we have moved to a post-modernist era turns out, in part, to be an argument they have challenged for years. To paraphrase Orwell, the eddies of history are being construed as tidal waves, for, as Callinicos argues, recent socio-economic developments (the so-called emergence of post-industrial society) can be understood within a classical argument concerning capital accumulation. Also, according to Callinicos, the post-structuralist critiques of Foucault and Derrida flow directly from the headwaters of the enlightenment and are therefore an old familiar idealist irrationalism. New lusty tongues engage, but we are invited to consider the familiarity of their sayings. We have, consequently, another new debate to boost the business of sociology.

Sociology can afford to play with 'new' ideas such as post-modernist and feminist[6] thought because the way in which it organises the questions does not undermine its foundational status as serious science, societal critique, or practical policy. The critiques and the proliferation of new ideas are organised in accordance with the properties of the 'stable foundations of sociology'. Theories such as 'feminist social theory', or theories about the cultural transformation of society, may challenge existing bodies of thought, but they do not challenge the very foundational act of theorising. Findings may be challenged but the methodological foundation through which those findings are generated remains intact.

Sociology is not isolated from the rest of the human sciences in this respect. Despite the arguments between bodies of thought in a discipline, and despite the claims made by the different human science disciplines to be addressing different phenomena, there is a common epistemological and methodological womb from which the bodies of thought in a discipline, and the human sciences in general, have sprung. This allows us to recognise a new face as a member of the family. The common womb is that of theorising, professional scepticism, and the application of mathematical reasoning to human phenomena. Theorising, the epistemology of professional scepticism, mathematicalising the social world, and other very related matters which are considered in this volume, are the foundations upon which the human sciences are built.

It is here, at the very foundations of the human sciences that a problem is encountered when considering ethnomethodology. Right from its very first introduction, sociology could not comprehend ethnomethodology because the foundations seemed to move whenever ethnomethodology was addressed. 'The stable properties of discipline's foundations' seemed to alarmingly shudder. Ethnomethodology was obviously a 'new turn'. Indeed it was once very fashionable to claim to be 'doing' ethnomethodology or, to be 'doing in' ethnomethodology. For ethnomethodologists, however, the often vitriolic attacks of the later group missed their mark because they really did not address the issues ethnomethodology was raising. They attempted to accommodate the arguments of ethnomethodology within the body of sociology and to nail ethnomethodology by reference to 'the stable properties of the discipline's foundations'. As I have tried to argue, 'new moments' in sociology can be incorporated into the business because they shore up the sociological enterprise even as they attack it. They do so by buying into the very sociological ways of addressing foundational issues, in *theorising* them. Ethnomethodology, however, never bought into the business of theorising, it was iconoclastic, it would not theorise foundational matters. This does not mean that it is not interested in foundational matters (this book testifies otherwise) but that it was interested in them in an alternate way: it wished to make them investigable, available for enquiry. In holding them up for scrutiny, and in working through the implications of that enquiry, ethnomethodology came to respecify foundational matters. Sharrock and Anderson put the matter very succinctly:

> In its own view, and, agreed, not everyone shares it, ethnomethodology has a 'foundational' relationship with more conventional sociology, i.e. it inquires into what they would regard as their foundations. These differences then work their way through such important aspects as the role of theory, the nature of data, the place of studies, and much, much more. (Sharrock and Anderson, 1987: 14)

In this idea of enquiry (as opposed to theorising) ethnomethodology bewildered, and still bewilders, many sociologists. An early exchange that took place at one of the first symposia on ethnomethodology, the Purdue Symposium on Ethnomethodology (Hill and Crittenden, 1968) and which is remembered by Mike Lynch in chapter 5, bears testimony to this. Ethnomethodologists seem to use the same terms as any other sociologist but not in the same way. The bewilderment that 'lay' persons display when they encounter sociology's strange uses of the terms that they are quite familiar with, and proficient in using, is experienced by sociologists when they encounter ethnomethodology. Mike Lynch reproduces a problem that arose concerning 'method'. One of the participants at the Purdue Symposium becomes frustrated at Garfinkel's seeming inability to state what he takes as 'evidence' in ethnomethodology. Garfinkel, and later on Sacks when he is asked a similar question about theory, obstinately turn to the social world in order to address the questions they are asked. This seems to be a typical ethnomethodological trick. When asked any questions about matters pertaining to epistemology, method, theory, meaning, rationality, thought, structure, action, and so much more, ethnomethodologists constantly appear to turn to specifics, to turn to some materials they have collected, or study they have conducted, in order to explain what they mean. Ethnomethodologists seem quite incapable of plainly stating how they see, for example, action, without reference to some study of action. Even that seems to be so damningly trivial for they end up talking about the structure of, for instance, greetings on, of all things, telephones, not *action*. This *is* bewildering for sociologists, because when sociology does address its foundations it does so by theorising them, not by reference to the details of accountable action. Sociology does not require reference to the details of accountable action in and as of the embodied practices of particular living breathing human beings – even though it is living breathing human beings who, in the details of what they do, are being sociable – when it considers how to apprehend sociality, or considers of what sociality consists, or attempts to actually describe sociality.

Other human sciences proceed likewise. For example, linguistics has often considered 'language' as somehow removed from its actual use by persons. As sociologists have discussed 'action' and 'actors' without reference to the fact that it is people who engage in embodied action in 'real time', so too has linguistics often discussed 'language' without reference to its use by speaking people. Model building in economics shuts out the confusing contingencies of real world irascible transactions. Anthropology has often glossed over the details of circumstantial action through having the occasioned account of the native informant stand as proxy for a society. Psychology would rather construct an experiment to, for example, examine people's reaction to authority and have subjects 'shock' accomplices 'to death', than enquire into how obedience to authority is relevantly built into their practical everyday lives, where random orders to administer people with electric shocks would be regarded with some scepticism. I will not go on, for this is not meant to be a crude indictment of methods in the human sciences. The point is that, by and large, when the human sciences examine such issues as method, theory, epistemology and the like, they do so without recourse to the situations and phenomena such matters are to apprehend. If sociology is bewildered by ethnomethodology, then in this respect ethnomethodologists are bewildered by sociology and the human sciences at large, for ethnomethodology cannot be free of circumstantial details.[7]

What ethnomethodologists mean by this is what was 'new' about ethnomethodology, and what continues to be 'new' about it, even if it is hardly intellectually fashionable to engage in ethnomethodological studies these days. Ethnomethodology *respecifies* sociology and the human sciences at large with respect to these details of what Garfinkel calls 'reflexively accountable action'. The attacks on ethnomethodology, and perhaps worse, its marginalisation within sociology, demonstrate to many ethnomethodologists just how fundamentally this respecification has been misunderstood, or has not even been seen to be relevant, by the main stream of sociological thought – despite ethnomethodology's inclusion in the humus of 'social theory today'.[8]

This book is about this respecification. It is not an introduction to ethnomethodology,[9] but an attempt to coherently and systematically develop what that respecification amounts to for the human sciences. In the second chapter, Harold Garfinkel addresses the idea of an ethnomethodological respecification. It is to make order 'in-and-as-of-the-workings-of-ordinary-society'. This idea begins in Garfinkel's exception to Parsons' specification of society in the results of human or social sciences investigation – Garfinkel takes Parsons as speaking for the human or social sciences in general. That is, for Parsons (and the human or social sciences), what order and society amount to can only be specified in the practices of the human sciences. As Garfinkel explains, ethnomethodology takes exception to this, and respecifies issues such as order and society in the details of their workings. That is, what they are is to be found not in the human sciences, but in their achievement. Garfinkel summarises the distinction with the term 'plenum'. For the human sciences there is no orderliness in the plenum, for ethnomethodology the phenomena of order are in and as of, Parsons' (the human sciences) plenum.

For Garfinkel, there is no beating about the bush. Ethnomethodology is not sociology as sociologists know it. Neither can it become part of what sociologists consider sociology to be. For Garfinkel it stands in contrast to what sociology is, it is incommensurate to sociology. He calls it an *alternate* sociology. This is a bitter pill for some to swallow, because it rules out many of the ways that 'new moments' in sociology have been traditionally accommodated. Ethnomethodology cannot be used by some, as they have used other arguments, as a corrective to the predominant 'positivist' methodology in the human sciences, because ethnomethodology treats their alternatives as it treats 'positivist' methodologies, as something to be enquired into. Ethnomethodology cannot be lumped together with other arguments it is taken as having a family resemblance to, it construes those arguments in different ways to their progenitors. Ethnomethodology cannot be used to solve problems 'constructively' specified, because ethnomethodology would constantly address the relationship between the construction and the problem, and never really get to grips with what is traditionally considered to be the problem. Ethnomethodology just cannot be built into sociology in the way in which other initiatives have, for it does not work the business of sociology by reference to the mutually constituted 'stable properties of the discipline's foundations' – it is indeed an alternate sociology.[10]

Ethnomethodology is an alternate sociology in terms of its *respecification* of order 'in-and-as-of-the-workings-of-ordinary-society'. This means, as discussed in chapter 7, that 'social actions are irreducibly events-in-a-social order and they cannot therefore be adequately identified independently of the social order in which they are embedded. Neither, on the other hand, can the social order in which the actions are sited be itself identified independently of the actions themselves'. An ethnomethodological respecification is, consequently, a respecification of action and order – order in-and-as-of-the-workings-of-ordinary-society.

In this volume I have attempted to consider what seem to be significant ways in which the human sciences, themselves, have specified action and order in their very foundations. The human sciences have specified action and order in 'theorising', 'logic', 'epistemology', 'method: measurement', 'method: inference and evidence', 'the actor', 'cognition', 'language and culture' and 'values and moral judgement'. The authors have addressed each specification and show what an ethnomethodological respecification of action and order amounts to in the ethnomethodological respecification of 'theorising', 'logic', 'epistemology', 'method', 'actor', 'cognition', 'language and culture' and 'values and moral judgement'. In respecifying these matters, ethnomethodology respecifies action and order as specified in the human sciences, and in so doing has constituted an alternate sociology.

Part of the reason for developing this book is that these matters have too often been summarily dealt with. Consequently I will not use this introduction to summarise the book, although I will make some brief general observations about its structure. First, the chapters consider action and order in the intellectual history of the foundational specification they address in order to show what an ethnomethodological respecification amounts to. Some of these specifications are particularly developed by other human science disciplines than sociology. In these instances although sociology is consistently examined and referenced, the specification is also examined with reference to that human science discipline; for example: cognition in psychology; language in linguistics; culture in anthropology, and linguistics, logic in linguistics and (dropping reference to 'science') philosophy, values and moral judgement in moral philosophy. Other specifications are germane across the human sciences, for example, theorising, epistemology, method, and the actor. Here, it is primarily by reference to sociology that the specifications are examined, though it is stressed that sociology is a vehicle for their consideration, which is as applicable to the human sciences as the specifications are.

Second, each of the chapters can be read independently. However, in as much as, together, they provide an ethnomethodological respecification of action and order as specified in the foundations of the human sciences, they are inextricably linked. This means that at places they inevitably shade into one another, and that there is also a self-explicating order to the chapters. Indeed, the book and the chapters have been designed to highlight both of these features, and there is a good deal of cross-referencing between the chapters.

Third, Harold Garfinkel originated ethnomethodology but two other names also consistently figure in this book: Ludwig Wittgenstein and Harvey Sacks. Although Garfinkel only makes passing reference to Wittgenstein, Garfinkel's concern with the entwining of method and finding resonates with important aspects of Wittgenstein's later philosophy. Harvey Sacks is probably most widely known as the originator of conversation analysis, and most will know of his work through his articles (some done in conjunction with Schegloff and others in conjunction with Schegloff and Jefferson), or the piece-meal publication of a few of his transcribed lectures. In order to understand the full force of Sacks' contribution to an ethno-methodological respecification, it is necessary to place these within the context of his transcribed lectures given between 1964 and 1972 at the University of California, Los Angeles and Irvine. In its entirety Sachs' work constitutes an alternate methodology which is an integral feature of an ethnomethodological respecification of foundational matters in the human sciences.

NOTES

1 I shall shortly take two examples of 'new bodies of thought' in sociology: 'feminist social theory' and 'post-modernism'. It should be apparent that the term 'new' must be understood relatively, for both bodies of thought have been lurking within sociology for some considerable time. In this respect 'new' may not so much be a matter of age, but truly a matter of fashion.

2 *Sociology*, 17 (4), 1983; *Sociology*, 18 (2), 1984, and *Sociology*, 18 (4), 1984.

3 This is illustrated again by the British Sociological Association's journal *Sociology* which in Vol. 23, No. 2, debates the concept of 'patriarchy' for the very reason that 'feminist social theory' is considered to be an important 'new turn' in sociology. As one of the contributors puts it: 'Because of the important theoretical consequences of feminist thought for sociology as a discipline 'patriarchy' has also achieved widespread sociological usage' (Waters 1989: 193).

4 See Ramazanoglu (1989) for a recent discussion, especially pp. 57–90.

5 See Lash (1990) for a consideration of this question.

6 I am not implying that the practical matter of feminist politics is a plaything. Hopefully those politics would continue should the British Government disband all sociology departments, in the same way that the hopes that Marxists have for class struggle in capitalist society is not dependent upon the debates that occur in the academic community. The point is that, although on the face of it a feminist challenge to 'malestream sociology' seems to be a radical shaking of the discipline's foundations, it is *not,* because, irrespective of the desirability of practical feminist politics, 'feminist social theory' as a sociological development does not challenge the foundational presuppositions of how to orient to and study sociality. In this respect it is not a challenge to the very business of sociology, the challenge of 'feminist social theory' is conducted *as* the business of sociology. Sociology is accustomed to this sort of debate, it trades in it, and consequently, it can not only tolerate it, it can actively promote it.

7 Strictly speaking I should say that ethnomethodology is not so much bewildered but *indifferent.* It is not that ethnomethodology is putting up alternatives, but that if sociology ignores the details of accountable action, then ethnomethodology is showing that certain things follow.

8 See Giddens and Turner (1987). The idea that ethnomethodology is *theory*, however, would perplex many ethnomethodologists.

9 There have been a number of very mystifying introductions to ethnomethodology. Three introductions, however, avoid the problem: Heritage (1984), Sharrock and Anderson (1986a) and Benson and Hughes (1983).

10 I do not mean to imply by this, nor by preceding remarks that have questioned the order of 'new' in sociology, that unlike other developments, ethnomethodology does not have any sociological antecedents. Of course, ethnomethodology is firmly rooted in sociology, even though it proposes an alternate sociology. Garfinkel directly confronts Parsons, in part, utilising selected questions he has culled and adapted from Schutz. Ethnomethodological worries about sociology develop in the process of trying to do sociology through investigation and enquiry. See Heritage (1984) and Sharrock and Anderson (1987), who discuss this matter at length.

2

Respecification: evidence for locally produced, naturally accountable phenomena of order*,[1] logic, reason, meaning, method, etc. in and as of the essential haecceity of immortal ordinary society, (I) – an announcement of studies[2]

Harold Garfinkel

At a recent symposium of the American Sociological Association celebrating the 50th anniversary of the publication of *The Structure of Social Action* (Parsons, 1937),[3] Jeffrey Alexander called attention to the book's continuing influence upon professional sociology. In the generosity of the celebration, he situated ethnomethodology's programme in the agenda of analytic sociology and offered ethnomethodology good advice.

From his place within the agenda, he identified for all ethnomethodologists the studies they do, advised them of studies they should do, and offered friendly advice about emphases they cannot avoid. In thoughtful reflections, he praised ethnomethodological studies for carrying on with the problem of social order that Parsons specified, and with which he instituted formal analytic sociology. In a spirit of generosity Alexander offered ethnomethodology an olive branch. Rather than pursuing their programme of current studies – which in another context he has criticised as 'individualistic' – ethnomethodologists should celebrate *The Structure of Social Action* by returning to the analytic fold.[4]

I disagree. There are good reasons for ethnomethodological studies to specify the production and accountability of immortal, ordinary society – that miracle of familiar organisational things – as the local production and natural, reflexive accountability of the phenomena of order*. Among those reasons is making discoverable *one* of those phenomena of order*, but only one, namely what analysis incarnate in and as ordinary society, as practical action's locally and interactionally produced and witnessed embodied details, could adequately be.

Although both formal analytic sociology and ethnomethodology address produced phenomena of order*, and although both seek to specify the production and accountability of immortal ordinary society, a summary play on Durkheim's aphorism reminds us of their differences.

For *The Structure of Social Action*, Durkheim's aphorism is intact: 'The objective reality of social facts is sociology's fundamental principle'.

For ethnomethodology the objective reality of social facts, in that, and just how, it is every society's locally, endogenously produced, naturally organised, reflexively accountable, ongoing, practical achievement, being everywhere, always, only, exactly and entirely, members' work, with no time out, and with no possibility of evasion, hiding out, passing, postponement, or buy-outs, is *thereby* sociology's fundamental phenomenon.

In his talk, Alexander properly reminded the profession that in *The Structure of Social Action* Parsons gave to professional sociology a way to find and exhibit the real production and accountability of immortal, ordinary society. Concerned with, and profoundly reasoned about generic, massively recurrent properties of human action in and as the properties of populations, *The Structure of Social Action* set an example for formal analytic sociology, and has become emblematic of analytic sociology and of the world-wide social science movement.

Ethnomethodology has its origins in this wonderful book. Its earliest initiatives were taken from these texts.[5] Ethnomethodologists have continued to consult its texts to understand the practices and the achievements of formal analysis in the work of professional social science.

Inspired by *The Structure of Social Action* ethnomethodology undertook the task of respecifying the production and accountability of immortal, ordinary society. It has done so by searching for, and specifying, radical phenomena. In the pursuit of that programme, a certain agenda of themes, announced and elaborated in *The Structure of Social Action*, has over the years offered a contrasting standing point of departure to ethnomethodology's interest in respecification. Found throughout the book, faithful to the book, and used by ethnomethodologists to read the book, these themes brought the book's materials together as its coherent and researchable argument that the real society was available to the policies and methods of formal analytic sociology. With these policies, concrete society could be investigated and demonstrated to indefinite depths of detail, with no actual setting excused from jurisdiction, regardless of time, place, staff, locality, skills, or scale.

In the brief remarks that space allows, I must reduce Parsons' agenda of themes from an argument to a recitation of slogans.

Endlessly seminal was sociology's stunning vision of society as a practical achievement. Affiliated to this vision were several technical specifics. A first one was the problem of social order formulated by Hobbes. Another, inexorably tied to it, were theorising's constantly undertaken and unfinishable tasks of requiring that the vexed problem of the practical objectivity and practical observability of practical actions and practical reasoning, *because* it was vexed, serve as the standing source and grounds for the adequacy of theorising's claims. Third, in every actual case of inquiry a priority of relevance was assigned, no matter how provisional, to empirical studies to specify the problem of social order's identifying phenomena. Altogether, sociology's standing job was to specify the issues that identified as society's workings – real workings, actual workings, and evidently – the ongoing production and accountability of ordinary society.

Deep policies and technical methods of theorising were stated explicitly with which to specify real, immortal, ordinary society in the methods of its production, and in the conditions of their effectiveness, as structures of practical action. Administering the unit act as if it were constitutive of practical action was one of these methods of theorising. Administering an in-principle difference between common sense knowledge of social structures and scientific knowledge of social structures was another. Theorising was directed to design and administer policies with which to specify real society as observable structures of practical action.

These policies were accompanied by concerns to design, develop, clarify, correct, criticise, and administer methods of constructive analysis. For one example, a recurrently used method consists of designing a formal scheme of types, giving their formal definitions an interpreted significance with which to develop and explain the orderly properties of the types as ideals, and then assigning the properties of the ideals to observable actions as their described properties of social order.

The book's policies of theorising, and methods of constructive analysis, emphatically provided for issues of immortal society's observability. Among these policies one policy dominated all the rest: the distinction between *concreteness* of activities and actions provided for *analytically*. The distinction inhabits every line of *The Structure of Social Action*. When the book was written, the distinction was omniprevalent in professional sociology and the social sciences, and it remains so today.

I shall call actions provided for *concretely* that Parsons provided for with his distinction, Parsons' *plenum*. His plenum is a constituent part of the pair, actions concretely and actions analytically. His plenum was administered as a constituent of the pair.

Parsons needed a plenum. He was not the first author ever to need one and he was not alone. Not only in the social science movement, but everywhere in intellectual history, authors have made use of plenums. Authors have designed plenums with which the tasks of recording, reading, writing, collecting, picturing, speaking about, remembering, marking, signing real world specifics, were accompanied by provisions for worldly things left over and worldly things left out, real world matters that remained unremarked. Webster tells us 'Plenum' has been used to speak of 'a space every part of which is full of matter – as opposed to vacuum', 'fullness', 'a general or full assembly', 'the condition of being absolutely full in quantity, measure, or degree; a condition of fullness, completion'. 'Plenty!' puts the case according to Webster. So does 'Plenarty'. So does 'Plenilunium'.

For what I want to get at, the question is *not*, what does plenum mean? And

Not, how is plenum to be defined? But *who needs a plenum*? I don't mean it is not needed. I mean *who has had what need of a plenum*? By whom has a plenum been needed? For what? To do what *with it*?[6]

William James' plenum, the blooming, buzzing confusion, was needed to specify distinctive generic properties of perception and attention. Alfred North Whitehead needed common sense that would sit in judgement on every version of itself. Edmund Husserl used his hyle as his plenum with which essential, invariant structures of consciousness – the noesis–noema structures – could be *found* and made findable without so assigning to a transcendental phenomenological ego its jobs that perception's things would have been lost. The circumstantiality of signs, another of Husserl's plenums, was needed to carry out his policy of the ideality of meaning. A beautiful plenum is Colin Cherry's soundful, noisy assemblages in, and with which, intelligible and remembered 'sounded doings' are demonstrable phenomena. Experimental perception's noisy assemblages – *its* plenum – permit published experimental studies of selective attention to be collected as specifications of the 'cocktail party effect'. A recent and compelling plenum is found in the intractability of common sense that exhibits itself in furiously numerous, but so far unsuccessful attempts in the computing industry to design computable representations of ordinary human jobs.

With his concreteness/analysis pair, Parsons demonstrated[7] there was no orderliness in concrete activities. With *his* plenum, Parsons specified the analytically empty concreteness of organisational things. With Parsons' plenum the concreteness of organisational things is not yet real organisational things. Nor is it yet organisational things produced according to, let alone consisting of, methodic procedures – call these 'actual' organisational things – nor is it yet organisational things evidently.

Established analytic sociology's big prize – and Parsons' big prize – is immortal ordinary society, and not just any imaginable society but (i) real society, the society available in coherent structures of inexhaustible details; (ii) actual society, society for just how it is produced, with just what causal texture; and (iii) real and actual society, evidently, i.e. real and actual society represented in claims that are offered by analysts for their truth and correctness, for their availability to correctability, for the claimed work of a socially organised setting's production and accountability that is available to autonomous assessments of truth, correctness, relevance, factivity, motivation and other adequacies.

For Parsons, real and actual society, evidently, *that* prize is *not* to be found in the concreteness of things. Many interesting things *are* to be found in the concreteness, but *not* real, immortal society. Instead, real immortal society is *only* specifiable as the achieved results of administering the policies and methods of formal, constructive analysis. Real society is specified distinctively, and in detail, and with everything that detail *could be* in the formal generic structures of practical actions. These are obtainable with the policies and methods of constructive analysis. These policies and constructive methods also furnish the correctable warrant for analysts' claims. Analysts' claims offer constructive methods to certify their status as objective knowledge of the work of producing accountable, invariant, essential structures of practical action, the great recurring, immortal, comparable structures of ordinary activities.

Orderliness in the plenum pose for formal sociological analysis[8] its tasks of detecting and specifying that orderliness, and demonstrating it in massively recurrent, distinctive, essential, invariant identifying details of formally analysed structures of practical action.

To review: from *The Structure of Social Action* we could learn there was no orderliness in the plenum. We could learn from *The Structure of Social Action* how to distinguish between actions provided for concretely, and actions provided for analytically, and we could learn how to administer this distinction over the vicissitudes and local contingencies of research and argument.

We learned from *The Structure of Social Action* that specifics in producing the phenomena of order are found, collected, described, explained, and demonstrated by administering a distinction between concreteness of organisational things on the one hand, and real society that methods of constructive analysis would provide on the other; that *only* methods of constructive analysis could provide – *only and entirely* – for any and every orderliness whatsoever, for every one of the endlessly many topics of order, meaning, reason, logic, or method; and for every achievement of any of these *topics* of order* after they were prepared for inquiry by formal analytic sociology by being respecified as *phenomena* of order* that are achieved in and as analytically represented generic workings of immortal, ordinary society.

Parsons' thematic agenda was in every respect answerable to the observability of immortal, ordinary society. It was therein everywhere sensitive to the difference between the concreteness of actions, and actions construed analytically. In *The Structure of Social Action*'s thematic agenda, and, in that the agenda was everywhere answerable to the distinction for all issues of adequacy, Parsons was spokesman for the social science movement. He was not its leader in this respect. And of course he did not originate the distinction. But with that distinction he spoke for the world-wide movement of professional social science which accords the distinction unanimous endorsement. In all these respects and, most pointedly, in respect of unanimous agreement that there is no order in the plenum, Parsons talked on behalf of professional sociology, and of the world-wide social science movement.

Ethnomethodological studies, in which I include of course, conversational analytic studies, *learned* to take serious exception without sacrificing issues of 'structure' and the 'great recurrencies', and now with results in hand they *take* serious exception.

Twenty years after *Studies in Ethnomethodology* there exists, as the work of an international and interdisciplinary company, a very large corpus of empirical studies of practical actions, so-called 'naturally organised ordinary activities'. These studies demonstrate locally produced, naturally organised, reflexively accountable phenomena of order*, in and as of Parsons' plenum, in detail.

In order that concreteness not be handed over to generalities, I shall mention several studies by ethnomethodologists. These may remind the reader of just what concreteness has been used by Parsons and the social sciences, among indefinitely many analytic arts and sciences of practical action, to insist upon.

Talking medicines among the Kpelle of Liberia so as to be heard by those who need to hear it that one is properly concealing secrets (Bellman, 1975 and 1981).

Mathematicians work of proving the schedule of 37 theorems and their proof accounts that make up, as instructions, Gödel's proof (Livingston, 1986).

The work of a local gang in neurochemistry lab making artifact recognisable and demonstrable in electron microscopic records of axon destruction and regrowth in rats' brains (Lynch, 1985).

Designing and administering a medical school curriculum in pediatrics, and evaluating the competence with that curriculum of medical students, interns, and residents (Robillard and Pack, 1976–82).

Administering federally funded mental health programmes in the US Pacific Trust territory, specifying the way these programmes design and administer, staff, finance, care for and analyse records with which to track in specific social and medical pathologies of Oceania (Robillard and Colleagues, 1983, 1984, 1986a, 1986b, and 1987).

Teaching English as a second language to pre-school children from immigrant families (Meyer, 1985 and 1988).

Teacher and students concertedly arranging for and spotting trouble-in-the-making in an inner city high-school classroom (MacBeth, 1987).

Providing to the teacher of an article on Goethe's theory of prismatic colour *this*: The work of reading the text *consists* of an instructable reproducible demonstration of Goethe's theory of prismatic colour. The work of reading the text exhibits in and as of the text, as an *in vivo* course of revealed details of a witnessable demonstration, Goethe's theory of prismatic colour (Bjelic and Lynch, 1989).

Finding in an afternoon the sequentially organised character of an experiment in undergraduate laboratory chemistry (Schrecker, in press).

Understanding among Australian aborigines learned by an American anthropologist by helping them document their sacred sites so that they can withstand legal controversies instituted by corporate interests (Liberman, 1986).

The use by parties at work (1) in the offices of an enterpreneurial firm in the fast-food business, and (2) in the operations room at the London air traffic control centre, of the on-site 'notion' of a working division of labour as a local means in each of interrelating and explicating the activities to be found there (Anderson, Sharrock, and Hughes, 1987).

Learning to play improvised jazz piano (Sudnow, 1978).

Talking the convict code in an inmate half-way house (Wieder, 1974)

Undergraduates achieving the definiteness of sense and the coherence of a text's details in reading introductory sociology (Morrison, 1976).

Collaborative writing at a computer on a Grade-One classroom collected and elucidated as two related production problems: where am I? and what next? (Heap, 1986a, 1986b).

Designing a Xerox copier to assure complaint-free operation by office personnel (Suchman, 1987).

Teaching civil procedure to first-year students in one of the country's leading law schools (Burns, 1986).

And then there are the seminal studies of Harvey Sacks. Among these are his extraordinary studies of conversation. Sacks, and many colleagues, established a domain of conversational phenomena that was unsuspected until their work developed it (Sacks, 1964–1972, Sacks, 1989, and Sacks, Schegloff and Jefferson, 1974).

I have listed a very small number of titles in the corpus of published studies that report radical phenomena.[9]

When I speak about the phenomena that they report as radical phenomena, what am I claiming about these phenomena? What is ethnomethodological about these studies and their results?

First, the phenomena they report are available to policies of ethnomethodology – for example, they are available under the exercise of 'ethnomethodological indifference' and they are available under a respect for the unique adequacy requirement of methods. But they are specifically *not* available to the policies and methods of constructive analysis. These phenomena cannot be recovered with *a priori* representational methods. They are not demonstrable in the established terms of classic studies.

Second, the social science movement, in carrying out its research agenda, as a systematic feature of that agenda, depends upon their existence as omni-relevant details of their agenda and makes use of them, finds them essentially unavoidable and essentially without remedy, but finds them specifically uninteresting and ignores them.

Third, the reported phenomena cannot be reduced by using the familiar reduction procedures in the social science movement without losing those phenomena.

Fourth, the reported phenomena are only inspectably the case. They are unavailable to the arts of designing and interpreting definitions, metaphors, models, constructions, types, or ideals. They cannot be recovered by attempts, no matter how thoughtful, to specify an examinable practice by detailing a generality.

Fifth, they were discovered. They are only discoverable and they cannot be imagined.

Sixth, they specify 'foundational' issues, in and as the work of a 'discipline' that is concerned with issues of produced order in and as practical action.[10]

Seventh, these phenomena are locally and endogenously produced, naturally organised, reflexively accountable in and as of details, and therein they provide for everything that details could possibly be.

Eight, not only do these phenomena provide for *details* as a topic of order*, but any, and every, topic of logic, order, reason, meaning, or method is eligible for respecification as locally achieved phenomena of order*. Not only the topic of *detail*, but every topic order* is to be discovered and is discoverable, and is to be respecified and is respecifiable, as only locally and reflexively produced, naturally accountable phenomena of order*. These phenomena of order* are immortal, ordinary society's commonplace, vulgar, familiar, unavoidable, irremediable *and* uninteresting 'work of the streets'.

To summarise: it is ethnomethodological about these studies that they show for ordinary society's substantive event, in material contents, that, and just how, members concert their activities to produce and exhibit the coherence, cogency, analysis, consistency, order, meaning, reason, methods – which are locally, reflexively accountable orderliness – in and as of their ordinary lives together, in detail.

A very large corpus shows in and as of Parsons' plenum, in detail, contrary to the entirety of the social science movement, in incommensurably asymmetrically alternate sociology, the local production and natural, reflexive accountability of immortal, ordinary society really, actually, evidently, and these ordinarily. A development of many years work in ethnomethodology and conversational analysis, these studies are founded on, they continue, and they depend upon, the work of a large company of colleagues.

It is the company's achievement that their studies, by composing a current serious situation of inquiry, provide access to a technical domain of organisational phenomena. These phenomena were not suspected until the studies established their existence, provided the methods to study them, and provided what methods and their accompanying issues of relevance, evidence, adequate description, observability, validity, teachability, and the rest could be.

Distinctive emphases on the production and accountability of order* in and as ordinary activities identify ethnomethodological studies, and set them in contrast to classic studies, as an incommensurably alternate society. My purpose in these remarks has been to sketch these emphases, and to identify the fact of a company whose existence furnishes these emphases their technical details, assures their consequentiality for the tasks in ethnomethodological inquiries of discovering the identifying issues of the problem of social order, and grounds my claims in the real-world practices of their craft.

NOTES

1 When, in this chapter, order* is spelled with an asterisk, but only then, it serves as a convenient proxy. I use order* as a marker to hold a place for any of the endless topics in intellectual history that speak of logic, purpose, reason, rational action, evidence, identity, proof, meaning, method, consciousness, and the rest. Any of the topics that order* is proxy for should be read with an accompanying suffix: (order*) – in-and-as-of-the-workings-of-ordinary-society. Then the *topic* of order* would be understood to speak of a *phenomenon* of order*, a practical achievement. When order is spelled without an asterisk it is used in its textually appropriate vernacular or technical meaning.

2 Based on my talk, 'The Seriousness of Professional Sociology' at the Annual Meetings of the American Sociological Association, Chicago, August, 1987. (See endnote 3). Prior versions were published in the *DARG Newsletter*, Fall, 1987, 3 (2), pp. 5–9; and in *Sociological Theory '88*, 6 (1), pp. 103–9.

3 Section on Theoretical Sociology, 'Parsons' *The Structure of Social Action*: Three Views Fifty Years On', Bernard Barber, Chair. Annual Meetings of the American Sociological Association, Chicago, August, 1987. I wish to thank Bernard Barber for his invitation to speak at this celebration.

4 Alexander's extended argument is found in Alexander (1988).

5 Of course, in deliberately reconstructive readings of them.

6 Obviously, much turns on what plenum is taken to mean. Having rejected the first two questions – 'What does plenum mean?' and 'How is plenum to be defined?' and insisting on this one: 'Who has had what need of a plenum?', I must risk the charge of wilfully having my way with it, no matter what way it is, by having left specifically unspecified what plenum is to mean. Temporarily, and just here, that is just what I want to do. To define and explain plenum would introduce a distracting excursion. I don't want to take up those questions, but insofar as we can, without taking up those questions, I want to ask, 'Who has used the notion of a plenum and for what?' The sense of what plenum means will emerge as I document that.

7 I use demonstrated respectfully, without irony, as Parsons' version of what he was doing with the pair. With his pair he took it to be showable, and to have been shown, he demonstrated, there was no orderliness in the plenum. Not only for his part, but on behalf of professional sociology, *and* as a stand-in for the analytic social sciences. For *their* part, with their pairs, with their administered distinctions, they are able to demonstrate the same things.

Caution: That does mean that *I* figure there is no orderliness in concrete activities. Because I say Parsons and the analytic social sciences demonstrate and demonstrated I fear that this will be treated as my real position and be used to read my subsequent text. In the rest of the paper I say otherwise. I must caution the reader *not* to use that reading to subsequently understand the remainder of my argument, which argues just the opposite.

8 As well as for the social sciences, among other countlessly many arts and sciences of practical action.

9 I regret that this list will lend itself to finding in it persons and studies that are not mentioned. I apologise to the company of ethnomethodologists for not knowing

how to spare them the unfair consequences of reading the list as a roll call. Whoever has tried to do ethnomethodological studies would be thereby equipped to recognise that the list testifies to a division of labour, and that the list is not a bibliography of all eligible, possible, relevant, or consequential work.

10 In 1987 I was invited by Richard Heyman and Robert Seiler to write an article for their *DARG Newsletter* to mark twenty years of work since the publication of *Studies in Ethnomethodology*. The materials in that reflection were later presented at the fiftieth anniversary celebration of *The Structure of Social Action* and published in *Sociological Theory '88*. In *Sociological Theory '88* the work was collected with the theme of that work's achievement, and was retitled as the claim that ethnomethodological studies offered evidence for locally produced, naturally accountable phenomena of order*, logic, reason, meaning, method, etc. in and as of the unavoidable and irremediable haecceity of immortal, ordinary society. The article in *Sociological Theory '88* reported: Part I, *An Announcement of Studies*. Part II, *The Curious Seriousness of Professional Sociology*, was presented during 1987 and 1988 in seminars and colloquia at UCLA, Boston University, The Ecole des Hautes Etudes, and the University of Wisconsin. Part III, *Instructed Action* was worked out in classes and seminars at UCLA in 1986 to 1988 and presented at colloquia during 1987 and 1988 at Temple University, the University of Oklahoma, and the Western Behavioral Science Institute. Part IV, *Pairs of Incommensurable, Asymmetrically alternate Technologies of Social Analysis* was presented at The First International Conference on Understanding Language Use in Every Life, 23–6 August 1989, under the auspices of the Discourse Research Analysis Group, The University of Calgary, Alberta, Canada. (To be published in the conference proceedings edited by Richard Heyman and Robert Seiler.)

3

Logic: ethnomethodology and the logic of language
Jeff Coulter

1 Introduction

In this discussion, I seek to consider various aspects of the historical divorce of Logic from a concern for the details of *praxis*, and the contemporary reassertion of that concern in various quarters. My purpose-built history will be designed to specify the important place of ethnomethodological studies within the current respecification of the proper object of logical inquiry broadly conceived.

2 Logic and practical activities: historical connections

In their splendid overview of the development of Logic, the Kneales address themselves explicitly to a range of relationships which obtained between everyday practices and the emergence of logical formalisms:

[I]t is argued that some logical thinking had been done before Aristotle which had its source in the criticism of everyday factual argument, and that this helped to give rise to a tradition independent of Aristotle, that of the Megarians and the Stoics. *The first tentative steps towards logical thinking are taken when men try to generalize about valid arguments and to extract from some particular valid argument a form of principle which is common to a whole class of valid arguments.* (W. and M. Kneale, 1962: 12, emphasis added)

Everyday discourse, and not only everyday factual arguments, generated various puzzles which prompted logical dissection prior to Aristotle (Kneales, 1962). The contemplation of such conceptual puzzles was developed by the Megarian school founded by a disciple of Socrates called Euclides. That this school enjoyed some success is attested to in the chronicles of Diogenes Laertius. The Megarians were widely reputed to be skilful in verbal controversies. Plato and Aristotle used the alternative designation for the Megarians, 'Eristics', to impute frivolity in argument, but the Kneales point out that Philo and Cronus, two Megarian thinkers after Aristotle, 'showed a genuine understanding of logical problems' (Kneales, 1962: 15). A second connection between logical formalism and social *praxis* was to be found in the sophistic 'amusements', noted by Plato, in which a group of performers gave public exhibitions of techniques of argumentation. These performers, the Sophists, deployed fallacious arguments having a misleading but compelling resemblance to valid arguments, whereby they would 'prove' outrageous points such that, e.g. the father of Ctesippus was a dog, or that no-one could ever tell a lie. The Kneales interestingly propose that many of these sophistic arguments could have been used in law courts to confuse juries faced with sound arguments: many instances from the *Euthydemus* or the *De Sophisticis* could have had such a use. Moreover, the practice of setting logical puzzles to juries was documented by Aulus Gellius (Gellius, *Noctes Atticae*, v. 10, cited in Kneales, 1962: 14). A third connection relates logical formalism to public debating contests. Here, Aristotle's *Topica* is essentially a handbook for contestants, and the final book adduces specific instructions for both questioner and answerer in such contests (Ross, 1958: Kneales, 1962: 13 and 33 *et seq*).

3   From formalisation to mathematicisation

Formalisation in Logic consists originally in the codification of rules of valid inference in arguments. The abstraction of *winning* argumentation forms becomes the major preoccupation of the Logicians, and the development of the *syllogism* as a specification of a 'formal structure' for valid argument stands out as Aristotle's most famous achievement in Logic: the rule-governed relationship between two or more 'premisses' and 'conclusion' in valid arguments. Various complications were later explored thoroughly: Aristotle himself developed the concept of the *enthymeme*, in which an argument rests upon *unstated*, but nonetheless assignable, premisses; and initiated the inclusion of modal terms such as 'necessary' and 'possible' in syllogistic schemes of inference, in his *Prior Analytics*.

A preoccupation with syllogistic inference exercised Logicians for centuries. In the Middle Ages, we encounter the first addition to syllogistic schemata of 'subaltern moods' and, eventually, we discern increased attention to the internal structural configurations of one of the components of a syllogism, the *proposition*. Rules for using logical connectives ('and', 'or', 'if', 'then', etc.), and rules for representing the conceptual content of propositions in the most perspicuous manner, the better to facilitate accuracy of deduction, required specialist attention. Subjects and predicates, quantifiers ('all', 'some', 'none', 'each', etc.), negation terms, modal terms, and an array of particular grammatical categories were analysed. Any identifiable component of a propositional form which had any apparent bearing upon considerations of truth-value, generated study aimed at specifying their general logical function. Aristotle had, before the development of algebra, employed letters to express generality, but it was Leibniz (1646–1716) who first articulated the idea of using a formal symbolism in logical studies. In pursuit of an *ars combinatoria*, or general theory of 'arrangements of elements' in constructing a logical formalism, Leibniz aspired to produce an alphabet of human 'thinkables' 'with which all possible thinkables might be constructed by suitable combinations and by which reasoning might be reduced to the quasi-mechanical operation of going through a list' (Kneales, 1962: 325). The first logician to espouse the notion of a philosophical language or *characteristica universalis* which could be designed to help men to think more clearly than with their own natural languages, Leibniz proposes a project for constructing a grammar for formal reasoning, a *calculus ratiocinator*. To this end, algebraic symbolisation was to be employed extensively (Styazhkin, 1969: 67–81). However, it was the singular contribution of George Boole (1815–1864) to have established an algebra for Logic, thereby effectively initiating Symbolic or Mathematical Logic as we know it today. Boole wrote:

We might just assign it as the definitive character of a true Calculus, that it is a method resting upon the employment of Symbols, whose laws of combination are known and general, and whose results admit of a constant interpretation . . . It is upon the foundation of this general principle, that I propose to establish the Calculus of Logic, and that I claim for it a place among the acknowledged forms of Mathematical Analysis . . . (Boole, 1847: 1948 edn, p. 2)

Boolean logical algebra, the descendent of the Leibnizian project of a *calculus ratiocinator*, was later employed in the first attempts to construct 'logic machines', the forerunners of modern electronic computers. By the mid-1930s, Shannon was deploying Boolean ideas in his study of relay and switching circuits, and we have in these efforts the origins of the now-familiar computational apparatus of 'AND'-gates, 'NOT'-gates and 'OR'-gates, etc.

Boole had construed Logic as a branch of pure Mathematics. Just as the Galilean mathematicisation of physical relationships had revolutionised the ways of our 'natural philosophy' and helped to create natural science in its modern form, so Boole had, by algebraicising logical relationships, made possible the project of computing machinery, and paved the way to the contemporary pursuit of 'artificial intelligence' technology.

Where Boole had sought to mathematicise Logic, it was Gottlob Frege (1848–1935) who sought to show that arithmetic is identical to Logic. As Baker and Hacker remark,

Where Boole had generalized algebraic principles and applied them to logic, Frege invoked a more avant-garde branch of mathematics, namely function theory, subsuming syllogistic [sic] with a much more logical system which sought to display all sound patterns of reasoning as theorems derived from a few function–theoretic axioms. He explicitly referred to Leibniz's idea of a *characteristica universalis* and viewed his function–theoretic calculus not as an analysis of natural languages, but as a logically perfect language which, for the restrictive purposes of deductive sciences, would replace natural languages. (Baker and Hacker, 1984: 32)

Frege construed his 'concept-script' as 'accurately representing the structures and articulations of contents of possible judgements (propositions) and of the concepts of which they are composed' (Baker and Hacker, 1984). The rise of propositional and predicate calculi, and the results of Frege and Russell and Whitehead in the twentieth century, heralded the following highly consequential disciplinary developments: firstly, the dominance of a conception of formalisation in the analysis of propositions and inferential relations in which essentially *mathematical* concepts of sets, variables and functions form the bases for symbolic formalisation; secondly, the hegemony of the goal of constructing a Logically Ideal Language within which reasoning, especially scientific reasoning, was to be expressed and developed; and thirdly, the gradual separation of Logic from the wider disciplinary home of Philosophy in the academy.

Russell, for example, made his attitude to the goals of logical analysis very clear in his characterisation of a major aspect of the achievement of *Principia Mathematica*:

In a logically perfect language the words in a proposition would correspond one by one with the components of the corresponding fact, with the exception of such words as 'or', 'not', 'if', 'then', which have a different function. In a logically perfect language, there will be one word and no more for every simple object, and everything that is not simple will be expressed by a combination of words, by a combination derived, of course, from the words for the simple things that enter in, one word for each simple component. A language of that sort will be completely analytic, and will show at a glance the logical structure of the facts asserted or denied. *The language which is set forth in Principia Mathematica is intended to be a language of that sort* . . . It aims at being that sort of a language that, if you add a vocabulary, would be a logically perfect language. (Russell, 1968: 1987–8, emphasis added)

In the course of the exposition of the 'philosophy of logical atomism' from which this passage is drawn, Russell is clearly (and explicitly) influenced by the early Wittgenstein, in whose *Tractatus* are developed the notions of atomic facts and atomic propositions, 'simples' and 'complexes', and the picturing conception of the relationship between propositions and their components on the one hand and 'states of affairs', 'world' or 'reality', on the other. Wittgenstein was later wholly to repudiate these conceptions of the relationship between language and its logic and the world, in large measure by stressing the contextual variability of sense and purpose-dependence of modifiers such as 'simple' and 'complex/compound', 'object' and 'proposition' itself, arguing as well that the sense of a proposition cannot be read off from its structure but requires reference to its *application* in real-worldly communicative contexts. Russell, however, even in this early statement, was alert to the fact that 'Actual languages . . . cannot possibly be [perfect in the above sense], if they are to serve the purposes of daily life' (Russell, 1968: 198) – yet he never fully attended to the consequences of this realisation.

Arguably, the work of the Frege, Russell, Carnap, Schlick, the younger Wittgenstein, and the whole Vienna Circle constituted the highest points of attainment for those pursuing the goal of an Ideal Language. Just as the details of actual, winning arguments had become progressively idealised, abstracted, and formalised in the history of the development of syllogistic and related logical schemata, so now were the details of actual natural languages (viewed as the instruments of thought, reasoning and judgement in general, and not just as the instruments of argumentation) subjected to *logical regimentation.* Actual languages were uniformly conceived of as suffering from vagueness, ambiguity, undecidability, redundancy, colloquialism, metaphor, and a multitude of contaminants which rendered them unfit for representing the theorisings and truths emerging from the Sciences. Not just the primary tools of argument-construction (propositions, predicates and connectives) were to be explored for their logical powers of representation and combination, but 'concepts' – the 'meanings' of words – were to be similarly subjected to formal analysis. Set-theoretic and componential schemes were to be used to render perspicuous the sense of words and sentences. The classical 'true/false' contrast class becomes elaborated into the tripartite 'true/false/nonsensical' distinction in respect of propositions. (Tarski was to expand the scope of the new distinction from 'propositions' to 'sentences'.) Only a proposition which has a 'sense' can be assigned a truth-value ('true' or 'false'): a nonsensical proposition cannot have one. The quest for principled demarcations of 'sense' from 'nonsense' in the construction of propositions becomes a preoccupation of the Vienna Circle school of logic, and famous contributions were made to this quest by Carnap, Ayer, Schlick and the younger Wittgenstein, whose early *Tractatus Logico-Philosophicus* became the 'bible' of the Circle.

Scientific Reason, it was thought, enshrined especially in the progress of Physics (still the paradigm 'science'), required formulating and assessing in something less vulgar, more pure, than 'Ordinary Language' itself, notwithstanding the fact that practising scientists actually reasoned and conducted their research in ordinary natural languages embellished with technical terms of art for purposes of common reference, economy of speech and the expression of *specialised* knowledge. For some proponents of the search for an Ideal Language for Scientific Reason, such a Language (Logical Calculus) was to become a criterion by which *all* other forms of reasoning was to be assessed. Logicians of this persuasion (such as A. J. Ayer, in his *Language, Truth and Logic*) announced that an idealised, logical language was to be a court of appeal for what could count as Intelligible Reason and Meaningful Speech beyond the confines of Science. Theological and ethical propositions fared notoriously badly when adjudicated against the deliverances of the Circles' guardians of reason in Logic, as did the locutions of Common Sense and Practical Reason.

4   From ideal language to communicative praxis: reactions to regimentation

It was against the deification of scientific criteria for what was to count as Reason and Intelligibility, and against the amnesia which railed against

Ordinary Language and Practical, Commonsense Reasoning, that Wittgenstein came to argue so intensely in his later work. So too, albeit in a different way, did Edmund Husserl, the founder of 'phenomenology'. Before considering the revolutions which these thinkers announced in regard to Logic, it is worth pausing to consider one major development in twentieth-century thinking about language and communication – Chomsky's transformational–generative grammar and associated psycholinguistics – which has its roots in the Leibnizian tradition of formal–logical systematisation. For this programme is often counterposed to the initiatives involved in the Wittgensteinian rejection of the pursuit of the logically-perfected Ideal Language as a prerequisite for proper reasoning, and its consideration will enhance our appreciation for the role of ethnomethodological conceptions of communicative *praxis* and common-sense reasoning in the contemporary reassessment of that pursuit.

In 1957, Noam Chomsky published *Syntactic Structures*, arguably among the most influential treatises on the study of language published in the twentieth century, having repercussions throughout the discipline of linguistics, and beyond into psychology and philosophy of language. Here, in this work, ideas drawn from recursive–function theory were applied to the study of the syntax of *natural* languages: the goal of linguistic analysis was to be the specification of the rules (expressed in algebraic formalism) governing the combinatorial possibilities of the syntactically most elementary units of any natural language. The concept of 'generative', in the designation 'generative grammar', was to be understood algebraically: the rules were finite, operating upon syntactical classes (noun, verb, noun-phrase, etc.), which would 'generate' the supposedly infinite set of grammatical sentences acknowledgeable as 'well-formed' for any given natural language by any competent speaker of that language. The analysis of the *semantics* of natural languages was considered by Chomsky and the 'generative grammarians' to be amenable to a similar programme of formalisation. This work was developed principally by Katz, Fodor, Postal and, within philosophy of language, by Davidson and Dummett, among others. The initial division of the domain of a 'language' into its 'syntax', its 'semantics' and its 'pragmatics' was due to the division of the subject-matter of semiotics by C. W. Morris, but its apparent utility for analytic compartmentalisation and manageability of formalisation extended its life within linguistics generally. Developments within the implementation of Chomsky's own programme, however, eventually resulted in controversies concerning the putative 'autonomy' of the distinguished 'components' of natural language. 'Syntactical' principles were increasingly difficult to separate out from 'semantic' ones (resulting in the coining by some of the neologism of 'semantax'), and, ultimately, although far more controversially, the 'autonomy' of semantics from 'pragmatics' became questioned. This latter move was already implicit in the contributions to the philosophy of language being made independently by Wittgensteinian thinkers, such as Stanley Cavell and others in the early 1960s (Cavell, 1971).[1]

Chomsky's goal of stating a set of combinatorial rules or principles for the elements of natural-language which could project or 'generate' all, and only all, of the (infinitely) many grammatically well-formed sentences possible for that language (Chomsky, 1957, 1964), and Leibniz's pursuit of an 'alphabet of thought' whereby it becomes 'possible to deductively derive new ideas by means of definite rules for combining symbols' (Leibniz, 1765, cited in Styazhkin, 1969: 65), are sufficiently analogous to justify referring to Chomskian linguistics as 'neo-Leibnizian' as well as neo-Cartesian. One major ostensible difference between them, namely, the postulation by Chomsky of a level of 'transformation rules' linking the canonical 'logical' rendition of the conceptual content of a sentence (its 'deep structure') to its actual 'surface structure' (its actually appearing form), should not blind us to the deep continuity of logical regimentation at work. However, in sharp contrast to the Chomskians, neither Leibniz nor any of his direct successors ever postulated a mental or psychological 'existence' for any part of the *calculus ratiocinator* they were attempting to formulate.

In the Chomskian project, marrying the interests and formalism of what we may call a Leibnizian logic to the subject-matter of linguistic theory, we encounter the modern apotheosis of one major line of development of Logic. From a concern for the formal properties and inferential structures of possibly valid *arguments* to the analysis of the 'laws of thought' expressed in the structure of *propositions* to the production of a formal–logical *calculus* or Language for Science, we move to the elucidation of the Logic of Natural Languages, construed now as an infinite set of possibly grammatical or 'well-formed' *sentences*. The transition had yet to be made to a treatment of the object of logical analysis – natural language – as consisting in sets of (linguistic) practices or *activities*. Indeed, in Chomsky's frequent insistence that the major purpose of natural languages is thought, not communicative action, we find still the implicit abstraction of language and its logic from the arenas of actual language-*use* characteristic of the entire tradition of logical regimentation.

Fundamentally at odds with the tradition within which Chomsky developed his thoughts about the analysis of language stood the work of the later Wittgenstein and that of its adherents. Based upon the repudiation of his *Tractatus* (1921), in which he had argued that all natural languages have a 'hidden' structure akin to that of a to-be-specified, formal–logical calculus whose rules articulate 'the essence of the world' (Wittgenstein, 1961 edn, p. 79), Wittgenstein's later writings contain a plethora of arguments *against* the notion that practices of logical regimentation can uncover the 'essence' of language and the world; *against* the notion that any actual language is a system of symbols whose rules are akin to those of any formal–logical calculus, and *against* the notion that speakers of a natural language, whose speech is intelligible, must perforce be operating such a calculus unconsciously. Such a position set Wittgenstein apart from the traditions within which his own *Tractatus* had been hailed as a crowning achievement and programmatic vindication. Schlick had written of this earlier work that it was 'the first to have pushed forward to the decisive point' (Schlick, 1959: 54) whose beginnings had been only 'dimly perceived' by Leibniz and developed by Frege and Russell (Schlick, 1959). His new work was greeted by bafflement and even sadness, particularly by Russell who had served as his supervisor for the *Tractatus* in the doctoral programme at Cambridge (Russell, 1959: 217).[2] To many of his former colleagues and mentors, it seemed that the older Wittgenstein was repudiating Logic itself.

It is, I think, beyond serious question today that Wittgenstein actually believed himself to be *preserving* Logic from transient and distorting ambitions. Engaging the twin pillars of his earlier work in a vigorous criticism, Wittgenstein railed against the notion that 'The strict and clear rules of the logical structure of propositions . . . appear to us as something in the background – hidden in the medium of the understanding' (Wittgenstein, 1968: para. 102), and against the *'preconceived idea* of crystalline purity' (Wittgenstein, 1968: para. 108) of Logic as a requirement of a properly satisfactory logical analysis of language and thought.

108. We see that what we call 'sentence' and 'language' has not the formal unity that I imagined [in the *Tractatus*] but is the family of structures more or less related to one another – but what becomes of logic now? Its rigor seems to be giving way here. But in that case doesn't logic altogether disappear? For how can it lose its rigor? Of course not by our bargaining any of its rigor out of it. The *preconceived idea* of crystalline purity can only be removed by turning our whole examination around.

We are talking about the spatial and temporal phenomenon of language, not about some non-spatial, non-temporal phantasm. But we talk about it as we do about the pieces in chess when we are stating the rules of the game, not describing their physical properties. (Wittgenstein, 1968)

Since the 'crystalline purity' of Logic was 'not a *result of investigation*: it was a requirement' (Wittgenstein, 1968: para. 107), Wittgenstein sets out to expose its deficiencies and inappropriateness *as* a requirement, pursuant to the development of a different conception from that of a logical calculus: a *logical grammar*. One major difference between a calculus in the Tractarian (as well as Russellian, etc.) sense, and a grammar in the new sense, is to be found in the conceptualisation of the object of 'logico-grammatical' analysis – it is no longer 'language' writ large (and thereby writ larger than life), but *language-games* (Wittgenstein, 1968: paras. 7–24 *et seq.*) (*Sprachspielen*, or 'speech-games'), in which language-use and practical conduct are seen as interwoven in complex ways. Another point of contrast is to be found in the nature of the 'rules' posited respectively by the Ideal Logical Calculus of Language, and a logical grammar of a natural language. The former's 'rules' were putatively exact, complete, and were supposed to be interpretable as wholly context-independent, operating to regiment intelligibility and to provide for full determinateness of sense. The latter's 'rules' are to be construed very differently, as a result of Wittgenstein's relentless attack on the former conception. In *Zettel,* he writes:

How should we have to imagine a complete list of rules for the employment of a word? – What do we mean by a complete list of rules for the employment of a piece in chess? Couldn't we always construct doubtful cases, in which the normal list of rules does not decide? Think, e.g., of such a question as: how to determine who moved last, if a doubt is raised about the reliability of the players' memories?

The regulation of traffic in the streets permits and forbids certain actions on the part of drivers and pedestrians; but it does not attempt to guide the totality of their movements by prescription. And it would be senseless to talk of an 'ideal' ordering of traffic which should do that; in the first place we should have no idea what to imagine as this ideal. If someone wants to make traffic regulations stricter on some point or other, *that does not mean that he wants to approximate to such an ideal.* (Wittgenstein, 1967: para. 440, emphasis added)[3]

Clearly linking operable standards of 'completeness' to purposes and contexts of practice, Wittgenstein elsewhere does the same for 'exactness':

'Inexact' is really a reproach, and 'exact' is praise. And that is to say that what is inexact attains its goal less perfectly than what is more exact. *Thus the point here is what we call 'the goal'.* Am I inexact when I do not give our distance from the sun to the nearest foot, or tell a joiner the width of a table to the nearest thousandth of an inch? (Wittgenstein, 1968: para. 88, emphasis added)

In his various remarks directed against the misleading search for the 'essence' of forms of expression or of concepts, Wittgenstein develops his famous 'family resemblance' analogy for analysing concepts formerly subsumed under the regimentarian requirement of specification in terms of sets of 'necessary and sufficient' conditions for their application (Wittgenstein, 1968: paras. 65–85). In this way, he undermines the 'craving' of formal logicians for seeking to characterise the 'essence' of language and thought, where 'essence' is construed independently of actual standards sustained and enforceable within practical domains of language-*use*. The general 'subliming' of Logic is held to be an illusory claim when it is advanced as a claim for the revelation of some decontextualised, but nonetheless unitary and fundamental, 'essential structure' of language. Furthermore, this putative 'essence' is then projected back into the world as *its* essence, but its locus therein becomes radically problematic. It is thence construed as 'something that lies *beneath* the surface' (Wittgenstein, 1968: para. 92) of actual use and actual contexts of use. A favoured space for it is the 'mind'. It is from this point that Wittgenstein develops his remarks on philosophical psychology in a sustained elucidation of the concepts of 'meaning', 'understanding', 'thinking', 'imagining', 'remembering', 'applying a word', 'following a rule', and 'introspecting', etc., many of which were part of his general attempt to undermine our temptation to 'think that if anyone utters a sentence and *means* or *understands* it he is operating a calculus according to definite rules' (Wittgenstein, 1968: para. 81). As he notes, 'All this, however, can only appear in the right light when one has attained greater clarity about the concepts of understanding, meaning and thinking' (Wittgenstein, 1968: para. 81).

It is not a hidden calculus of determinate 'rules' which enables us to speak together and understand one another in our practical, social intercourse, but, rather, our commonality of judgement:

If language is to be a means of communication there must be agreements not only in definitions but also (queer as this may sound) in judgements. *This seems to abolish logic, but does not do so.* It is one thing to describe methods of measurement, and another to obtain and state results of measurement. But what we call 'measuring' is partly determined by a certain constancy in results of measurement. (Wittgenstein, 1968: para 242, emphasis added)

Logic has its place as the domain for the *elucidation* of methods of reasoning, but it does not describe any 'underlying' or 'mental' structure or mechanism or 'grammar' which makes intelligibility possible. *That* is made possible by our simply making common judgements and sharing (sufficiently) a form of life characterised by common forms of training and reactions to training.

Edmund Husserl, the creator of 'phenomenology' as a rigorous 'science of essences', also developed a concept of 'logical grammar' (Husserl, 1970b: 52b), although with a different focus. In particular, Husserl tended to construe our understanding of linguistic expressions as 'peculiar act-experiences' (Husserl, 1970a: 302), a mistake which Wittgenstein avoided in his general attack on Cartesian misconceptions of our psychological language-use. By stressing the role of public conduct and circumstances as criteria for distinguishing between 'thinking that' and 'actually' understanding an expression (etc.), and by noting that concepts of 'experience' are used quite differently in avowals and ascriptions from concepts such as 'understanding', 'knowing', 'being able to . . . ' and the like, Wittgenstein successfully avoided making any concessions to mentalistic stories in which 'understanding' is viewed as an operation of the mind (Baker and Hacker, 1980: Ch. 6; 1984: Ch. 9). For Wittgenstein, in contradistinction here both to Husserl and to Chomsky, although not in direct argument with them, 'understanding' is analysed as a predicate of personal capacity rather than as a mental 'action'-verb (Wittgenstein, 1968: paras. 138–55).[4] Nonetheless, Husserl joins Wittgenstein in deploying the analogy between linguistic *praxis* and games in the following:

Chessmen are not part of the chess-game as bits of ivory and wood having such and such shapes and colors. Their phenomenal and physical constitution is quite indifferent and can be varied at will. They become chessmen, counters in the chess-game, through the game's rules which give them their fixed *games-meaning* . . . signs taken in a certain *operation* or *games-sense* do duty for the same signs taken in full *arithmetical meaningfulness*. (Husserl, 1970a: 305).

Despite their many differences, for both thinkers it is in the *Lebenswelt*, or domain of ordinary, practical, social affairs, where rules for using linguistic symbols, signs, concepts, are to be revealed in operation. The proper methodology for a Logic concerned to elucidate the structures of conceptual *praxis* – 'free phantasy variation', 'bracketing', 'the search for *eidos*' in Husserl, but 'surveying' actual use, deriving 'perspicuous representations', seeking the connections between uses and contexts of use in Wittgenstein – separated them. The Cartesian residues in Husserl's thought also prevented him from coming to embrace a Socio-Logic for *praxis*, whilst Wittgenstein's radical anti-Cartesianism, both in philosophical psychology and in epistemology, enabled him more fully to grasp a proto-sociological conception of a reconstructed project of logical analysis of language.

After the end of World War 2, there arose in Britain some further developments of what one could loosely term a post-Wittgensteinian sensibility in the work of J. L. Austin, Gilbert Ryle and others. Austin in particular developed further the insights involved in reconnecting language with practical, social conduct in his celebrated concept of the 'illocutionary act' or 'speech act' (Austin, 1955; 1981 edn), and Ryle was to propose a fundamental distinction of permanent usefulness between Formal (Symbolic, Mathematical) Logic, and what he called 'Informal' Logic, arguing persuasively for the analytical priority of the latter (Ryle, 1954). He wrote:

Since Aristotle, there has existed a branch of inquiries, often entitled 'Formal Logic', which has always adhered more or less closely to general philosophical inquiries. It is not easy to describe this liaison between Formal Logic and philosophy. The systematic presentation of the rules of syllogistic inference is a very different sort of activity from, say, the elucidation of the concept of pleasure. The Aristotle who inaugurated the former is the same thinker who considerably developed the latter, yet the kinds of thinking in which he was involved are very widely different. The technical problems in the theory of the syllogism have a strong resemblance to the problems of Euclidean geometry; the ideals of systematisation and rigorous proof are at work, questions of switches and shades of significance are barred, false moves are demonstrable fallacies. The problems in, say, the theory of pleasure or perception or moral responsibility are not like this. (Ryle, 1954: 111)

He continued, lamenting the gradual separation from philosophical questions of what had become Formal Logic:

You have converted the words 'logic' and 'logical' to your private ends, and now you invite us to cease exploring the moors to become conductors on your trams. And for what? For nothing, apparently, but the proliferation of truistic formulae. No philosophical problem of any interest to anyone has yet been solved by reducing it to the shape or size that suits some slot in your slot-machine. Your cash-register is indeed quite impeccable and totally neutral, and for that reason it cannot be appealed to for aid in the settlement of any bargaining-disputes. (Ryle, 1954: 113–14)

Concluding that just as fighting cannot be reduced to drill, nor trading to account-balancing operations, problems of philosophical interest cannot be reduced 'to either the derivation or the application of theorems about logical constants. The philosopher is perforce doing what might be called "Informal Logic"' (Ryle, 1954: 124). However, in spite of his continuous appeals to 'use', 'usage' and the 'logical *behavior*' of concepts, Ryle was less self-consciously *praxiological* in his logical inquiries than were either Wittgenstein or Austin. For example, Austin's famous auto-critique of his original 'constative/performative' dichotomy for the classification and analysis of linguistic forms had turned upon a recognition that the constative nature of an expression (note: *not* solely a *proposition*), its fact-stating or describing function, is available only within the *activity* of describing or stating. If a performative utterance is one which can be used to perform an action, so also is a constative utterance. Describing or stating a fact are as much activities, as much parts of human *conduct*, as baptising, marrying, vetoing, promising or sentencing, even though there may be no 'function-indicating device' (Searle, 1969) such as 'I hereby describe . . . ' conventionally prefacing the act of describing, as there can be one such as 'I promise' as a part of the uttering/making of a promise.

Austin elaborated upon the traditional logician's concept of a language as a set of possible 'propositions' tied together by 'logical constants', or as (even an 'infinite') set of possible 'sentences' structured by syntactical, combinatorial rules, by placing at centre-stage the notion of a 'speech act'. Subsequent interpreters and developers, however, returned to fetishise the 'proposition' by insisting that *all* speech-acts (interrogatives, commissives, verdictives, etc.) or *any* illocutionary act (command, warning, threat, apology, complaint, etc.) housed some fundamental (if grammatically 'disguised') 'propositional content'.[5] Such an error (of conflating the activity of making a proposition with the quite different *activity* of making a promise) has its germ in Austin's own discussion. However, for Wittgenstein,

It would produce confusion if we were to say: the words of the communiqué – the proposition communicated – have a definite sense, and the giving of it, the 'assertion' supplies something additional. As if the sentence, spoken by a gramophone, belonged to pure logic; as if here it had the pure logical sense; as if here we have before us the object which logicians get hold of and consider – while the sentence as asserted, communicated, is what it is in *business*. As one may say: the botanist considers a rose *as a plant*, not as an ornament for a dress or room . . . The sentence, I want to say, has no sense outside the language-game. (Wittgenstein, 1980: para. 488)

Commenting insightfully upon the ways in which logical relations between propositions and their component parts have appeared to possess a 'compelling' hardness, a rigidity quite impervious to the pragmatic and contingent features of actual communicative *praxis*, Winch remarked:

One thinks of propositions as something ethereal, which just because of their ethereal, non-physical nature, can fit together more tightly than can be conceived in the case of anything so grossly material as flesh-and-blood men and their actions. In a sense one is right in this; for to treat of logical relations in a formal, systematic way is to think at a very high level of abstraction . . . But like any abstraction not recognised as such, this can be misleading. *It may make one forget that it is only from their roots in this actual flesh-and-blood intercourse that those formal systems draw such life as they have.* (Winch, 1958: 126, emphasis added)

The exclusive preoccupation of logicians with propositions, predicates and logical connectives, or later with sentences and their syntactical structures, had led many to deny that inferential, presuppositional, implicational and other logical properties could be determined for other phenomena, and even to deny that new forms of orderly, conventionalised relations holding between *utterances*, *activities*, and *contexts* of utterance/activity constituted *logical* relations. There was a tendency to maintain that a 'proposition' had the logical properties it did in virtue of its *structure* independently of its *application*, the latter being consigned to the intellectual dustbin of mere 'pragmatics', a domain held to be in a state of intrinsic disarray. To speak of a 'logic of language' that embraced such putatively disorganised phenomena as 'use', 'application', 'speech' (as contrasted to 'language') was to be taken to abuse the very concept of 'logic'. Yet, of course, this was exactly what Wittgenstein was proposing to do, as Dilman remarks in the course of his Wittgensteinian treatment of Quine's work on logical necessity:

The idea is not that we cannot speak of the logical structure of propositions or of the rules of syntax that govern logical inferences, but that these are what appear in the employment of propositions, of language, in the course of conversations, discussions, investigations and reasonings in the weave of our lives. They are not something that can be identified *a priori* and in abstraction from what we actually do with language in our lives. (Dilman, 1984: 81)

Propositions which we regard as *necessary* (e.g. 'red is a colour', 'promises oblige the promissor', 'no bachelor who is a human being is married', etc.) are not so regarded purely in virtue of some *intrinsic* nature of such propositions (such that their absolute immunity to falsification is transcendentally guaranteed); rather, such propositions 'are rules of our language-games. They are formulations of established practices with words, and it is these practices which give meaning to our words' (Dilman, 1984: 95).

If Logic took a thoroughly 'Linguistic Turn' and, with that, moved in the direction of re-discovering its ancient moorings in *praxis*, it was yet fully to embrace a Sociological Turn. However, if the 'Formal' designation of Logic was now to be shared with the 'Informal' designation, after Wittgenstein, Austin, Ryle and their protagonists, it was soon to be extended further and more deeply into the analysis of the intersubjective, communicative, and essentially practical sphere of the social world.

Perhaps the most important figure in the history of the (renewed?) relationship between Logic and Sociology is Peter Winch, whose observations about the grounds of propositional and logical relations in the sphere of social relations we have already noted. In his famous, but widely misinterpreted monograph, *The Idea of a Social Science and Its Relation to Philosophy* (Winch, 1958), Winch developed the argument, drawing his inspiration from Wittgenstein's later writings, that social actions and social relations may be investigated as logical relations between concepts, since the rules and criteria governing the use of the concepts of human conduct and social behaviour are the rules which accord intelligibility or meaning to human behaviour. Winch claimed:

It will seem less strange that social relations should be like logical relations between propositions once it is seen that logical relations between propositions themselves depend on social relations between men. (Winch, 1958: 126)

Since 'the ways of thinking embodied in institutions govern the way the members of the societies studied by the social scientist behave' (Winch, 1958: 127), and since those ways of thinking are made possible by concepts and their 'grammars' (and where the 'institutions' Winch has in mind include, most prominently, natural languages), then it follows that actions are the expressions of concepts and rule-governed accordingly, and the analysis of social conduct is in significant measure the elucidation of the 'grammars' of the concepts of social conduct. In this way, Winch sought to 'dissolve' sociology into conceptual/grammatical analysis of a Wittgensteinian kind, and, at one stroke, to settle the *verstehende* problem of 'interpretive' sociology.

It was perhaps this perceived 'threat' to the project of an 'autonomous' sociology, sought after academically since Durkheim, and the associated arguments against the possibility of a truly 'nomological' form of inquiry into social phenomena, which alienated many sociologists from Winch's arguments, and it was undoubtedly Winch's invocation of the notion of truth-relative-to-a-language-game which misled many into thinking of him as a 'radical relativist' who abjured the notion of 'absolute truth'. (As if there couldn't be an 'absolute truth' *within* a language-game but only, *mirabile dictu*, outside of any of them. A similar misreading of Wittgenstein's proposal that 'logical necessity' is bound up with language-games and their essentially contingent rules has led some to argue that Wittgenstein had mistakenly 'relativised' the concept of 'necessity', thereby supposedly depriving it of its 'transcendental' authority. However, for Wittgenstein, as for Winch, the criteria for truth, necessity and certainty are *essentially* language-game- and purpose-dependent, which does not in the least argue for their non-existence nor for their 'arbitrariness' or *unconstrained* variability of meaning. In no sense does it commit them to the absurd view that 'truth' is *whatever* it is taken to be, nor to the equally absurd view that 'truth' or 'rationality' or 'logical necessity' are *subjective* notions. I mention these matters in parentheses for they are given close attention in the next chapter when the respecification of epistemology by ethnomethodology is turned to, and in chapter 10 when the respecification of values and moral judgements is taken up.)

5   The ethnomethodological extension of informal logic in sociology

Ethnomethodology developed independently of Winch's contribution, but was nonetheless the first clear indication of a recognition, on the part of some sociologists who developed its initiatives and its promise, of the power of adopting neo-Wittgensteinian and phenomenological conceptions of logical analysis in their studies of social conduct, of action and interaction in the real, social world.

Garfinkel drew upon the work of the logician Yehoshua Bar-Hillel for one of his major concepts, that of 'indexical expression' (Bar-Hillel, 1965; 1970; Garfinkel, 1967: Ch. 4 *et seq.*). Noting also the remarks of Husserl, Russell and Goodman on 'occasional expressions', 'egocentric particulars' and 'indexical tokens' as precursors to his own use of the concept of indexicality, Garfinkel makes only two explicit references in his early published writings to the later Wittgenstein, but his influence is clear enough. He begins by observing that, whenever logicians and linguists encounter 'indexical expressions' – locutions whose sense, reference and/or truth-value vary contextually – they are 'repaired' in various ways in order to facilitate formal analysis. Either ideal-types are postulated for which actual indexical expressions function as 'tokens' or 'instances', or 'context' is held constant, thereby privileging *some*, usually unspecified, possible context over others.

Structures are then analysed as properties of the ideals, and the results are assigned to actual expressions as their properties, though with disclaimers of 'appropriate scientific modesty'. (Garfinkel and Sacks, 1970: 339)

For example, in theoretical linguistics, the grammarian's 'sentence' is analysed in terms of the requisites of grammatical theory, but the results are then tacitly assigned to actual *utterances* as part of their methods of production or 'generation' (Coulter, 1973a; Baker and Hacker, 1984, *passim*). Similarly, arguments and propositions considered by logicians are rarely embedded within a discourse-context explicitly, so that their logical properties may come to have an unknown relationship to any *actual* or *situatedly assignable* processes or achievements of inference-making, implication-drawing, presupposition-detection or illocutionary-force specification. 'Indexicals' pose obstinate problems for formal logicians and linguists operating in the traditions of logical regimentation, and Garfinkel notes the 'unsatisfied programmatic distinction between and substitutability of objective for indexical expressions' (Garfinkel, 1967: 4). After all, even a Quinean 'eternal sentence' (such as 'ice melts in water') still requires *some* context (occasion, situation) for its intelligibility to be vouchsafed to a competent hearer. One cannot say just anything anywhere, even if in some sense what is said is 'syntactically' well-formed, and expect to be (expect that one's sentence/utterance will be) 'understood' or 'intelligible'. Garfinkel and Sacks

(1970) go on to note that paraphrasings, idealisations and other formal methods for 'repairing' the contextual-dependency and purpose-relativity of sense and reference of indexical expressions only 'preserve in specifics' the original problems, and they contend that, since no expression in a natural language can have *any* intelligibility *without* a context (where semanticists' so-called 'zero contexts'[6] are simply rhetorical ways of tacitly assuming *some* particular context), this will include *also* 'formulations' designed to repair the indexicality of expressions used or encountered. For 'formulations' of sense will themselves have indexical properties (context-dependence and purpose-relativity). There can be no real-worldly 'meaning-invariant and context-free' *praxis*. However, people manage to communicate effectively by any practical standards of comprehensibility and orderliness for the most part in the routines of their daily lives. Therefore, indexical expressions do not require 'cleaning up' prior to analysis. Indeed, such efforts risk considerable distortion of the phenomena as they are produced and monitored by speakers and hearers, by practical reasoners. Rather, *analysis must begin with the actual, situated properties of communicative conduct itself.* Garfinkel and Sacks posed the issues thus:

Are there practices for doing and recognising (the fact that our activities are accountably rational) without, for example, making a formulation of the setting that the practices are 'contexted' in? . . . What is the work for which (definiteness, univocality, disambiguation, and uniqueness of conversational particulars is assured by conversationalists' competence with speech in context) is a proper gloss? (Garfinkel and Sacks, 1970: 355–6)

That there *are* analysable practices for 'doing and recognising' the intelligibility of practical actions (particularly communicative actions), without the need constantly to invoke or presume full-fledged 'formulations' of their sense, is at once the claim and the programme for that part of ethnomethodology which developed into the study of the 'rational properties of indexical expressions and indexical actions' (Garfinkel, 1967: 34) viz, Sacks' 'conversation analysis'. In various respects, this accumulating body of work is designed to exhibit 'the work' for which the expression: 'rationally-accountable communicative *praxis*' is a proper description or 'gloss'.

In arguing that indexical expressions do not *need* 'purification' for logical analysis to proceed upon their properties, Garfinkel and Sacks are making a very similar point to Wittgenstein's in his insistence that properties such as '(in)exactness', 'ambiguity', 'indeterminacy', 'vagueness' and 'uncertainty' are *not* generic characterisations true for all ordinary-language expressions, thought of now as the poor cousins of the logician's 'proposition', 'sense' or 'Thought', poor cousins which now stand in need of generic purification or even replacement by the construction of an Ideal Language devoid of such features. Rather, these properties of vagueness, ambiguity, inexactness, etc., are assignable to ordinary-language expressions only for specific contextual purposes (Wittgenstein, 1968: paras. 88–109). Take, for example, a logician's criterion for fully rational sense, that of 'completeness of expression', as contrasted to 'elipsis', rhetorical 'enthymematic' usage, etc., and now consider the following example, furnished by Bittner:

(A) person shouting 'Police' is heard calling for any policeman; but a child crying 'Mother' is heard calling *its* mother. Had the child, however, made this fact explicit by crying 'My Mother' it would surely have been heard as implying some kind of urgency concerning its parent rather than itself. Thus, *it would appear that in some communicative context, to make known what we mean we must refrain from expressing it fully, lest we be taken to mean something else.* (Bittner, 1977: 6, emphasis added)

This example also nicely illustrates the earlier point about 'formulations' as potentially generic 'remedies' for the indexical features of expressions: 'My mother' may be a 'logical formulation' of the child's desired object – of the 'sense' of what the child was saying – but if articulated as such, it could be radically misleading in its context. Indeed, it could result in a *mis*understanding rather than a clarification.

Returning to the topic of 'truth-value' and its assignability, let us consider how an extension of focus from decontextualised 'propositions' to contextually embedded speech-acts affects the logical analysis of truth-conditions. First, classically, the true/false contrast class was available for 'propositions'. Statements, declarative assertions and 'constatives', etc., which could be accorded the property of 'having a meaningful propositional content', could be subjected to assessment in terms of such a contrast-class. However, as soon as *other* illocutionary acts are examined, it becomes clear that the conditions under which such a contrast-class becomes *relevant* encompass considerations broader than determining a 'propositional content'. Sacks argued:

Let us suppose that a first contrast class relevant upon the occurrence of a statement is whether it is intended to be serious or a joke. Then it may be that the relevance of true–false is conditional on the determination that it is intended to be serious, whereas if it is intended to be a joke the contrast class true–false is not relevant in dealing with it. (Sacks, 1975: 61)

Truth-determinations, as well as intelligibility-determinations, are contingent upon the *activity* which any utterance can be heard to accomplish in a context of its use. From these observations, it becomes clear that a further, analytical specification of the gloss 'context' is required if formal analysis is to proceed upon the praxiological data of communication. Sacks was among the first to notice that, among the array of possibly relevant aspects of 'context', *sequential location* was paramount, and furnished a crucial constraint upon considerations of relevance to an utterance's possible intelligibility, illocutionary force *and* (thereby) susceptibility to assessment in terms of the true–false contrast class. He argued:

Sequential relevance can involve sorts of actions that utterances can accomplish. In the case of actions like *complaining* or *offering an excuse*, one recurring type of utterance that goes directly after the action is an utterance that proposes either its truth or falsity. Also, such utterances seem to implicate the effectiveness of the proffered complaint or excuse. Given a complaint or an excuse, a sequentially relevant next utterance can be concerned with acceptance or rejection of the excuse or complaint, and one way acceptance or rejection of a complaint or an excuse can be done is by reference to assertions of the truth or falsity of the *complaint* or the *excuse* . . . Then, as acceptance or rejection is relevant on the making of the complaint [or excuse], the contrast class true–false is thereby relevant, that is, sequentially relevant. (Sacks, 1975: 62)

Austin had much earlier proposed adding to the concept of 'truth-condition for statement/proposition' a notion of 'felicity condition' for a speech-act. By this he intended to indicate not only that the intelligibility of any given utterance is a function of its appropriateness of use in a given speech situation: he wanted to point out that its illocutionary force (the action it could be heard to be accomplishing in its context) is a function of its being produced according to conditions of *warrantability*. Thus, if I am neither an ordained minister of the church nor a secular authority endowed with certain rights, no matter how often or how sincerely I may say: 'I now pronounce you man and wife', I have *not* succeeded in performing the act of *marrying* them. Austin gives many similar examples (Austin, 1955). One has to be a judge in order to sentence someone by saying, in appropriate circumstances, 'I sentence you to N years imprisonment': one has to be a superordinate authority in order to veto something by saying, in appropriate circumstances, 'I veto that resolution': one has to be a police-officer (or a citizen effecting a citizen's arrest) in order to arrest someone by saying, in appropriate circumstances, 'I arrest you in the name of the law', and so forth. However, Austin nowhere considered a crucial, a massively general, constraint upon 'appropriateness' and 'felicity' conditions for speech-act intelligibility and warrantability: *the sequential location of an utterance* with respect to other utterances. In Sacks' hands, this feature becomes a major analytical focus, enabling him to begin to map out a *combinatorial logic for illocutionary conduct*.

Consider, first, the range of illocutionary acts which Austin treats: most of them may be characterised, in Sacks' terms, as 'first parts of adjacency pairs' (Schegloff and Sacks, 1973; Sacks, Lectures, *passim*). That is, questions, but not answers; requests, but not grants or denials; invitations, but not acceptances or rejections, etc., are the primary topics of investigation. By ignoring sequential location, Austin fails to discern a whole array of logical properties of utterances-in-context, including, centrally, the very possibility of determining illocutionary force. For example, an utterance, or turn-at-talk, like: 'What time did you arrive home?' may look like a *question* (in virtue of syntactical, intonational and kindred features), but located after (adjacently to) an utterance such as: 'And then what did she ask you?', it takes on the illocutionary potential of a (direct) *quotation*. Such examples can be ramified.

Austin claimed to be interested in elucidating the properties of speech-acts in the 'total speech situation' (Austin, 1955, 1981 edn: p. 148). It is apparent, however, that such elucidations had to await the contributions of the ethno-methodologists in sociology.

Identifying the logical properties of sequentially organised communicative practices naturally included a concern for the *sequential constraints on inferential options*, as well as sequential constraints on illocutionary force, 'sense and reference' and truth-value assignability. Whereas the Aristotelian syllogism emerged as a 'formal structure' for possibly valid arguments understood (initially) through a step-wise arrangement of turns (i.e. Turn 1: All men are mortal. Turn 2: Socrates is a man. Turn 3: (THUS) Socrates is mortal), the notion of analysing actual communicative exchanges in social interaction for their inferential–logical properties, encompassing *any* sequence or series of sequences (or even 'speech-exchange systems' such as courtroom trials, psychiatric diagnostic interviews, classroom lessons, employment interviews, etc.), was the original contribution and major insight of the ethnomethodological analysts of naturally occurring practical conduct.

Since there exist abundant compendia of studies in conversation analysis (*inter alia*, Sacks (1964–72), Sudnow (1972a), Turner (1974), Schenkein (1978), Psathas (1979a), Atkinson and Heritage (1984), Button and Lee (1987), Psathas (1990)) I shall not attempt here to review the many contributions available in this corpus of research to 'informal–logical' interests.[7] I shall illustrate the issue of 'sequentially controlled inferential option' with one, hopefully perspicuous, example – that of 'pre-sequence constraint on inference-potential'. It is at once elementary and powerful in its operation, and it captures a property which is *actually* orientable-to by any natural-language-using member of the communication community from which it is extracted as an instance. Take the following sequence of naturally occurring turns-at-talk:

PRE-INVITATION: 1. A: What are you doing tonight?
SOLICIT: 2. B: Nothing.
INVITATION: 3. A: How about taking in a movie?
ACCEPT: 4. B: OK, let's do it.

Although turn 1 is hearable as question, a hearer can infer that it may be accomplishing an initial 'try-out' prior to the possible production of an invitation. It stands as a conventionalised form of question designed to be oriented to in that way by a hearer in this particular communication community. In saying: 'Nothing' as an answer to the 'question', the second speak cannot conventionally be heard literally to signify a prospective state of complete immobility. Rather, the appropriate inference, contingent upon hearing the opening 'question' as a prelude or 'pre-' to a possibly forthcoming invitation, is to the *potential* availability of the speaker for being invited, or, minimally, to being prepared to consider some course of action about to be proposed by the first speaker. The appropriateness of issuing the invitation, which is accomplished in turn 3 by the first speaker, is contingent upon such a hearing/inference. However, note that the hearability of turn 3 as indeed an *invitation* or proposal for *joint* action rather than, say, a *suggestion* about what B ought to do him/herself, may be contingent upon the set of inferences so far achieved through the interchange. The second speaker's production of 'let's do it' – an acceptance in the acceptance–rejection slot adjacent to the heard-invitation – exhibits his inference that joint action is being proposed which includes the one heard as having made the invitation. Of course, such inferential operations are *defeasible*. Many cruel jokes turn on the transformation of such a conventionalised system of inferential options via the production of fifth turns such as: 'Me? Oh, I'm far too busy: I was just seeing if you were working or interested in a movie. It would do you good!', etc. But the very nature of the 'joke' itself turns on the exploitation of the sequentially controlled inferential options just outlined.

Formalisations of such matters as sequential organisations for illocutionary actions, inferential optionalities, presupposition-assignability constraints, preference orderings in speech-turn production and design, relationships of illocutionary conduct to assignable membership category, display/detection of orientations of speakers and hearers, topic organisation, and many other considerations, now become possible. This work constitutes a genuine expansion of the analysis of the Logic of Language, but, unlike most previous efforts, it constitutes a contribution to an Endogenous, rather than Exogenous, Logic for Linguistic Conduct.

6   Ethnomethodological analysis of practical action as endogenous logic

The project of logical regimentation may be contrasted to that of logical explication, and that of a correspondingly exogenous logic to one of an endogenous logic for practical reason. There are many differences between these projects, and at least some features of work within the latter mode of analysis may be found to undermine various assumptions and principles belonging to the former mode. The relative neglect of *symbolic* formalisation and axiomatisation within Endogenous Logic will not be discussed here: suffice to say, much of the narrowness of scope of traditional formal–logical studies of language may be attributed to attempts to preserve the consistency of a notation system at the expense of discerning fresh and actual logical relationships and connections orientable-to, and made by, practical reasoners in the course of conducting their everyday affairs. Further, an exclusive reliance upon supplementing the classical logical (particularly 'formal semantic') concepts with mathematical ones (especially the concept of 'set'), and a related (Carnapian) insistence upon distinguishing between a 'logical' and a 'nonlogical' vocabulary or conceptual apparatus in natural languages, can both be seen now as unnecessary restrictions upon the logical investigation of language-use and cultural *praxis*. The exact extent of the revisions necessary in relation to former conceptions of logical analysis remains an open question. Certainly, though, the Wittgensteinian tradition established subsequent to the publication of *Philosophical Investigations* has generated a range of novel analytical constructs alien to preceding formalist analysis of language: 'criterial' and 'symptomatic' evidences now complement 'deductive' and 'inductive' evidences in logical analysis; 'defeasible criteria' coexist with 'entailments' and 'material implications'; 'polymorphs', 'family-resemblance concepts', 'open-textured categories', 'essentially contestable concepts' and 'fuzzy sets' now coexist with (sometimes supplanting) 'definite descriptions', 'necessary-and-sufficient conditions *definienda*' and 'semantic components (markers, distinguishers, etc.)'; 'logico-grammatical relations' take the place of 'meaning postulates'; 'language-games', 'indexical (deictic) expressions', 'illocutionary acts', 'speech-exchange turns' and 'turn-constructional units' supplement 'propositions', 'sentences' and 'predicates'; and 'membership categorisation devices', supplant 'names', 'person-referring expressions' and 'roles' in the compendium of praxiological inquiry.

I shall discuss one exemplary contribution of ethnomethodology in terms of what is here being referred to as an endogenous logic of praxis: the logic of 'membership categorisation'. This topic is given a complementary examination in the discussion of *moral inferential logic* which forms part of Lena Jayyusi's examination of values and moral judgements in chapter ten, and readers are invited to read the two in conjunction with one another. The topic has been selected for extended, summary review primarily because of its perspicuous and relatively well-developed status. It is also possible to specify its major elements without reproducing substantial segments of transcription data. I make no claims for comprehensiveness, only for succinct illustration.

A fundamental question confronted quite early in the development of ethnomethodological studies of practical action and reasoning concerned the orderliness and intelligibility of *person categorisation*. Sacks, who pioneered the formal analysis of person categorisation *in vivo*, eschewed a semantic–componential analytical approach in favour of an interactionally-sensitive one. Existing schemata for representing the 'semantics' of person reference and attribution simply could not handle the many properties discovered by inspecting actual, *in situ*, instances of the *practices* from which the semantic components and rules had been abstracted.[8] Moreover, the primary purpose of these abstracted formal schemata was to establish 'rules for *correct* use' – a typically restricted truth-conditional enterprise, and one which often culminated in the imposition of closure by fiat upon specifications of cultural categories which, in actual use, were open-textured, polymorphous and/or family-resemblance concepts.[9] Adherence to both a 'lexicographic' conception of 'meaning' and a restrictive conception of 'rule of use' both informed the 'compositional theory of meaning of expressions' derived from Frege and the early Wittgenstein. Sacks noted that 'correctness' criteria alone (however they may be formulated) could not elucidate a major 'problem' solved routinely for practical purposes by practical categorisers: given the availability of an indefinitely extendable array of possibly 'correct' categories for use on any given occasion of categorisation, how could 'correctness' criteria alone illuminate the logic of *actual* categorisations? (Sacks, 1966). At a minimum, one must take stock of a distinction between 'possibly correct' and 'appropriately correct' categorisation of persons. Simply because a category or series of categories may in *some* sense be formally ('logically', 'strictly', etc.) correctly predicable of someone, and some criteria may be stated to justify that claim for 'correctness', does not mean that one has revealed thereby the principle(s) for its use. You may 'correctly' be referred to or categorised as, *inter alia*, 'female', 'teacher', 'white', 'Protestant', 'Republican', 'veteran', 'bookworm', 'professional', etc., and yet any accomplished selection or use of any one or more of these categories on some actual occasion of categorisation cannot be construed as a rational practice purely on the basis of its 'correctness', however substantiated. Considerations (amenable to formal treatment) extending beyond canonical 'truth conditions' must enter into the analysis of the logic of actually accomplished and rationally accomplishable categorisation *praxis*. One such additional consideration may initially be glossed as 'appropriateness'. But in what could 'appropriateness' consist?

One facet of Sacks' decomposition of 'appropriateness' criteria was 'orientation to the presumed local distribution of knowledge' in respect of categoriser and categorised. Here we encounter a particularisation for the case of membership categories of a more general principle informing the conduct of social and communicative *praxis*: 'recipient design'. A general constraint upon the design of one's communicative conduct is an orientation to the presumed local knowledge/beliefs of interlocutors. In the domain of person categorisation, this is instantiated by a 'preference for recognitionals over non-recognitionals' in using categories to name or refer to persons (Schegloff and Sacks, 1979). Thus, as a general intelligibility principle, reference-forms are used which maximise hearer-recognition even at the expense of proliferating categories beyond those elsewhere satisfactory for successful identification. Let us consider the 'preference for recognitionals' first, and focus on the use of 'proper names'. If I announce to you that I am going to see 'Miss Jones' this afternoon where I know, and know that you know, that the person so-categorised is your sister, and where I know, and know that you know, that we routinely call her 'Sally', then something beyond merely routine categorisation is being done, and, in various contexts, my usage of the 'Title + Last Name' reference-form risks ambiguity at best and unintelligibility at worst. Note, however, that your sister Sally *was correctly* categorised: she is unmarried and her surname is Jones. Conversely, if I announce to you that I am going to meet 'Joe' this afternoon, where I know or discover that you do not know anyone whom you call 'Joe', and where you do not know that I know someone called 'Joe', then, although the person in question has been *correctly* categorised by the use of the name 'Joe' (he *was* christened 'Joe' and has not changed his name), my categorisation will require supplementation by *further* categories until recognition or adequate characterisation has been achieved. Thus, I may continue with: 'You know, Joe – the janitor – the black guy who lives next to Peter – *Mr DuBois*,' until I attain common ground with you. Note, however, that occasions in which recognitionality or mutual comprehension fails constitute an orderly class of exceptions to an otherwise very general convention for person categorisation: the use of minimal reference-forms. To speak of Joe to you as 'Joe, the janitor, the black guy, Mr DuBois', i.e., to 'proliferate' categories, in circumstances of presumably mutual knowledge of him is to engage in something *other than* routine, ordinary categorisation. There is a 'preference for minimisation' or an 'economy convention' for person-categorisation such that 'on any occasion of categorising Members . . . the task *may* be complete if (the Member) has had a single category applied to (him/her)' (Sacks, 1972a: 34).

Further aspects of 'appropriateness' or 'relevancing rules' in respect of person (or 'membership') categorisation may be specified. Sacks proposed a 'consistency' rule or 'device co-selection' convention as organising the intelligibility of uses of a first plus (a) subsequent category (categories) in an utterance or exchange of utterances. In order to appreciate the force of this principle, we must first introduce the concept of a collection of categories in a device, or a Membership Categorisation Device (Sacks, 1972a: 31–2). Categories such as 'father', 'mother', 'son', 'uncle', 'grandmother' are found to 'belong' to a naturally acknowledged grouping of categories which could be termed a Device. In this case, the Device is that of 'Family'. Similarly, categories such as 'doctor', 'teacher', 'lawyer', 'professor' belong to the Device 'Occupations', some of them also to the Device 'Professions'. Categories such as 'Catholic', 'Pentecostal', 'Moslem', 'Jew' belong to the Device 'Religion'. Categories such as 'Democrat', 'Socialist', 'Liberal', go together as components of a Device such as 'Political Affiliations', and so on. However, categories within one Device may also be categories in other Devices. Thus, whilst 'English', 'French', 'Chinese' may belong to the Device 'Nationalities', they may also belong to the Device 'Natural Languages', and whilst 'Protestant' and 'Catholic' may belong to the Device 'Religion' or 'Religious Faiths', they may also belong to the Device 'Church'. Let us, then, introduce Sacks' 'consistency' rule in respect of first-plus-subsequent uses of membership categories. He states: 'If two or more categories are used to categorise two or more members of some population, and those categories can be heard as categories from the same collection, then: hear them that way' (Sacks, 1972b: 333). In this way, we can represent a logic for significant domains in the routine achievement of understandings *and* misunderstandings which turn upon hearing category uses. 'He's a solid right-winger, but she's still SWP' can be heard, whether or not a hearer has ever heard the term 'SWP', to refer to the Political convictions of *both* parties categorised in those terms. Naturally, hearings predicated upon such a logic for hearing can incur errors: inferences such as these are defeasible. Nonetheless, *first* hearings/candidate-understandings can turn upon such a spontaneous orientation to the relationship between membership categories. My introduction of someone to a friend as 'a lawyer' can provide for my friend's subsequent self-categorisation with a term of occupational or professional reference, where a follow-up with a term of Nationality or Geographic Location (e.g. 'Hi, I'm Vietnamese' or 'I'm from Denver Colorado') can signal either a mishearing, or a deliberate piece of obtuseness, etc. Sometimes, persons can successfully figure to what Device an otherwise unknown reference form belongs upon hearing its juxtaposition to a known category usage. For example, a person speaking to another remarks that he has been a Born-Again Christian for several years, whereupon her interlocutor observes that he is now a 'convinced Zoroastrian', and, without prefacing her inquiry with a request for clarification, the first speaker launches right into: 'Hmmm, where did you come across that religion?' even though it transpires through the conversation that she had never heard of the term at all in any previous context. Sacks noted a prototypical example in which the propensity to hear categorical identifications as belonging to a single unifying Device resulted in a *mis*understanding. A speaker was delivering news of his vacation activities, and remarked that he had heard 'Pete Seeger, Joan Baez and Wayne Morse'. The list was heard by an interlocutor as a set of Entertainers or Folk Singers, in virtue of his not knowing the identity of Wayne Morse (a former US Senator) and in virtue of his grouping all of the members of the list under the auspices of the Device implicated by the initial names (Sacks, *Lectures*, 1967).

In addition to these procedural principles, Sacks specified several further properties of membership categorisation. Two of these, 'inferential adequacy' and 'programmatic relevance', are introduced as relevant primarily to what he terms 'Standardised Relational Pairs', a subset of the set of Membership Categorisation Devices (MCDs). In this subset, the collections of categories logically related together have only *two* categories each, as distinct from the collections of several comprising the larger set of MCDs. The S–R pairs comprise such groupings as: 'friend–friend', 'neighbour–neighbour', 'parent–child', 'husband–wife', 'boyfriend–girlfriend', 'stranger–stranger', etc. To say that the pairs are 'standardised' means the following:

(1) If any Member X knows his own pair position with respect to some Member Y, then X knows the pair position of Y with respect to himself. X also knows that if Y knows what pair position Y has to X, then Y knows what pair position X has to Y.

(2) If any Member Z (neither X nor Y) knows what X takes to be X's pair position to Y, then Z knows what pair position X takes it that Y has to X. Z also knows that X takes it that if Y knows that X stands to Y in the pair position X supposes, then Y takes it that Y stands to X in the pair position X supposes. Z knows too that the converse holds for Y. Z knows further, as X and Y know, what the rights and obligations are

that obtain between X and Y given a convergence in their determination of their respective pair positions. (Sacks, 1972a: 370)

Simply grasping a pair-relation, then, may be, for various practical purposes, 'inferentially adequate' in terms of assigning moral requirements and rights to incumbents, as well as adequate in terms of other assignable properties. We shall consider various inferential affordances of categorisation further on. The notion of 'programmatic relevance' as a property of the use of S–R pairs makes reference to the enthymematic availability of one part of the pair given the other, and to the non-incumbency of one part as a potentially accountable *issue* for members. Given, for example, 'child', one projects 'parent(s)' and, whether through explicit topicalisation or latent presupposition, a non-incumbency for the S–R pair-part 'parent' can be constituted as a lack, something 'missing', a *noticeable* absence.

In the course of a discussion of conversational 'truth-conditions' (Sacks, 1975: 63–4), Sacks develops an interesting treatment of a compound concept, *everyone*, in which *every* is found to operate quite differently from its status as a Universal Quantifier in predicate logic.[10] Sacks observes that there are some occasions for which 'everyone' operates *summatively*, ranging over categories or persons, and yet not requiring for its operation an especially large number of categories or persons: e.g., an advertisement reads 'Something for everyone: An X for Dad, a Y for Mom, a Z for Brother, a T for Sister', and it is perfectly intelligible to discern a scope for 'everyone' as restricted here to 'family'. In addition, however, Sacks proposes that 'everyone' can operate 'programmatically' in circumstances in which comprehensive summation might otherwise generate a paradox. Thus, someone's saying something like: 'Everyone's going: why can't I?' as a complaint, may be heard to be interested in *bringing it about that* he is included in the 'everyone', and *not* to have uttered a self-contradictory remark.

In the course of an elaboration of the logical apparatus sketched by Sacks for relational-pair categories, Jayyusi (1984: 124–7) argues for an orderly variant of the S–R pairs which she terms Asymmetric Relational Pairs. Noting that members link such categories as 'doctor' programmatically to 'patient', 'teacher' to 'student', 'judge' to 'defendant' and 'policeman' to '(category of offender)', etc., Jayyusi proposes that such pairs exhibit, in many routine uses in account construction, the property of 'asymmetrical rights and/or knowledge'.

Whereas simple principles of set-inclusion would allow that a doctor's patient can himself be a doctor, a student can himself be a teacher, a thief can be a policeman, and a judge can appear as a defendant at a trial, where any such possibility is actualised in practice some special accounting or other contextual provision is expectably to be made in virtue of the *exclusionary* hearings/readings to which members conventionally orient. Incumbents of first-parts of asymmetrical relational pairs (e.g., 'doctor', 'judge', 'policeman') are *not* conventionally oriented to as incumbents of second-parts such as 'patient', 'offender' or 'defendant'. One finds frequent references in ordinary conversational accounts, as well as in media reportage, to such asymmetrical categorisations as 'army' and 'people', 'government' and 'people', etc., where a formal semantics would accord primary recognition to the fact that armies and governments are themselves composed of people. It is perfectly intelligible to hear/read of armies clashing with the people of the same nation without our taking it that they are fighting themselves in the process, and of governments oppressing the people where we do not take it that in so doing they necessarily suffer from the same oppression. This is due to our conventionally exclusionary ways of orienting to such categories *notwithstanding* their actual extensional identity under a semantic–componential representation. Jayyusi considers the following interrogative extracted from the Scarman Tribunal into the Northern Ireland civil disturbances:

Q: Would you agree, Father Mulvey, that there are people, be they calling themselves civil rights workers, or revolutionaries or anarchists, who have been deliberately placing the people of the Bogside in conflict with the police for the past twelve months? (Jayyusi, 1984: 124)

Although it is possible to take the 'police' in the conflict also to have been (part of the) 'people of the Bogside', and even to consider the possibility that the variously categorised persons putatively involved in stirring up the conflict were themselves (part of the) 'people of the Bogside', the 'natural' hearing is an exclusionary one. 'Police' and 'people' form an asymmetric relational category pair.

At this point, it is appropriate to consider Sacks' concept of category-bound activities (Sacks, 1972b). Once more focussing upon the fact that there are many possibly correct categories predicable of persons, Sacks argues that our socialised seeing and hearing in *praxis* enables us to make connections to 'relevant' or 'operable' categories by virtue (in part) of the conventional 'ties' or 'boundedness' of activities (activity-categories) to membership categories. Thus, for example, when witnessing a scene in which someone is crying, and that individual cannot be seen to be an adult, then 'without respect to the fact that it is a baby, it could be either "male" or "female", and nonetheless I would not, and I take it you would not, seeing the scene, see that "a male cried" if we could see that "a baby cried".' (Sacks, 1972b: 338). From these and other observations, Sacks extracts a 'viewers' maxim or 'relevance rule' for membership categorisation:

If a member sees a category-bound activity being done, then, if one can see it being done by a member of a category to which the activity is bound, then: See it that way. The viewers' maxim is another relevance rule in that it proposes that for an observer of a category-bound activity the category to which the activity is bound has a special relevance for formulating an identification of its doer. (Sacks, 1972b: 337)

The activity (-category) 'crying' is thus tied to 'baby', even though the 'baby' may be correctly described as 'male', 'black', 'Jewish', 'son' or by a variety of other categories. (Moreover, an adult who 'cries' *may* be categorised as a 'baby', and a 'baby' who no longer cries as babies do as now a 'big boy/girl' etc.) Similarly, it is the 'police' who make arrests, not 'Protestants', 'veterans' or 'democrats', even though any given police-officer may also be an incumbent of any or all of these membership categories. Examples ramify: teachers/ professors (etc.) 'teach', voters 'elect', judges 'sentence', doctors/physicians/ psychiatrists (etc.) 'diagnose', employers 'fire', and so on, where the activities and the categories are *conventionally* (although by no means indefeasibly or exclusively) bound, both for the organisation of our seeing/hearing and for the construction of accounts. Further, a woman who picks up a baby who is crying and who happens to be the 'mother' of the baby will preferredly be so categorised, notwithstanding her categorisability as, *inter alia*, 'dress-designer', 'free-lance writer', 'daughter', 'socialite', 'secretary', 'Born-Again Christian' and so forth. Descriptors of agents and their activities are characteristically *co*-selected to exhibit an orientation to category-boundedness. Indeed, as Jayyusi notes, many activity-categories are category-*constitutive* for membership categories, and the establishment of any binding relation, or its transformation to a constitutive one, may be consequentially negotiable matters for members (Jayyusi, 1984: 35 *et seq*).

Sacks (1979) introduced a further set of considerations in regard to membership categories and their logic of use, which Jayyusi developed into the concept of *attribute transitivity for category incumbents* (Jayyusi, 1984: 47–9). Sacks notes that although most categories do not constitute 'groups' in the ordinary sense of self-organised collectivities with known-in-common membership, rules and locations, nonetheless for many of them (e.g. 'women', 'teenagers', 'old people', etc.),

... any member is seen as a representative of each of those categories; any person who is a case of a category is seen as a member of the category, and what is known about the category is known about them, and the fate of each is bound up in the fate of the other, so that one regularly has systems of social control built up around these categories which are internally enforced by the members because if a member does something [deviant] . . . then that thing may be seen as what a member of some applicable category does, not what some named person did. (Sacks, 1972b)

In Jayyusi's terms:

The operation of a transitivity of attributes depends, in the first place, on this: whether, for some course of action or activity by a person who is a member of some collectivity, that 'collectivity' can be produced as an endogenous feature to that course of action . . . One way of accomplishing the defeasibility of such work, then, is to provide that 'collectivity' (in whatever relevant specific) was an exogenous or incidental feature to that course of action. (Jayyusi, 1984: 49)

From here, we can readily see how invocations of minimal person-categories can function at once as inferentially and judgementally rich usages in practical contexts. Thus, prototypically, an utterance embodying a single category as in: 'They're militants' could count as a possibly adequate (albeit defeasible) *explanation* in response to a query such as: 'Why are they on strike?' or 'I'm a doctor' could stand as a possibly adequate explanation when asked at the scene of an accident, say, 'What are you doing here?'

A final aspect of the logic of use of membership categories in practical discourse to be considered in this schematic review is the relevance rule of Opaque Attribution as a Hearers' Maxim for their use in object-complements of activity/orientation verbs in account construction. Consider an account of a scene delivered by a reporter (lay or professional) as follows: 'The Protestants encircled their Catholic adversaries at the Falls Road.' Independent of whatever background knowledge or belief a hearer may have pertaining to the events described in the account, it may be heard as a *first or preferred way of being heard* (whether intendedly so or not by its producer) as asserting not just that the victims of the attack ('Catholic adversaries') *happened to be Catholic* (i.e., that it is merely correct to predicate 'Catholic' of them) but that their victimhood is (partially at least) being *explained by their incumbency in that category*. This operates in virtue of the following convention: the persons described in the object-complement are hearably described with the particular categories used, not simply because those categories happen to be true of them, but because they are the categories under whose auspices *the subjects* (here 'Protestants') of the report would relevantly describe them in connection with the activity (or orientation) being reported. Using Quine's terms (Quine, 1960), predicating categorial identities in *opaque contexts* (e.g., as object-complements to the use of verbs of propositional attitude and action-orientation) can generate hearings in which such categories as are used may be construed as the categories which would be relevantly used of those persons *by the subjects of the accounts within which they appear as grammatical objects* (as subject–objects), and not merely as those useable by a(ny) reporter in virtue of their *transparent* truth.[11]

Immensely powerful resources, membership categories and their logic of use can organise our perceptions,[12] knowledge, belief,[13] discourse and other forms of practical conduct in thoroughly routine, expectable, conventional – in a word, orderly – ways. Although arguments can be initiated and/or organised with reference to topically invoked membership categories which are 'open-textured' in Waismann's terms (Waismann, 1965),[14] nonetheless, they are used as implicatively, inferentially, and presuppositionally conventional pieces in the language-games of everyday life.

It has not been my purpose in this discussion to detail every claim available in a now-extensive literature in ethnomethodology on the endogenous–logical properties of person or 'membership' categorisation, nor to burden the reader with fully detailed renditions of the transcription data sets and fragments which inform such claims as have been presented here. All that is being proposed is that existing formal–logical and formal-linguistic approaches to this domain of language-use, from Russell's treatment of proper names and reference to Donnellan's (1971) dichotomy of 'referential' and 'attributive' uses of 'definite descriptions' to currently popular 'causal theories of reference', singularly fail to reveal many central and significant facets of the *socially situated activities* of person categorisation. As a result of a similar neglect of the socially embedded character of linguistic usage, traditional Logic of Language (even including Austin's otherwise iconoclastic work on speech acts), failed to grasp and adequately represent so many of the ordered possibilities of practical reasoning and communication. Although we still have much to learn from such a traditional conception of the analysis of the logic of language, there are several characteristics of earlier modes of inquiry from which we must part company in the service of advancing a wholly cognate goal: the elucidation of the (various kinds and modalities of) rules governing the use of our linguistic apparatus. It is time to set out these points of difference explicitly.

7 Concluding remarks

Among the many respecifications required of extant Logic of Language if it is to regain its relationship to (linguistic/conceptual) *praxis* in its detailed orderliness as social-communicative phenomena would be the following:

(A) An extension of analytical focus from the proposition or statement, sentence or speech-act, to 'utterance design' or 'turn-at-talk'.

(B) An extension of analytical focus to encompass indexical expressions as components of *sequences* in terms of their logical properties and relations, especially their *inferential affordances*.

(C) A respecification of the concept of 'illocutionary act' to exclude *a prioristic* efforts to isolate 'propositional contents', and more fully to appreciate the socially situated availability of 'what an utterance could be accomplishing' *in situ*, especially in respect of its properties of design, sequential implication and turn-allocation relevances; in other words, its *interactionally* significant properties.

(D) A development of the concept of a *combinatorial* logic for illocutionary activities *in situ*.

(E) A development of an informal or endogenous logic for the *praxis* of person (Sacks, various; Watson, 1975, 1978, 1981; Drew, 1978; Jayyusi, 1984), place (Schegloff, 1972; Psathas, 1990), activity (Twer, 1972; Jayyusi, 1984), mental predicate (Coulter, 1973b, 1979a, 1983a) and collectivity categorisations, and their interrelationships, among other domains of referential, classificational and descriptive operations. This requires *abandonment* of formal semantic theoretic schemes deriving from set theory, extensionalism, generative- (transformational) grammar, truth–conditional semantics, and componential analysis as resources.

(F)   Abandonment of the preoccupation with 'correctness' defined as usage in accord with any rule specified *independently* of an analysis or orientation to ascertainable members' situated relevances, purposes and practices (Garfinkel, 1967: 33 *et seq*).

(G)   Abandonment of *a priori* invocations of mathematical concepts in the analysis of the informal logic of reasoning and communication; only those concepts warranted by studies of actual, *in situ* practical orientations of persons may be employed.

(H)   Replacement of the goal of logical regimentation in favour of logical *explication*.

(I)   Awareness of the varieties and modalities of what could count as 'rules of use' of linguistic/conceptual resources.

(J)   Abandonment of intellectual prejudices and generic characterisations concerning the putative 'vagueness', 'disorderliness', 'ambiguities', 'indeterminacies', 'imprecisions' and 'redundancies' of ordinary language use.

(K)   Formalisation, but not axiomatisation, becomes an objective, but not necessarily the production of an *integrated system* of formalisations.

(L)   Adherence to the constraint that formulations of rules of practical reasoning and communication be sensitive to *actual*, and not exclusively hypothetical, cases of *praxis*.

(M)   Extension of the concept of a 'logical grammar' to encompass the diversity of phenomena studied as components of conceptual *praxis*, requiring the de-privileging of 'strict categoricity rules' and the fuller exploration of the ties between Logic and Rhetoric.

(N)   De-privileging of all decontextualised standards for the ascription of 'rationality' and 'truth' without sacrificing their position as components of real-worldly reasoning in the arts and sciences of everyday affairs.

(O)   Recognition of the priority of *pre*-theoretical conceptualisations of phenomena as constraints upon 'technical' renditions of them.

If this purpose-built history has any merit, then I believe that these injunctions preserve the spirit, if not the letter, of the foundations of Logic as an exploration of the properties of *logos*; as Wittgenstein argued, although it may appear that we abolish Logic, indeed we do not – we recast its focus by rediscovering it afresh. In Sacks' terms, there once existed, long ago, a 'rather deep relationship between logic and [what we now understand as] sociology' (Sacks, 1975: 58–9). In ethnomethodology, we have found our way back to these ancient moorings in the interest of advancing our understanding of social phenomena. There are many other ways of grasping the intellectual significance of ethnomethodology for our times, as is examined throughout this book: surely, however, the link with the exploration of *logos* is one such way.

NOTES

1 For some discussion of these theoretical developments, see Coulter, 1973a.
2 For further details on Russell's relationship to Wittgenstein, see Blackwell (1981).
3 Also see Wittgenstein (1968: paras. 80–4).
4 Ryle had also elaborated a similar analysis, Ryle (1949).
5 See, e.g. Searle (1969: 30) on 'promising' as analysable into both 'function-indicating device' and 'propositional content' even for an expression such as: 'I promise to come', where the former is specified as the component: 'I promise' and the latter as the ('elided') component: 'I will come'.
6 See for instance, Fodor and Katz (1963).
7 For a brief review and discussion, see Coulter (1983a). For a more elaborate overview, although informed by an adherence to 'linguistic pragmatics' as a point of reference, see Levinson (1983).
8 See various contributions to Tyler (1969). Cognitive anthropology, and the general issues that are involved here, are given detailed consideration by John Lee in chapter nine when he exclusively addresses the relationships between language and culture.
9 See Coulter (1974).
10 See McCawley (1981: 98–104) on standardly recognised properties of quantifiers.
11 For a fuller discussion of these properties of account construction in terms of the logic of categories, as well as for their relationship to *de re* and *de dicto* reportage, see Jayyusi (1984: Ch. 6).
12 See Coulter (1975).
13 See Coulter (1979b).
14 For some analysis of categorical open-texture as an argumentative resource, see Coulter (1990).

4

Epistemology: professional scepticism
Wes Sharrock and Bob Anderson

1 Introduction

In our view, the epistemological arguments over 'objectivity and relativism', the relationship between 'commonsense and pure reason', the issue of 'a paramount and multiple realities', the relationship between 'objects and appearances' and other related epistemological issues in sociology and the human sciences seldom get beyond first base, not least because it is hard to get the lines of division identified well enough for there to be agreement on what are indeed the points of difference. Here we attempt a first base treatment of these issues by reverting to consideration of them in terms of Schutz's argument, and other basic phenomenological considerations. We do this because reasoned presentation of the issues in simple terms may help with the uphill struggle that, as Margolis (1986) observes, confronts anything that looks like a 'relativist' position – and we add, any which might be construed as 'subjective' in approach – because it will be typically presented by the opposition as blatantly stupid. Our objective is to display how Schutz, then Garfinkel and ethnomethodology, transforms the formulation of epistemological criteria into the topic of describing the properties of social organisation.

2 Examining social reality

It is a serious mistake to set philosophical scepticism on all fours and head to head with common sense understandings as though one straightforwardly and directly challenged the other. It is a usual characteristic of that scepticism that it seeks to operate at another level than the one on which our ordinary claims to knowledge get made. The epistemological sceptic, who denies that we can ever really know anything, has no interest in getting into dispute with someone who, say, claims to know where to find a good Chinese restaurant in a strange town, over whether they can in fact find such a restaurant. The philosophical sceptic is typically willing to grant that people do in the ordinary sense in which they make their claim, know what they say they do. The epistemological sceptic's case is that even when our ordinary standards of knowledge have been fully satisfied so that everyone would normally agree that, indeed, in this case it is right to say that someone knows something, still there is reason to question whether, at a *stricter, more demanding, level*, we should want to allow that this is truly knowledge. Descartes (1971 edn), the initiator of modern philosophical scepticism, consistently maintained that he had no intention of raising doubts with any practical effect, that his were philosophical doubts, raised within the context of a distinctive form of investigation, the 'pure enquiry', which aimed to determine what could be established as certain by the wholly unaided power of thought, through the application of pure reason.

The way disagreements over 'objectivity' in sociology are expressed is such, it seems to us, that in important ways they often reproduce the mistake just described, with ethnomethodology being one unfortunate victim of confusion on this point. Reducing the diversity of sociological views to a dichotomy, the contrast between sociologies conceiving 'social reality as objective', and those conceiving 'social reality as subjective', provides a handy but potentially misleading categorisation. It *has been* seriously misleading insofar as it has encouraged the idea of ethnomethodology as being of the 'social reality is subjective' school which can be dismissed peremptorily because it results in – if it does not depart from – a scepticism which conflicts with the patent objectivity of social phenomena – perhaps even natural, physical phenomena – as we ordinarily experience these. Saying that social reality is 'subjective' supposedly means that people can do anything they like, that the only thing stopping them from flapping their arms and flying, for example, is that they do not try to fly strenuously enough, but they could do it if they really believed in their power to do so. Indeed, they will have succeeded if they really believe they have. The individual will is sovereign and can dictate the nature of reality. If this *is* what is meant by saying that social reality is subjective, then the simple exposition of the point of view can be relied upon to reveal its absurdity. A sturdy sense of reality tells us that it is nonsense to suppose that anyone can fly like a bird. The law of gravity and other laws of physics tell us they cannot do this. It is an impossibility. The applicability of the laws of physics is an objective matter, something very different from a matter of personal preference or of even the most determined conviction.

The mistake which is being made, then, is in pitching the opposition between the views of social reality as 'objective' and as 'subjective' at the level at which this could make a difference to what ordinarily observably goes on in the everyday world. At that level the 'subjective' predilection is notably disadvantaged, for its vindication would apparently require that people do the impossible – at least, that they do what we generally regard as impossible, and do it at will. Because of this we will rigorously dissociate ethnomethodology from this idea of what saying 'social reality is subjective' means for this idea is indeed implausible. Continuing to use it as though it contrasted with our everyday use of 'objective' will make it seem that we are indeed setting out to dispute (amongst other things) the laws of physics. At the very least, continuing compliance in such a usage gives other sociologies the opportunity to arrogate to themselves a position to which they are not entitled, namely, that making them the distinctive and staunch defenders of the reasonable and plausible. Who, just by taking thought, can add one cubit to their stature?

In the light of the role that phenomenology has played as inspiration to ethnomethodology, some adversion to Husserl's own project is relevant and spells out this point. It was surely not Husserl's (1970a and 1970b) aim to make the truths of logic, mathematics and science 'subjective' in the sense that they could be treated in a cavalier way, with people arbitrarily deciding, if they felt like it, to accept that two plus two equals four, but refuse to assent to two plus three equals five. If the objectivity of mathematics *is* manifest in the fact that two plus two *does* equal four, regardless of whatever personal preferences any one might have, then Husserl does not contest the objectivity of mathematics.

The same applies to the findings of science. Husserl is not out to challenge or restrict the universality of the law of physics as we *ordinarily* understand those. In other words, it is integral to those laws that they apply across the board, not in random ways, here but not there, to you but not to me. If *this* is what the objectivity of the laws of physics consist in then, again, Husserl leaves this intact. The crux of Husserl's project was, as it has been for many twentieth-century philosophers, to understand the nature of logic, to comprehend the inexorability of its supposed laws. Husserl concurred in a widespread view that these were iron laws, ones which 'are more strict, more coercive, more general, and *in their sense* more unalterably "objective" than any of the generalizations of science or everyday common sense'[1] (Edie 1987: 37).

This is hardly the premise which should commit a project to the conclusion that everything is open to a 'take it or leave it' treatment, that matters are within the arbitrary discretion of each individual. On the contrary, Husserl's project is to understand, *not contest*, the 'objectivity' of (especially) logic, but also mathematics, science and so forth, and the target of his opposition is not the truths of mathematics or the findings of science, but (amongst others) the 'objectivist' interpretation of these. For Husserl the problem with objectivism is its *philosophical starting point*. It tends to take the findings of science and the suppositions of common sense at face value to the extent of assuming with them that the external world is already there, already given, but this, for Husserl, is to take for granted the very thing that ought to be up for *philosophical* inspection. Not, however, because there is a need to take a sceptical attitude toward the existence of the external world but because of the philosophical necessity to demand the full and explicit justification of assumptions, meaning that one cannot take the assumption of the givenness of the external world as the unexamined basis for a philosophy. A thorough philosophy must distance itself from the assumption, *suspend* (not deny) it, the proper task being to understand the sense of the supposition, to understand what it consists of. Starting from there, it ought to be clear that at the level of our ordinary experience the phenomenological investigation *makes no difference* to the ordinary experienced objectivity of social or natural phenomena, even in their character as exhibitions of the inexorability of the logical 'must', or invariance in the application of natural laws.

But Husserl's phenomenology *does* lead toward what is very widely – and, surely, rightly – called 'subjective idealism', does it not? Well it may, so long as it is borne in mind that in this context 'the subject' is a 'transcendental ego' that we *ultimately* encounter only through the rigorous and persistent application of the method of phenomenological reduction, through the suspension of ever-deeper layers of presupposition, and that this ego is very different from the empirical persons we encounter in the course of, and as the focus of, sociological and psychological studies. It is only at this remote level, and *only at this level*, that it is really possible to say that (social) reality is subjectively constituted in this sense, a level which is very remote from that at which people ordinarily talk of the objectivity of the law of gravity, the truths of mathematics or the impersonality of social arrangements (and a level to which many phenomenologists – including Alfred Schutz – have declined to follow Husserl). The undeniable fact that ethnomethodology has drawn more or less directly upon phenomenology does not entail that it must, in order to be sufficiently consistent with Husserl's work for its own legitimate purpose, be itself identified as a form of 'subjective idealism'. Insofar as ethnomethodology operates at the level of *sociological* investigation, it is a long way indeed from the level at which such a characterisation would be relevant, and, therefore, any reading of it which tries, on the grounds that phenomenology is, sooner or later, a *metaphysical* subjectivism, to project ethnomethodology as 'subjectivist' in this way at the level of our commonplace experience, is misguided.

3   Common sense and pure reason

The adoption and adaptation of Alfred Schutz's work made a crucial contribution to ethnomethodology's initial formulation, and it is, therefore, relevant and helpful in the development and clarification of the theme of the 'objectivity' of social phenomena to return to Schutz's arguments and their connection with the Cartesian method of systematic doubt, the basis of modern philosophical scepticism.

In Cartesian terms, true certainty exists only where there is no *conceivable* possibility of doubt (given, of course, that one recalls that this standard is seriously applicable only in the context of the 'pure enquiry'). Possession of certainty on this scale requires that every *conceivable* possibility of doubt be eradicated – which in turn requires, of course, that every conceivable possibility of doubt be identified, and so the attempt must be actively made to doubt everything to determine whether doubt proves to be impossible in the sense of being inconceivable.

Alfred Schutz's reflections (Schutz, 1962, 1964 and 1966) take note that the organisation of *practical action* cannot proceed on the basis of systematic doubt.[2] Some other auspices must be identified as those under which action-in-society takes place. The systematic application of the method of doubt would (at least on Cartesian assumptions) result in complete paralysis, and not just to practical action but even to philosophy itself, as the arguments of the sceptic show.

If a philosophically rigorous demand for certainty is unrelentingly applied, action will be interminably postponed whilst all conceivable possibilities of doubt are identified and thoroughly investigated. The Cartesian method is, then, utterly corrosive, for it opens up endless possibilities of doubt and at the same time undercuts the very procedures which could close them down. Within the context of ordinary affairs there is sometimes the possibility that something is not as it might appear to our eyes, a possibility which the Cartesian method ruthlessly generalises, but in *that* context (i.e. that of every-day affairs) we *can* very often resort to closer or more careful visual inspection to determine whether something is indeed as it appears to be. The Cartesian method, however, denies us legitimate confidence even in our eyesight[3] for we can on its terms conceive that our eyes might systematically deceive us: we can doubt not only appearances but also the very efficacy of eyesight itself and, given that, the most scrupulous visual inspection will be of no avail in dispelling the possibility that all things might be quite otherwise than they look to us. The point is generalisable beyond eyesight: any and all of our ordinarily acceptable ways of checking things out can be shown to be exposed to unresolved, and probably unresolvable possibilities, of doubt.

The simple fact about life-in-society, though, is that it does not exhibit the total paralysis that is to be expected if everyone were engaged in the endless pursuit of Cartesian certainty. Action goes on, things get done. Doubts occur, but (relative to the Cartesian possibility of their utter ubiquity) only occasionally, and are typically short lived, being speedily resolved.

To achieve explicitly formulated contrast with the Cartesian frame of reference we can identify the auspices under which social action is conducted as those of 'the natural attitude', an attitude which is most centrally characterised by its orientation to the possibility of doubt. The 'natural attitude' does not involve the total suspension of the possibility of doubt, but differs from the pure, systematic philosophical doubt in that it cannot cast doubt comprehensively, but only selectively, from within the assumption of the givenness of the external world as a whole. The philosophical doubt can indeed put the very existence of the external world itself into question, but the natural attitude can only question the existence of this or that thing within the context of assuming the existence of the external world as a whole.

The kind of caution we are about to give should not need making, but experience proves that unless – and even when – such clauses are explicitly entered the whole sense of these arguments will be misconstrued. We heavily stress that we are not proposing that consideration of the orientation under which daily life is conducted *must* begin from the Cartesian problematic, only that in this instance it has *happened* to do so. Without implying that 'the natural attitude' provides the inexorable place to initiate reflection on the character of conduct, by differentiating some of its kinds with respect to their orientation to the possibility of doubt, we nonetheless maintain that *given* the starting point of an interest in Cartesian issues, *then* it is entirely natural to pay attention to the differential possibilities of doubt, being forcibly struck with the way in which action in society requires taking things for granted.

Those acting under 'the natural attitude' turn away from the general possibility of doubt, allowing doubts only where they are specifically occasioned, where there is reason for them: the specifically motiveless, for-its-own-sake, doubting of the philosophical sceptic is actively excluded. It will be helpful if it is borne in mind that talk is at a very broad and abstract level of orientation here, that we are making comparison at the level of 'attitude' where this is absolutely not to be identified with the specific opinions of particular individuals, the psychological sense of attitude, but refers rather to the general orientation, or frame of reference, of conduct. 'Attitude' in this sense is manifested in the way people react to, and treat, situations, the fluent way in which they go about most of their activities, seldom if ever hesitating, only very occasionally showing any disposition to check anything out, to confirm that something is indeed what it appears to be. Anyone who would call the appearances of everyday phenomena into question 'just to see' runs every risk of getting a dismissive response for the futile, foolish, offensive and/or time-wasting character of their effort (unless, of course, they have specific grounds for doubting appearances.[4] The point, here, though, is not to develop the contrast of the 'natural attitude' with the Cartesian method of doubt, but to introduce a consideration of the 'scientific attitude' as an instance of the natural attitude. It is, of course, the contrastive treatment of 'common sense' and 'science' which provides the problematic crux of much sociological agonising, and Schutz's reflections on common sense are often seen as germane to this. Science may be more extensively sceptical than common sense, but these two fall together within the natural attitude, for both raise doubts against the background assumption of the external world. *Both* lack the capacity to put the world as a whole into question.

Much agonising occurs over the counter-posing of common sense and scientific understandings. *On the supposition* that 'common sense' and 'science' are both modes of knowledge and that they have one and the same object of knowledge (viz. the external world) the question is: where the two conflict (as they allegedly very visibly do) which of them is to be adjudged correct? The argument is then joined, with some (for example, Gellner, 1985, contributions by MacIntyre, Lukes, and Hollis in Wilson, 1970, and Hollis and Lukes, 1982) being thoroughly confident that the frame of reference of science must be taken as the setting for all our deliberations, that its specifications identify what is really there and that, therefore, any respects in which 'common sense' (or any other scheme of knowledge) fails to agree with those specifications, then so far does it fail to represent reality.

Others (for example, Winch, 1958 and 1970, Collins, 1982 and 1983, Collins and Cox, 1976 and 1977, Feyerabend, 1975, 1987 and 1988) are less than convinced by this. It seems deeply unsatisfactory because it degrades whole groups of persons relative to scientists and to those who, though not themselves scientists, overweeningly pride themselves on embodying a 'scientific culture'. The only way out of this often appears to be to maintain that *even though* the specifications of science and (for relevant example) common sense differ considerably, both must be considered as cognitively adequate, which means that some form of relativism appears necessary. We are not going to follow out the 'relativism' controversy here.[5] We only mention it at all because Schutz's characterisations of 'common sense' are often treated as though they initiate arguments which lead us in a relativist direction. However, Schutz's arguments *fall entirely outside* the framework of choice just outlined, *for they simply do not involve attempting to match the substantive specifications of common sense with those of science to begin with.* The kind of substantive matching which we are talking about is the sort that is famously exampled by the 'two tables' problem. Here is a table: common sense tells us that it is a solid object, made of wood, but science tells us that it is not solid, that the table is made of atoms and consists, in large proportion, of empty space – which of them is right? This practice of counterposing 'what common sense would say' about a particular object and 'what science would say about the same object' finds much favour in sociology, where it is often automatically assumed that what science would say about it would be the right thing.[6] Whatever the actual utility of putting what common sense says against what science does, it certainly is not the case that Schutz is setting out on another exercise of the same kind, though one which might reverse the usual verdict, finding that what common sense says is to be preferred over (or at the very least held to be just as good as) what science says. Schutz is not interested in matching the specifications of science and common sense at all, in invidiously comparing what they respectively have to say on any particular topic. Already we have noted that Schutz's investigations are at the level of 'attitude' and it is at this level that 'common sense' and 'science' are to be counterposed, as variants of the natural attitude. Consistent with the characterisation of the natural attitude in terms of its level of doubt so 'science' and 'common sense' may be contrasted with respect to the extent to which they accommodate doubt, albeit within the common restriction on doubting the existence of the world as a whole.

What Schutz does invite us to consider are the common-sense and scientific outlooks in terms of the possibility that they might be substituted for each other, especially that the scientific outlook could be substituted for the 'common-sense' one *in conduct.*

The idea that there is a superior correspondence between science's specifications and the 'real world' feeds into what we will call the 'canonical conception of reality'. Assuming that science is the optimal *cognitive* instrument,
it will be natural to suppose that, since there is a substantial cognitive element
in *practice*, then the optimal organisation of action will involve the incor-
poration of not merely the specifications that science provides but, more
fundamentally, the adoption of science's procedural standards as maxims of
practical conduct, rather than simply as procedures for theorising. This
canonical conception typically assumes that those engaged in practical conduct could actually make such a substitution (and thereby achieve more
effective action), but Schutz sees reason to doubt this. He holds that the attitudes of common sense and scientific theorising are not interchangeable.

The world of scientific theorising is constituted through *modification* of the
practical, common sense one. Naturally, given the terms of Schutz's comparison, one at the level of attitude, instituted with reference to the Cartesian
frame of reference, the scientific attitude is also to be characterised primarily
with respect to the possibility of doubt, and in that connection it falls between
the Cartesian one of methodic doubt and the 'practical' one of suspending
virtually all possibility of doubt save that occasioned by things failing to turn
out as it had been taken for granted that they would. The scientific attitude is
exempted from common sense's prohibition on doubt 'for its own sake', and
is licensed to raise and pursue doubts where there is no pragmatic necessity for
them, to raise them 'just to see' where these might lead. It is difficult to
formulate these comparisons both briefly and in a way which does not allow
(let alone invite) the reading into them of rather more than is either intended
or allowable.

The presentation of the difference between 'common sense' and 'science' as
one at the level of attitude is not misread as an attempt to insinuate (if not say
right out) that this difference is essentially one in the personalities of individuals. The impression that this is what we are saying may be reinforced by the
way we continue the case, but even our arguments so far should not foster such
impressions. That it will do so perhaps testifies to the fact that within contemporary sociology there is an overdeveloped sense of the threat 'individualism' poses, with correspondingly over-zealous searching out of instances of
the supposed offence (Althusser, 1971, 1976 and 1979, and Foucault, 1979).[7]
The comparison at the level of 'attitude' we already said does not apply in a
psychological sense, and it ought also to be apparent that much that we have
said about 'attitude' could easily be recast as remarks about 'norms of conduct', a phrase which identifies non-individual, socially provided requirements. The emphasis is, throughout, surely upon *the differential legitimacy* of
asking otherwise unmotivated questions in the respective contexts of (say)
scientific theorising and business practice, in the laboratory and the school
room.

When we go on to elaborate further on the contrast of common sense and scientific theorising, by describing the common-sense outlook as ego-centred, we will, if our previous comments are taken in unduly 'individualist' terms, be compounding our imagined offence, falsely presenting the individual's standpoint as though it were the centre of the universe. Again, though, to say that the 'common-sense' outlook is ego-centred is a long way from saying that people are more than ordinarily egotistical, or that in any way they overestimate the extent to which things revolve around them. It is a *very long* way from saying that the individual in the common-sense outlook views the world with him/herself at its centre, *to saying* that this same individual imagines that everything revolves around him. The fact that someone speaks of a place as 'my home town' indicates, in plain English, that this is the town in which they grew up and/or in which they live, and their speaking of it as *'my* town' indicates the place that it has in their relevances, accounts for the differential, perhaps the preferential, interest that it has for them over other towns. 'My town' does not say that the town belongs to the speaker, but that the speaker belongs to the town. In other words, the user of the saying is not expressing conviction that the home town's affairs are organised for and around him: though it is the centre of his life, *he is not the centre of its.* There is, then, no attribution of heightened possessiveness to the locution 'my town', nor any hint that we treat this expression as manifesting an unacceptably monomaniac standpoint to its user. It is, therefore, in very much the same sense to talk of 'my town' that we speak of 'my world' when we take up Bittner's (1973) contention that the social world is, in the common-sense attitude, fundamentally and irreducibly encountered as 'my world'. This formulation highlights the fact that persons structure their experience around the focal point of their particular situation, that they view things from their individual 'here and now' (with – of course – its associated history and prospects), that it is the world within which they are at home and within which events have their meaning relative to how they fit into their relevances.

To re-emphasise: that someone views events from their centre does not mean they are unduly insensitive to others, for it is an elemental feature of the ego-logical orientation that it is relativised, not absolute. It involves recognition that others comparably structure experience, placing themselves at the centre of their (so to speak) system of coordinates. We hasten to add that individually developed co-ordinates are not being invoked to eliminate socially provided ones, as will shortly be seen. However, the task in hand is to continue the 'scientific'/'common sense' contrast.

The attitude of scientific theorising certainly contrasts with common sense on the dimension of ego-centredness. It goes to the opposite extreme. It is constituted through the displacement of the ego-centred frame of reference, which is accomplished through the adoption of a conception which idealises the theorist as one who examines matters as 'from no particular point of view' or, in other words, from the standpoint of eternity. Such an idealisation certainly makes a difference to the way events are viewed, for its adoption means the methodic elimination from the portrayal of events the things which give them their very character when regarded in terms of an individual's common-sense coordinates. The scientific theorist, then, operates within a different kind of frame of reference to that which is employed in common-sense situations, with the scientific discipline providing an impersonal standpoint from within which things are to be viewed, within which problems are to be formulated and their solutions sought. The investigator takes as problematic those matters which are recognised as such by the discipline, which have not already been resolved within its frame of reference. In exchange for exemption from the prohibition on pragmatically unmotivated doubt, the scientific investigator is subjected to exceptional requirements of logical consistency and semantic clarity. To put the contrast as starkly and simply as we can, the common-sense outlook is directed toward practicality, dominated by the need to *get things done*, and the acquisition of knowledge is overwhelmingly subordinated to this. The result is that the practical actor's 'stock of knowledge at hand' will be a heterogeneously organised collection of (pre-eminently) recipes for effective conduct. The natural attitude is certainly not suitably designed for the pursuit of *systematic knowledge*, whilst the scientific attitude provides a far superior environment for the single-minded pursuit of this, providing a setting within which individual inquiries are conducted within a coordinating framework and their results may therefore be incorporated in a unified whole. The common-sense and scientific attitudes are not so much in conflict with one another, as they are incongruous, to the extent that the systematic substitution of either for the other would be disruptive.

This stark contrast of the practical and scientific attitudes is devoid of all implication that the worlds of common sense and science are hermetically sealed against one another, so much so that it would be impossible for any 'common-sense conceptions' to be dislodged by 'scientific findings'. We nonetheless maintain that the fact that piecemeal transplantation of scientific ideas into common sense can and does occur, it just fails to bear upon the argument here, which has been about whether there might be a *thoroughgoing* substitution of the scientific for the common-sense attitude.

Doubtless there are many different lessons which could be drawn from Garfinkel's 'classroom demonstration' or, as they are otherwise known, his 'experiments' (Garfinkel, 1967), but the ones which are often drawn – that, as Giddens (1976), Craib (1984) and Gilbert and Mulkay (1984), allude to, these demonstrate the fragility of social order, for example – often have little real relevance for ethnomethodology, and certainly do not draw the most useful conclusions. Amongst the lessons which can, we think, most usefully be taken from some of the experiments are those which implement the case just developed. For brief example mention of two such exercises will suffice. The first involving the relentless interrogation of the conversational partner, the second requires students to act as though they were lodgers in their own homes. Both of these can be understood as simple, economic, above all *unpretentious* ways of illustrating incongruity between the common-sense and the scientific attitudes.

Garfinkel's students were sent out to engage people in conversation (Garfinkel, 1967: Ch. 2). On any possible occasion in the conversation on which they can see the opportunity they are to demand clarification of the other's remarks, persisting in that demand until all possible ambiguities or obscurities are eliminated. These attempts did not get very far, the conversational 'subjects' quickly becoming impatient and irritated, denying any need for further clarification of their remarks despite being challenged, and even terminating the conversation. This exercise can be seen as a way of introducing into the context of the common-sense outlook a requirement appropriate to that of scientific theorising, namely that of semantic clarity for its own sake. The implementation of that requirement does not, however, result in better organised, more rationally conducted conversation but in the disruption, even destruction, of the conversation itself.

Comparably, the 'experiment' with students casting themselves in the role of lodger within their own homes (Garfinkel, 1967: Ch. 2) can be seen as inviting the adoption of something akin to the de-personalised standpoint that the scientific attitude imposes, removing the student from involvement in the specific context. The students did not, however, find that this distancing from their involved, personalised standpoint gave them a more objective comprehension of those same circumstances but, instead, deprived them of some essential features. The capacity to see what was really happening before their eyes as events in a household – more, their own home – required reference to knowledge of the circumstances, of persons and the history of their mutual relationship which were acquired by full participation in the household.

Like Garfinkel, we decline to promote these simple illustrative devices to anything more than that, claiming for them only that they offer *prima facie* support for the view that the scientific and common-sense attitudes are incongruous, at least to the extent that the attempt at the progressive, and eventually complete, substitution of the former for the latter is an impracticable project.

4   Paramount and multiple realities

Though we have previously set aside the 'relativism' question and have implied that Schutz's treatment of the common sense/science issues gives no reason to develop that as an issue, it is nonetheless probably as well to spell out why these arguments do not support relativism.

There are still important points of clarification about the nature and implication of Schutz's argument which are essential to the forestalling of relativistic interpretations. The fact that Schutz's thoughts are largely devoid of these will be the more readily appreciated if it is seen that the move is being made from 'epistemological' to 'organisational' mode, and that first Schutz, then

Garfinkel and ethnomethodology, are attempting to respecify topics by transforming them into ones which involve describing properties of social organisation, rather than formulating epistemological criteria. It will not remotely help the comprehension of the work to read it as if it attempted to formulate properties of social organisation *so that they can serve as epistemological criteria*, either securing or undermining ordinary claims to knowledge, let alone vindicating or invalidating the philosophical sceptic's challenge. Wittgenstein (1978) remarked that (legitimate) philosophy could only leave everything as it is, meaning (particularly with reference to the sciences and mathematics) that philosophy *could not possibly* either enhance or diminish the support for these. It was beyond the capacity or competence of philosophy to make any difference to the findings of science and the results of mathematics. A comparable thing might be said about ethnomethodology, that it too leaves everything as it is, is capable of making no alteration to the cognitive value of either common-sense understandings nor scientific theorisation: these are neither more nor less certain as a result of ethnomethodology's investigations than they were before.

One of the difficulties with which one must contend in contemporary sociology (and social thought throughout the human sciences more generally) is that strong contemporary prejudice condemns political quietism (and, in accord with Durkheim's argument about strong, widely shared sentiments, that prejudice is quick to be outraged), with the result that remarks like Wittgenstein's and our reiteration of them are likely to be singled out as evidencing that such approaches to philosophy and sociology are reprehensible invitations to quietism. Our remarks here, and the related arguments concerning values and moral judgement in general that are made by Lena Jayyusi in chapter 10, are certainly out of sorts with those views of philosophy and sociology which make it incumbent upon these pursuits to achieve the revaluation of phenomena, to reveal that they are more or (more usually) less than they are cracked up to be, but those same remarks are (if read *without prejudice*) quite neutral about the desirability of political quietism. The critical supposition is that 'leaving everything as it is' contributes support to the political *status quo*, but the conclusion that Wittgenstein's (or ethnomethodology's) approach does this omits to notice what is being said, which is that (properly executed) Wittgensteinian philosophy and ethnomethodological inquiry *make no difference* to these things, so they certainly cannot make them stronger or weaker, more or less defensible etc. than they otherwise might be. Just as it is outside of the competence of these approaches to re-evaluate cognitive schemes, so it is equally beyond their reach to re-evaluate other kinds of legitimacy, hence it would be less the fulfilment than the violation of their conviction that they must leave everything as it is if they were to make phenomena out to be more legitimate than they otherwise would be.

It ought, then, to be obvious from the outset of our argument that any version of ethnomethodology which seeks to see it as substituting an inferior 'socially constructed object' for 'the real thing'[8] has somewhere along the line gone off the rails. One point at which such derailing can occur is in taking Schutz's discussion of 'multiple realities' as leading in the direction that relativists like them to go, which is that of setting up premises for arguments about a plurality of cultural systems, with the implication that what we are confronted with is a plurality of autonomous and competing 'realities'. Schutz's own thoughts on 'multiple realities' have little to do with this, and if taken *in conjunction* with those on the reciprocity of perspectives and the interchangeability of standpoints definitively show how far he was from going that way. Sure enough, Schutz does talk of 'multiple realities' and does identify the world of daily life (as comprehended through common-sense understandings) as 'paramount reality', but this does not indicate either an incipient relativism *nor* (in the opposite direction) an inclination to grant incorrigibility to common-sense understandings.

It is important to recall that Schutz is not concerned with 'common sense' as a determined collection of specifications, that his notion is a *formal* one: 'common sense' is the social correlate of the individual's demonstrable disposition to take things for granted. At the level of the premises of conduct (so to speak) it is inevitable (*given* the origins of the argument in Cartesian issues) that anyone who would act *must* leave a multitude of things unexamined, *must* be taking all of these for granted. To reiterate, the Cartesian method of doubting everything that can possibly be doubted must result in the paralysis of action, in its endless postponement pending the resolution of the vast multiplicity of possible doubts, but the very existence of social life entails that *action does occur*, which means that possible doubts must be being extensively disregarded. The capacity of persons to take things for granted on this scale is enabled through inheritance of the socially distributed stock of knowledge, the acquisition of a set of received recipes for practical life that are socially sanctioned and which delimit the possibility of doubts by institutionalised insistence that there are matters which cannot legitimately be inquired into. Those who attempt to raise doubts with respect to these matters will typically find that their attempts reflect not on their intended targets, but react back upon the questioner, casting doubt on their practical competence, even their sanity. Others will be mutually supportive in rejecting such doubts. Obviously, in order to illustrate one may speak from one's own pre-theoretical point of reference of things which *amongst us* are taken as certainties and which stand outside *legitimate* examination, but this manner of presentation must not be mistaken for an analytical parochialism.

Things that might be pointed to as having 'common-sense' status in such illustration are not, thereby being awarded any universal and generally incorrigible character, for *analytically speaking*, talk of 'common sense' merely intends the fact that *amongst any given collection of persons organised into anything that can meaningfully be called a collectivity*, there will be a corpus of matters which those persons will find 'obvious', as 'going without saying' and as 'beyond doubt and investigation'. What those matters will be will vary, of course, from one collectivity to another. It will not do, either, to suppose that these matters are the equivalent of Durkheim's sacred conceptions, *protected* from investigation by their sanctity, for they are instead prevailingly matters of utter mundaneity, such that inquiry into them embodies less the transgression of boundaries into the forbidden than it does the investment of energy into the pointless, the time wasting and the unnecessary. In other words, the perceived futility of such inquiries is what ensures that they reflect negatively upon their maker.

The world of daily life, comprehended under the auspices of common sense, is picked out by Schutz as 'the paramount reality' but, again, this only indicates the organisational position which 'the world of daily life' occupies amongst the various 'finite provinces of meaning'. The initial objective of distinguishing amongst 'finite provinces of meaning' is to put the spotlight on the episodic nature of the flow of experience. The differences which talk about 'multiple realities' is designed to capture are those between waking and dreaming, between walking the streets and being engrossed in a theatrical performance, between engaging in practical pursuits and theoretical reflection. Over any period of time the individual can alternate between episodes of these kind, passing from wide awakeness into sleep and dreaming then awakening again, moving from attentiveness to the daily world into an imaginative daydream and so on.

The *first* point Schutz is making is that the transition between these episodes is abrupt, with the respective spheres of the wide-awake world, the dream, the fantasy and so on being self-contained. *Second*, he emphasises that *within* each sphere an 'accent of reality' is assigned to the things experienced there. *Whilst we are undergoing them* the things which happen in the dream seem real to us, just as those which take place before our eyes on the stage of the theatre do. *Thirdly*, the transition from one episode to another is typically via the world of daily life: we enter the world of dreaming from the waking world, and we return eventually to the latter; we go to the theatre from the streets, are caught up in the world of the play but eventually the play will end and we return to the streets and the concerns of daily life (remembering where the car is parked, wondering if we left the umbrella in the theatre, etc.). *Fourth*, the standards of reality which are applied in daily life pre-empt those in the other 'provinces of meaning'.

Thus, to repeat, *whilst we are dreaming* the occurrences in the dream are real to us, the dream of winning a vast amount of money engenders the euphoria we should doubtless feel if such an event occurred in real life, but, however real the events in the dream might seem, upon wakening they will be (regretfully, in this case) consigned to the category of 'only a dream'. Try telling the bank manager that you have dreamed you won a million pounds and that you would like to use this million to clear off your overdraft. Similarly, try telling the police complaints desk that you have just seen the murder of Julius Caesar and that you are fortunately able to name the killers: Brutus, Cassius and so on. However strongly the accent of reality may have been placed upon the events in the play, *in the context of daily life* these events did not really take place. It is by virtue of its two characteristics, as the environment for other provinces of meaning and the role of its standards as arbiters of reality, that common sense is dubbed 'the paramount reality'. This is not to offer any endorsement of its position on Schutz's behalf, merely to note the typical manner in which relations amongst waking, dreaming, fantasising and theorising (to name but a few) are dealt with by the members of society.

One further point is necessary in connection with Schutz, pertaining to the vital but easily neglected qualification which he sets upon the assumptions of 'the reciprocity of perspectives' and 'the interchangeability of standpoints'. *Given* that Schutz is attempting to reconstruct the generic properties of the social world out of the structure of individual experience, and *given* that the argument involves the 'relativising' of the environment to the extent that the world is, for each individual, *my* world, then the risk is that this will be taken to involve the decomposition of the social world into a vast multiplicity of ego-centred realities, each substantially and irreconcilably different because of the exigencies of individual positioning and experience. However, to project such a possibility of proliferation is to neglect the fact that Schutz is throughout responsive to the pre-theoretical givenness of the world as a social world, as an intersubjectively available 'one and the same' world for different persons. The aim was certainly not the decomposition of the social world into unrelated subjectivities but, rather, one the experiential underpinning of the *socially sanctioned* unity of the world, of the mutual *demand* that we recognise the commonality of circumstance.

The provision Schutz makes for this is, first, in terms of the socially distributed stock of knowledge. It is necessary to distinguish between actually identifiable persons and the theoretically reduced creatures that are devices of Schutz's own theorising. For the purposes of expositing the structure of socially organised experience Schutz envisages a drastically reduced consciousness, a pure stream of experience which is unstructured and into which socially provided structures will have to be installed. The wisdom of employing such a method of exposition may be debatable, but the fact that it is employed should not lead us to suppose that the experience of actual persons is *conceivable independently of socially provided structures*, for it is not.

Any actually encountered person will, of course, be the possessor of a handed-down body of knowledge in terms of which their circumstances and courses of action will be conceived. Hence, it is just not possible to conceive the real members of society as a collection of mutually independent standpoints. Further, Schutz builds into his analysis of the structure of experience two 'theses', which are those of 'the reciprocity of perspectives' and 'the interchangeability of standpoints'. These are assumptions that the respective standpoints of ego and alter will be complimentary, that the way things seem to A will not be strictly identical with the way they are for B, given that the two occupy different standpoints, but that they will reciprocate each other, to the extent that differences between them can be discounted against their separate locations.

This first assumption of the 'reciprocity of perspectives' is reinforced by that of 'interchangeability of standpoints' which is that if A and B were to change position then what A would find from his/her new vantage point would be identical with what B had previously found in that position *and vice versa.* These are, note, assumptions built into the common-sense attitude, their presence evidenced in the multifarious and multitudinous ways in which the flow of activity in society simply presupposes orientation to a commonly known environment. There is not, on Schutz's part, any attempt to make unduly optimistic assumptions, to dispose of, let alone, minimise, possibilities of divergence and dissent, for the reciprocity of perspectives and the inter-changeability of standpoints are assumptions and *are not guaranteed.* They hold good *until further notice* – they can, and do, break down. Conduct which begins on the presumption of a commonly known environment may find that its presumption must be reviewed. Furthermore, and this is the point at which the above mentioned vital qualification needs to be entered, these assumptions are ones which have legitimate application only when it can be *assumed that biographical differences can be set at zero.* If this qualification is overlooked then it will appear that Schutz's characterisation gratuitously overestimates the homogeneity of experience in the face of cultural diversity but, to the contrary, Schutz makes ample provision against such overestimate: allowance for the diversity of experience and culture is built into the socially distributed stock of knowledge itself, as citation of the cases of children and strangers unequivocally illustrates.

5   Objects and appearances

The challenge of scepticism is not absent from contemporary sociology,[9] but is still strong there, perhaps more prominent than ever. Cartesian scepticism directed itself toward the identification of necessary certainties and an exercise in that spirit will be moved to despair if it cannot find any certainties, for Cartesianism holds a 'foundationalist' conception of knowledge. A sound edifice of knowledge can be erected only if it stands in secure foundations: if there can be doubts about even its founding assumptions, then the whole construction is affected. However, 'foundationalism' is now in poor repute and the idea of the search for certainty itself is inimical. The reaction against Cartesianism means nowadays not a disappointed resignation to the fact that there are – can be – no certainties of the kind it seems, but an enthusiastic, even joyous acceptance of the absence of certainty, the abandonment of whose schemes of thought have been informed (or infected) by Cartesian aspirations.

This is celebratory scepticism and, though it may not have the upper hand in contemporary sociology, it is certainly a pro-active force, vigorously cultivating equivocality, irresolution, and doubt, delighting in the ultimate and utter indeterminacy of reality. Though those who follow out the most developed forms of this scepticism are apt to regard ethnomethodology as joining them on the sceptical side, but as doing so only timidly and without taking the possibility of doubt anywhere near far enough.[10]

Appreciating that the roots of contemporary sociological scepticism are diversified and more complex, certainly, than can be properly acknowledged in comments as concise as ours, we will incautiously but flatly assert that much of this scepticism is propelled by rejection of the possibility of any 'final interpretation'. The 'achievements' of reason are now 'recognised' to be the production of interpretations, and there is always a multiplicity of these. No matter how convincing any interpretation may appear, some other (equivalently effective) interpretation is *always* possible, the pursuit of any 'final' one being futile because the sequence of possible interpretations is endless. The obligation is, therefore, to reveal interpretations for what they are, unravelling any pretensions they may have to finality, and proliferating the alternatives to them, this activity of course being wholly alive to its own inherent lack of finality and requiring, therefore, the development of the means of its own eventual destruction.

Ethnomethodology (and Wittgensteinian philosophy) also are seen as initial moves in this direction. They are anti-Cartesian certainly, and are imagined to have contributed their share to the erosion of 'reality' and to the supposed realisation that *there is only interpretation*. Ethnomethodology has established that 'social reality' is (merely) an ensemble of interpretations, but it does not take this insight seriously enough (in the judgement of its would-be surpassers, for example: Blum and McHugh 1986, McHugh *et al.*, 1975, Woolgar, 1988, Silverman and Torode, 1980), to throw itself into the constantly self-destabilising proliferation of interpretations which is the *sine qua non* of adequately self-conscious contemporary theorising. In other words, ethnomethodology has started on, but failed to go very far down, the road to the realisation that theorising is essentially a self-expressive activity, which – unless it is conducted as a continuously self-deflating self-scrutiny – will become gratuitous assertiveness, intrusion into the other's interpretive space. In the manner of all those who regard one set of values as a provisional but partial step toward their own, those who subscribe to contemporary scepticisms perhaps consider themselves to be paying ethnomethodology a compliment by allowing that it is on the right side of the sceptical divide – just – but failing to subject itself to a sufficiently searching, self-doubting scrutiny.

However, compliments of this sort may not be gracefully received, and may even be flatly rejected with a tart comment like Bittner's, because they have as their source 'the pallid ideology of cultural relativism' (Bittner, 1973).

Bittner, appraising the situation in field-work studies of a quarter of a century ago, wrote with continuing relevance, for though he might have been expected to welcome the 'turn to subjectivity' which was then taking place in sociology, giving a new centrality to 'the actor's point of view', he proved highly critical of the way this turn was being taken, declaring that it implemented an 'abortive phenomenology'. Abandonment of the previous ideals of 'objectivity' should not mean the relaxation of strong standards of investigation and analysis in favour of a relaxed, casual, perhaps self-indulgent approach to these, though this was the direction in which the move-ment away from aspirations to 'objectivity' was taking. The opportunity was there for the maintenance of standards of rigour, but in the service of realism, a commitment to capturing the phenomena under investigation through scrupulous study and accurate description had the opportunity to replace the previous, 'positivist' commitment to the supposed requirements of scientific method. The opportunity might however be missed for,

although the attacks on positivism were mounted from positions that involved strong commitments to philosophically well-grounded and rigorous scholarship, the argu-ments of the attack were often invoked as the aegis for studies of a loose, impression-istic and personal nature. (Bittner, 1973: 117)

Bittner wanted to hold these studies to what they were apt to put up as objectives for themselves, but from which they were tending to deviate because they were short-circuiting the process of understanding 'the actor's point of view':

if the fieldworker's claim to realism and to respect for the actor are to be given serious credence, then it will have to be made clear when they are a function of a natural atti-tude of the actor but of a deliberately appropriated 'natural attitude' of the observer. (Bittner, 1973: 119)

Fieldwork methodology was recommended because it brought researchers into close contact with those whose setting and life was being investigated, and supposedly ensured that the researcher would be more intensively, vividly aware of the actor's point of view, and therefore able to give the most faithful rendition of this, but, if Bittner's judgement was right, immersion in the field was producing only an attenuated characterisation of the actor's sense of social reality. Indeed, the very nature of fieldwork itself could be the very thing producing this attenuation with the fieldworker's relation to the phenomena encountered in fieldwork experience being conflated with those encountered from within the social worlds under study. The world of daily life comes to appear to the fieldworker 'merely' as a corpus of exhibits, with the conse-quence that:

[the fieldworker] tends to experience reality as being of subjective origin to a far greater extent than is typical in the natural attitude. Slipping in and out of points of view [the fieldworker] cannot avoid appreciating the meanings of objects as more or less freely conjured. Thus [the fieldworker] will read signs of a future from entrails of animals, believe that the distance objects fall is a function of the square of time, accept money in return for valuables, and do almost anything else along this line; but the perceived reality of it will be that it is so because someone is so seeing it, and it could be and probably is altogether different for someone else, because whatever necessity there is in a thing being what it seems to be is wholly contained in the mind of the perceiving subject. Hence, without it ever becoming entirely clear, the accent of the fieldworker's interest shifts from the object to the subject. (Bittner, 1973: 122)

Again we have the spectacle of an ethnomethodologist setting himself well apart from a viewpoint which many would be convinced must be his own, but the history of ethnomethodology's public life, at least since the appearance of *Studies in Ethnomethodology* in 1967, is full of comparable ironies. The decomposition of social reality into a phenomenon within the mind of the subject is a failing (to those who allow this *is* a failing) for which ethnomethodology is regularly criticised. The double irony is that remonstrations like Bittner's receive scant attention when these criticisms are made.[11]

A united front of ethnomethodologists is too much to hope for, and is not in any case really needed. Evident disagreement between them on the issues under review at least reinforces our general case – a shift of attention to 'the subject' *at the expense of* 'the object' is not what all ethnomethodologists see as the inexorable outcome of their point of departure, though the prospect of unwittingly making such a transition/transgression is no doubt one ethnomethodologists run. Unless the distinctive standpoint which is identified in investigation as 'the actor's point of view' is understood to be rooted in the natural attitude, and itself interpreted against its background, then in all probability they will fall foul of that risk.

Though the passion for fieldwork has now abated, acknowledgement of the contingency of social phenomena now engenders similar difficulties. First Bittner again, and at some length:

For the fieldworker, as noted earlier, forever confronts 'someone's social reality'. And even when [the fieldworker] dwells on the fact that this reality is to 'them' incontrovertibly real in just the way 'they' perceive it, he knows that to some 'others' it may seem altogether different, and that, in fact, the most impressive features of 'the' social world is its colourful plurality. Indeed, the more seriously [the fieldworker] takes this observation, the more [the fieldworker] relies on his sensitivity as an observer who has seen firsthand how variously things can be perceived, the less likely he is to perceive those traits of depth, stability, and necessity that people recognise as actually inherent in the circumstances of their existence. Moreover, since [the fieldworker] finds the perceived features of reality to be perceived as they are because of certain psychological dispositions people acquire as members of their own cultures, he renders them in ways that far from being realistic are actually heavily intellectualized constructions that partake more of the character of theoretical formulation than of realistic description. (Bittner, 1973: 123)

Now dulled, the passion for fieldwork has been succeeded by a fascination amongst sociologists more generally with the contingent character of social arrangements, a fact which in all likelihood has indeed been understated by many social theories and which is, therefore, rightly given corrective acknowledgement. Unfortunately, over-compensation is not unknown, and the successor to Bittner's anxiety is the worry that, in seeking unequivocal demonstration of the contingent nature of some phenomenon, the 'traits of depth, stability and necessity that people recognise as actually inherent in the circumstances of their existence' may continue to be excluded from the picture.

Surely, though, phenomenology itself recommends paying attention to the appearances, leaving the question of how Bittner's strictures can be applied in the name of that cause? If phenomenology aims to close altogether the gap between reality and appearance, then what is the source of Bittner's dissatisfaction with the view that reality is as it appears to individuals?

Once again large and important differences hinge much upon how one understands slogans such as 'there is nothing behind the appearances'. 'Behind the appearances' there were supposedly objects, so if someone claims there is nothing behind the appearances then they will be understood as saying that there are no objects, only appearances. Hence, one is saying that appearances have displaced objects, that there are *only* appearances. The 'only' here can rapidly acquire, if it does not from the very first possess, distinct overtones of diminishment: objects have been replaced not by appearances but by *mere* appearances: reality has certainly been down-graded if it has been reduced from solid objects to mere appearances. This move, the disposal of objects in favour of appearances, surely encourages the view that objects are matters of appearance, of being 'merely' how they appear to particular observers?

To construe the slogan 'there is nothing behind appearances' in that way, however, is to continue to speak the language of the very conception we are trying to get away from, to accept their terms in which objects and appearances are distinct, in which one provides the substance that is covered by the other. What we experience are appearances and (presumptively) *behind* those appearances are the objects. Construed in those terms, phenomenological arguments which invite us to confine our investigations 'within experience' thereby perhaps unavoidably deny us access to objects themselves, for they stand outside experience. It is feared that if we do not preserve the separation of objects from their appearances then we will inevitably lose that vital distinction between how things appear to us and how they really are, independently of our perceptions. This kind of argumentation, surely, is familiar enough in recent sociology, where the insistence that this latter distinction is vital not only to the prosperity of sociology but to the continuing strength (and superiority?) of our civilisation.

There is, though, no reason why phenomenology should be understood in the terms of its predecessors' conception, as placing itself within the terms of the distinction they want to make. Why should it continue to speak their language, and why, therefore, should the slogan 'there is nothing behind the appearances' be meant in a way that makes the naïve mistake of supposing that we can never be wrong in our identification of the thing we are (say) looking at? Instead of *directly* controverting the assertion that there are objects behind appearances, the case is that this received way of talking makes it seem that we should only say that we see the surface of a chair or the front of a house, and never that we see the chair or the house. Seeing-a-house-from-the-front is, in phenomenology's submission, a much more adequate description of our experience than is 'seeing only the front surface of a house' and this latter, inadequate description is forced on us because of the way philosophers have attempted to separate objects from their appearances. Once again, the phenomenological position begins from, rather than goes against, the objectivity we ordinarily find in things. It does not seek to *reduce* objects to appearances in this inimical sense because it does not respect the contrast of 'object' and 'appearance' that was previously in place. The slogan can now be seen to mean something quite different than that objects do not exist, that only appearances do. Rather than putting appearances where objects used to be, one may be seen to be drawing attention to the way in which (so to speak) *objects are found in their appearance*. The 'objects' have been 'relocated' and are to be found from amongst the appearances.

Two very simple but persistently employed examples which are designed to show the difference between the appearances and the object are those featuring the stick-bent-in-water, and the-disk-that-is-seen-to-be-elliptical. The (object?) lesson in both cases is that exclusive reliance upon appearances, the strict confinement of our inquiries within the domain of experience, will deny us a distinction that we should otherwise consider indispensable. It is that between the stick which *appears* to be bent in water but which *in reality* is straight. Similarly, the disk that is seen to be elliptical is a disk which is seen to be elliptical but which is in fact (in itself) round.

The possibility of such instances, of a disjunction between how things appear and how they really are, between how things are in our experience and how they are in themselves, is one we are allegedly deprived of if we give credence to the phenomenological slogan, but this is not so. On the terms of phenomenology it is entirely conceivable that persons will find that things which appear bent when submerged in water will prove straight when extracted from the water, that a disk viewed from an angular perspective will look elliptical but upon closer inspection will be found to have been all along round. The apparent incapacity of 'appearances' to reveal the true character of the stick and the disk – as straight and round, respectively – is not, for phenomenologists, evidence that we need to go *outside* experience in order to determine the actual nature of phenomena – from the phenomenological point of view there is, after all, nowhere 'outside experience' to go.

The idea of a standpoint which is not *someone's* standpoint is equally nonsensical (though this does not, as we have already strongly stressed in our discussion of Schutz, deprive anyone of the capacity to use the standpoint of 'no particular point of view' as a cognitively invaluable device). Our apparent incapacity to determine *through* appearances, from *within* experience, the difference between something which 'merely appears' to be one thing but is 'in fact' another, is not inherent in the supposed 'restriction' of phenomenology to the merely subjective, perspectival or experiential domain. It is, rather, a product of the distinctly *impoverished description* which will inevitably be given of the character and dimension of the world-perceived-from-someone's-standpoint, if the conceptual apparatus of phenomenology's opponents is retained. In phenomenological terms, the stick which appears bent is not necessarily a stick which *is* bent, for the stick *as a properly assembled and described ensemble of appearances* to be precisely a-stick-which-appears-bent-but which if we go-over-extract-it-from-the-water-and-then-look-at-it-will-appear-straight which, for us counts as *being straight*.

An alternative possible way in which the stick can appear, is as a stick which looks bent but, allowing for the fact that it is partially immersed in water, we know even without examining further that it would prove to be really straight if we did look at it. However, does this not bring us back to the difficulty which both would-be friends and enemies see affecting the preservation of 'the object' in terms of 'appearances'? Is there not a (fateful) symmetry between 'the stick which appears bent (when in water)' and 'the stick that appears straight (when extracted from water)', and so how are we to determine which – bent or straight – the stick really is? Do we not have to say either that the stick is both-bent-and-straight, or that the stick is in itself neither-bent-nor-straight? Do we not have to accept that such determinacy as people find in reality is only that which they have imposed upon it? This, though, remains within the very framework from which phenomenology has withdrawn, one which puts in place a distinction between reality as it is in our experience, and reality as it is in itself. In phenomenology's own terms, however, there is no such distinction between reality as found in experience, and reality in itself.

An irresolvable symmetry appears only *if we withdraw* from assumptions which are otherwise already in place. There is a deep-rooted ambiguity in the presentation of both the case of the disk and the stick, which is that it has been presented as though each one of us was being invited to decide *for the very first time* what shape the disk was, what shape the stick was. To decide for the very first time *for everyone* that is, as though we were without any pre-given basis whatsoever on which to resolve the problem. We are being presented, therefore, not with the problem of deciding *for one particular case* what shape this disk is, or whether that stick is straight or not. It is not, that is, a *problem of perception* to resolve the general problem of the relationship between 'reality' and 'appearances', since it will be only in terms of some pre-given 'solution' to that problem that one is able to determine the character of particular perceptions. The ambiguity of the example results because the inherited ways of deciding what we see are built into their construction: the fact that we know about the effect of perspective on shape, and about the refracting effects of light in water, is presumed in describing the very situations themselves. When invited to consider the case in which a disk looks round to one observer, and elliptical to another, we are supposing that readers will imagine a familiar situation, one in which a something which, viewed head on, looks round will, when viewed at another angle, look elliptical. We do not suppose they take the example as one in which they are invited to consider the possibilities of the disk looking round and elliptical, as one in which these two are just the first in a long line of equivalent possibilities: that, for example, the disk might look like a triangle to a third party, like a fly to a fourth, like a caterpillar tractor to a fifth and so on and on.

If our supposition about the likely reading of the examples is correct, then this shows that the perceptual possibilities are *already* pretty well restricted, are restricted in terms of a pre-given conception of the possibility of relations between appearances and realities. The apparent choice being constructed on *that very basis*, then the apparent symmetry between the disk's being round and elliptical and the stick's being bent or straight is a fake one, for the basis of choice between them is built into that same pre-given conception: on its terms, the shape that a disk looks when viewed straight decides what shape it really is, and a look at the stick out of the water settled whether or not it is straight (if, in fact, there is any real doubt about the stick's shape).

We have come back by another route to Bittner's point about aborted phenomenology. Many philosophers and sociologists want to challenge the adequacy of our ordinary experience as a source for knowledge of reality, which, by an almost Newtonian law of equal and opposite reaction, inspires others to set out to defend that experience. From the standpoint adopted here, however, *both* sides of that argument are inclined to start with largely unexamined preconceptions about the character of that commonplace experience, and, further, that there is a critical issue not about the adequacy of our ordinary experience but about the possible inadequacy of *the descriptions* of that ordinary experience. The simple examples of the disk and the stick together highlight the difference between partial and wholesale withdrawal from the framework within which 'everyday experience' is gained, suggesting that:

(1) the character of any ordinary person's supposed experience of a disk viewed from an angle, or of a stick partially submerged in water, is described in an over-simplified way,

and

(2) that the examples which are supposedly constructed to allow us to distance ourselves from the 'prejudices' of our ordinary experience, and to invite us to critically reflect on these, are examples whose very construction presupposes, and employs for its basic intelligibility, the very apparatus of presuppositions that it ostensibly suspends.

The acceptance that there might be something to these two points, makes enormous differences to the whole agenda. The first, and major, difference is that it turns attention to the issue of *description*. Of course, the question of what counts as an adequate (or more adequate) description of our common-place experience is not to be dogmatically resolved in favour of a 'phenomenological' style of approach, but our simple examples and their perfunctory discussion are introduced merely to show that *there is a problem here*. On superficial inspection, there is reason to argue that the versions of 'everyday experience' are, if nothing else, over-simplified, giving truncated descriptions of the perceptions from which we *all* (philosophers, sociologists and everyone else) begin. Though we have given only very simple-minded and very basic examples, we see no reason to expect that, if the examples were 'scaled up' in terms of both complexity and sophistication, the problem would significantly change.

The standard question is put: are phenomena real in the sense that persons take them to be? Because of the pivotal role which scientific knowledge is imagined to play in defining our contemporary concept of knowledge, it is supposed that examination of the case of science will resolve many epistemological issues. This perhaps accounts for the interest which has recently been taken in the sociology of scientific knowledge.[12] It is, for example, regularly asked whether the phenomena 'discovered' by natural science are real *in the way practitioners of science and commentators on the history of science* typically take them to be? Though they may not necessarily be meant to carry such a connotation, the concern to say that they are 'socially constructed', that they are *real in a social or cultural sense*, such descriptions nonetheless carry strong overtones of the suggestion that these phenomena are less real than they are presumed, by scientists, commentators and laypersons, to be.

Ethnomethodology need not step up to defend the conception of the reality of the science's phenomena in the sense in which the sociology of scientific knowledge typically challenges this. The issue is not whether scientists are right or wrong to hold 'realist' conceptions of their work, but whether the *fundamental* sense in which scientists find 'the reality of their phenomena' has anything to do with holding realist views at all. The question whether scientists are right in their 'realistic' construal of their achievements gives way to the question of whether the *scientists' sense of the reality of the phenomena* they deal with has in fact been identified at all. Ethnomethodology prefers to look into the ways in which scientists *encounter* their phenomena, to examine the ways in which they 'come upon these' in the course of their investigations, to see how – for example – their activities in a laboratory comprise – *as far as the scientists are concerned* – the disclosure of a hitherto undiscovered phenomenon (or, alternatively, the routine reproduction of a well established one). (See for example, Garfinkel *et al.*, 1981, Garfinkel *et al.*, 1989, Lynch *et al.*, 1983, Lynch, 1985 and Livingston, 1986.) It is, after all, in the laboratory, the observatory and comparable places of work that scientists satisfy themselves about the *bona fide* character of findings, and ethnomethodology's question is about the ways in which, within such settings and *through their disciplinary work practices*, scientists determine the 'reality' of what they have found. It is only through (minimally) fuller description of the ways in which scientists conduct investigations and discover phenomena that one will have begun to specify the sense in which the phenomena of science are real or the scientists themselves.

6 Conclusion

If there is anything to the argument we have just made, then it has more severe consequences for the agenda than meaning just that description is given much higher priority on it but that, otherwise, the list remains the same. The implication is that if the problems of description are more seriously treated then the rest of the agenda may be obviated. If a more thorough description of our 'ordinary experience' is given, then it may transpire that standard suggestions about the way in which our commonplace experience might 'misrepresent reality' originate in very bare descriptions of the structure of that experience, and that they cannot, therefore, be regarded as initiating *serious* problems.

Now there is a fundamental difference in judgement. Does one take the problems of description as being merely incidental? Should we simply bypass them, taking it for granted that taking the problems of description seriously would not change the basic problems and that, therefore, to make description crucially problematic would merely lead us into a detour? The challenge to move the issues to the level of description will then simply be declined. It has not been answered, merely set aside. The other judgement is, of course, that there is no way around the problem. Far too much *depends* upon casual presuppositions about the nature of ordinary experience, about the appearance of the world of daily life, for it simply to be granted that these presuppositions are apt. Before making judgements as to whether the (social) world is the way it appears to be, there does seem to be room to ask: but how exactly does it appear to be? An important part of ethnomethodology's peculiarity within sociology is that it takes the answering of that question to be a serious and problematic task.

NOTES

1 Whether Husserl overstates the objectivity of logic or misunderstands its basis for it is irrelevant to the assertion. If he *did* conceive the world and the leading expressions of our knowledge of it 'subjectively', then it was certainly not in the sense that sociologists worry about.

2 Since Schutz's objective was the clarification of the presuppositions of the 'social sciences', it is a natural consequence that he should put the examination of the

premisses of conduct in the central place, not those of the acquisition of knowledge.

3   In fact, it only denies us this for philosophical purposes. For all practical purposes we can continue to count on our capacity to 'look and see' at its usual level of reliability.

4   We take it that, in this sense, the presence of the natural attitude in the orientation of the general run of 'everyday' conduct is *indubitable*.

5   See Wilson (1970) and Hollis and Lukes (1982) where the debate is engaged.

6   See Ryle's (1954: Ch. 6) discussion of technical and untechnical concepts.

7   See James (1984) for an examination of this issue.

8   We are reluctant to use the expression 'social construction' to characterise ethnomethodology's view of 'social reality', though not because of deficiencies inherent in the expression itself. It is widely used in a way which is contrastive with 'real' such that, classically, the demonstration that a social problem is a 'social construction' carries the implication that it is not really a problem: cf. Spector and Kitsuse (1977). However, this contrastive use of 'socially constructed' against 'real' or '*bona fide*' is not the only possible employment, and in all probability represents a theoretical short-circuiting of the idea of 'social construction' itself. The demonstration of something's 'socially constructed' character need not be – in our view, should not be – at the expense of its 'reality'.

9   Three concerns illustrate this: deconstructionism (for example, Derrida, 1976 and 1978), Quine's scepticism (Quine, 1961, 1966, 1981 and 1990; see Roth, 1986), reflexivity (for instance, contributions to Woolgar, 1988, Barnes, 1974 and Bloor, 1976).

10   For example, there is much scepticism about meaning; ethnomethodology's early stress upon the 'indexical' character of commonplace expressions is thought to show that these expressions are without determinate meaning. This disregards Garfinkel's (1967) overt insistence upon the way in which the everyday users of indexical expressions find plain sense, determinate meaning in each other's talk, writing and so forth.

11   Ethnomethodologists may be less than unanimous on this point – consultation of *some* of Melvin Pollner's work, for example, would amply support the locution that social reality is 'a mere construction', cf. Pollner's *Mundane Reason* (Pollner, 1987). Even so, Pollner's writings do not consistently sustain this view; contrast the above work with his 'The Management of Meaning in Traffic Courts' (Pollner, 1979).

12   Kuhn (1977) and contributions to Knorr-Cetina and Mulkay (1983) are illustrative of this interest.

5

Method: measurement – ordinary and scientific measurement as ethnomethodological phenomena[a]

Michael Lynch

1 Introduction: the classic view of measurement

Measurement in science traditionally is defined as an assignment of numbers (or, in some definitions, numerals) to fundamental attributes of an object or event studied (Kyburg 1984). Once such a correspondence between numbers and objective properties is established, the numbers can be manipulated via mathematical operations and the results assigned back to the measured phenomena. The classic conception of measurement can be elaborated to include the entire range of techniques through which geometric models mediate the interpretive relationship between theory and data: 'Using a geometry, the abstract objects and events of physical theory are composed into models which give a picture of reality and which are used to connect theory by experimental and nonexperimental investigation to sense impressions' (Willer, 1984: 243).

This broadened definition of measurement comprehends a more complex array of practices than simply attaching numbers to objective attributes. The construction of an 'interpreted diagram' or model articulates the relevancies under which theoretical expressions are brought into correspondence with empirical properties. A model's constituent symbols and imagery can enable progressive generalisation of a family of models for mapping and measuring diverse phenomena. Despite its emphasis on the dependence of models on theory, this definition retains the classic concept of measurement as a bringing together of symbolic imagery and 'small bits of information which we receive from the world' (Willer, 1984: 247).

The idea that measurement is constructed (and its validity assessed) in terms of an inherent isomorphism between mathematical symbols and empirical data is widely assumed by social scientists. Even critics of measurement practices in the social sciences often avow that the natural sciences are blessed with

[a] I am grateful to Bob Anderson for his helpful suggestions while I was preparing this chapter, and to David Bogen for his comments on an earlier draft. I was also aided by recent discussions with Harold Garfinkel, and I rely heavily upon what I have learned from him over the years.

phenomena already fit to be measured. Wilson, for instance, opens his 'ethnomethodological' account of measuring in the social sciences with the following assertion:

It is an astonishing fact that when the material universe is addressed as an attitude divorced from human emotions, sentiments, or practical purposes, its fundamental structure can be described in mathematical form, whether this be the sophisticated algebra and analysis used in the grand unified theories of physics or the more humble mathematics of set theory that could be employed for classifications in biology if formal representation were wanted. (Wilson, 1984: 221)

Although Wilson goes on to argue that measurement in the social sciences may never describe 'fundamental' structures of the social world, he takes for granted the 'astonishing fact' that measurements in the physical sciences correspond precisely to their objective referents. By doing so, Wilson passes over the topic of how such correspondences are achieved in situated scientific work. So, for instance, he never raises the issue of 'reasonable agreement' that Kuhn (1961, 1977 edn) treats as an irreducible feature of measurement in the physical sciences. Kuhn argues that what counts as an adequate correspondence between theoretically predicted values and experimental data is not governed by general criteria, but depends upon the state of the art within any historical discipline. So, for instance, a discrepancy between the predicted and observed orbit of a planet can be accepted as reasonably accurate given current observational techniques, or it may be viewed as a minor perturbation due to yet-to-be-measured gravitational influences from other planets. Under exceptional circumstances, such a discrepancy can be treated as an anomaly that problematises the geometric model of the orbit assumed in the theory. For Kuhn (1977: 185), 'the only possible criterion' for assessing the agreement between predicted numbers and observed measures 'is the mere fact that they appear, together with the theory from which they are derived, in a professionally accepted text'. In the absence of criteria, 'reasonable agreement' is achieved locally, in reference to singular constellations of technique and equipment, and as an inextricably communal affair. This does not imply that the achievements in the physical sciences are any less astonishing than Wilson asserts, but it raises the topic of their disciplinary and praxiological foundations. In other words, the 'astonishing fact' is more than a *fait accompli* of interest only as a basis for assessing the relative imprecision of social science measurement techniques; it is an *ethnomethodological phenomenon* to be investigated in its own right.

Wilson (1984: fn. 4, p. 237) correctly argues that ethnomethodology 'is a particularly confused scene' with regard to the central methodological debates in the social sciences. He notes that some ethnomethodologists repudiate the possibility of scientific sociology and become liable to accusations of subjectivism, while others like himself attempt 'to forge links between ethnomethodology and conventional sociological inquiry'. In this chapter, I will argue that ethnomethodology's treatment of measurement differs radically from both of the alternatives Wilson mentions. Ethnomethodology is neither a *Lebensphilosophie* denying the very possibility of measurement in the social sciences (Bloor, forthcoming) nor a source of positive methodological advice for social scientists. Instead, it topicalises measurement and respecifies its methodological significance for studies on the production of social order.

Wilson's couplet – Fundamental Structure <--> Mathematical Form (where <--> articulates an isomorphism or correspondence between elements from separate domains) – expresses the classic view of measurement that Garfinkel's ethnomethodology *respecifies* (Garfinkel *et al.*, 1989). Such respecification does *not* amount to an outright rejection of the possibility of social science measurement, nor does it provide a normative basis for quantitative methods in the social sciences. Instead, to put it simply, ethnomethodology treats measurement as a *phenomenon* to be investigated in an endless variety of ordinary and professional settings. The initial aim of such investigations is neither to demonstrate, nor to dispute, the possibility of devising valid measures of social phenomena; rather, it is to discover how situated practices of measurement constitute orderly social activities.[1] Rather than presuming Wilson's couplet to be an historically achieved structure, ethnomethodology raises the question, 'What is the *work* of Wilson's couplet?' The following schematic representation marks Wilson's couplet as an ethnomethodological phenomenon:

{Fundamental Structure <--> Mathematical Form}

The 'tick brackets' { } are a notational device for identifying Wilson's couplet as a 'classic' issue from intellectual history calling for ethnomethodological respecification (Garfinkel *et al.*, 1989). This device is similar to Garfinkel and Sacks' (1970) use of square brackets [ ] to topicalise the production (or *doing*) of activities formulated by expressions within the brackets. In the present instance, the tick brackets mark the classic isomorphism {Fundamental Structure <--> Mathematical Form} as an ethnomethodological phenomenon whose identifying details are inextricable from the 'vulgar competences' concertedly relied upon and taken for granted whenever measurements are produced and assessed.

In what follows, I shall argue that an ethnomethodological respecification of Wilson's couplet implicates much more than the issue of whether or not sociologists can ever hope to achieve valid and precise measures of social phenomena. It transforms the very conception of 'method' deployed in conventional sociology. By 'conventional sociology', I mean the pre-theoretical organisation of the discipline and its topics exhibited in the chapter headings of any of the established introductory texts; in the 'methods' sections of publications in mainstream journals; in the schedule of headings (e.g., 'Hypothesis', 'Methods', 'Significance', etc.) in standardised forms for social science grant applications; in the designs of multi-variate models and the advice for constructing them; and in the coherence of the programme for annual meetings of the American Sociological Association. Although sociology continues to be riven with fundamental disputes about whether quantitative methods offer a viable approach to sociology's phenomena, few sociologists question the assumption that *some* set of methodological prescriptions can be spelled out in advance of any inquiry. By treating methods and the entire roster of topics associated with methods as discoverable phenomena, ethnomethodology problematises the fundamental unity of the social science disciplines. The implications of this move can be utterly baffling, and I cannot hope to do justice to them here. Instead, by briefly reviewing some examples of ethnomethodological studies of measurement, I aim simply to convey a particularised appreciation of ethnomethodology's respecification of methodological phenomena. In the following chapter Doug Benson and John Hughes take up a particular aspect of measurement that has fascinated the human sciences, 'inference and measurement', and readers will hopefully read the two chapters in conjunction with one another. Before reviewing relevant ethnomethodological studies, I will, however, sketch a background for ethnomethodology's respecification of Wilson's couplet.

2   An historico-praxiological genealogy of scientific measurement

Let us first consider Husserl's (1970c) account of Galileo's 'invention' of the *mathesis universalis*. Like Wilson, Husserl is astonished by the achievements of the mathematical natural sciences. But unlike Wilson, he is not content to lay his astonishment at the door of nature. Instead, Husserl attempts to disclose the praxiological foundations of mathematical natural science. He does so by explicating Galileo's 'surreptitious substitution of the mathematically substructed world of idealities for the only real world, the one that is actually given through perception, that is ever experienced and experienceable – our everyday life-world' (Husserl, 1970c: 48–9). As Husserl reconstructs this genealogy, Galileo inherited the ancient legacy of geometry, and along with it the Platonic view of mathematical forms as ideal and permanent essences lying behind the world of appearances. Husserl's genealogy traces the ideal geometric forms – the perfectly straight line, dimensionless point, angular figure and regular curve – back to the proto-geometric practices of surveying and measuring. The measuring instruments embody relatively 'pure' lines, scales, curves, and angles, and act as templates for shaping and polishing surfaces or reckoning material alignments and lengths. The purified shapes represented in Euclidean geometry not only enable descriptive or mapping functions, but also provide the generative models for extrapolating, predicting, and planning yet-to-be realised architectures. The elaboration of a constructed object, built environment, or project of action thus takes shape on an approximately axiomatic foundation, and in approximate accord with the purified forms and established theorems of geometry.

Initially, there is no essential demarcation between the artisan's craft and the mathematics of the phenomenal field constructed in and through that craft. A vivid historical account of this is given in Edgerton's (1975: 38) treatment of the 'rediscovery' of linear perspective by Brunelleschi and Alberti in fifteenth-century Florence. Edgerton documents how the skills of the 'artisan–engineer' Brunelleschi, combined with the optical theory of Alberti, articulated the new representational conventions. The artisan–engineers of Florence 'were called on for two requisite talents: skill in mathematics and the ability to draw'. In a development roughly akin to Husserl's (1970c: 376) account of the 'primal geometrer's' craft of 'polishing' the artifact to align its surface with the limit forms of geometry, the artisan–engineers were attuned to 'pure' geometric forms in the course of their constructive praxis. Where Brunelleschi invented a mirror-device for perspectival painting, Alberti later articulated the principles through which the lines of sight embedded in the design and operation of the device could be exposed and reckoned with in an abstract mathematical operation.

Alberti's optical treatise articulates a plane geometry for painters, where each 'point' on the field is simultaneously 'a sign'; a sign being 'anything which exists on a surface so that it is visible to the eye' (Edgerton, 1975: 80). Alberti's *signum*, a textual 'figure' or 'mark' is 'something tangible like a dot on a piece of paper' (Edgerton, 1975: 80). The features of the image apparently are displaced outward onto the canvas. Sign–referent relations take the place of the point-by-point correspondence between visual image and object. Moreover, the painter's construction of a plane of signs is seen to take place in a concrete geometrical field. Painting thus becomes a kind of embodied mathematics, trading in hybrid objects (e.g., dots and marks) which concretely approximate geometric limit forms. The 'plane' a painter composes is organised as an empirical graph where a grid of lines link up 'like threads in a cloth' (Edgerton, 1975: 80). Galilean science takes this artistic achievement one step further, attributing the plane of signs and the grid upon which they are inscribed to nature's authorship.

For Husserl, Galileo's distinctive achievement was to identify the idealised forms and calculative resources of geometry with an infinite expanse of natural space, ultimately subsuming the entire 'plenum' of magnitudes and 'secondary qualities'[2] found within that space. The limit forms no longer act as ideal tools for reckoning and modelling, since a coherent tissue of mathematical laws encompasses the entire sensory manifold. The couplet {Fundamental Structure <--> Mathematical Form} no longer formulates the piecemeal achievements of constructive praxis; it becomes the irreducible foundation of an independent nature, a nature that remains indifferent to human historicity and purpose. Henceforth, it is the goal of a Galilean science to use mathematics to discover the inherent structure of the world; an inherent structure that is *always and already* mathematical.

Having identified Galileo's achievement, Husserl seeks to retrieve the 'lost' praxiological foundation of the natural sciences' phenomenal field. He argues that the apparent correspondence between mathematical form and natural properties is less a ground for rational certainty than a mystery at the heart of Galilean science. This is because any such correspondence, established as a singular achievement in the course of a scientific project, secures its self-evidence only as long as it rests upon the unexplicated foundation of the intuitively given surrounding world. As complex *worldly* interventions, acts of measurement and calculation in the physical sciences presuppose the stability and meaningfulness of the life-world (*Lebenswelt*) within which they are secured. The calculative techniques of any science depend upon an intuitive grasp of the distinctive subject-matter of that science.

One operates with letters and with signs for connections and relations (+, ×, =, etc.), according to *rules of the game* for arranging them together in a way essentially not different, in fact, from a game of cards or chess. Here the *original* thinking that genuinely gives meaning to this technical process and truth to the correct results (even the 'formal truth' peculiar to the formal *mathesis universalis*) is excluded . . . (Husserl, 1970c: 46)

For Husserl, the foundations of natural science cannot be secure until rigorous explication is given on the 'original thinking' that gives rise to the presumed isomorphism between calculative 'games' and the subject-matter of a science. His phenomenological science of the life-world provides a preliminary move toward such an explication. Although I cannot go into the details of Husserl's conceptual apparatus, for present purposes it is sufficient to point out that he never entirely abandons the idea that scientific truths can be traced back to a unitary foundation. But, rather than treating technical 'rules of the game' in the specialised sciences as the basis for a universalised grasp of the intuitively given structures of the life world, Husserl subordinates these 'games' to the acts of a transcendental consciousness.

Transcendental phenomenology has not fared well under criticisms by later philosophers, including Sartre (1957), Heidegger (1967), Merleau-Ponty (1962), Gurwitsch (1964) and Schutz (1966), all of whom were variously indebted to Husserl's philosophical initiatives. What remains viable through all the critiques, however, is the idea that rules of method and calculative techniques obtain their efficacy and adequacy on the basis of an unexplicated foundation in the embodied and socially organised praxis of a discipline. Contrary to Husserl, this 'foundation' is no longer treated as a *unitary* source of intuition and practical certainty. Instead, 'it' devolves into the discursive and embodied activities of situated social praxis. For Merleau-Ponty and Heidegger, there is no 'transcendental ego' outside the world that endows it with meaning, there are only acts situated within discursive and embodied access to a world that is always and already shot-through with meaning.

Despite these criticisms, two initiatives from Husserl remain viable for ethnomethodological studies of science: (1) that an historico-praxiological genealogy of scientific measurement begins with 'ordinary' arts of measurement, and (2) that the question of how numbers (or, more precisely, numerals, equations, and mathematical models) correspond to objective properties is to be addressed by investigating the practical and contextual production of measurable phenomena. Ethnomethodology abandons Husserl's reflective mode of inquiry, and in a peculiar fashion it treats the life-world as a domain of 'discoverable' phenomena.

In what follows I will review ethnomethodology's approach to measurement. While doing so I will need to elaborate upon ethnomethodology's 'indifference' to *Method* in the social sciences. Ethnomethodological discussions of methods in the social sciences are often viewed as attacks on the validity of quantitative representation in sociology, to the effect that quantitative methods are insufficiently sensitive to 'actual' social actions. Although there are many reasons to question the validity and aptness of social science measures (Turner, 1986; Krenz and Sax, 1986), I will argue that ethnomethodology's indifference poses a more radical threat to the programme of professional sociology.

3   Proto-ethnomethodology: Cicourel's method and measurement

Any review of ethnomethodological work on measurement must start with Cicourel's (1964) *Method and Measurement in Sociology*. Twenty-five years after its publication, Cicourel's text remains the most extensive and widely recognised ethnomethodological study on the topic. In several important respects, however, *Method and Measurement* is a proto-ethnomethodological account of measurement. Cicourel does not bill his volume as an ethnomethodological study, and, while he cites Garfinkel many times in the text, especially in the concluding chapter on 'Theoretical Presuppositions' (pp. 189–224), he does not undertake what *now* should be regarded as an ethnomethodological study. Because Cicourel's book can easily be mistaken to be an exemplar for ethnomethodology, it is worth re-examining its treatment of measurement in light of later ethnomethodological studies. My aim in doing this will not be to cite failings in Cicourel's study, but to clarify a distinctive approach to measurement opened up by his text, and developed primarily in Garfinkel's and Sacks' subsequent researches.

Given the circumstances of its publication, *Method and Measurement* was in no position to elaborate the approaches to measurement that I shall discuss later in this chapter. 'Ethnomethodology' was not yet the field it later became, and this can be appreciated by comparing, for instance, Garfinkel's paper on 'trust' (initially delivered in 1957, and published in 1963) with Garfinkel and Sacks' paper 'On formal structures of practical action', published in 1970. Cicourel (1964: 203ff.) cites the former paper as one of his main theoretical sources. The latter paper made a more complete break with many of the basic premises about scientific theory and method embodied in the earlier work.

Like Garfinkel's earlier work, Cicourel's study uncritically adopted Schutz's (1943; 1953) conceptions of natural and social science inquiry which were given extensive examination in the previous chapter. The abstract themes under which Schutz elaborated the attitude of daily life, and the contrasts he drew between the natural and human sciences – as well as between the pre-suppositions of the attitude of scientific theorising and those of the 'natural attitude' of daily life – were incorporated wholesale into Cicourel's and Garfinkel's proto-ethnomethodological studies. Schutz's writings, in turn, relied heavily on Kaufmann's (1944)[3] and Whitehead's (1925) philosophies of science, and in my view he de-radicalised many of the Husserlian initiatives discussed above.[4] There were good reasons for doing so, of course, since Schutz, Garfinkel and Cicourel all faced the daunting task of establishing phenomenologically inspired investigations at a time when neo-Kantian structural functionalism dominated American sociology. It was more than a matter of gaining acceptance for a distinctive and critical approach, since many sociologists found, and continue to find, phenomenology and ethno-methodology to be pointless and unintelligible unless translated into more familiar idioms.

(1) The 'remedial' register

The 'remedial' register is exhibited in Cicourel's repeated assurances that his various critiques of ethnographic observation, interviewing, content analysis, and survey research identify *remediable* problems. However biting and relent-less its critical implications, Cicourel's discussion of the various methods never entirely rejects the possibility of developing 'rigorous measures' of social phenomena:

> The sociological observer . . . who fails to conceptualize the elements of common-sense acts in everyday life, is using an implicit model of the actor which is confounded by the fact that his observations and inferences interact, in unknown ways, with his own bio-graphical situation within the social world. The very conditions of obtaining data require that he make use of typical motives, cues, roles, etc., and the typical meanings he imputes to them, yet the structures of these common-sense courses of action are notions which the sociological observer takes for granted, treats as self-evident. But they are just the notions which the sociologist must analyze and study empirically if he desires rigorous measurement. (Cicourel, 1964: 22)

Cicourel explicitly sets-up a 'straw man' (p. 2) for his analysis, which he calls the 'seldom attainable' ideal of *literal* measurement. This he defines (fn. 6, pp. 225–6) as 'an exact correspondence between the substantive elements and relations under study and the ordered elements and relations of the measurement system' (or, in other words, Wilson's couplet). Literal measurement contrasts to 'arbitrary or forced correspondence between elements, relations, and operations'. Cicourel goes on to suggest that fixed-choice questionnaires and other measurement instruments become 'grids' through which sociologists' understanding of social processes can be 'distorted' (p. 105). By subscribing to the in-principle possibility of literal measurement, along with the reciprocal possibilities of bias and distortion cast into relief by that ideal, Cicourel's treatment echews a more radical critique of the correspondence 'theory' of representation. Cicourel's critique takes the form of 'good advice' for sociologists to the effect that a more explicit attention to language and common-sense reasoning can enable researchers to eliminate sources of bias and construct more rigorous measuring instruments.

Despite the promise running throughout his text, Cicourel delivers virtually nothing of *technical* value for the committed survey researcher. Unlike, for instance, Blalock (1984) or Lieberson (1985), who also criticise quantitative methods but from a position sympathetic to the overall programme, Cicourel does not elaborate specific suggestions on data reduction strategies, question-naire design, or other techniques for avoiding bias and enhancing viability. However, he does offer a positive theory of practical action and practical reasoning. In the final two chapters of his book, Cicourel draws upon cognitive anthropology, linguistics, Wittgenstein's later philosophy, Garfinkel's (1963) 'trust' paper, and Schutz's phenomenological sociology to elaborate what he argues are key constituents of the language and practical reasoning that survey researchers and other methodologists take for granted. He argues that 'measurement in sociology at the level of social process cannot be rigorous without solutions to the problems of social meanings. Understanding the problem of meaning requires a theory of both language and culture' (Cicourel, 1964: 173). The 'theory' Cicourel offers draws from sources as diverse as Chomsky and Husserl, and encompasses several levels of linguistic structure and language use, as well as explicit and unstated norms of action and the constitutive features of the 'natural attitude'. Although Cicourel sometimes refers to these orders of language-in-action as 'variables', for the most part they identify entire domains of linguistic structure and everyday action. It remains unclear how sociologists could hope to correct for potential sources of 'bias' by taking account of how their measurements are situated within such ubiquitous features of common-sense reasoning and ordinary language. Unless we grant sociology the privileges of transcendental analysis, it is hard to imagine how sociologists could avoid complying with the constitutive rules of everyday reasoning, since these describe what 'taking account' of social reality consists of in the first place. To inform sociologists that their measurement techniques make use of an unexplicated 'logic' of ordinary language, or that they and their research assistants tacitly rely upon common-sense reasoning and ordinary modes of communication, can only misleadingly imply that an explicit study of such matters would help them to construct more valid measures. What the suggestion offers, instead, is a massive change of topic.

(2) The 'subversive' register

The 'subversive' register is fully 'visible' only in light of later developments in ethnomethodology. Nevertheless, it can be elucidated in retrospect by reading Cicourel's text, as well as Schutz's methodological writings, as tentative movements into a distinctive domain of study. The key to this reading is to regard Cicourel's remedial register – his suggestion that a study of constitutive structures of common-sense action will enable sociologists to develop more rigorous measurements – as an attempt to smuggle a change of topic under the guise of methodological advice. The social praxis of measuring simply becomes the phenomenon of interest, aside from whether studies of that praxis have any methodological payoff for quantitative sociology. Although Cicourel does not explicitly recommend such a topic shift, his study effectively accomplishes it. The unease some sociologists may feel when reading Cicourel's complex theory of meaning and communication ('How could we *ever* take all of *this* into account?') gives way once they are seduced into taking an interest in everyday discourse and common-sense reasoning as topics in their own right.

4   Ethnomethodological indifference

The subversive register is associated with the policy that Garfinkel and Sacks (1970) later call ethnomethodology's 'indifference' to the project of analytic sociology. Rather than addressing whether sociologists ever can achieve adequate or acceptable measures of their phenomena, the policy of indifference opens up the alternative topic of how 'members' conduct measuring activities by producing local judgements on the practical adequacy, accuracy, and appropriate correspondence between measuring devices and measured phenomena. Sociologists' methodological troubles and remedies are thus placed within a vast field of practical activities within which 'measures' are generated and used. The policy of 'indifference' not only applies to questions on the 'ultimate' validity and reliability of sociologists' measures, it also covers Schutz's (1953) normative proposals about the 'special' character of scientific cognition, including the theoretical contrast he draws between the natural and social sciences. Since 'indifference' is not equivalent to 'denial', the policy does not imply that social scientists' measurements have no more than a 'common-sense' basis or that there are no distinctions to be drawn between sociologists', coroners', physicists' or any other lay or professional efforts to measure phenomena. Rather, it is proposed that any such differences remain to be discovered as ethnomethodological phenomena.

Garfinkel's (1967: 18ff.) study of 'following coding instructions', which was cited by Wes Sharrock and Bob Anderson in the preceding chapter, provides an early case in point, and we can now take up the methodological plight that they introduced. Although the routine social science practice of using a standard set of categories to 'code' observed or recorded activities, interview responses, and so forth, is not a matter of measurement in the sense of assigning numbers to events, it is often a necessary step in the quantification of social science 'data'. In Garfinkel's study of selection criteria in a psychiatric outpatient clinic, two sociology graduate students were given the task of coding standardised information from a large collection of case folders. Each folder contained a 'Clinic Career Form' upon which clinic personnel were supposed to record information about their initial contact with the patient, to specify any tests they administered and treatments they recommended, and to note when the case was 'terminated'. The two research assistants were then given a set of instructions for extracting standardised information from the folders and recording it on a 'Coding Sheet', and a reliability procedure was used to assess the amount of agreement between the coders' judgements. Rather than simply relying upon the coders' training and skills to produce adequate data for the study, Garfinkel investigated how the coders managed to accomplish this mundane research task.

A procedure was designed that yielded conventional reliability information so that the original interests of the study were preserved. At the same time the procedure permitted the study of how any amount of agreement or disagreement had been produced by the actual ways that the two coders had gone about treating folder contents as answers to the questions formulated by the Coding Sheet. But, instead of assuming that coders, proceeding in whatever ways they did, might have been in error, in greater or lesser amount, the assumption was made that *whatever* they did could be counted correct procedure in *some* coding 'game'. The question was, what were these 'games'? (Garfinkel, 1967: 20)

By way of an answer to this question, Garfinkel (1967: 21) formulates a list of '*ad hoc* considerations' coders used to decide 'the fit between what could be read from the clinic folders and what the coder inserted into the coding sheet'. Garfinkel (1967: 20–1) designates these with a short list of rhetorical terms, including 'et cetera', 'unless', 'let it pass', and '*factum valet*' (an action that is otherwise prohibited is counted as correct once it is done). Coders used these practices to assess the substantive and 'reasonable' fit between folder contents and the categories on the Coding Sheet, without getting bogged down by a 'literal' assessment of what was, or was not, 'in' any folder. That is, the coders relied upon what they 'knew' about the clinic and the staff, including the exigencies of patient presentation and record keeping, to make-out what each folder 'said' in more than so many words. Their competence thus presupposed an understanding of the state of affairs the Coding Sheet categories formulated; indeed, what they entered into a Coding Sheet was essentially tied to what they 'knew' the respective clinic folder *must have* contained in addition to, and in despite of, its literal contents. As Garfinkel points out (1967: 21–2) such reliance on *ad hoc* practices is the very sort of 'common-sense' practice sociological methods seek to replace with disinterested and objectively defensible judgements. He adds, however, that every attempt to upgrade the coding procedure in order to restrain or eliminate such practices itself relied upon and reproduced them. Garfinkel later (pp. 66ff.) makes a similar, although more general, point about the relation between 'common understandings' and social science 'models of man'.[5] He clearly does *not* offer methodological advice for evaluation researchers or survey analysts, since he explicitly argues that *ad hoc* considerations are irremediably a part of routine social science research, as well as more 'ordinary' modes of practical sociological reasoning. He argues instead that coding instructions, along with the *ad hoc* practices used in following them, 'furnish a "social science" way of talking so as to persuade consensus and action within the practical circumstances of the clinic's organised daily activities, a grasp of which members are expected to have as a matter of course' (Garfinkel, 1967: 24). This is not to say that social science discourse amounts to little more than a fancied-up version of 'common sense'; instead, it is to recommend a *constitutive* rather than a descriptive analysis of the relationship between 'measurement' (or, in this case pre-measurement categorisation) and the social activities measured. Or, in terms we have used here, Garfinkel's study suggests an indifference to questions on the validity and reliability of the presumed isomorphism between clinic folders and Coding Sheet, while respecifying that relationship as the aggregate product of coders' *ad hoc* procedures for handling each file's singular contents. This ethnomethodological respecification can be expressed with a variant of Wilson's couplet: {Structure of Clinic Activities <--> Standardised Code}. We can now see that {<-->} is a key 'term' to be translated as 'coders' work over the singular exigencies of each case in hand.

Readers might ask why I would propose that ethnomethodological indifference would be 'subversive' of quantitative sociology. At first glance, the policy suggests little more than a re-orientation to the detailed practices through which measurements are accomplished in sociology and other fields of endeavour. Presumably such a programme of study could co-exist with sociology, and perhaps be of some technical use for sociologists' continuing efforts to improve their methods. The subversion operates on another front, however. Rather than confronting sociological methods in terms of an immanent concern with validity and reliability, ethnomethodological indifference turns away from the *foundationalist* approach to methodology that gives rise to principled discussions of validity, reliability, rules of evidence, and decision criteria. The implications of this move can be threatening and even incomprehensible for sociologists.

A vivid indication of sociologists' consternation over questions of 'method' in ethnomethodology can be found in the transcribed dialogue between ethnomethodologists and sociologists presented in the *Proceedings of the Purdue Symposium on Ethnomethodology* (Hill and Crittenden, 1968). The sociologists' questions and complaints about 'method' persistently punctuate the dialogue. While Garfinkel, Sacks and others present a series of examples

and demonstrations of ethnomethodological studies, the sociologists with-
hold judgement while waiting for an *a priori* warrant, decision rule, or
criterion of correctness, relevance or acceptability:[6]

HILL: Hal [Garfinkel], you have not told us yet what rules of evidence you accept or
employ. (Hill and Crittenden, 1968: 27)

HILL: You have to be able to tell us how you make such distinctions in terms of
decision rules. I believe this illustrates a kind of question many of us have with regard
to how one presents a warrant for the evidence that one uses to reach a decision. (Hill
and Crittenden, 1968: 28)

DEFLEUR: . . . What are the rules by which you unravel who is right?
We have been asking for methodological information and you have been giving us
subject matter. A moment ago, Hal said, 'Well, we don't have any new science up our
sleeve.' How about some old science? (Hill and Crittenden, 1968: 39)

DEFLEUR: How do you reject a thing? What are the rules of evidence on which you
reject or accept an explanation? (Hill and Crittenden, 1968: 40)

Such questions persist throughout the symposium, and are never given
satisfaction. The questions presuppose a set of methodological standards
independent of the 'subject matter' under investigation, and they imply that a
description or demonstration cannot be sensible or plausible until compared
to such standards. In effect, the sociologists immobilise the dialogue by defer-
ring acknowledgement of the sense and intelligibility of the ethnomethodologists' descriptions until given a set of general methodological precepts.
Although there is not yet any question of how numbers might be assigned to
the properties of the described phenomena, the sociologists demand extrinsic
measures of the truth and intelligibility of what the ethnomethodologists tell
them. Their questions and complaints embody Lord Kelvin's memorialised
dictum, 'If you cannot measure, your knowledge is meagre and unsatisfactory'
(quoted in Kuhn, 1977: 178). Or, to translate this in terms of the sociologists'
questions and complaints, 'If you cannot tell us what rules of evidence and
decision criteria you respect, your claims are unfounded.' By demanding such
epistemic guarantees, the sociologists become apt targets for a distinctive form
of rejoinder (Hill and Crittenden, 1968: 34):

MCGINNIS: What criteria would you accept as grounds for arguing that it [a conversationalists' rule for identifying persons, which Sacks had just discussed] is false? What
criteria would you require from me to assess my assertion that your claim is false?
GARFINKEL: Why don't you just state your objection?

Garfinkel's rejoinder casts McGinnis' academic question into a 'vulgar'
conversational frame. The question proposes that an earlier observation made
by Sacks should be tested in reference to a criterion of falsification. By sequentially treating the question as a roundabout 'objection', Garfinkel's rejoinder
cuts through McGinnis' hypothetical voice; disregarding the question's

deference to a criterion that *would* justify subsequent belief, and implicating it as an allusion to what McGinnis *already is prepared to argue* with or without 'criteria'. Garfinkel's 'vulgar' move situates his interlocutor within a conversational competency that requires no extrinsic criterion. The entire edifice of 'method' is thus challenged, not through an explicit argument, but in the *way* it is submerged within a 'vulgar' competency. *That* is ethnomethodology's indifference; it is a move that simply leaves the scene of sociology's methodist discourse. Such a move does not leave 'knowledge' behind, nor does it place ethnomethodology within a realm without sense or reason; instead, the move *pivots* upon the demonstrable fact that both McGinnis and Garfinkel are acting, have acted, and will continue to act, with no time out, within a dialogue that is already intelligible, mutually recognisable, and identifiable. It is not that Garfinkel's 'professional expertise' as an ethnomethodologist enables him to recognise what McGinnis has just said and to identify it as a 'pre-objection'; rather, his rejoinder acts contentiously within, while making an issue of, the *ordinary* grounds of McGinnis' demand for a criterion. McGinnis' privileging of criteria is cast into ironic relief as an 'academic' posture within an unremitting and already intelligible conversation.

A related implication is produced by Sacks' response to a similar demand by a sociologist (Hill and Crittenden, 1968: 41):

HILL: . . . Could you tell us without reference to the subject matter what the structure of [an ethnomethodological] demonstration would be?
SACKS: Do you know what that is asking? You are asking, 'Could you tell me, without knowing what kind of world we are in, what a theory would look like?' . . . I do not know in the first instance what it is that sociology should look like to be satisfactory. That is not an available phenomenon.

Sacks' reply undercuts Hill's distinction between 'method' and 'subject matter', and situates 'sociology' within the substantive field investigated. Sacks is not advocating an 'inductive' procedure; rather, he is questioning Hill's programmatic separation between a unitary method of scientific inquiry and the particular subject matter investigated in any science. Sacks' refusal to go along with this picture implicates an alternative view of science, where 'methods' are situated within distinctive constellations of activity, equipment. investigative sites, and investigated phenomena (Feyerabend, 1975). In 1968 this was a radical view of method for a sociologist to espouse, and while it is now familiar to students of the sociology of scientific knowledge (Knorr-Cetina and Mulkay, 1983), it has not yet seriously dented textbook accounts of sociological method.

The 'subversion' here is clear. Questions of method and measurement are now off the table, except as 'subject matter' for ethnomethodological studies. 'Methods' are implicated, but only as endogenous constituents of the practical activities studied. There are no *a priori* guarantees, and the initial requirement for an investigator is to find ways to elucidate 'methods' from within the relevant competence systems in which they are bound. With regard to measurement, two subsequent lines of ethnomethodological research can be elaborated. One is mainly associated with Sacks' studies of conversation, and the other with Garfinkel's and his colleagues' studies of work in the sciences and professions. A third development, which will be of no interest here, is the practical use of numerical indices for purposes of coding and record keeping by professional conversational analysts. To construct measurements in such a fashion is no more distinctive of ethnomethodology than is the fact that ethnomethodologists make use of written texts to render descriptions or transcribe conversations. Although it can be studied, it would be of no greater interest than any other ethnomethodological phenomenon.

5 Ordinary measurement and the 'pragmatisation' of mathematics

Cultural anthropologists and cognitive psychologists recently have taken interest in 'folk measurement': situated uses of numbers and measures, and mundane calculations using other than pencil and paper methods (Scribner, 1984; Lave, 1988; Brown *et al.*, 1989). Their work is roughly aligned with anthropological and historical investigations on calendrical and other endogenous modes of temporal reckoning (Geertz, 1973; Zerubavel, 1985), but shows greater attention to the contextual organisation of singular actions in a variety of practical activities. A frequently cited example from Lave's (1988) study of ordinary mathematical reasoning concerns the efforts by an American man attempting to measure a serving of cottage cheese in accordance with a diet plan. In this case the dieter attempted to measure three-quarters of the two-thirds cup his Weight Watchers programme prescribed. After some deliberation, but without figuring out the calculation (e.g. $2/3 \times 3/4 = 1/2$) he hit upon a way to do it. 'He filled a measuring-cup two-thirds full of cottage cheese, dumped it out on the cutting board, patted it into a circle, marked a cross on it, scooped away one quadrant, and served the rest' (Lave, 1988: 165).

The substantive solution to the problem was achieved through a manipulation of the singular materials embodying it. The cottage cheese was both an object upon which arithmetical calculation was applied and a means for measuring *what* was measured. The approximately circular wad of material, and the rough division of quadrants inscribed into it, did not constitute a geometric model separate from the problem, so much as a materially embodied solution simultaneously revealing the pragmatic mode of its 'calculation'.[7] In other words, the elements of Wilson's couplet {Fundamental Structure <--> Mathematical Form} emerged as the indissoluble product of an act. This, of course, is a far cry from the sort of procedure Lord Kelvin had in mind, and it should not be viewed even as an approximation of what would be obtained by means of a paper and pencil calculation or a measurement with standardised scales. Indeed, the point made with the example is that such 'folk' measures are performed for all practical purposes and without need for comparison with a more 'exact' or academic paradigm of measuring.

The topics of situated measurement, of counting, and of various other ordinary uses of numbers, have long preoccupied ethnomethodologists, although much of the relevant work remains unpublished. In an unpublished research note, Garfinkel (1962) contrasts the routines used by staff at a mental hospital for 'counting' patients, to a mathematical model of the 'same' activity using set theory. He dramatises this contrast by imagining a confrontation between a researcher devising the set-theoretic model and a staff member whose job it is to assure a proper count. The staff member finds nothing of practical interest or relevance in the researcher's model; he *cannot have* nor *can he want* the paper model, since his job depends upon an intimate knowledge of patient ploys, evasions, and mishaps. His record of 'present' and 'absent' cases implicates his competent access to the same organisation of daily schedules and hospital routines the 'count' elaborates. Although the activity makes use of a roster of names to provide a public document of the count, no mathematical analysis of the order of signs on that record can assure what a competent staff member is responsible for doing when he checks names off the roster. The activity for which he is held responsible is more than an operation performed in his head or on paper, since it includes an entire organisation of activities *in the ward*.

In his transcribed lecture notes, Sacks also touches upon several topics having to do with 'measurement' and number-use in conversation.[8] His discussions include remarks and examples on conversationalists' pragmatic and poetic uses of temporal and place formulations, with a focus on the local relevancies associated with 'approximate' and 'precise' uses of measurement terms.[9] Sacks' discussion of measurement terms in conversation does more than demonstrate that these terms are used contextually. This is particularly clear in the way he elaborates the issue of 'precision' in time-of-day references:

> . . . there are 'approximate' numbers and 'precise' numbers; one sense of which is, if you were to say to someone 'I'll meet you at five twenty-seven' and you arrive at five twenty-nine, they might well say 'You're late.' If you say 'I'll meet you at five thirty' you may well arrive at five forty and they won't figure you're late. Or, if you tell them you'll meet them at five twenty-seven, they might ask why you're being so precise - where in terms of just a series of numbers, five thirty is no less precise than five twenty-seven, or vice versa. It's just a different class of object.(Sacks, Lecture, 23 January 1970: 17–17; also see Sacks, 1988/89: 54ff.)

In another lecture, Sacks (Lecture 24, Spring, 1966) makes a similar point about formulations of speed in driving. He argues that the non-numerical formulation 'fast' in the utterance 'You like to drive cars fast', can be preferred over any numerical account of miles per hour read off a speedometer. The standard against which 'fast' is measured is 'the traffic', where 'traffic' is produced *in situ* by drivers who drive so as to be 'with' the traffic; drivers who, in effect, constitute the very traffic they are 'with'.[10] The expression 'fast' translates into no single numerical formulation, since the measurement device – 'fast/slow'/'with the traffic' – is flexibly used in reference to the vicissitudes of traffic, local speed limits, and police surveillance: 'The stability of the terms, and the conditions under which they're usable, are then such that time, place, speed laws, whatever else, are all irrelevant to their use. Changes in speed laws, changes in the capacity of the car, changes in the personnel, new generations, new places – this thing can hold' (Sacks, Lecture 24, Spring 1966: 9). In still another example, again having to do with driving but in this instance referring to the way the 'aftermath' of a car wreck on the freeway is described in a phone call, Sacks coins the term 'usualness measures', by which he means formulations that rely upon a competent sense of what one 'usually' or 'normally' can observe under the circumstances:[11]

It's not like you're telling the story of the first wreck you've ever seen, and are now seeking out ways to characterize it. That you know how to characterize a wreck is something you can show from the way you describe one, and if you show that you know how to describe one, then the recipient, by virtue of that, can take it that you've possibly correctly characterized this wreck.

That is to say, it's perhaps not incidental then that one doesn't get a more precise characterization of how small a space the car was smashed into, or how long we were parked there [in the traffic jam]. It's, in a fashion, better to not use those, which can be equivocal – in the sense of it, 'Is that a long time for a wreck?' or 'Is that a small space for a car?' – instead, what one does is offer the product of an educated analysis, that can then be seen to have been specifically done as an educated analysis, and thereby be seen to have been done by someone who knows how to look. If it's told to someone who knows how to hear. So that this possible 'vagueness' of the report, quite a while – well how long was it? is not a defective kind of vagueness but is the way to show that you measured the thing in an appropriate way to measure being caught in a traffic jam. (Slightly edited for punctuation – M.L.) (Sacks, Lecture, 16 April 1970: 16–17; also see Sacks, 1988/9: 59–60)

The singular relevance and appropriateness of any 'measurement' term – whether a number or a non-numerical expression like 'enough', 'full', 'empty', 'more', or 'less' etc. – is clearly not governed by rules defining an isomorphic relation between the term and an independent object. It is not even a question of a situationally determined 'reasonable agreement' between measurement term and object, since that question depends initially on what conventional *activity* is implicated when a measurement term is used. Indeed, in many circumstances, to assume a 'classic' relation between a measurement term and an object's properties is to invite confusion, such as in the following instance of a teacher's use of the expression 'how many' in a question to a class.

Here's the sort of thing I mean by the 'possibility of confusion'. A teacher in class says 'How many people don't have paper?' some people stick their hands up; one kid sits there, looks around and says 'Five'. Now the question 'How many people don't have paper?' provides for an answer, but the question isn't intended as that sort of thing. (Sacks, Lecture, 21 November 1967: 13)

The question is a recognisable constituent of classroom routines for distributing supplies. The question in this case is competently 'answered' by a show of hands from those students wanting paper, so the teacher can then distribute paper to each of the relevant students. The kid's confusion consists in his treating the question as though it were occasioning a spontaneous arithmetic exercise, and while his answer may be correct for arithmetic, it comes off as a minor blunder in the present episode. A *competent* use of measurement terms is more than a matter of calibrating 'precision' to the requirements of the circumstances, since what is *said* with a numerical or non-numerical expression of, for example, time, length, quantity, distance or speed depends upon the immediate pragmatic environment. In addition to sequential, narrative, and other pragmatic considerations, the circumstances can include the poetic relevances exhibited in what Sacks (Lecture, 11 March 1971) called a 'flurry' of measure terms. In such a case, any next term's selection can be organised poetically in relation to the sound-qualities, semiotic oppositions (such as between 'full' and 'empty'), and other qualities exhibited by the words in the local 'flurry'.

Given the array of considerations involved in such ordinary uses of measurement terms, we might wonder how salient is the traditional view of measurement for the analysis of such activities. In contrast to the Husserlian mathematisation of the life-world, we see an entirely different 'pragmatisation' of mathematics. Numbers, standardised scales, standard time, geographical place formulations (Schegloff, 1972; Psathas, 1979b), and other mathematical or 'objective' references are submerged and dispersed within a dense contexture of ordinary conversational activities. Like Garfinkel and Sacks' (1970) contrast between 'objective' and 'indexical' expressions, the contrasts between 'precise' and 'approximate' measures, between numerical measures and 'usualness measures', and between dates and the specifications on 'private calendars' (Sacks, 1987) are strictly of local rhetorical value. The contrasts do not specify stable ontological domains; it is not as though some measurement terms are inherently precise while others are approximate. 'Precise' and 'approximate' expressions are not placed along a continuum defining the degree of correspondence between numbers and measured properties, since to propose, for example, 'I'll meet you at 4:03' is to presume a *qualitatively* different state of affairs than would be the case for 'I'll meet you at 4:00.' In other words, the 'precise' time '4:03' indexes a particular kind of conjoint activity for which time pieces are synchronised and a minor lapse can make a difference; otherwise, the proposal is likely to be heard as non-serious. Again, it is not as though numbers and measurement terms, *lose* their precise functions when the 'folk' get hold of them, they function *precisely* as 'usualness measures' for particular activities and social scenes. Following the policy of ethnomethodological indifference, a study of ordinary uses of measurement terms need not involve invidious comparisons between inherently

responds by professing not to recollect when the particular documents were shredded. As his subsequent elaboration makes clear, he is not claiming to have a 'faulty memory', nor is he denying outright that he shredded the documents on *some* date or that on 21 November 1986 he shredded *some* documents. Instead, he offers a biographical reference ('my return from Europe in October') as an approximate starting point for daily shredding, and later adds that in any case he shredded documents 'almost every day that I had a shredder'. He thus embeds his 'failure to recall' within the 'usualness' of shredding at his National Security Counsel office. The 'precise' reference is significant in this instance since 21 November had previously been established as the date on which North was informed about an impending investigation of his activities by the Attorney General's office. If North were to admit to destroying key documents on that date, a strong presumption could be drawn about his 'unusual' motives for doing so. By refusing the 'date' the interrogator offers, North does more than give a mere 'approximation' of when he shredded the key documents; he disavows the motivational horizons implied by the 'precisely dated' juxtaposition of shredding, particular documents, and organisational activities. That is, he refuses a chronological 'binding technique'[12] for collecting his activities. Nields then attempts to pursue North's confirmation of an undated temporal reference to 'publicity' about the Iran–Contra affair in 'early November'. Again, this attempts to frame the 'shredding' as a motivated reaction to impending public scrutiny of North's and his administrative colleagues' covert activities. North also disavows any specific recollection, and explicitly objects to Nields' attempt to 'fix' him 'with a date' (a lovely pun on Nields' manipulative solicitations). Both the interrogator's solicitations and the witness' disavowals make use of a distinction between relatively 'precise' or 'approximate' ways of formulating events; but in this case we can see that these 'measures' are not selected for an overhearing analyst's disinterested assessment of the degree of correspondence between measures and events. Rather, the work of 'fixing North with a date' is part and parcel of the committee's task of making a 'disinterested' historical record of North's motivated actions. Again, we can use the tick brackets { } to mark the phenomenon for ethnomethodological respecification: {date <--> North's activities} where <--> can be translated as 'is a disinterested record of'. Respecified, {<-->} becomes salient as a binding technique through which the committee's interrogators try to constitute {date <--> North's activities} for the record and as part of a 'master narrative' of 'the Iran–Contra affair' (Bogen and Lynch, 1989). The phenomenon of interest for ethnomethodology is the interactional work through which the committee attempts to 'fix North with a date', and this includes contingent interrogative uses of the 'mathematical' grid constituted by a chronology of dates, times, and activities; and, relatedly, of the 'ordinary' pragmatic resources through which such terms of reckoning can be plausibly substantiated or resisted.

6   Science (again): enframing measurables in an assemblage of haecceities

Modern science's way of representing pursues and entraps nature as a calculable coherence of forces. Modern physics is not experimental physics because it applies apparatus to the questioning of nature. Rather the reverse is true. Because physics, indeed already as pure theory, sets nature up to exhibit itself as a coherence of forces calculable in advance, it therefore orders its experiments precisely for the purpose of asking whether and how nature reports itself when set up in this way. (Heidegger, 1977: 221)

Conventionally understood, Wilson's couplet – Fundamental Structure <--> Mathematical Form – is a fact in the physical sciences, although perhaps not in the social sciences. Ethnomethodologically respecified, {Fundamental Structure <--> Mathematical Form} becomes a contingent achievement. Consistent with the overall stance on 'methods' in ethnomethodology, 'measurement' becomes the phenomenon of interest rather than a source of methodological security. The policy of ethnomethodological indifference requires that we put aside strong professional urgings to 'ground' inquiry in a set of *a priori* rules and standard techniques, while examining the uses of measurement in varieties of lay and professional circumstances. The conventional distinction between scientific and common-sense measurements – which holds that the former are precise, disinterested, and correct to the extent permitted by the state of the art, while the latter are approximate, interested, and often erroneous – is no longer of any use for ethnomethodology. Following Sacks' remarks on 'approximate' measures and measurement terms, we can see that such terms are not weak or distorted versions of 'scientific' measurements, since they serve adequately in circumstances where 'precise' numbers, dates, and measures would be strange, incorrect, or even incriminating. Relatedly, 'scientific measurement' is not to be treated as a homogeneous set of methods and standards, but as an ecology of techniques through which locally recognisable and locally adequate measures are attained in the very way a distinctive subject matter is elucidated. Each science is now to be treated as a distinctive science of practical action (Garfinkel *et al.*, 1989). As such, each discipline itself generates 'measures' of its own praxis as an indissoluble 'property' of its social organisation; or, in Latour's (1987) terms, each laboratory locally generates a 'sociology of science' integrated with the investigation of its phenomena, promotion of its enterprise, and application of its results.[13]

It clearly would not be appropriate in light of these considerations to suppose that the diversity of disciplines that call themselves 'sciences' are unified by a common set of measurement techniques or standards of adequacy. The particular practices used, for instance, in particle physics do not necessarily inform or exemplify what sociologists (or, for that matter, geologists, field ecologists, or molecular biologists) ought to do. 'Measurement' is a familiar term of trade but not necessarily a coherent practice from one discipline to another. Although the term implies a domain of practice shared in the various natural and human sciences, *just how* equipment is set up, calibrated, and de-bugged, *just how* specimen materials are prepared to expose thematic configurations, and *just how* equipment is handled and readings are taken in one run of an experiment after another, remain to be discovered in the hands-on work of a discipline.[14]

Several ethnomethodological studies have investigated the '*just how*' of discovering practices in the natural sciences and mathematics (Garfinkel *et al.*, 1981; Garfinkel *et al.*, 1989; Lynch *et al.*, 1983; Morrison, 1981, 1990; Livingston, 1986; Lynch, 1985; Schrecker, forthcoming; Bjelic and Lynch, 1989). These studies emphasise the singularity, *quiddity*, or as Garfinkel puts it in chapter 2, the *haecceity* ('just thisness') of discovering practices. This emphasis differs remarkably from the prevailing aim in the social sciences to explain general patterns of events rather than single episodes, but to put it this way is to misunderstand the issue. The point of studying *haecceities* is to disclose an order of local contingencies of the day's work: unique assemblages of equipment for recording and enframing data,[15] improvised methods for getting experiments to work, uncanny procedures for selecting 'good' data and cleaning the data of artifacts, expedient ways of getting results and getting them again, situated rhetorics for instructing colleagues how to see the results etc. and etc. Assemblages of haecceities gloss the embodied and interactional work of doing experiments and demonstrating results. They identify *Lebenswelt* practices, although they do not index a foundational centre – a transcendental consciousness – intentionally related to a coherent phenomenal field.

For simplicity's sake, consider a slogan: 'There's no time out from society.' To seriously consider scientists' measurement practices in light of this slogan, we need to turn away from questions on the objective validity of measurements in order to wonder how a society can be so ordered that 'measurement' becomes a mathematically accountable and reproducible activity. That is, we need to wonder how a society makes itself 'knowable'; how 'it' becomes accountable *in, of, and as* a society with distinctive and measurable features. If 'there is no time out from society', then measurements of things are measurements in, of, and as social practices. This is not a question of the depth structure of consciousness, or even of a general rationalisation of the lifeworld, but of the mundane, taken-for-granted orders of affairs through which members produce the accountability of their activities.

Ethnomethodologically respecified, 'measurement' is a hopelessly vulgar competence, and it is no less vulgar when encountered in the scientific laboratory than it is when performed on the streets, in the market, or at congressional hearings. As noted above, in Garfinkel's (1967) 'coding' study, the research assistants made use of a vulgar competence through which the clinic's organisation was already 'known' before its activities were quantitatively assessed.

However accurate, inaccurate, valid or invalid, the code simultaneously conflated 'clinic activities' with 'coders' practical competence with 'clinic activities'. A similar point can be made about the many routine technical practices accomplished in scientific laboratories. For instance, in the following transcript of a tape-recorded episode two research assistants in a neurosciences laboratory argue about how to add a small amount of a chemical reagent to a solution. The measurement is botched, and the ensuing dialogue is very instructive for our purposes, since it unravels the lab members' attunement to an environment of practical activities. The breach exposes how a measurement glosses a practitioner's competence with a mundane order of laboratory things at the same time that it selectively renders those things accountable. In the following sequence, researcher 'L' has just made an attempt to 'shake' a small amount of powdered ingredient from a vial into a liquid solution when 'J' confronts him. 'G' is a research assistant from another lab who 'L' has been instructing on the use of the technique:

J: Jesus Christ! You made up a bunch didn't yuh.
L: I know.
J: How concentrated?
L: I made it too concentrated. I was trying to shake just a little bit.
L: A big glob fell in.
J: When you make that up –
L: I know.
J: Use uh, a silver spatula. Us a –
L: Y'use spatulas in it?
J: Yeh. Yeh use five milligrams with ten milliliters.
L: Uoh- oh kay.
J: That's more of the order of twenty milligrams and five milliliters.
L: No, that's thirty milligrams.
J: Yeah, but y'got oh (   ) but y'got hundreds of milligrams in there –
J: Not hundreds
L: Oh no
J: Ye have about (   )
L: (to G) What he's saying is that I added way too much.
G: Yeah.
L: Oh kay.
G: W' about five milligrams you put into twenty
L: Almost as little bit as you can get into there.
J: Five milligrams in ten something.
G: You don't necessarily need to weigh it out?
J: Ten milligrams – yeah
L: I don't weigh it out. It says thet yer not supposed to
G: Oh
J: Yeah I
L: D'you weigh it out?
J: The way to do that is to take your plastic thing and set it on there. Get a clean metal spatula take it there and add it while that thing's on there (tarr . . . tarr) the plastic

like that and that way you don't have to touch anything but this thing, and then wash that thing off really well.

L: Oh kay I'y was just – I'd heard that you're not supposed to do it on our balance – you're not supposed to take the stuff in there. That's what it is.

(Taken from Lynch, 1985: 237–8)

The 'amount' of the chemical is formulated in very interesting ways as the sequence develops. Initially, J and L use non-quantitative formulations ('a bunch', 'too concentrated', and 'a big glob') displaying apparent agreement that L added too much of the chemical to the solution. At first, L attempts to head-off J's incipient advice on how to do the technique by asserting that he already knows that he added too much. However, when J begins to give advice on using a spatula (presumably to dole out a precise amount to be weighed), a discrepancy begins to emerge between his and L's version of measuring. Stated in simplest terms, the discrepancy is between a quantitative and a non-quantitative technique: J elaborates a technique for producing a 'precise' ratio of weight to volume, while L uses a non-quantified 'approximate' measure. L initially resists using the numerical formula when he translates J's ratios for G's benefit into non-numerical expressions: 'What he's saying is that I added way too much . . . Almost as little bit as you can get into there.' It becomes clear, however, that the discrepancy is more than a question of alternative ways of *talking* about the amount in the solution. The discrepancy is a matter of technique; and the alternative techniques reflexively implicate practitioners' understandings of the chemical agent being constructed and of its potential reactions to available equipment for constructing it.

When L says 'I don't weigh it out. It says thet yer not supposed to', he invokes an unspecified authority for his non-quantified technique of shaking-in '[a]lmost as little bit as you can get into there'. From the way he justifies his technique, we can infer that the issue he raises is not 'accuracy' so much as the potential contamination of the equipment and possible hazards to the researcher arising from a reaction between the chemical agent and the metallic surfaces of the scale. J then demonstrates a measurement technique that gets around the problem by dishing out the powder on to a plastic sheet and then placing the sheet on the balance's surface. The instructive demonstration is riddled with deictic references individuating its terms in an assemblage of haecceities:[16] 'take your plastic thing'; 'set it on there'; 'Get a clean metal spatula'; 'take it there'; 'add it while that thing's on there'; 'like that'; 'that way you don't have to touch anything but this thing'; 'wash that thing off really well'. The assemblage is enunciated through an order of 'thisses, thats, and theres' immediately tagged to the equipment at hand. This string of haecceities simultaneously articulates a practical basis for the molar solution and a 'molecular' emplacement of the chemical agent within the lab's collective routines. The assemblage is a 'unit act' incorporating a chemical *agent* as an irreducible 'element' (Parsons, 1937).[17] The action is thus hopelessly and irremediably *scientific* in its every detail, but this 'science' is nothing other than a vulgar competence in a singular laboratory environment.

This example suggests a way we can reconsider our slogan, 'There's no time out from society.' The assemblage of haecceities laid out by the demonstration of a measuring technique acts simultaneously as a 'binding technique' for the practitioner's 'narrative' and a locally organised chemistry lesson (cf. Schrecker, forthcoming). But, unlike a story told over the phone or inscribed in a text, the narrative's structure is bound to the material assemblage it articulates. In its immediate form it does not travel. The story reports from no other place than the assemblage of 'thisses, thats, and theres' it traverses; just as a pianist's fingers have no other place to 'sing' than the keys they play on a keyboard (Sudnow, 1979).

7   Days in the life of an embalmed rat pack

The above instance documents how a laboratory's measures can be unravelled in an assemblage of haecceities. But, this still leaves unanswered how Wilson's couplet {Fundamental Structure Mathematical Form} can 'come true' as a members' achievement. How does an assemblage of haecceities[18] become a set of measures subject to 'abstract' operations? To address this, let me introduce a very primitive example, that of 'days' used as a unit of measure for a laboratory demonstration. 'Days' are, of course, among our most familiar measurement terms for organising activities. A vulgar competence with 'days' is an unquestioned prerequisite for membership in virtually every concerted social activity. 'Today' is an archetypal haecceity: 'a mode of individuation that is distinct from that of a thing or a subject' (Deleuze and Guarrati, 1987: 541). Although, when we think about it, it is an astonishing fact that we can assign a date to 'today', for the most part we do this without any sense of having made a profound translation. 'Today *is* 4 January 1990.' Like the fingering gestures, '*Here's one!*'; '*Here's another!*' the expressions act as primal haecceitic movements that already constitute members-in-a-series. The finger that points also counts. We simply pass over a concerted *trafficking* in such 'digital' gestures when we start our inquiries with the mathematical orders they achieve. The units, segmental joints, rigor, and resoluteness arising from a massively concerted and densely articulated organisation of pointing and counting collapses into an order described by a cardinal number series: 1, 2, 3, 4 . . . .

The beauty of laboratory experiments is that the social order of the lab regularly re-creates its objective circumstances. That is, it is a feature of discovering work to articulate the hidden conditions that have operated, all-along, at the heart of the practice (Eglin, 1974). The seamlessness of the pointing-that-also-counts is painstakingly reconstructed in a halting and deliberate operation. So, when we wonder how a society can be so ordered that measurement becomes a mathematically accountable and reproducible activity, a lab's experiments give us an 'experimental' case of such a society. 'Days' in the lab take on unique configurations, once they are used as measures for the phenomena under study.

As an unremarkable fact of life, a lab's work is enumerable in an order of days (1, 2, 3, 4, 5, . . . n). A day's work consists in an assemblage of contingent temporalities, some of which can be enumerated in an order of days and others not (Lynch et al., 1983). The design, enactment, and fulfilment of a project largely consists in a struggle to align assemblages of temporalities from one day to the next. Sometimes, the conventional orderliness of the 'day' (e.g., waking and sleeping times, eating, work schedules) gives way to the lunacy of experimental demands. Researchers often live 'crazy' schedules, out of phase with the rest of society, while tending their specimens, tracking phenomena in the night sky, or taking advantage of 'off hours' at the computer centre. The conventional enumeration of days nevertheless remains in force, and is convertible into a scale of events. So, for instance, in one neurosciences project 'days' were used as an index of regenerative processes in the rat brain (Lynch, 1985; 1988b). Cohorts of rats were subjected to an operation that selectively destroyed a region of the cerebral cortex. Anatomical studies had established that axons from neurons in the destroyed region terminated in particular layers of cells in the hippocampus. The study was designed to assess whether axons terminating at adjacent regions of the hippocampus would send 'sprouts' into the regions previously enervated by the axon terminals from the destroyed region. Theoretically, the 'sprouts' would reoccupy some of the dendritic sites previously occupied by the degenerating axons. It was believed that this process took place in a matter of a few days, and that careful comparison of electron micrographs of the hippocampus taken at different 'time points' after the lesion would demonstrate the timing and distribution of the regenerative process.

A scale of 'days' for reckoning axon-sprouting was constructed as follows. The origin of a series was marked by the lesion. To produce a 'five-day animal', a rat would be operated upon and given an experimental brain-lesion on, for example, a Monday, and then sacrificed on the following Saturday at approximately the same time of day. The brain would presumably have begun its regenerative process in the days since the lesion, and the sacrifice would arrest that process at the specified point. The hippocampus would be dissected and preserved, and later prepared for electron microscopy. All micrographs produced from that specimen would be indexed by the animal's identification number and by the number of days following the lesion. The condition of cells exposed by electron microscopy would then be compared to those from other animals at different time points.

Animals were lesioned and sacrificed in batches, so that several animals were used for each of the time points constituting the 'day' scale. A sequence of events was thus elaborated in and through the series of micrographs at the different time points (e.g. 2 days, 3 days, 4 days, etc.). The series was designed to be like a time-lapse photograph of a section of the hippocampus, showing a gradual darkening and shrinking of degenerating axon profiles, followed by a rapid proliferation of glial cells moving into the region to engulf the degenerative material, and then a sprouting of neighbouring axons which snake their way into the degenerating region to reoccupy vacated synapses. This was to be a territorial drama enacted upon a micrographic plane, where a degenerative retreat would be followed by an advancing army of neuronal rhizomes. But, unlike a time-lapse photograph, each still-frame required the sacrifice of its subject and a distillation of its bodily materials. The camera angle necessitated a lethal operation, and the corpse was embalmed and recomposed to simulate a stage in a generalised life. The day for the portrait was literally the day of reckoning for its organic subject. So, instead of a transparent rat gradually recovering from its injury, a pack of rats[19] was deployed in a rigormortic assemblage. 'Regeneration' was enframed in the passages between the corpses.

The scale of days had peculiar properties. Different versions of this scale could be reconstructed during different phases of the project. A minimal series (4, 11) was used in a preliminary draft of the project report, while a more elaborate series (2, 4, 5, 6, 7, 9, 11) appeared in the final draft. A still more elaborate series (2, 2$1/2$, 3, 4, 5, 5$1/2$, 6, 8, 9, 11) emerged from the project's corpus of micrographs. Each series told a distinctive 'story': the minimal series documented the cellular distributions 'before' and 'after' the regenerative event evidently took place. That is, it enframed the central event of axon sprouting. The two more complicated series not only enframed the central event more 'precisely' (at around 5 days), they both exhibited other events such as, e.g., the beginnings of degenerative decay at around 2 days, and a proliferation of glial cells between 2 and 4 days. Particular 'days' also became significant as sites for *non*-events, documenting continuous changes in the distribution of materials rather than discrete events. The lab's data archive documented an uneven span of intervals between 2 and 11 days. Exploratory forays interpolated the intervals between 2 and 3 and 5 and 6 days. Key events were believed to take place within these intervals, whereas the larger gaps between, for example, 9 and 11 days testified to a less eventful temporal environment. The half-day intervals were dropped in the published series; apparently because they showed nothing that was not resolved by the whole-day intervals, and too fine an interval was likely to confuse the resolution of the 'events' from one animal to another. In some respects, the temporal series documents a substantive 'interest' in a product, like a pattern of exploratory oil wells drilled on a Texas plateau.

All of these 'day' scales contrasted to a series of cardinal integers (1, 2, 3, 4, 5 . . . n), and the gaps did not resolve into a coherent *mathematical* series (e.g., 2, 4, 6, 8 . . . n). To reckon a 'day' was to undertake an extensive project, rather than simply to count-out the next number in a series. Since there was a cost to such undertakings (in time, labour, rats, materials), the undertakers designed the series in terms of a substantive economy, where intervals enframed the events they anticipated. There are well-known fallacies associated with such enframings of events by instrumental readings (Langmuir, 1968), but in this case it may be more pertinent to consider the features of the scale as a part of the collectively achieved 'grasp' of a phenomenon.

We can now see that in this case Wilson's couplet {Fundamental Structure Mathematical Form} comes true, but not because nature 'is addressed in an attitude divorced from human emotions, sentiments, or practical purposes'. On the contrary, it comes true through the undertaker's craft, in a morbid cartoon of regeneration. The still-life kinetic ensemble of the embalmed rat pack embodies a mathematical form, but the passage from an assemblage of haecceities to an order of things is already pre-figured in the day of reckoning.

8 Conclusion

For Husserl, Galileo's mathematisation of nature involved a 'surreptitious substitution' of idealised mathematical forms for the one real world of immediate experience. The picture emerging from ethnomethodological studies of measuring praxis is somewhat different. Studies of work in the sciences demonstrate that this 'substitution' is very much out in the open when practitioners go about their work. Galileo's 'invention' of the *mathesis universalis* is not a forgotten legacy, since it is reproduced whenever scientists set up their instruments and begin to record data. There is no secrecy or deviousness to it, as it is 'hidden' within the 'thisses and thats' of routine laboratory praxis. Nor is embarrassment necessarily entailed by its redis-covery. It simply does not travel from its primordial site since it *is* the assem-blage of haecceities that makes up that site: it *is* preparing materials for an experiment, tuning the equipment, tracing a biochemical marker, sacrificing the animals on schedule, coding the data, taking care of noise, and plotting the data on a graph (Garfinkel *et al.*, 1989; Lynch, 1988c). Or, as Livingston's (1986) study demonstrates, the substitution of idealised mathematical forms for *Lebenswelt* praxis is internal to the embodied performance of a math-ematical proof.

To say that 'vulgar competencies' are unavoidable and irremediably part of measuring is not to say that science is based on 'mere' common sense. Although laboratory practitioners take for granted an ability to count unerringly, keep track of time, speak sensibly, and know what anyone should know about the world, their immediate actions compose singular contextures of their own equipment, their own projects, and their own findings. In other words, vulgar competencies are bound to a local historicity of practices, understandings, and previous research, and their organisation is far from transparent to anyone who might happen to take a casual interest in them. This is not to say that vulgar competencies are 'scientific knowledge' in the usual sense. To be able to handle laboratory animals so that they do not die from the trauma of an experiment, or to be able to fix bulky equipment and to know when not to trust the results of experiments using such equipment, is not necessarily based on 'scientific' theories or methodological doctrines, and yet such abilities are cultivated as indispensable laboratory routines.

There may be nothing special about measurement in the natural sciences, taken as a whole. The question for sociology is not, 'How can *we* obtain the precise correspondence between mathematical models and empirical data achieved in the natural sciences?' Such a question gives too much away. It supposes that 'the natural sciences' can be treated as a methodologically unified field, and it assumes that general criteria exist for assessing 'precision' without regard to subject matter. The question raised in ethnomethodology is, instead, 'What are the games?' That is, what are the locally organised practices through which {Fundamental Structure <--> Mathematical Form} becomes an adequate and acceptable expression? The expression does not come true simply because it is targeted to a 'material' universe.

In closing, I should add that my arguments about ethnomethodology's indifference to conventional sociological methods do not imply that ethnomethodology is thereby a 'common-sense' approach. To an extent, Feyerabend's (1975) slogan, 'Anything goes!' may be particularly well-suited for ethnomethodology, since it militates against any preliminary attempt to delimit what scientific methods must be in order to be scientific. Relatedly, it warns against the kind of self-imposed exile from interesting phenomena entailed by too 'rigorous' an adherence to preconceptions about what 'data' must look like in order to stand as records of 'actual' social activities, or what 'analysis' must involve in order to surpass mere 'intuition'. But by throwing-off *Method* ethnomethodology enacts less of a move into eclecticism than a radical turn away from scientism. This entirely transforms conventional sociology's preconception of what it means to undertake a 'study' of social phenomena. A 'study' no longer requires that the analyst devise ways to take the measure of objects or mechanisms in the extant society; instead, it becomes a matter of perspicuously exhibiting the society's hold on the very measures that take account of it.

NOTES

1 The 'reasonable agreement' Kuhn speaks of can be viewed as a special case of social order within a larger field. As Kuhn (1962) elaborates, scientific disciplines are communities bound by concerted agreements on theories, measuring techniques, and characteristic modes of demonstration. What Kuhn said of science was, in part, based on what Wittgenstein (1968) had previously identified for ordinary practices; that the techniques and adequacy of measurement are inseparable from the organised forms of life in which they have a role.

2 For an illuminating discussion of the distinction between primary and secondary qualities see Hacker (1987). The distinction is perspicuous in the Newtonian conception of colour, where colour is said to be a secondary effect based on sensory stimulation by colourless 'rays' travelling at different speeds and obeying mathematical laws.

3 Helling argues that 'whenever Schutz uses methodological concepts or rules in the strict sense, he relies on either Max Weber or Felix Kaufmann.' (Helling, 1984: 142). She states further that her study of Schutz's long-standing relationship to Kaufmann shows that 'Schutz's methodological position is compatible with conventional sociology and that the more radical of his followers have not read him correctly.' (Helling, 1984: 142). I read this as an allusion to Garfinkel's ethnomethodology, and while Helling seems to suggest that a 'radical' departure from Schutz's methodological position is not warranted, this is only the case if we continue to treat Schutz's texts as unquestionable guidelines. It is clear from ethnomethodology's history that Schutz's writings were relied upon as a way-station but not a final authority.

4 See Lynch, 1988a for an elaboration upon this idea.

5 The issues that are involved here are given explicit and elaborate attention in the consideration of 'action' and 'the actor' in chapter six.

6 The human science specification of 'inference and evidence' that is invoked in some of the following excerpts is exclusively examined in the following chapter.

7 Palincsar (1989: 7) points out that this example of measuring illustrates the dieter's ineptitude with fractions, since it would have been simpler initially to measure-out half a cup of cottage cheese. While this objection may be true, the important feature of the example is the method for 'dividing by four'. Such a procedure is hardly remarkable, since it is much like the mundane art of folding a sheet of paper or cloth to divide it in fractions. It is not so much that such practices are superior or more 'authentic' than pencil and paper calculation, but that they are *used*, and their use produces 'measurements' without requiring a separation between measuring device (or model) and what is measured.

8 Some of Sacks' previously unpublished lectures on ordinary measurement systems were recently published in an edited paper (Sacks, 1988/9). Some of the materials are also touched-upon in another paper edited from lectures (Sacks, 1984a). In my discussion of Sacks' remarks on measurement, I refer to the original lectures as they are indexed for Sacks (1964–72).

9 Also see Churchill (1966) on ordinary quantitative usages, Schegloff (1972) on place formulations, and Psathas (1979b) on sketch maps and formulations of direction. Although I will not pursue the issue here, it might also be argued that a kind of numerical reckoning is inherent in the typical three-part composition of lists and bursts of laughter, and also perhaps in the normative duration of conversational silences (Jefferson, 1979; 1988a; 1990).

10 Garfinkel (lectures and colloquia, UCLA) frequently uses the example of traffic as a social order *sui generis*. He stresses that this order is constituted in no other way than by each driver's driving *in and as* the traffic. Sacks may very well be invoking Garfinkel's emphasis on the concerted achievement of traffic when he points out that, in effect, though hardly as a laudable achievement, many drivers drive so as to constitute the 'traffic' against which others can be said to be driving 'fast' or 'slow'.

11 Sacks' remarks are based on the following transcript (Sacks, 1984a: 424):

> MADGE: *Say* did you see anything in the paper *la*st night or hear anything on the local radio, 'hh Ruth Henderson and I drove down, to, Ventura yesterday
> BEA: Mm hm,
> MADGE: And on the way home we saw – the most gosh awful *wreck*.
> BEA: Oh:::
> MADGE: we have ev– I've ever seen. I've never *seen* a car smashed into sm– such a small space.
> BEA: Oh:::
> MADGE: It was smashed, – 'hh from the front and the back both. It must have been in – caught in, between two car: :s,
> BEA: // Mm hm, uh huh
> MADGE: // Must have run *in*to a car and then another car smashed *in*to it and there were people laid out and covered over on the pavement,
> BEA: Mm
> MADGE: We were s– parked there for *quite* a *while*. But *I* was going to, listen to the local r-*news* and haven't *done* it.

12 Sacks (Lecture 3, Spring 1970; 16 April, '70) discusses how place-indexical references in a story can also be part of a 'binding technique' for building a coherent scene for the listener to follow. In the present case it is worthwhile to consider 'binding' as operating along two fronts: the various references to dates and activities bind together a coherent narrative, and at the same time the references implicate the teller's placement in the scene constituted by those particulars. Implications of innocence and guilt can turn on just how the narrative voice reflexively places itself within a sequential assemblage of such terms (Sacks, 1984b: 423).

13 Although there are significant differences between ethnomethodology and the semiotic approach to science and technology developed by Latour (1987; 1988) and Callon (1986), there is at least one strong point of convergence, and that is the acknowledgement that each scientific field studied by sociology is itself an endogenous 'sociology of science'. Accordingly, no initial commitment is made to a body of sociological methods extrinsic to the field studied, since this can conflict with an effort to discern the locally produced sociologies within the discipline studied.

14 Consider an analogy to athletic events. The fact that pole-vaulting and equestrianism are both recognised as Olympic sports should not lead us to figure that 'methods' of pole-vaulting would be very instructive for participants in equestrian events.

15 'Enframing' (*das ge-stell*) is Heidegger's (1977: 19ff.) term for the essence of modern techno-science; a pre-theoretic 'ordering' that constitutes a stark landscape in which persons and things simultaneously assume their places as mechanistically structured and calculable forces. My use of 'enframing' refers to the mundane praxis through which 'data' are uncovered and ordered as 'measurable information'. Accordingly, enframing is an in-forming of what is too easily treated as *given* information.

16 In this discussion I 'misread' Deleuze and Guattari's (1987: 260ff.) discussion of 'memories of haecceity' in light of Garfinkel's exemplary treatment of 'haecceity'

in chapter 2. Deleuze and Guattari's essays include evocative terms like 'assemblage', 'pack', 'emplacement', 'rhizome', 'molar', and 'molecular'. I have lifted many of these terms from their textual context while disregarding Deleuze and Guattari's enigmatic and elusive use of them. I am also assuming that such unscholarly violence to the authors' original intentions is entirely in the spirit of their text.

17 Latour (1988) successfully brings-off a word-play on the analytic category of 'agent' when he demonstrates how Pasteur retrospectively incorporated a new social 'agent' – the microbe – within the fields of agriculture and hygiene. In the present context, the term 'chemical agent' can suggest how an assemblage of actions and equipment incorporates a chemical agent, not only as a substance with tangible effects, but as a functional ordering of actions and equipment presupposing those effects.

18 Needless to say, an assemblage of haecceities is not equivalent to an order of 'sense data', even though the assemblage subsequently describes a structure of appearances. To treat an assemblage as 'original information' requires a sleight of hand (as well as a slighting of the hand's work).

19 The 'pack' of animals is a key term in Deleuze and Guattari's (1987) account of 'becoming animal'. They argue that to *be*, e.g., a rat or a wolf is not to be an individual but to become a being dispersed within the presence and movements of an assemblage, a pack. Also relevant is the sense of a 'pack' of cards. This recalls the Husserlian (1970c: 46) 'game of cards' through which an assemblage of signs becomes a mathematised field. The term 'cards' is also explicitly used by Goethe to refer to the textual figures that make up intrinsic elements of the *Farbenspiel* ('colour games') through which he demonstrates a distinctive theory of colour (Bjelic and Lynch, 1989). In laboratory usage, the term 'animal' refers both to the laboratory rat and the micrographic documents indexed to the specimen (Lynch, 1988b). Each sacrificial animal becomes a card (or frame) in a pack of micrographic documents, which, in turn, enframes each animal's analytic transparency.

6

Method: evidence and inference – evidence and inference for ethnomethodology

Douglas Benson and John A. Hughes

1 Introduction

One of the more notorious of Garfinkel's methodological recommendations, exemplified in his early 'breaching experiments', was the importance of rendering the familiar strange in order to make visible the work necessary to sustain the common understandings and practical reasoning that is the basis of the social order (Garfinkel, 1967). For Garfinkel, of course, no activity could, in principle, be exempt from this proposal, least of all sociology itself. The radicalness of Garfinkel's recommendations is manifested and celebrated in the contributions to this volume and, of course, elsewhere. Our concern in this chapter is to develop in depth a methodological issue which is deeply rooted in the human sciences and which arises from out of the general concern with measurement as considered by Mike Lynch in the preceding chapter: the structure of evidence and inference as exhibited in that family of techniques known by a name popularised, though in condemnation, by Blumer, as 'variable analysis'[1] (Blumer, 1956). These techniques encompass not only the standard means of data collection in social research, such as questionnaires of all types, interviewing, the organisation of the inferential basis of these in survey designs and the principles of sampling, but also the sophisticated, and increasingly esoteric arsenal of statistical analysis. For most practising sociologists, and social researchers more generally, variable analysis is the familiar set of methods of social research against which all other approaches have to be judged and weighed. Even participant observation, a research method with a lineage which is, if anything, older than variable analysis, is relegated to a small sideshow in the methodological fair or, at best, a useful exploratory method to use as a prelude to more systematic investigation by the methods of variable analysis.[2]

Some years ago, and there is no reason to believe that matters have changed overmuch since then, Phillips (1971) quoted an estimate to the effect that some 90 per cent of published empirical sociology was produced using the statistical manipulation of interview and questionnaire data. Of course, especially in hindsight, it is not difficult to see why the promissory note variable analysis offered in the early pioneering days of Lazarsfeld and his colleagues should have been accepted with such alacrity. Its espousal of quantification and, as discussed in chapter 5, its ingenious solutions to problems of measurement in the human sciences; its claim to emulate the experimental controls regarded as the *sine qua non* of the scientific method, and through this conformity to the hypothetico-deductive reasoning taken as the hallmark of science, suited the mentality of the time and ensured variable analysis its paragon status in social research.[3] One unfortunate consequence of this which we simply note here is the way in which methodological debate, especially, but not only, in sociology, has been polarised between opposing camps, usually debated as qualitative versus quantitative methods. So much so that serious methodological discussion has become obscured by the need to attack, defend or otherwise justify general stances, rather than trying to deal with the problems of securing adequate empirical reference.[4]

Variable analysis is more than simply a haphazard collection of techniques. It is a collection which obtains a unity through a way of thinking about investigating human behaviour empirically. Most of the familiar techniques comprising the collection were begged, borrowed or stolen from a range of disciplines, including market research, genetics, biology, statistics, and psychology. What provided them with their methodological unity was, though this is to put it too bluntly, the familiar motivation to secure the scientific status of the social sciences. In this respect, providing a sound basis of dealing with the problems of evidence and inference was of paramount importance.

Of course, questions about evidence and inference have been an enduring theme of Western philosophy in its search for the indubitable grounds of human knowledge; an inquiry which has taken as many forms, offered as many conclusions, as schools of philosophy have disputed in a shifting battle of ideas. The growth of natural science, however, with its claims of producing knowledge of the constitution of the world by empirical rather than rational means, heralded the end of metaphysical philosophy: a predicted demise which proved premature. Nonetheless, the advent of science did force philosophy to concede ground in making it recognise that its own search for the foundations of human knowledge would, henceforth, have to focus on the nature of science itself.

Although it is not our purpose here to contend more than we need to with philosophical arguments about the foundations of human knowledge, it is important to single out one important theme for our purpose, namely, the tension between the general and the particular. In brief, and with no little avoidance of the variations and detailed arguments, scientific knowledge was seen to be universal across space and time as represented in its general laws. Yet, the evidential material for such laws was particular in its instantiation. As Campbell (1969) aptly put it in quoting the case of Nicholson and Carlisle who, in 1800, took a very parochial sample of Soho water, inserted into it a very biased piece of copper wire through which flowed a very local electric current. At one electrode oxygen was given off, at the other, hydrogen. Despite the particularities of all the elements that went into the experiment, they went on to generalise about the constituents of all water, past, present and future. Quite how natural science managed to transcend knowledge of particular cases to produce universal descriptions of phenomena was a matter of considerable debate centering on the nature of the scientific method stressing the importance of experimental controls, the *ceteris paribus* conditions placed on the statements of a law, and the abstractive properties of scientific concepts.

As is well known, whether or not the human sciences should, or could, aspire to the ambitions of the natural sciences, a question largely posed in terms of philosophical versions of these rather than from a more direct acquaintance with their practices, was to prove a contentious issue; one perhaps dominating their history. But, even for the advocates of the natural-science model of the human sciences, the endeavour to translate ambition into achievement was to prove less than straightforward, not least because of problems about characterising the nature of science itself. Nonetheless, one key assumption, again one largely uncritically derived from philosophy despite its constant arguments about such, was the idea that the superiority of science over other forms of knowledge was its use of *a* method; in a word, the scientific method. It was this which enabled scientists to uncover the laws of nature which linked seemingly unconnected empirical and particular events into general patterns. Thus, and very obviously, falling apples, planetary orbits, tidal movements, and more, were all shown to be the result of gravitational force.

Three further points are relevant. The first concerns the connection the scientific method established between empirical evidence and the truth status of theories. The truth claims about the nature of the world are not veridical by reason alone, as in metaphysical and philosophical speculation, but by empirical evidence. Second, and closely related to the first, is establishing a systematic connection between *particular* empirical events and the general claims of the theory; a matter of 'inferring' from the empirical evidence to some general statement. It was this as, variously, the problem of induction or deduction, that constituted, and still does so, one of the central problems of philosophy.[5] Third, the success of science, though whether this is a contingent as opposed to a necessary feature of science is arguable, was associated with the 'mathematisation of nature'.

Galileo had said that the 'book of nature is written in geometrical characters'; an apothegm which captured the difference in outlook between himself and most of his contemporaries. Nonetheless, though probably more is owed to Descartes than to Galileo, it is this which is regarded as the 'Galilean Revolution' in science. The 'mathematisation of nature' that Mike Lynch discussed in the preceding chapter was a major historical moment in the development of science, for science henceforth became, in Koyre's word, Platonic; that is, according to mathematics a superior and real value in the furtherance of scientific knowledge (Koyre, 1986: 36–7). The success of the generalising impulses of a discipline, and thereby its claim to scientific status, became associated with the extent to which it was capable of mathematising its theoretical endeavours. Mathematics was seen as the abstract, general, and universal discipline above all others and harnessing its 'certitudes' – irrespective of the fact that these 'certitudes' were the source of much philosophical puzzlement – to the scientific method provided a machinery for making and securing the connection between the particular and the general.

As far as the human sciences were concerned, of course, their mathematisation was to prove difficult in a number of ways.[6] One disadvantage they suffered was from was the very success of the natural sciences which themselves had encouraged the development of a mathematics more suited to the problems and the phenomena of the natural rather than the human, sciences. Another, and one hinted at in the previous remark, was the very real problems of applying mathematical reasoning to human phenomena. Prior to the rise of the social sciences, there were already moves toward developing a quantitative descriptive apparatus of social accounting. For one example, Wiles (1971: 198) cites the case of William Petty (1623–85) who had been engaged in the analysis of 'bills of mortality'. Petty argued that the government ought to collect what we would now call official statistics in order to better understand the state of the nation and, through this, make more considered decisions. 'By the number of people, the quality of inebriating liquors spent, the number of unmaryed persons between 15 and 55 years old, the number of Corporall sufferings and persons imprisoned for Crimes, to know the measure of Vice and Sin in the nation.' Some century and a half later, Petty's proposals, though he can hardly be held responsible, were adopted by most European governments as 'moral statistics' and, later, as the modern census and officially produced statistics.

The development of this aspect of modern, and indeed more ancient, statehood has been well documented.[7] For our purposes what is important is that these beginnings of national statistics heralded a growing stimulus to social scientific inquiry into the 'state of society'. For not only were these statistics general in the sense of covering a large population (a confusion over the notion of 'general' which still bedevils the social sciences, as if the problem of scientific generalisation involved the statistical concept of population), they also displayed, in some part at least, the regularity and stability of population characteristics. It was, of course, these properties which led Durkheim to claim that suicide rates could be indicative of the moral state of society (Durkheim, 1952).

This is not the place to review the details of Durkheim's study of suicide, except to note one distinctive feature of his method, namely, taking official figures of such as crime, mortality, unemployment, etc., and suicide of course, and their covariation as the evidence from which inferences can be drawn about the real social processes and patterns which the figures, though not in an unmediated fashion, reflect. It is this move from what we might term a descriptive to an analytical use of quantification which presages the orthodox machinery of social research. That is, using quantitative data and quasi-experimental reasoning in order to identify what he thought of as causal patterns among 'social facts'.

It is, of course, Paul F. Lazarsfeld who inspired the development of that collection of techniques referred to earlier as variable analysis. Lazarsfeld is surprisingly relatively unsung, despite the fact that he it is, probably more than anyone, who is responsible for the character of much of contemporary social research. By a judicious borrowing of techniques including questionnaires, cross-tabulation methods, the logic of statistical inference, surveys, and moulding them into a justifiably coherent approach, Lazarsfeld and his colleagues bequeathed to social research its current orthodoxy of practices.[8]

2   The Lazarsfeldian format

What Lazarsfeld proposed was nothing less than an inferential apparatus for the 'discovery' of patterns in social research data. Kantian in its conception, Lazarsfeld argued that 'No science deals with its objects of study in their full concreteness' (Lazarsfeld and Rosenberg, 1955: 15). Certain properties are selected as the special province of each science about which it seeks to discover patterns of relationship, the ultimate being, of course, those of a law-like character. Science's empirical connection to the world is an abstracted, or selective, one dealing with the properties, attributes or qualities of phenomena rather than with phenomena themselves. Accordingly, he proposed that persons (though the units of analysis need not be restricted to persons) be treated as 'objects' displaying general properties. Thus, and for simple illustration, social actors can be considered as possessing the properties of age, gender, social class, status, intelligence, etc., as well as those pertaining to attitudes, opinions, beliefs and so on. But, for Lazarsfeld and his colleagues, the trick was to think of these properties as mappable onto a mathematical space. To this end he ingeniously deployed a metaphor from mathematics, the variable, to create 'devices by which we can characterize the objects of empirical social investigation'. A variable, as opposed to a constant, can take one of a range of values which can be expressed numerically even, as in the simplest of cases, where 0 signifies to the absence of a property and 1 its presence.[9] At a stroke, one of the classic objections to the quantification, hence the mathematisation, of the human sciences, namely, that much of their phenomena are qualitative in character, was seemingly resolved in a practicable manner. (See Lazarsfeld and Barton, 1951.) Provided that an investigator could determine whether a qualitative attribute was present or absent, then it could be treated as a variable. Although, and as Lazarsfeld recognised, this is a modest requirement, it is nonetheless a route toward more sophisticated mathematisation. But even at this level, by being able to count the frequencies of the property-variables recorded among a collection of persons allows for the empirical identification of any stable patterns of association among the property-variables. Using the numerical values given to the variables, such as frequency counts, they can be mapped onto a coordinate property space, cross-tabulated in a word, and made amenable to statistical partitioning in order to search for stable linkages in the data set. The relative frequency with which combinations of different variable values occur, their covariation, is the basis for determining the degree of association among variables and, therefore, among properties.

As we said earlier, the basic principles Lazarsfeld and his associates enunciated, modest beginnings as they were, have been built upon and developed until we have the current state of social research technology with its mathematically more powerful measurement systems, causal modelling, inferential statistics capable of dealing with larger and larger data sets and more and more complex partitioning of the variables, and so on (Blalock, 1982, 1984).

Before proceeding to examine the basics of the Lazarsfeldian strategy, there are a number of further points worth drawing out. First, social research, on this view, becomes a matter of seeking relationships among indices. Properties are not directly measured, but represented in 'indicators' which are generated by the researcher with an eye on both the conceptual and logical connections of the indicator to the property, and the exigencies of the research situation itself. Lazarsfeld himself conceived of this as a process of translating the 'vague images' suggested by 'immersion' in a theory into observables that could 'stand for' the underlying property, and appropriate to the practical context in which the research is to take place (Lazarsfeld, 1958). In practice, a property is likely to be measured by a combination of indicators; as we shall see, the possible reasons for this are central to the ethnomethodological critique of such methods as well as to its own methodological proposals.[10]

Second, and as already suggested, the measurement of properties is indirect. The mathematics, even as elementary as counting, is brought to the data as an organising principle to work on the indicators, *rather than arising from the structure and character of the phenomenon itself*. A point to which we shall return. On the Lazarsfeldian view, indicators are what social research works with. No indicator will reflect all that a concept might mean, of course. The 'looseness' of social science concepts, the difficulty of operationalising them in a variety of circumstances, errors of all kinds, contribute to an imperfect match between concept and indicator. The relationship, Lazarsfeld argued, is essentially a 'probabilistic one'.[11] However, this is no reason for despair; it is merely focussing attention on the need for measures to improve the validity of indices. In practice, however well or badly an indicator 'stands for' a property it is intended to reflect, is resolved by the operationally expedient criterion of conformity to more or less stable patterns of association with other indicators (Pawson, 1989; Costner, 1972). In other words, the 'stability' or otherwise, of the relationship between indicators arises not from the phenomena themselves but from criteria derived from the techniques, mainly statistical but also those associated with questionnaire and survey design.

Third, the patterns found among the data sets are not, of course, laws in the sense in which natural science would understand this. They are, at best, empirical generalisations and, on this conception, a route to the formulation of law-like statements by the accumulation of empirical results and the identification of the causes at work. In other words, it is a model of scientific work which emphasises the patient accumulation of data gathered by an agreed upon method as the route to better, more predictive, more all-embracing theories. Thus, by what is essentially an iterative process, the relative importance of key independent variables on dependent ones is tested out by partitioning techniques within data sets, and further testing out in other studies. The quantitative values of the correlations being the measure of the relative importance of the variables.[12]

Fourth, and an important point, the method for determining the patterns of association between variables are designed to handle not the individual case but a collection of units. In other words, the question to be answered is not, say, is 'age' associated with 'conservatism' in person A? but in this collection of persons is 'age' associated with 'conservatism'? That is, the route to claiming an association between properties for *particular* units of analysis has to be via the association for the collection.

Fifth, the logic of variable analysis is not restricted to searching for patterns among data. What Lazarsfeld and his colleagues offered was a format for thinking theoretically as well as for data analysis. As one textbook advises, 'it is necessary to translate your ideas . . . into the language of variables before you can carry out or evaluate research. The experienced sociologist develops the habit of routinely translating the English he reads and hears into variables . . . ' (Davis, 1971). Similarly, and for another example, the earlier modes of generalising in social science, perhaps best represented by Weber's 'ideal type' method, was subsumable in the format as a collection of dimensioned properties, hence variables, open to quantitative estimation and, through this, empirical refinement. The format of variables, or property spaces, of association, is intended to provide homologies of inferential structure at both the theoretical level and at that of data[13] (Barton, 1955). It is essentially an empirical approach to theory building by trying to secure stable associations in data which can be hypothesised about and generalised upwards as relationships are discovered to be stable across more and more studies.

Finally, the use of mathematical procedures, even those of simple arithmetic (though these days it has gone way beyond this), to extract patterns from what are, in effect, putative descriptions of the properties of particular cases, offered the possibility of finding general features of specific cases. But, as said earlier, the route to general features of specific cases is by the determination of patterns of association among a collectivity of units. Nonetheless, the question as to what is to constitute data in the social sciences is, now, commonly answered in terms of materials which conform to the requirements of variable analysis.

The approach has not been without its critics, of course, the most widely known in sociology being, perhaps, Blumer's eloquent invective, referred to at the beginning of this chapter, to the effect that variable analysis fails to capture the interpretative and processual character of social life. More recently, some 'insiders', too, have expressed profound disquiet about the ability of variable analysis to deliver on its earlier promises. Despite many years of development there is still what Blalock, one of the foremost exponents of causal modelling, refers to as the 'gap between theory and method', the failure of sociological theories to be strictly responsive to empirical test (Blalock, 1982, 1984). For Blalock, the problem can only be solved by devoting more effort to the development of what he calls 'auxiliary measurement theories' to effect a better fit between theory and data. Lieberson, on the other hand, believes the problem is wider than this, having its roots in the very attempt of variable analysis to emulate the logic of the experiment by means of statistical controls. Such methods, he claims, produce a corpus of data which is both sadly deficient and often wrong by its own criteria (Lieberson, 1985). Turner, too, in pointing to the arbitrariness of the assignment of variables to any statistical modelling of that data, and the consequences this has for the values of the coefficients, results in a radical underdetermination of any theoretical conclusions that might be offered (Turner, 1987). Nonetheless, despite such misgivings, perhaps more widespread than is commonly supposed, the Blalockian view seems to prevail, namely, that variable analysis is broadly on the right lines as a way of constituting an empirical social science. What is needed is more directed effort in refining the techniques. The problem is not one of conception but of technology.

So far we have concentrated on describing the key elements of the Lazarsfeldian format for effecting an inferential link between particular data and general associational relationships in that data. By format, we mean some of the following. First, variable analysis establishes a framework for data. Second, in effect it proceduralises data gathering and analysis, by imposing constraints on the procedures, hence the data and its analysis, in order that it can be accommodated to the framework. Third, and an aspect of the feature just mentioned, the format is not especially sensitive in its constraints to the character of the phenomena with which it deals; on the contrary, it shapes the way in which the phenomena are to be described. In this connection it is worth noting that many of Lazarsfeld's own pronouncements on variable analysis suggest that he saw himself as proposing a ubiquitous method for empirical social science research not just for sociology: a method which, he felt, corresponded to the practices of the scientific method itself. That is, the Lazarsfeldian programme, to call it that, is not a cavalierly expedient choice about the methods of social research, but embodies a claim that in this way the objectivity of social research procedures can be achieved. This apart, it is qualities such as these that provoke us to speak of variable analysis as a 'mentality' embracing not only the nuts and bolts of empirical social research, but also its very way of thinking about phenomena and the empirical problems of the respective human sciences; a 'mentality' that is often described as positivistic (Halfpenny, 1982).

3   Variable analysis as a descriptive apparatus

One feature that is fundamental to variable analysis is that not only is it offered as an inferential structure for determining the relationships among properties and, through these, facilitating explanation, it is also intendedly a descriptive apparatus, and one with special qualities. Lazarsfeld's methodological proposals require that social actors, or any unit of analysis for that matter, be treated as an 'object' possessing certain attributes or qualities.[14] In this he was explicitly drawing upon an analogy with the formal and highly abstract structure of mathematics and logic in which variables and constants are uninterpreted and, as remarked upon in chapter 5, 'stand for' objects in the mathematical domain, and only that. What qualities and properties they possess is defined formally by the axiomatic structure of the mathematical system itself. To the extent to which a mathematical system is applied, 'objects' in the target domain must be mapped onto 'objects', that is numbers, in the mathematical domain.[15] If the mapping is successful then manipulation of the mathematics is equivalent to the manipulation of the 'objects' of the target domain. Of course, the 'objects' in disciplines other than mathematics have attributes and qualities given by their theories and, presumably, by the nature of the world they investigate. For physics, its 'objects' possess mass, size, velocity, and so forth, while other disciplines, perhaps less strictly than physics, have their own distinctive collections of conceptualised phenomena abstracted from the concrete objects of the experienced world. But, for physics and other mathematised disciplines there is, again as Mike Lynch has mentioned in chapter 5, an established and fundamental homology of structure between the mathematical and the substantive domains. What variable analysis proposes is that this homology be achieved by what can only be described as the working through of the methodological *stipulation* that the social domain be homologous to the mathematical. The 'object–attribute' structure of variable analysis requires that social phenomena be described as 'objects–attributes' irrespective of whatever other character they might possess. As Wilson (1971: 72) puts it, it is an attempt to produce 'literal descriptions' which amount to 'asserting that on the basis of those features the phenomenon has some clearly designated property, or what is logically the same thing, belongs to some particular well-defined class of phenomena'. Thus, and for example, all persons possess the property of gender which can be categorised as either 'male' or 'female' but not both. Providing that there are available rules for determining in which of these two categories any particular person is to be uniquely placed, this would, on the face of it, satisfy the conditions of literal description. In this way a particular characteristic of a person, namely their gender, is made to appear a general characteristic by using the 'object–attribute' apparatus and deploying this upon a collection of persons.

The aim of such a structure is to facilitate quantification. The indicators of properties or attributes, considered as variables, must satisfy the basic mathematical requirements for counting, basically, those of identity and equivalence. That units being classified in terms of their properties must be uniquely classifiable as belonging to a category or not, and that all attributes so categorised as belonging to that category or not are equivalent.[16] Simply illustrated, if these requirements are met, each mark on a questionnaire indicating some attribute can be counted as the number 'one' and then added together to give a total of such marks for the collection of questionnaires. By comparing the relative totals (usually expressed as percentages) between various subgroups, and with respect of similarly counted properties, allows variable analysis to detect associational patterns among attributes.[17] That is, to put it another way, if the conditions of identity and equivalence are met, then the mathematical operations, such as counting, can be used, so turning statistical 'results' into sociological 'findings'. Statistical results are the mathematical outcomes of applying the procedures of statistical formulae to events in a mathematical domain. The 'object–attribute' descriptive apparatus, allied to the notion of a variable, turns the sociological domain into a mathematical one. Once the descriptive apparatus is in place then the inferential structure of statistics can be deployed to produce the quantitative expressions of relationships in the data. As Lazarsfeld remarked, the cross-tabulation is the 'automatic' research procedure employed in social research when faced with a relationship between two, or more, variables (Lazarsfeld, 1955).

However, to the extent that sociological 'findings' produced in this way can stand as such depends upon a strict correspondence between, respectively, the statistical and the sociological domains. The postulates of identity and equivalence must hold for the structure of the sociological domain. The classification of sociological objects must satisfy the postulates of identity and equivalence, otherwise the mathematical procedures employed will be meaningless. It is not that the descriptive apparatus cannot be used, and all that follows from that deployment: the issue is, to remain within the ambit of variable analysis, whether these operations constitute the quantitative manipulation of the sociological domain.

It is at this point that difficulties arise over the extent to which social researchers allow themselves to be limited by the constraints imposed by the requirements of the mathematics. Take, by way of example, this comment about the Ethnic Origins Survey with regard to categorising a person's race or ethnicity.

The kind of difficulty facing someone of mixed descent whose forebears have been long domiciled in Britain is best illustrated by an example. One can but sympathise for instance with the complaints of the West Indian born resident who asked us how he should describe himself and his Welsh born wife whose grandfathers had both been West Africans who had married local Cardiff women. (p. 16)

Sillitoe regards these matters as, first, marginal in that they occur only in a small minority of the sample and, second, resulting from the 'diffuse nature of the concept "race or ethnic origin" '. But these two issues are related. Defining the property 'race or ethnic origins' is to provide a classification rule for interviewers and coders who need to apply that rule consistently and accurately to the relevant and particular replies given by the respondents. This is necessary, according to the Lazarsfeldian programme, in order that the classification of respondents satisfies the postulates of identity and equivalence, so allowing for the deployment of the mathematics. The rule is to be deployed to decide the equivalency of events, persons, actions, etc. The complaint of the Cardiff respondent, however, testifies to the kind of problems that can arise here. How is such a respondent to be classified? It is not that a decision cannot be made, for this is, in part at least, consequent upon the richness of the classificatory scheme.[18] The issue is whether the responses offered by any respondent do, in fact, satisfy the requirements of the classificatory scheme in terms of equivalence. The Cardiff respondent is, in effect, raising precisely this issue as a practical matter in the context of completing a questionnaire. The implication is that cases in the categories are not the same and that the equivalency required does not hold. In other words, the problem is not one which affects only a small minority of the sample since we do not know, and cannot know, in each and every case, whether equivalence holds. Or, to phrase it another way, even in situations in which researchers and respondents find little difficulty in classifying a phenomenon, they do so by attending to, and using, unexplicated features of the case/person/event in arriving at some classification *for the purposes at hand*. So, other purposes, other relevancies, other classifications. As Garfinkel keeps reminding professional sociologists, the research activity itself is conducted under the auspices of situated reason and, hence, bears unknown and unexplicated relationships to members' activities undertaken for other purposes.

What the rules provided in the format for determining the equivalency of events, persons, actions, etc., ignore, or at best underplay, is that members of society also deploy 'rules' for the determination of equivalency within their contexts of action. (See, for example, Winch, 1968; Baccus, 1986.) The concept of 'race' or 'ethnic origins' means different things in different contexts. In which case the sociological structure of race and ethnic divisions is such that the demands of category equivalence as variable analysis requires, cannot be met.

This is relevant to the second point Sillitoe raises about the 'diffuseness' of, or as it is sometimes referred to, the 'inexactness' of social science concepts and the problems this raises for sociology's empirical reference. For variable analysis this is recognised in its stress on the importance of multiple indicators of some specified property on the supposition that no one indicator is likely to capture all that a property might possibly show. The 'probabilistic' relationship between an index and the property it is designed to measure inevitably will reflect errors of all kinds which further research should aim to control. This is the burden of Blalock's urging, as we said earlier, that more effort should be devoted to controlling measurement error in order to make data more decisive for theory.

Nonetheless, people do answer questionnaires, and researchers offer conclusions based on this evidence which are not by and large, without sense. Indeed, Lazarsfeld, in a discussion of the process of constructing indices to determine the factors influencing why women buy certain kinds of cosmetics, urges that the classificatory scheme eventually arrived at must:

match the actual processes from which the respondent herself has derived her comments; the classification, so to speak, puts the comments back where they came from.[19] (Lazarsfeld and Barton, 1951: 55)

The results of using the format procedures produces accounts of social phenomena which constitute 'their objects of discourse as real-worldly, that is, as actual, objectively extant phenomena' (Baccus, 1986: 3). The results, the relationships found among the variables, the measures calculated, the theorising done on the basis of the results, are recognisable as features of the real social world. The question is, how is this achieved?

4   Making the apparatus work

Cicourel (1964) refers to measurement, and we can add the categorisation procedures prior to this, in much of social research as, quoting Torgerson, 'measurement by fiat' which 'depends upon *presumed* relationships between observations and the concept of interest . . . This sort of measurement is likely to occur whenever we have a prescientific or common-sense concept that on *a priori* grounds seems to be important but which we do not know how to measure directly' (Torgerson, 1958: 21–2, itals. in original). The link is made by using implicit assumptions and common-sense knowledge made about the social actor and about the social world in which he/she lives, as a resource to secure the connection between an indicator and a concept. Cicourel, for example, elaborates the point in connection with fixed-choice questions used in many questionnaires (though, again, the point is generalisable). These are designed to elicit common-sense meanings from the respondent but, at the same time, provide a format for categorising responses into a small number of alternatives to facilitate categorisation and, through this, data processing. The form of the question is an integral part of the classification procedure. What we have is a formalisation of both the question and its response through 'obvious' and 'reasonable' coding procedures and which 'thereby manage, through progressive classification operations, to keep one foot in the common-sense world of everyday life and the other foot in the quasi-acceptable (in a practical sense) measurement procedures' (Cicourel, 1973).

It is not always easy to appreciate quite what the problem here is. After all, fixed-choice questions are a standard procedure in social survey research; a procedure which, it could be argued, has stood the test of time in that it has produced a massive amount of findings. And, to repeat an earlier observation, Lazarsfeld, as did Durkheim, from the onset recognised the necessary reliance of index construction on a common body of understanding; an understanding assisted, for Lazarsfeld, by training researchers to perform classification with a high degree of agreement and consistency, communicating with other researchers, duplicating and extending studies, and so on, in order to systematise the correspondence between indicators and theoretically derived categories (Lazarsfeld and Barton, 1951). But, it is the fact that measurement in social research is rooted in a 'common body of understanding of everyday life' that is the problem, in that the properties of this understanding and of everyday life are taken-for-granted. The problems this poses are obscured but not eliminated when a measurement system, even something as modest as a classification of ethnic origins, is imposed on 'data' which is elicited from respondents required to report on their experience in a manner detached from the circumstances in which those experiences were made relevant, and played their part, in constructing social activities. In short, we know little about the properties of the underlying phenomena; only how it looks through the imposition of the format.[20]

The interview method, perhaps the most widely used of social research techniques, is a social encounter in which a respondent, under the stimulus of questions put by an interviewer, provides verbal materials in the form of answers which are later coded and processed, usually to provide tabulated quantitative results. The data produced by interviews, then, consist of the processed reports of what a respondent said on the occasion of the interview itself. It is these replies, presented as attitudes, beliefs, opinions, reports of past and intended actions, present circumstances, and so on, which are transformed into data about particular types of social actors. The responses, in other words, stand as indicators of social facts and processes which social actors exhibit, or in which they are involved; they are incorporations and measures of Lazarsfeldian properties or attributes. The fact that the interview is a social encounter is, of course, recognised, but treated as a potential source of various, and unwelcome, 'instrument' or 'experimenter' effects which may prevent the respondent from offering 'valid' replies.

In the briefest of terms, the interviewer's job is to make sure that the respondent reports his/her views, attitudes, facts about their life, etc., accurately. Questions must avoid ambiguity, be clear, not threaten the respondent's self-esteem, or lead in any way, and so on. The interviewer must try to create an encouraging atmosphere so that the respondent can talk freely in the knowledge that what is said is in private and without personal consequences. (See, for example, Benney and Hughes, 1956.) In detail, the lore of interviewing contains highly varied and extensive guidance on the conduct of interviewing in the face of various possible 'contaminating effects', the aim being to provide instructions for the interviewer on how to manage this social encounter to produce 'something that springs from the soul of the respondent to the notebook of the interviewer without encountering any contaminating influence en route' (Kahn and Cannell, 1952). In effect, the rules of interviewing are practical procedures for managing a social encounter in order to get the interviewing done; all focussed, we might say, to achieve meaning equivalence in the material. Thus, the interviewer, and later the coder, out of all the interchanges that take place on the occasion of the interview, have to select those which can be taken as valid replies to the questions asked, reject those which are 'chatter', make judgements about the consistency of replies, and so on; all the myriad of practical decisions, judgements and interpretations that have to be made to get the material to speak in the way required. The neat tables that are the end result of such research conceal the interpretative work done by interviewers and coders; work that is not explicated in any of the rules of interviewing except in some general, abstracted and decontextualised fashion. In doing their best to do the work in accordance with the rules, interviewers and coders have to 'resolve ambiguities', 'let certain remarks pass', 'allow propriety to constrain lines of questioning', 'hold meanings in reserve', and more; in sum, use their own common-sense knowledge of social structures to make sense of the replies, the coding task and, later, make sense of the tables (Cicourel, 1973). The very activity of categorisation upon which the counting itself depends, provides for and accomplishes, in each and every instance of categorisation as an instance of 'this', as another case of 'that', the necessary equivalence and identity characteristics. The features of the categories are constituted in terms of local decision-making about the particularities encountered as the 'same' or 'different', so accomplishing what Baccus calls 'interphenomenal integrity' (Baccus, 1986: 4).[21]

Of course, the point is of wider import than arguments about the techniques of interviewing and the design of questionnaires. Indeed, it is not about technique at all, but very much about how the results of variable analysis are produced by the socially organised activities of social researchers to achieve the appearance of 'real-worldly reference'. The implication of this, however, is that the putative sociological findings are not so much discoveries elicited by the deployment of the format, but versions of sociological phenomena organised through the efforts of researchers to meet the constraints of the format.

5 Variable analysis as camouflage

One of the images Garfinkel uses to characterise the point of much research is that of trying to find the animal in the foliage. For our part, what we want to suggest is that variable analysis creates the foliage that hides the animal in the first place (Garfinkel *et al.*, 1981).

An important part of the argument is that, in doing the work of interviewing and coding in ways required by variable analysis, researchers are making use of their common-sense knowledge of social structures in order to get the work done in ways required by the format. The complexity of the putatively 'real' social world is 'reduced' in compliance with the requirements of the format itself. The description of persons – their attributes and their activities – is the outcome of the methods, procedures and policies embodied in the format. This has major implications for the kind of inferences that can be drawn about the data. We said earlier that what the format provides is a way of mapping the properties of phenomena onto a mathematically conceived 'property space' which allows for the use of the inferential apparatus of statistics. Specifying actors in terms of 'objects–attributes' devices, along with the use of statistical modelling, allows researchers to empirically discriminate and disentangle from the complexities of the real world those relationships which are significant from those which are not. What is missing from this essentially formalised empirical procedure is any sense of what properties should be the object of investigation. Earlier we drew attention to Lazarsfeld's characterisation of the process of index construction as beginning with a 'vague image' of what the problem to be researched is, what theories suggest, and so forth. For him the problem is to translate these into the language of research, the language of variables and, having done so, invoke the iterative and eliminative procedures of statistical analysis to determine which of the many possible relationships that might be hypothesised are the ones that have empirical significance.

It is not that variable analysis, least of all in what is commonly referred to as the 'data collection' phase, is totally devoid of any reference to the social world. On the contrary, it is stressed that indices, questionnaire items, attitude scales and the rest, have to be based on observables; it is this principle or rule which is intended to secure empirical reference. So, in this respect at least, 'interphenomenal integrity' is preserved by taking into account and using the 'visible' properties of phenomena within the format (Baccus, 1986: 4–5). However, as we have said, the 'visibility' of the phenomena is a function of the format and the natural theorising of researchers, rather than of the phenomena.

Unfortunately, and as is widely recognised by practitioners themselves, the use of such statistical models speaks to no particular sociological theory, and one major reason for this, again, has to do with descriptive matters.[22] The choice of independent variables, it could be one of the standard 'perduring attributes' as Rosenberg (1968) calls them, such as age, gender, class, ethnicity, education, or anything else that captures the researcher's imagination, is, sociologically speaking, arbitrary. As Sacks (1963), among others, has pointed out, there are an infinite number of ways in which persons may be described and categorised, and to select a few which are susceptible to variable analytic procedures or assume a version of society in advance of investigations of that society, says little about how persons themselves in constructing social activities use categories in the accomplishment of their activities.

It can be argued that the problem is not so much one of categorisation at all, or at least not in the sense in which variable analysis understands this, but of explicating social activities. Given the indefinite number of ways in which persons can be potentially categorised, the question becomes one of the relevance or purpose of the categorisation (Ryle, 1966; Taylor, 1985). For variable analysis the point of categorisation is, as we have said, to identify the factors which best explain (though this often is a confusion of theoretical explanation and the statistical) the distribution of values of some dependent variable. What is concealed is the way in which members use the categories they do in order to make the social world visible and organisable in ways relevant to them. Dorothy Smith alludes to this in connection with the term 'single parent'. This term, she notes, is not one which has the features of a generalised description usable on indefinite occasions, though it can be made to appear so. Rather it has a particular set of social *loci* of operation and use. One such place is in relation to 'parenting' and 'schooling':

This category 'single parent' names, from the perspective of the school, a particular type of defect in the conditions of effective classroom work organisation. The category provides an interpretative procedure regardless of the mother's actual practices. (Smith, 1987: 173)

Similarly, categories devised and used in variable analysis provide a common-sense basis for the interpretation of statistical results involving those categories, without ever once coming to grips with the actual organisation of social activities for which these categories may or may not be relevant. To treat the categories as 'properties of objects' operating in conjunction with other 'objective properties' is to claim that these categories have a trans-situational quality *independently of how real persons use and make relevant or disattend to such features in the accomplishment*. The tables, graphs, procedures used become a document, as Livingstone says:

for something that has not yet been exhibited and, by being this, provides the grounds for their exegesis . . . Who knows what sociologists' tables and mathematical procedures would be about, as wordly descriptions, if sociologists were not forever labelling them, explaining them . . . In turn, this activity becomes the source and aim of further explication and labels and arguments. (Livingstone, 1987: 47)

Thus, it is not that variable analysis fails to make 'adequate' reference to the world, rather what becomes of interest is the manner in which it does so.

Baccus (1986) uses the notion of 'signs' to explicate the procedural manner in which indices reference the social world. Sign-reading is a mediated account with the sign standing 'between' the interpreter and the object; the object being known 'through' the sign. The sign allows the 'unseen' to be made visible. This is what variable analysis, as a mode of constructive sociological theorising, accomplishes. Thus, indicators, such as questionnaire items, and the properties they 'stand for', are constructed as signs and referent, the latter being, normally, a theoretical construct which is unobservable directly. The construct's features, however, as an account of the real world, are indicated by the indices and variables as data. The indicators are not equivalent to the construct but display its features, provide for its visibility as referencing real events, actors, attitudes, actions, etc. The construct is indexical to the data which 'reflexively gives it life and only imaginably indexical to wordly things' (Baccus, 1986: 17). In other words, the theoretical construct, the theories themselves, the interpretations of the data, has a relation only to the data and 'its empirically demonstrable existence as *world-sensible*, as real worldly, but that data is not the world's events' (Baccus, 1986: 18, italics in original). The constructive theory gives meaning to the data, though from the point of view of variable analysis itself the data provide the basis for the theory as an explanation of it. But the constructs of the theory are 'indifferent' to their cases because they only 'indicate'. What is not provided for is the essential reflexivity of theory and method. As Baccus concludes, 'Cases and data, indicators and measures, have only a "probabilistic" relation with their constructs because the natural account of indicators makes them signs' (Baccus, 1986: 19).

We have already alluded to some of the problems of variable analysis, including the way in which the results of social research are almost endlessly debatable, both in terms of what the results theoretically signify and on methodological grounds. Although there are many reasons offered for this state of affairs, the burden of the ethnomethodological critique is, as far as variable analysis is concerned, that it sets the conditions for sociological description in advance so that we look at the phenomena through a grid that we impose upon them, *irrespective of whatever properties the phenomena might otherwise display*.

The problems of social research are not so much about theory and data, as variable analysis would have it, but involve three elements: theory, research and phenomena (Anderson and Sharrock, 1986a: 40). Research, and the methods deployed, produce materials which are the objects of theorising because they display the features, or the properties, of the phenomena which it is the purpose of theory to understand. Sociology's task is to come to terms with the social world in an empirical manner. It makes studies about, and produces theories about, the social world in which we live and which exists independently of each of us. Sociology's topic, as might be said of a number of the human sciences, is to study patterns of social life. This, of course, says very little about how this might be done and it needs to be acknowledged, obvious though it may be, that there are many ways in which this topic can be undertaken as an investigative programme. What the Lazarsfeldian programme proposes is the importance of describing the phenomenon objectively, quantitatively, determining the patterns among phenomena empirically, and explanation as the objective of theory. It is this apparatus which enables a researcher to make claims about how well theories correspond to the facts of the social world; the facts being proceduralised in terms of the format proposed. Whatever properties the phenomena of the social world display are camouflaged through, as Baccus argues, a conception of indicators as signs. The requirements of objective data, measurement systems, consistency, and the like, lead to the disguise of the phenomena by the artifacts of the format. Yet there is a necessary and unavoidable reliance by the format for its sense, its intelligibility, its very ability to do the work required of it, on the knowledge of the features of ordinary life as understood and accomplished by members, but which are not made a topic of inquiry in their own right (Zimmerman and Pollner, 1973: 85–9).

6   Ethnomethodology: evidence and inference[23]

The upshot of the ethnomethodological critique is that sociology's methodological troubles are not merely technical, to do, for example, with selecting the right statistical procedure, but fundamental. In order to describe, categorise, understand or explain the activities of social actors, sociologists have to secure some understanding of the research data and how they are produced, be they questionnaire responses, transcripts of interviews, observations or official statistics, or whatever (Lee, 1987). They can do no other but to find the sense of such data by deploying their own common-sense knowledge and reasoning to relate the material to some context. This means that common-sense reasoning is unavoidably built into the research process as a means for getting the research done. The result is, as Lee remarks, that:

characterisations or descriptions of events and activities acquired by unexplicated, commonsense reasoning are not translatable into the status of objective events or indices as required by traditional methodology or by any discipline requiring *formally* decontextualised data. (Lee, 1987: 24)

A major consequence of this is that, despite its aspirations to become a generalising discipline, sociology's 'general' descriptions of social phenomena not only fail to capture rigorously the particularities of these phenomena, but has to secure any such connection by recourse to the familiar *ad hocing* features of common-sense reasoning such as illustration, epitome, claims to typicality, to representativeness, and so on (Sacks, 1963). Sociology's general descriptions do not allow for the systematic recovery of particular cases from the properties of the putatively more general characterisation. Thus, while any general description of some sociological object can be offered, the 'etcetera' problem means that its particularities cannot be recaptured except as a 'version' of the general description. The conditions necessary for inferring from the particular to the general cannot be met. In which case, there is as much to gain in pursuing the detailed analysis of particular cases as in trying to produce generalisations which are, in the end, unrigorously formulated.

As both Garfinkel and Sacks repeatedly point out, an indispensable feature of any science is to describe its phenomena as faithfully, as rigorously and as formally as possible.[24] It is this which gives the issues of evidence and inference their point. But these requirements for description cannot be achieved by importing an external and mathematically derived technical language for sociology, as in the Lazarsfeldian programme, which fails to preserve fidelity to the phenomena. While the sociologist surely seeks to provide findings about the social world, and this will involve relating and preserving a connection between members' use of categories and any technical vocabulary for sociological analysis, any procedure which fails in its fidelity to the former produces an array of concepts and findings which have an indeterminate relationship to what members ordinarily understand and, in addition, runs the risk of creating an ironic sociology.

The production of an ironic sociology, or of structural incongruities between members' actual practices and mathematical formulations of social structure, can be avoided. This can be done by attempting to describe the operational theories, or theories-in-use, that members deploy in attending to the appearances of their surroundings, in constructing their situated courses of action. Instead of working from the 'outside', as it were, trying to produce mathematical techniques which 'fit' the activities of members, we can examine instead the actual practices which members engage in when they go about their local purposive business of, say, making a 'count' of members. What we can see then is that the various 'troubles' encountered by the Lazarsfeldian approach are encountered again as part of the very methods through which members attend and produce the visible appearances of rational, accountable features of the social order. If our interest is in the way in which members produce, and account for, social phenomena, then it is their 'operational procedures' which stand to be described rather than those of professional sociology; the latter has to take the former as its subject matter.

As an alternative to attempting to force social phenomena into pre-selected categories in order, for simple example, to count the total number of members in those categories, we can, rather, examine the counting practices that persons use in the many varied situations that arise; that is, an interest in the way in which members count *by reference to the appearances of the social order* so as to make their count demonstrably rational or *accountable*.

Consider some common examples. It is perfectly possible to be present in a room and count two people on one side and ten on the other and yet have the two 'count' for more than the ten. Or we could have a long list of the names of members of the cabinet who were in favour of a particular measure, and a much shorter list of those opposed. The latter list, however, contains the names of the Prime Minister and the Chancellor of the Exchequer. In terms of the social order of the cabinet, the longer list may 'speak with one voice' and 'one voice' may be all that they total.[25] In terms of social organisational arrangements, the quantitative expression says nothing about how they 'count' within some decision-making setting.

For further example: who is to be considered as a member to be counted can be constituted through the activity of being counted. From sociology's standpoint it is assumed that the simple enumeration of persons constitutes a count; but from the perspective of the situated activities of members there are occasions when the making of a count could decide whether a person was a member or not, and a concern with the possible consequences that might arise in the course of their activities. Would one count male slaves as potentially part of a defending armed force? If one did, would they then be regarded as competent for other matters? Or, if one wanted to enumerate citizens for the purpose of raising taxes, then one might wish to cast the net as wide as possible to create a large tax base. This might have the consequence that persons so counted might wish to be also counted for other purposes, such as voting: 'no taxation without representation'.

It can also be the case that a person may be counted as a member for some purposes but not for others. Departmental secretarial and part-time academic staff may be counted for some matters, such as being permitted to attend departmental meetings and being kept informed of relevant matters, but would that entail their eligibility to vote in the election to the departmental Chair? These, and related, matters are features of counting procedures that members encounter in and through the course of conducting their affairs; methods used as and when they are rational and accountable for the relevant activities. From this point of view, 'making the count' becomes an activity available for description and analysis, where the analysis is controlled by the features of 'making the count'; features which the analysis aims to reproduce. The rigour of Ethnomethodological analysis is, thereby, controlled through the reproduction of features of the phenomenon.

Far from ethnomethodology's criticism of variable analysis being a criticism against rigour or, indeed, an invitation to abandon sociology altogether as a rigorous pursuit, the aim is to pursue it from another direction. Unlike the Lazarsfeldian solution, the problem for ethnomethodology is not operationalising some theory in terms of the requirements of scientific-cum-mathematical description, but of making the world investigable in terms of the theory and the phenomena that the theory specifies.[26] One constraint this methodological stipulation places on the investigator is that nothing can be assumed to be known about the phenomena specified in advance of investigating the world through the theory. To do otherwise would be to transgress the requirements of rigour in failing to establish that the world *can* be investigated by the theory to produce findings about the phenomena. Rigour, then, is served by sticking to the methodological election to treat the social order as a members' accomplishment through and through. This direction does not involve the concealment of common sense, but of finding ways of making common-sense reasoning, and thereby social organisation, available for study.[27] What this means, as Schutz (1962) argued, is that sociology is, along with the other human sciences, a 'second order' discipline using the concepts of ordinary language. In which case, an important constraint on sociological inquiry is that the categories, the concepts used, and the methods for using them, must be isomorphic to the ways in which they are used in common-sense reasoning.

This respecifies the issues of evidence and inference by recognising these as themselves issues in practical reasoning. 'Inferring', 'providing evidence for', 'describing', and so on, are features of members' own methods for rendering the sense of activities and, as such, orderly properties of interaction. According to Garfinkel's programme, they must, as respecified for measurement in the prior chapter, be turned into a topic of study whose aim is to reveal, display, describe the common-sense methodology of members' construction of the everyday world in all its particularity. Ethnomethodology is not concerned to stipulate what the world of members is like, in advance of inquiry into how that world is constructed, or to produce versions of that world which are in competition with those of members. In which case, what counts as a 'warranted inference', 'evidence for', an adequate 'description', is a matter of investigation for ethnomethodology. Thus, and for example, Pomerantz (1987) shows, in connection with a hearing in a Small Claims Court, how descriptions of the 'facts' are shaped so as to simultaneously perform activities such as 'telling what happened', 'correcting misinformation', 'making arguments', 'connecting points', 'attributing blame', etc. Descriptions, as features of members' sense-making machinery, are done to display a speaker's orientation to the purposes at hand on this occasion to what is being described. For brief example, 'the eleventh of March', as an Official Identification, is preferred for the written record as an indicator of the 'basic facts', whereas 'last year', as a Relational Identification, or 'for a very long time', as a Characterisation, provides for a sense of fact displaying understanding of what the events concerned, the flooding of the flat, meant in the plaintiff's life. However, the variety of ways of describing the 'facts' are not to be regarded as an opening to questions about whether any one form of describing them is superior to any other, as if such matters could be determined independently of some contextual specification, but rather seen and treated as the orderly accomplishment of parties to the occasion attending the task in hand.

Sociology begins with the assumption that daily life is an orderly, predictable affair and is experienced as such by members; in short, it makes sense.

But rather than seek for some 'general principle' which provides for social order (Sharrock and Anderson, 1987: 253), ethnomethodology, by addressing the practical production of social order as the accomplishment of members, means that the classical methodological problems represented by issues to do with evidence and inference, inferring from the particular to the general, and vice versa, take on a different set of considerations. What these might be can be gained from some of Sacks' own methodological remarks (Sacks, 1984b). In ruminating about how sociology could become a 'natural observational science', he proposes that if nature ensures that persons are 'workable things in a society', encountering from their infancy only small, and random, segments of a culture, then one of the ways in which order could be achieved is by seeing the culture as so arranged that this more or less random experience makes persons 'come out in so many ways much like everybody else and able to deal with just about everybody else'. In which case, we get the methodological maxim: 'Tap in whomsoever, wheresoever, and we get much the same things' (Sacks, 1984b: 22). So, despite the failure of survey research to satisfy proper statistical procedures, orderly results are produced. Anthropologists, by asking and observing one or two persons in a culture, also obtain generalisable results. 'We get an enormous generalizability because things are so arranged that we *can* get orderly results, given that for members encountering a limited environment they have to be able to do that, and things are so arranged as to permit them to' (Sacks, 1984b: 23). So, the point of working with 'actual occurrences', single instances, single events, is to see them as the products of a 'machinery' that constituted members' cultural competence enabling them to do what they do, produce the activities and scenes of everyday life. As is examined by John Lee in detail in chapter 9, the explication, say, of some segment of talk in terms of the description of the 'mechanism' by which *that* talk was produced *there* and *then*, is an explication of some part of our culture.

There are one or two points worth bringing out here. The first is the emphasis, noted before, on the instance as the locus of analysis. Instances are not specified as instances of anything other than that they 'happened'. They are not samples of anything, nor selected as 'typicalisations', illustrations, or whatever: they just happened. Second, and following on from the first, approaching the data with as few preconceptions as possible, not knowing whether anything of interest can be found, not knowing whether what can be found is likely to be 'typical' but knowing simply that 'it happened', requires that the analyst tries to recover the 'machinery' that produced the interaction 'as it happened'. Third, one consequence of this methodological election is that in explicating the 'machinery' that produced the instance of, say talk, the number of cases, any sampling procedures, is irrelevant. The fact that the occurrence happened, whatever on analysis it may turn out to be, is sufficient to regard it as the product of the proficient use of the cultural 'machinery', and this includes every 'competent language user'.[28] In other words, persons acquire the methods to make the social world sensible by deploying the cultural resources, the methods, to make the world, to make experience, a 'sensible' achievement. If it happened, then it happened according to a method. That the talk, that the action, was produced using a cultural mechanism means that the mechanism is available within the culture to produce that action, whatever it might be. The 'mechanism' is an oriented to feature of the culture to produce *that* action, and it is this which provides for the trans-situational character of an ethnomethodological description. In making visible the methods by which persons assign sense to their environment, one has secured a characterisation of what methods are utilised by persons in everyday life to produce its orderliness in all its fine detail.

Inferring from the particular to the general does not arise in the form in which it surfaces in variable analysis. The frequency of the occurrence of some phenomenon is not germane to whether the description of the 'machinery' is adequate or not. If the 'machinery' has been used at all, it is a part of our culture, our methods, for producing action. Once the 'machinery' is described, any more instances do not provide any more evidence for the description. What more instances do is provide yet another example of the method in action, rather than securing the warrantability of the description of the machinery itself. Given this attention to naturally-occurring instances, there is no sense in trying to specify a collection of data in advance, as required, say, by sampling procedures, since prior to investigation it cannot be known what an instance is a sample of. What sense could it make, for example, to attempt to sample conversations in other than a weak sense of the term, relying on our own common-sense knowledge of what conversations look like, and selecting on the basis of this. This would be equivalent to collecting together 'things that happened'. And this is what Sacks' and Garfinkel's methodological election proposes, namely, that analytic attention is paid to the instances in order to see what the instances are instances of and, through this, describe and explicate the 'machinery' that enables analysts to 'reproduce the data' as it happened. The analyst is endeavouring to discover the structure of social phenomena instead of imposing it. So, what is taken as an analytical feature of a fragment of talk, an extract from a folder record, or a video of an interaction, is generated from the material itself; that is, by examining the material at hand in an unmotivated fashion in order to see what questions might sensibly be asked. Instead of orienting to a collection of cases with an eye to producing abstracted generalisations from which the features of the individual case cannot be recovered rigorously, the ethnomethodological objective is to generate formal descriptions of social actions which preserve and display the features of the machinery which produced them (Garfinkel and Sacks, 1970). This requirement of 'unique adequacy' stipulates the aim of describing in detail members' competences in producing everyday social action.

This is not to say that other cases, other data, are of no use, but that the number of instances, the quantity of the data, is irrelevant to the grounding of the description of the 'machinery'. Thus, and for example, what the description of the turn-taking machinery in conversation (Sacks, Schegloff and Jefferson, 1974) describes is the methods members use for organising the sequential order of turns at talk, and can be shown in many, many cases of naturally occurring conversation not as an empirical generalisation to the effect that, as a matter of fact, in a very large number of cases conversation has been found to be organised this way, but as a 'mechanism', a set of *a priori* methods (Coulter, 1983a), members orient to and use in order to produce naturally occurring conversation in the 'way conversation happens'. The frequency is not the point: this is the way members produce conversation as an orderly phenomenon. The rules of chess, for want of an analogy, are not grounded in the frequency of chess games which contingently, as it were, exhibit these rules; the rules of chess allow us to play chess games and no amount of counting chess games to see if these rules apply is relevant to grounding the description of the rules of chess. Chess games, any chess games, are played, are done, according to the rules, the 'machinery' for playing them.[29]

Given that ethnomethodology is not concerned to stipulate, and thereby ironicise, members' experiences, then the evidence for a description also changes. Issues of what 'really happened' do not arise. There is no question of, as Durkheim among many others did not, treating members as other than experts in the production of social order. Therefore, the analytic task is, as said earlier, to explicate and describe the members' methods that could have been used to produce 'what happened in the way that it did'. So, in characterising some action, some setting, the description is warranted by showing how the 'machinery' being described can 'reproduce' the data at hand. The evidence for the description is to be found in the activities described rather than, as with variable analysis, in the procedures of mathematisation.

Our discussion of the nature of 'rigour' in ethnomethodology has been articulated in terms of conversation analysis. This is understandable since, as a new field opened up by ethnomethodology, it is now the one most firmly based. But it is not the limits of ethnomethodological concerns, however, as the increasing list of empirical studies shows. The structure of the social world is demonstrably heterogeneous, and it would be surprising if one approach alone were sufficient to enable the structure to be described in all its richness and detail. The abiding interest of ethnomethodology resides in its concern to produce formal descriptions of members' methods for the production of the social order. That social order is all around us and one can begin anywhere.

NOTES

1 Any discussion of variable analysis has to invoke the human sciences' concern with measurement. In this respect we rely upon the specification of measurement in the human sciences, and the idea of an ethnomethodological respecification of measurement, as detailed in the previous chapter. At places it is, though, necessary to briefly continue to elaborate on the idea of measurement in order to firmly anchor the points we wish to address. For a full appreciation of important aspects of ethnomethodology's methodological respecification, readers are encouraged to read this and the previous chapter together.

2 The history of social research methods perhaps deserves a rather better and more central place in the history of social thought which, on the whole, concentrates on theoretical and philosophical issues. A good model is that of Turner (1986). Also what we are referring to as variable analysis is more often referred to as 'positivistic methods' (see Halfpenny, 1982). Since we are concentrating on research practices, we prefer our term rather than positivism which also embraces philosophical considerations. Though both sets of ideas are closely intertwined, they are by no means equivalent. The statistical methods known as the analysis of variance are only part of variable analysis itself.

3 Of course, the use of experimental reasoning was, and still is, mostly *post hoc* and mathematical using sampling design and/or statistical controls on partitioned data.

4 Although we speak critically of variable analysis' attempts at quantification, we are not claiming that quantification in sociology is impossible, only that it is extremely difficult and unlikely to be attained through current procedures.

5 More recent philosophy of science plays down the importance of problems of induction and deduction in scientific theory. See, for example, Hacking (1983) and Cartwright (1984).

6 See Anderson, Hughes and Sharrock (1988, 1989) for a discussion of the way in which Economics endeavoured to become a mathematised discipline.

7 See, for example, Duncan (1984) for an extensive and important review of this and, as an extra, a critical exposition of some of the current measurement presupposition in social and psychological research.

8 We are not claiming that Lazarsfeld is the 'onlie begetter'. The technology of variable analysis owed debts to many. Nonetheless, in using his name we are paying a small homage to an innovative thinker.

9 Of course, with respect to many properties it was envisaged that levels of measurement higher than the classificatory, or 'nominal', level of measurement, would be attainable using the full range of qualities of number systems such as ordinality, distance and origin. The influential figure in this specification of levels of measurement is Stevens (1946). See also Duncan (1984) and Pawson (1989).

10 For many social researchers, the use of indicators is the *sine qua non* of science. See, for example, Blalock (1983). Lazarsfeld's own formulation is explicitly a two 'language model' of social research: the language of theory and that of data structures. The major problem of research methodology is to effect satisfactory translations between the two, largely through the development of appropriate measurement systems. Cicourel (1964: 16–17) suggests that most of Lazarsfeld's

ideas about measurement owe much to his commitment to survey research. Also Lazarsfeld (1958). See Pawson (1989) for a critical but otherwise innovative review of the problems of measurement in sociology.

11 It is not clear quite what Lazarsfeld means by this, since there is no claim that the precise statistical character of the probability distribution is known. However, he cannot say that the relationship between an indicator and its property is haphazard. In practical terms, variable analysis makes assumptions about the distribution and character of the property based on the requirements of statistical theory, for example, that IQ is normally distributed in a sample of all possible samples. Once again, it is statistical considerations which inform assumptions about the character of the underlying phenomenon.

12 Pearson, the great innovator and propagandist of correlational methods, argued that the precise and pristine laws of the more advanced of the nature sciences were, in actuality, idealisations, the product of averaging, and not descriptions of the real universe in which all kinds of 'contaminations' were present. For him the distinction between a causal relationship and a correlation was spurious. The former is simply the conceptual limit of the latter. See Pearson (1911) and, for critique Turner (1987).

13 Baldamus notes the formal parallels between Parsons' (1951) method of theoretical exposition with cross-tabulation. The similarity consists of treating a qualitative unit as a property infinitely divisible along a continuum as if it were a quantitative thing and is, for Baldamus, a 'feat of bold imagination' on Parsons' part (Baldamus, 1976: 105).

14 Lazarsfeld himself took up the issue of units in Lazarsfeld and Menzel (1969) and also see selections in Lazarsfeld and Rosenberg (1955). In effect, what is proposed is that various units, from the individual to the group, to the collective, to the aggregate, be defined in terms of indices and measures appropriate to the level of the unit. Thus, and for example, an 'ecological unit' would be indicated by an average measure of the lower level units comprising it. This is, of course, a major technical issue in statistical theory. See, for example, Robinson (1950), Hannan (1971).

15 Strictly speaking, one is mapping objects from a social realm onto *numerals* not numbers. In order to assert that the mapping constitutes the phenomenon in a mathematical domain, then certain axioms, such as those of identity and transitivity, need to be demonstrated as holding in the domain of the phenomenon being mapped. See below.

16 Formally these are referred to as the properties of symmetry and transitivity. Symmetry means that a relation holding between A and B also holds between B and A, and transitivity that if A = B and B = C, then A = C. Together these mean that if A is in the same class as B, B is in the same class as A, and that if A and B are in the same class, and B and C, then A and C are in the same class. These are rules for classification rather than for the assignment of a number system. Strictly, although numerical values can be arbitrarily assigned to the categories, the standard arithmetic operations are not permissible, though counting the frequencies of cases in categories can be. However, though there is some argument as to whether this nominal level is measurement, the procedures are fundamental to 'higher' levels, such as ordinal and ratio scales, or to measurement proper.

17 As we say, these are basic requirements of all the later quantitative embellishments.

The explicitness of categorisation procedures are set out in Lazarsfeld's and Rosenberg's (1955) 'Introduction'.

18 In any event, most questionnaire items contain an 'other' category to cover some of these kind of eventualities. The hope is, of course, that these are a very small minority of the responses, otherwise doubts have to be raised about the exhaustiveness of the substantive categories themselves.

19 Durkheim's strictures on social scientific definition also rely on this feature (Durkheim, 1952). See also Wilson (1972).

20 Lieberson (1985), a critical 'insider', makes a similar point about many of the assumptions invoked by statistical modellers about the underlying character of the relationships indicated, statistically, in the data, such as about the direction of causal paths, etc., that the mathematics are supposed to reflect; assumptions necessary in order for the available mathematics to be deployed in the first place. Most social research, he claims, implicitly assumes symmetrical and reversible relationships among variables, whereas, as is commonly the case in natural science, there are examples of both reversible and irreversible processes. Irreversible processes erroneously treated as reversible means that, at times, the data will appear to validate the incorrectly stated hypothesis and at other times not. See also Pawson (1989).

21 In a later study, Cicourel (1976) shows how the determination of juvenile delinquency, hence the rates recorded, is the result of common-sense categorisation and practical reasoning procedures deployed by the professionals concerned.

22 There are matters also to do with statistical techniques relevant here. In effect, determining the importance of variables amounts to calculating the amount of statistical variance accounted for in the dependent variables. In multivariate correlational models, redundancy sets in early. But there are always alternative ways of estimating the coefficients in a model's equations. As Turner (1987) concludes, 'different assumptions . . . produce different results, hence the conclusions are assumption-relative, and the assumptions themselves cannot be determinatively decided between'. This irrespective of the very important problems posed by measurement error. Lieberson, after an extensive examination of statistical modelling, concludes that, 'It is impossible to use empirical data in nonexperimental social research to evaluate the relative importance of one theory vs another (or, if you will, one independent variable rather than another)' (Lieberson, 1985: 106).

23 For an extension of some of the following arguments also refer to the discussion of the social actor by Wes Sharrock and Graham Button in the next chapter.

24 As Harré (1972) points out, the notion that science is explanatory as opposed to descriptive is an unwarrantable assumption. Anatomy and biology, for example, are as much descriptive activities as they are explanatory. Further, and again as Harré points out, the hypothetico-deductive model of explanation, usually offered by empirical sociologists as the paradigm of scientific explanation, can only work where detailed descriptive knowledge of the phenomena is available. Lieberson (1985) makes a not dissimilar point from another direction and tradition. See also Lee, 1987: 27.

25 The examples are culled from unpublished comments by Sacks.

26 Kaufmann (1944), whose work was a great influence on Garfinkel, codified some rules of theorising, summarised by Anderson and Sharrock (1986, p. 18) as, use

only terms defined in the theory; use only coherent, consistent and rigorous theories, and use only theories which yield studies of real phenomena.

27 This relates to a point made by Sacks (1963) when he argues that the social sciences are not so much stunted by their attachment to philosophy, but rather by their links to common-sense issues and questions, such as, 'why do working-class children "fail" at school?', or 'what is the cause of juvenile delinquency?'. Until the social sciences, he goes on, break the mesmerising hold of common-sense thought in regard to their questions and problems, then it will remain as a version of members' theorising.

28 This way of working is not especially different from the way in which practitioners in a number of other disciplines work. Anatomists, to use this example again, are not impelled to collect thousands of bodies in order to determine the structure of the body. One body may well suffice and the detailed description of that can lead to discoveries and non-intuitive findings.

29 We stress that this is an analogy only. 'Rule following' is, of course, for ethnomethodology another social action and, as such, a feature of common-sense reasoning and the accomplishment of sense.

7

The social actor: social action in real time
Wes Sharrock and Graham Button

1 Introduction

If social theory is going to pay any attention at all to the nature of 'the social actor', then how is that actor to be conceived? For some approaches to social theory (the structuralism of Althusser, 1971, 1976 and 1979, and Lévi-Strauss, 1963 are notable examples) there is little if any need for such a conception. The human sciences, for them, are not concerned with 'individuals' but with social wholes, and insofar as any conception of the social actor is needed then its development will be low priority, and the needs of its theorising can perhaps as well be served by leaving any conception of the social actor largely implicit.[1] Other approaches to sociological theory think that a conception of the social actor is their necessary and fundamental basis, that they must found their understanding of society in 'the actor's point of view'.[2] These two broad orientations have a long-standing, even traditional, opposition, though they have relatively recently been joined by another position (Derrida, 1976 and 1978; Foucault, 1972; and Lyotard, 1979, being significant examples) which calls a plague on both their houses, telling us that both 'the subject' and 'the social totality' are mere fictions, by-products of the play of discourse and text.[3]

Though the concern with social wholes regards the issues of the social actor as low priority, its very attempt to justify this evaluation contributes to direct controversy about the nature of the social actor, for making the case on behalf of locating sociological analysis primarily at the level of the totality involves arguing against the idea that social actors could possibly be self-determined.[4] The standard argument is that analysis at the level of the totality is more than just an autonomous level, and that it is the one which dominates 'lower' levels of analysis, such that the explanation of the actions of individuals will be in terms of properties of the encompassing system. Those who propose to examine social reality 'from the actor's point of view' are allegedly prone to overestimate the extent to which it is in the actor's own hands to decide what to do, and the extent to which it is within the actor's power to understand the nature and sources of his/her action. The attempt to make 'taking the actor's point of view' a critical move in understanding social reality will in all likelihood result in sociological analysis itself being confined within the limits of the actor's own understanding, thus obscuring from itself the existence and nature of the large-scale organisation of society and the operation of determinants of conduct of which the actor is unaware.

A common response, most elegantly present in the labelling theory of deviance as outlined by Becker (1963), is, of course, to argue the opposite: that social reality is *made up* of actors' points of view and that, therefore, to treat social wholes as phenomena *sui generis* simply means reification. Further, taking the actor's point of view is the way to correct the bias which virtually denies the member of society all character as 'actor', which makes the member a merely passive reactor to causal influences. Talk of 'constructing social reality' implies a creature deserving the title 'actor', one who acts rather than merely responds to pressures, one who positively contributes to the nature of social reality.[5]

The controversy between these two traditional opponents is frequently and fairly accurately summed up as setting up 'structure' versus 'agency', and it may seem that ethnomethodology is best understood as falling squarely on the 'agency' side. If it does not actually go completely to the limit at which the 'agency' conception effectively dissolves itself into the view that agents themselves are socially produced fictions only, then it comes close to this. It is normally counted a radical variant of the 'agency' conception. The traditional controversy calls for a decision as to which side is right. Does, for example, ethnomethodology 'overdo it' and exaggerate the independence of individuals from 'structural determination'? Would a position which would recognise that social reality is to some extent a product of structure but also, in part, a product of agency be nearer the mark? These, and other related questions repeatedly asked about the 'reducibility' of social structures to individual actions are, it must be noted, usually framed on the assumption that answers should service the objective of explaining social structural phenomena and/or explaining social actions.[6]

We should be wary, then, of treating them as the basic questions whose answers will set the subsequent course for all our thinking, for they are questions which depend upon the prior adoption of a conception of sociology's character, which is of it as an *explaining* enterprise. Thus, the questions about whether social reality can be 'reduced' to individual actions is essentially a question about whether apparent properties of the social whole can be explained by individual actions. Similarly, the objection to making the actor's point of view focal is that the individual's own actions cannot be adequately explained in terms of his/her intentions and reasons. Naturally, then, given (at least in the diatribes of Gouldner, 1970, and Gellner, 1975; and in Giddens' (1976) ill-founded examination) that ethnomethodology is supposed to be a variant on the standard 'agency' case, it is usually assumed that it is open to the objections that have been made to other and earlier variants of this case.

However, if ethnomethodology is an exercise in radically respecifying sociological views, it is not best understood as attempting this by taking the agency conception to extremes. Its other views will be better understood as consequences of its abandonment of the assumption that sociology is a form of empirical scientific inquiry, letting go the assumption that it should attempt to 'explain' social phenomena and social action through the construction of an apparatus of generalised theory and associated, specialised methods of inquiry, as examined in chapters 5 and 6.[7] The problem in understanding ethnomethodology is very often to appreciate that it is prepared to, has already, let go of assumptions which remain the common ground for a wide range of sociological positions that *otherwise* might be in the profoundest disagreement.

In other words, we here take seriously ethnomethodology's explicit claims that it is a determinedly 'unconstructive' enterprise (succinctly reiterated by Harold Garfinkel in chapter 2 of this volume), protestations which – if noted at all – are invariably disattended, thus allowing its arguments and studies to be read as straightforward exercises in sociological theorising, directed toward constructing a sociological apparatus and, inevitably on this reading, found to be inadequate for the purpose.

2   Is ethnomethodology a science?

Ethnomethodology is a heterogeneous enterprise, and there are within it very different views on its proper character, with nowadays many practitioners who think of it as a conventional scientific venture, conducted in much the same spirit as other forays into theory building, perhaps best viewed as complementary to those other theories.[8] We do not therefore offer an argument which thoroughly dissociates ethnomethodology from any such venture as the 'correct' position, but simply as one which is licensed by some, even a great deal, of Garfinkel's own writing. That view is that ethnomethodology is a science only in the sense in which phenomenology intends to be when it declares itself 'a rigorous science'.

The claim to be a rigorous science on phenomenology's part was anything but a bid to be on the same footing with the empirical (mainly natural) sciences. Its making was, rather, a gesture of protest against the way that the forms of understanding were being increasingly restricted, coming to be almost exclusively identified with the theories of the empirical sciences. Phenomenology's self-identification as a rigorous science is an attempt to reclaim the notions of 'rigour' and 'knowledge' from positivist and other philosophies which have attempted to identify these with the achievements of the sciences. This is, then, a gesture of dissociation from, not an affiliation with, the broad objectives of the empirical sciences. Those are dedicated, after all, to 'discovering' and 'explaining' and to doing this via the construction of general theories and standard methods.

Dissociation from these objectives is not the same as disparagement of them, and certainly cannot legitimately be taken as downgrading the substantial achievements of (some of) those sciences. However, there is a fateful difference between having a proper respect for the assorted achievements of the various sciences, and the fetishing of an imagined something dubbed 'the scientific point of view'. Whilst it is acceptable to expect and approve the idea of scientific progress in the sense that the various scientific disciplines will continue to extend their body of findings and develop generalised theories, it is much less so to construe the particular directions in which these disciplines individually go as comprising the concerted forward movement of a unified 'scientific point of view'. The notion of the progress of the scientific point of view typically carries the implication that one should fall in with it but, if this 'scientific point of view' is itself an illicit reification of the activities of the sciences, then that implication has absolutely no force. There is no need to assume that this supposed 'scientific point of view' comprises the sole context within which understanding can be sought and achieved; certainly one should refrain from unquestioningly taking over such assumptions. In other words, rather than setting out with the conception of 'the scientific point of view' already in place as a basis for deciding what counts as understanding and knowledge, there is the possibility, perhaps the need, for reflection upon that concept, which, if it is to be truly independent reflection, cannot afford to take anything about that received conception for granted.

A withdrawal on this scale will not result just in differences with 'positivists' and those close to them who, in modelling their conception of science closely on that of the more leading natural sciences, pride themselves on espousing the most apt and rigorous expression of the so-called scientific point of view, but also from those who are undoubtedly determined opponents of positivism. The latter may be satisfied that there are differences between natural and social phenomena; that the methods of inquiries into these two kinds of phenomena must be significantly different; that the idea of 'social science' is quite distinct from that of 'natural science'. This said, they can often remain contented to talk of 'social science', for though they envisage different kinds of concepts and quite different sorts of methods as differentiating their sciences from the natural ones, they nonetheless retain the notion that what justifies those concepts and methods is precisely in the development of generalised theoretical schemes which serve the job of explaining.

Though they differ on their pre-conceptions of the nature of the apparatus they are intending to construct, the general run of sociological approaches is underpinned by a consensus as to the objective of constructing such an apparatus.[9] Any expectations that ethnomethodology intends to construct some theoretical apparatus, or that it will yield – at least in any *conventional* sense – a collection of findings, are likely to be disappointed.

Since, further, it makes no effort toward the construction of a theoretical/ explanatory scheme, it has no requirement for a conception of 'the social actor' or, correspondingly, of 'social structure', in the sense in which sociologists dedicated to theory construction require these. Our theme is that discussion of these issues is pitched at an ontological level, such that controversy focusses upon the affirmation or denial of the *reality* of certain phenomena. This is undoubtedly a bonus for sociology in the sense that it is certainly eye-catching to deny that 'society' or 'the individual' exists, but the truth about such controversies is that they usually boil down to rather less than meets the eye. Those who deny the existence of society or of the individual are, if taken at their word, found to be implausible,[10] but as often as not their actual ontological claims prove far less drastic than they sound – apparent denial of reality to society or individual turns out to be rather less than that.[11]

Our preference is to see the issues treated primarily as methodological ones, in which case our main points are:

(a) that ethnomethodology has no need for the constructs 'social actor' and 'social structure'[12] because it has no work for these to do;[13] and

(b) that abandonment of constructivist ambitions means that it is enough for ethnomethodology's purposes to conceive 'social actors' as 'courses of treatment', to propose that – *from its point of view* – persons are neither more nor less than the ways they are treated. Ethnomethodology's equivalent of 'the social actor' is not a person equipped with any definite, specifiable ensemble of understandings, skills, principles etc. but simply one who is left to get on with his or her own affairs.[14]

The reason why there is 'no work' for the concepts of 'social actor' and 'social structure' to do, is that they are to be viewed, as suggested above, relative to a problematic, and these notions have a role in the traditional conception of the problem of social order. It is just this problem which ethnomethodology respecified to get its own enterprise off the ground. The classic conception of the problem requires its solution by means (stable arrangements of social relations or stable arrangements of the characteristics of persons) which are external to the orderliness observable in the sites of everyday activity. Ethnomethodology's respecification is, however, to treat the solution to 'the problem of social order' as completely *internal* to *those sites*. It conceives social settings as *self-organising* and for just that reason has no further need for the received concepts of 'social actor' and 'social structure'.[15]

One way to view ethnomethodology is to take note of its historical attachment to the work of Husserl and Wittgenstein, two thinkers who could not in many ways be further apart but who did share a concern, that of re-achieving theoretically unprejudiced perceptions.

Both were critics of our 'Western' culture, in which the success of physical science had led to the commitment to theory building getting out of hand; one prominent effect of that being that the relationship between the theories and the phenomena which they purported to cover had become obscured, even distorted. There was a confusion about the relationship between the world described in our theories and the world that we meet in the context of our

ordinary lives. This is a widely acknowledged confusion to which the predominant response was to continue laminating layers of theory. Against this,
Husserl and Wittgenstein sought to construct methods which would inhibit
the construction of further theories, and which would enable the recovery of
pre-theoretical perceptions of phenomena.

It is easy to read many ethnomethodologically derived critiques of other
sociological studies as reiterating this point: that their methods make it
impossible to perceive, even to reconstruct, the phenomena as they would be
encountered prior to the adoption of a set of theoretical and methodological
'prejudices'.[16] For both Husserl and Wittgenstein it has been deeply problematic to get theories to attend to that which is plainly before them, and ethnomethodology's standing concern is to bring into focus matters which are, in a
bit of its own jargon, 'seen but unnoticed', or, where those things do receive
the attention of theorists, to achieve a more perspicuous portrayal of them.[17]

3   Actor into analyst

The pivotal issue is that of the character of 'social reality'. This is often conceived in terms of the relationship between 'the actor's point of view' and 'the
theorist's point of view', and this issue is, in its turn, typically conceived in
terms of the *content* of the respective points of views. The sociological
theorist seeks to develop a generalised conception of 'social reality' according
to the requirements (supposedly, the *strict* requirements) of logical coherence
and empirical grounding. The members of society, however, are also usually
credited with a conception of social reality, but since theirs has not been constructed according to the rules which regulate the theorist's construction, it is
only to be expected that the contents of the two will differ significantly. And,
of course, since the theorist's conception has been constructed according to
the procedures which *define* objectivity, it seems that this conception must
identify objective social reality, and that the actor's conception – insofar as it
deviates from the theorist's – must be counted a (merely) subjective one. Not
everyone accepts that this position is right, but the overwhelming majority do
accept this view as presenting the problem. It is widely seen, that is, as a matter of either going along with this view of finding an alternative to it.

Both the theorist and the member of society, then, are attempting to
conceive the actor's environment. Simply, the actor seeks to identify his/her
external environment for pragmatic purposes. The actor seeks to understand
what that environment is and what principles regulate its workings, in order
that his/her actual circumstances may be adjusted by his/her interventions and
manipulations in the direction which more suitably satisfies his/her requirements. The theorist is, of course, seeking a generalised understanding of the
actor's conduct, and presumes that this will be a function of the environment,
and not only of the actor's *perceived* environment, but of properties of the
environment itself, for the principles which regulate its workings will apply to

the actor's conduct also, and will therefore play a critical role in determining the efficacy of the actor's conduct. Unless the actor *correctly* perceives the environment, then projected courses of action are likely to be frustrated, at the best only ostensibly succeeding. However, since the definition of 'correct perception of the environment' which has been adopted is that which is specified through the application of logico-empirical methods, and since the actor's point of view has not been constructed through the employment of such methods but is (only) 'socially derived' (i.e. substantially picked up from others; is mere rumour and hearsay) it follows almost by definition that the actor cannot be correctly perceiving social reality (except, perhaps, coincidentally). Such arguments which tend to be in both the Durkheimian and Marxist traditions, are often combined with 'holistic' considerations in developing notions of the actor's objective *social* environment. The actor's life goes on within some social organisation and it must be, therefore, the molar properties of that organisation which determine the efficacy of conduct, and so a concept of society-as-a-whole is indispensable.

The way in which to understand social action, then, is to *begin* from the point of view of 'objective social reality', to understand action against the background of the social whole, whether or not the actor is at all, let alone correctly, aware of the nature of this environment. Insofar as, further, the actor is not aware of the true nature of social reality, then it will follow that there will frequently be conflict between explanations the theorist gives for the actor's actions, and any explanation the actor himself might give, with the discrepancy being resolved in the theorist's favour.

All this is familiar enough, and it is the defence of something like this conception that has generated many of the objections to ethnomethodology. Clearly, it is seen that since ethnomethodology makes no attempt to construct a conception of the social whole, then ethnomethodology is *denying* existence of any such whole. Ethnomethodology has, therefore, no means of presenting the way social reality is in itself, independently of the actor's own perception of it, and so social reality must, therefore, be identical with the way the actor perceives it. This has consequences. For example, if two social actors conceive social reality differently, then since social reality is identical with what they conceive there must be different social realities. Also, if social reality is identical with the actor's perception of it, then the actor's projects cannot conceivably fail: the actor correctly perceives his/her environment, and forms his/her projects on the basis of that perception, and since there cannot be features of social reality unknown to the actor there is nothing to *prevent* the course of action going exactly according to the actor's plans.

Conceivable objections like this to ethnomethodology are of the sort found in the English nursery rhyme, which advise us to continue to cling to nurse for fear of finding something worse. Plainly the sociologies which are constructed on the basis of this 'objectivist' conception are less than generally compelling, but we are exhorted to continue under that conception because the only alternative to accepting that social reality is objective is, for example, supposing that people never make mistakes.[18] The sociologies constructed on the basis of objectivist sociologies are less than compelling in that whilst for some they have immense (albeit often very temporary) appeal for some others they are entirely unattractive. A minority may find any one or other of them compelling, but nowhere near enough to make up the consensus necessary to count any of them as soci-ology's paradigm.[19] Others find these same sociologies unattractive, even alienating, so much so that they may be willing to accept the alleged absurdities in order to oppose these schemes. There is, however, no necessity to counter the objectivist conception by stating the opposite to it. Indeed, to do this is generously, and perhaps mistakenly, to credit the objectivists with accurately identifying the choices before us.

It is all very well to say that we *begin* the understanding of action from the point of view of objective social reality, but this must surely involve the logical inversion of the actual historical sequence. 'Social reality', we are told, is identified through the procedures and investigations of theoretical activity, but this means that social reality is *the end product* of our studies. 'Social reality' will, on these terms, be specified as the outcome of a *successful* programme of sociological work, so there is more than a hint of paradox about any suggestion that the understanding of social action begins by viewing it relative to objective social reality. On the very terms which constitute the notion of 'objective social reality' such a conception can become available to us only at a late date in the sociological enterprise, when the discipline has prospered in ways which it certainly does not yet do. If one accepts the objectivist viewpoint, then, we are up against this disconcerting fact: that the social actor may not know what the objective reality of his/her social existence is, but *no more does the sociological theorist*.

The mere fact that someone appoints himself/herself to the role of theorist and even accepts the binding requirements of rigorous scientific enquiry (whatever these might be thought to be) does not automatically provide them with an *acceptable* conception of 'objective social reality'. Continuing and intense insistence on the legitimacy, no! the necessity, of such a conception as a precondition for understanding social action hardly puts us in possession of one. Nor will the arbitrary affirmation of a candidate conception of this sort put us in any better position, especially when the objectivist position prides itself upon upholding reason against authority, and in denouncing the arbitrary assertion of one's own perceptions and preferences, no matter how veridical they seem. Within sociology, it seems, one can only avail oneself of the 'content' of an objectivist conception *at the expense* of its methodological requirements, but such a sacrifice is not seriously conceivable, for the content can only legitimately claim representation of 'objective' phenomena if it has been constituted according to those rules.

If ethnomethodology is 'without' a conception of objective reality, then this is, in the first instance, because it *cannot avail itself* of any such conception, and if it is then in a bad position, it is in no worse a one than that in which any other sociology finds itself. Any conception of 'objective social reality' currently in circulation – unless treated strictly as a heuristic device – will seem from ethnomethodology's point of view to have been illicitly 'smuggled in' rather than procedurally (and properly) constituted. In terms of Kuhn's (1962) history of the sciences, sociology is unquestionably in the 'pre-paradigmatic' phase, when persistent attempts at 'fresh starts' are made. Ethnomethodology is fully aware of this, attentive therefore to the fact that sociological inquiries – its own included – are invariably at the stage of 'beginnings'. For it, then, it is hardly a matter of either denying or affirming the existence of 'objective social reality' but of asking how we can get on in the absence of a sound version of such a conception?

The question of the relationship between the sociological theorist's conception of social reality and the social actor's conception also seems to be prematurely raised (to put it as mildly as we can). The simple fact is that within sociology the first unresolved question must be that about the relationship between 'social reality according to the sociologist' and 'social reality'. The massive theoretical and evidential problems which the discipline is almost universally acknowledged to face (when it is considered in terms of any supposedly scientific standards, that is) suggest that the sociological theorist's conception of social reality is apt to be as far adrift as that of the social actor. Hence, the contrast the theorist intends to make will not actually take place. The contrast between 'social reality' and 'the actor's conception of social reality' is the contrast that is intended, but the actual contrast which is made involves (illicitly) telescoping 'the sociologist's conception of social reality' and 'social reality'. The actual contrast, then, is between 'the sociologist's conception of social reality' and 'the actor's conception of social reality', where, *for all anyone can tell* the latter has every bit as much likelihood of being correct as does the former.

It is certainly possible to dismiss these arguments as trivialities, obtaining in the short run but carrying no weight against the conviction that, in the long run, sociology will be able to say definitively what the nature of that social reality must be as a reality in itself. Of course, the only way to try to block *this* conviction is to argue that it *never can* be realised, that social reality is not a 'mind independent reality' – at least, not in the required sense. But whatever the ultimate rights and wrongs of this conviction they are not *legitimately* consequential in the current situation. Demanding that theorists line up for or against the proposition that social reality is 'mind independent' really only functions as the equivalent of a loyalty oath, for no sociological scheme can compellingly claim to be able to represent that mind independent reality.[20]

Though it may at first blush seem strange to say so, many of ethnomethodology's difficulties with other sociologies may be due to its proclivity to treat as matters of scheduling those things which they treat as issues of ontology.

For them the important question is whether there really is a social reality out there or whether it is 'only' in the mind of the individual. Ethnomethodology, by contrast, treats theorising, as it treats social action generally, as a step-by-step real time pursuit, and so it is centrally concerned in examining sociological theories, in asking what they have to start with and how they make, from what they have to start with, the constructions that they have derived. It reflects on itself in similar ways. Given that it is (relatively speaking) a 'beginning' enterprise, it could not conceivably claim, at that stage, to be in possession of an established and adequate concept of 'objective social reality', so it cannot resort to that in order to get its inquiries under way. To say it is 'deprived' of such a concept is to concede the assumption that such a concept is indispensable. It remains to be seen whether this concept proves indispensable, whether ethnomethodology will be prevented from getting on with its inquiries without having to make play with the concept.

It is important to bear in mind the difference which, somewhat uneasily, we will put as between 'adopting a concept' and 'talking about the things the concept is designed to identify'. The fact that one does not make reference to 'objective social reality' or 'the social structure as a whole' could be taken as a sign that there are things which one is thereby and necessarily incapable of speaking about, but it may just as well be that there are other ways of speaking of the phenomena that these concepts are designed to pick out, though one surely could not formulate them in that way, nor necessarily connect them in the way these concepts are designed to do. Certainly, for example, ethnomethodology's reluctance to put the notion of 'mind independent reality' into play does not prevent it from allowing that people make mistakes. After all, the fact that people 'make mistakes' is available *pre-theoretically*. One cannot, perhaps, talk of people making mistakes of the sort that theorists try to specify (confusedly and with debatable effect) with the notion of 'ideology', but it would be the most dubious, even dishonest, move to identify doubt about the sociological utility of the notion of 'ideology'[21] with a naïve assumption that it is impossible for people to make everyday mistakes.

Ethnomethodology's attention consequently turns away from consideration of relations between 'the social actor' and 'the sociological theorist' as if they were putative cognitive rivals with conflicting views of 'the same thing', namely, social reality, to pay more attention to the fact that they are *both* social actors, for, after all, the sociological theorist is a social actor operating under a distinctive attitude.

The standard construal of the problem develops because of its dependence on an assumption of 'object constancy'. It supposes that it is one and the same 'social reality' which is differentially conceived by actor and theorist (and then, if we look into the matter more closely, is differentially conceived amongst actors themselves). This provides 'conflicting versions' of social reality. Our insistence that the problem ought to be treated at the level of theorising here begins to pay off, for at this point we can dispense with the assumption of 'object constancy' without at the same time having to engage with the perplexities of multiplying realities. We can simply acknowledge that 'social reality' *for the purposes of sociological theorising* is not 'the same object' as 'social reality' *for the purposes of everyday life*. The difference neither originates in, nor gives rise to, a multiplication of realities (in any relevant ontological sense, that is) but only in the recognition of the diversity of people's purposes and, in turn, the specificity of the theorist's purposes. As argued in chapter 4, the theoretical and natural attitudes are not in cognitive conflict with each other because they are profoundly incongruous so there is no need either to accept the 'privileging' of the sociological theorist's stand-point over the actor's, nor to resort to the desperate contortions of relativism.[22]

Consistent with the treatment of Alfred Schutz as ethnomethodology's influential precursor (as discussed in chapter 4) we respecify the issue by giving up the fixation on the cognitive correspondence of actor's with theorist's standpoint (and of both, one or neither with 'external reality') in favour of refocussing on the derivation of 'sociological theorist' out of 'member of the society'.[23] The sociological theorist is, after all, a member of society *before* adopting the attitude of theorist, and so the attitude which regulates the theorists' reflections involves the *modification* of the natural atti-tude under which the theorist operated prior to adopting the theoretical attitude. The natural attitude which prevails in daily life, and in terms of which the events *of daily life* are definitively identified, is turned into 'the world according to sociological theory' through modification. The comparison of the 'world of daily life' and 'the world of scientific theory' is widely conducted in terms of comparing the way the world is conceived within daily life with the way it is conceived in scientific theory, but this is not the kind of comparison intended here. The comparison is, rather, between 'the world of daily life' and 'the world of scientific theory' as different 'worlds of activity' so to speak, a comparison in terms of the kinds of things involved in getting their business done.[24]

Because Schutz leads from this into talk of 'multiple realities' (see, especially, 'On Multiple Realities' in Schutz, 1962) and stresses the extent to which there are discontinuities between the different 'finite provinces of meaning' (that the transition between these worlds involves a 'leap') it is prob-ably worth warning against taking this to mean that any two are totally dissociated in the sphere of observable conduct. After all, Schutz cannot have intended his account to preclude the possibility of eating your lunch whilst dis-cussing theoretical issues (he is not eliminating the possibility of 'brown bag' seminars) or blowing your nose whilst watching a play. Hence, the transfor-mation of member into theorist is not total, with the theorist abandoning *all* requirements of the natural attitude. It is one which involves the partial modification of that attitude, the *exemption* of the theorist from many of the requirements of 'real world practicality' but which correspondingly involves the *imposition* of other requirements (such as those of logical consistency and semantic clarity for their own sake).[25]

There is, as Lena Jayyusi examines at length in chapter 10, a long running controversy over whether 'the sociologist' should abstain from judgements of fact and value relative to the affairs of the society, but this is debated as though it were a matter of election, as though the theorist could choose (on pragmatic, ethical, or other grounds) to refrain from making judgements where, otherwise, he/she could freely do so. The implication, here, though, is that this is by no means a matter of choice, that the adoption of the theoretical attitude, *if undertaken consistently rather than erratically*, specifically divests the person *acting strictly as theorist* of any standing in the matters of fact and value which are to be decided. The theorist is effectively *disqualified* from making such judgements.

Careful note should be taken of the nature of the argument. It involves, first of all, distinguishing between *sociologist-qua-role* and *sociologist-qua-individual*. We do not want to deny that sociologists, as individuals, are as entitled as anyone else in society to make judgements of fact and value, but want to highlight that their capacity to do this is entirely due to their *enfranchisement* as members of society, not derivative purely from their specific resources *as theorist*.[26] The adoption of the role of theorist involves a calculated (though *partial*) withdrawal from the status 'member of society', and therefore from the entitlement to make independent determinations of fact and value with respect to the affairs of daily life. Of course, the sociologist *qua individual* will be able to make many determinations of fact and value. This will be because of his/her continuingly extensive immersion in the natural attitude, and attendant enfranchisement in the social environment, which is not to be conflated with his/her strict entitlements *qua theorist*.

The issue of 'value freedom' is not really the topic here (though it is examined in chapter 10), for discussion of this typically assumes that social values must either be assumed to be consensually held, or diversified along antagonistic lines, and the problem is: can the sociologist either simply concur in the agreed values, or achieve neutrality between contested ones? Our issue is different, and we are raising the question of the *competence* of the sociological theorist to 'intervene' in these matters *on the strength of his/her standing as 'theorist' alone*, and are proposing that the overwhelming mass of the affairs of daily life are simply none of the sociological theorist's business (above and beyond that which he/she may legitimately have with them *from a specifically theoretical point of view*). It is somebody else's business altogether to decide whether an insurance policy should be honoured, whether someone is guilty as charged, whether the child's subsequent behaviour is reparation for their previous misconduct, whether to have the car repaired and so on.

The point can perhaps be made more strikingly at the level of sociological theorising with respect to the 'labelling theory' of deviance (Becker, 1963). The labelling theorists rightly see that sociological theorists have no independent basis for deciding whether persons are as a matter of fact guilty of offences for which they have been convicted and so forth, that the collection of a group of 'deviants' makes them necessarily parasitic upon the procedures of those who run the police patrols, organise bureaucratic paperwork systems, and who administer courtroom justice. But having rightly seen this they suppose that they have lighted upon an epistemological difficulty, have discovered something problematic and indeterminate about the nature of deviance. What they have, of course, encountered is the simple fact that they are persons without competence to decide matters of guilt and innocence *for the community at large*, that it is the exclusive business of certain specific kinds of people (certain specific people, in the end) to say definitively whether someone is or is not a criminal, and that sociologists, as both theorists and citizens, simply are not empowered to say anything *officially* on these matters; their sayings count for nothing.

Some illustration of these points can be given through recalling Garfinkel's discussion of the use of psychiatric clinic files (Garfinkel, 1967: Ch. 6). It is a commonplace sociological exercise to attempt the reconstruction of a social organisation from its residua, as for example, with the attempt to reconstruct the ways in which psychiatric treatment in a clinic is administered from reading the organisation's own records. These records, however, repeatedly prove to be poor materials for the *scrupulous* conduct of such a reconstructive exercise. One of the problems that readers of such documentation recurrently encounter is the equivocality of the documents as reports of events. It is possible to combine the materials in a file in a variety of different ways, with a correspondingly different interpretation of their contents and there is no basis *in the reading of the documents alone* for deciding amongst the possibilities which the document will allow.

Is the conclusion we are to draw from this that reading is inherently indeterminate, that for any text there is always a plurality of other possible readings? Only if we fail to appreciate that there is a difference between identifying possibilities between which there is *no possibility of choosing*, and that of being in a position in which you cannot possibly choose between one candidate reading and another. The sociological theorist, *as theorist*, is in no position to choose between the ways in which documents in a folder may be combined to 'make sense'. This is because there is no rule which dictates a unique combination for the materials assembled in a file, and so one can combine the file contents in a plurality of different ways. However, this does not indicate the metaphysical plight of the reader, eternally condemned to endlessly multiplying possibilities, for there is, first and foremost, no such creature as 'the 'generic reader' within ethnomethodology's frame of reference. That figure is a product of a tradition of theorising which, initially at least, was motivated to devise general methods for determining the meaning of texts, though its failure to realise this motivation has resulted in reaction formation, to the effective denial that texts have determinate meanings. The very attempt to derive general solutions to the problem of reading and meaning suppose that the way to do this involves systematic abstracting away of the features of 'readers' in the hope that this will reveal the characteristics of the 'essential' reader. But this is just a very different assumption from ethnomethodology, which assumes that (forgive the paradoxical sound of this) the specifics of readers *are* the essentials, that any actual reader will have specific relevances, purposes, procedures for reading, stocks of knowledge at hand, and that these will be integral to any determination of sense that the party will make.[27]

The problem of 'the reader' arises quite specifically from a tradition of literary theorising which, setting out to provide a generalised solution to the problem of meaning-in-texts (assuming, in this that there is a matchingly generalised problem) may well find that the impracticality of the task it has assigned itself drives it into scepticism. But this doubt does not arise in 'working' sociology because of the evident difficulties that researchers have had in arriving at 'readings' of documents, for it is evident that sociological researchers typically have no sustained difficulty in arriving at quite definite interpretations of the 'texts' they employ as research materials; they have no *general* problem in choosing between conceivable readings of some document, have no difficulty in sorting 'fact' from 'fantasy'. It is Garfinkel's point that the sociologically motivated readers of psychiatric records will overwhelmingly arrive at definite conclusions about what these say, and that they will do so despite the facts that the contents of those documents may be only marginally adequate to what those selfsame readers regard as necessary for determining the meaning of them, and that there are no definite, uniquely specifiable set of methods for reading these records. They will be able, there and then, to contrive ways of dealing with these difficulties, and are able to do this because they are able to draw upon their understandings of what things may possibly, and actually, happen in places like psychiatric clinics.

Garfinkel's point is that the introduction of 'determinacy' into an assortment of theoretical possibilities takes place through the invocation of understandings available *from the social setting itself*, not those derived purely from sociological theory. The sociologist who seeks to reconstruct the order of affairs within a psychiatric clinic from its records must, that is, anticipate the very thing that the study is intended to determine, namely the ways in which 'such places' (or even 'this place') work as grounds for deciding what the evidential materials could possibly mean. The members of psychiatric clinics may encounter the indeterminacy of file contents, but as an *occasional*, not a chronic, problem. They require of each other that they read records *under the auspices of their involvement in, and familiarity with, the circumstances under which the records were created*, and under those circumstances, by appeal to 'knowledge' of how 'such places work', of 'how this place works', of what kinds of things can actually rather than conceivably happen, of what as a matter of fact did happen in connection with the case described in the file and so forth, they can determine what the writer of some file entry must have meant and which of the possible readings of the file is the 'correct' one.

To say this is so is not to say that it is *invariably* so, that everyday users of clinic records will not encounter records where they are able to generate several plausible readings of a file and are unable to choose between these (no one can recall any details of the case etc.). Correspondingly, it is not even to say that the sociological investigator cannot achieve determinate readings of clinic files, for the investigator can, likewise, appeal to a good sense of how things happen, what is possible in the real social world, what happens in psychiatric clinics, what must have happened in this one etc. In short, the investigator has to anticipate the very thing the investigation of the records is designed to determine, which is how the clinic generating the records is organised.

The claim is: at the very least, sociology has failed adequately to clarify the relationship between 'knowing' and 'doing'.[28] More likely, there is a serious unresolved tension between 'knowledge for its sake' and 'knowledge for practical purposes', which shows itself in the deeply uncomfortable contortions that go on around the problem of whether members of society might be said to 'know what they are doing'.[29]

The big assumption is that the social actor, if he/she is to be a 'rational actor' at least, ought to conduct himself/herself on the basis of the theoretical standpoint. Note, there's not much question as to whether the actor ought to aspire to be 'a rational' one, for the term is heavily, positively, evaluative. So, social actors *ought* to aspire to rationality.[30] It is not, however, that most sociological schemes follow our line and suppose that the social actor is *de facto* operating under a distinctive orientation to the theoretical standpoint – such as the natural attitude. The theoretical orientation is, for most sociological schemes, a 'default' mode, and it is assumed that the actor is operating in compliance with the objectives of a theoretical standpoint, albeit, inadequately, incompetently, in a confused or dishonest way. That is, first, it is assumed that the social actor's activities are usefully judged relative to a theoretical orientation and, second, that the actor is *primarily* occupied with 'knowing' his/her environment. Thus, the actor is conceived as 'theoriser' in much the same vein as the sociological theoriser, such that the actor's constructions can be reviewed by the professional theoriser as though those constructions were candidates for inclusion within the theoriser's eventual production.

Here, however, is where the tension between 'knowledge for its own sake' and 'knowledge in service of practicality' reveals itself. In chapter 5 Mike Lynch has adverted to Garfinkel's ploy of envisaging a sociological issue as an encounter between persons, between member and theorist. Envisage, then, the standard issue of theoretical and natural attitudes as a matter of, necessarily, the theorist remonstrating with the member. The theorist must point out to the actor the inadequacy of his/her ways of conducting himself/herself for the acquisition of *bona fide* knowledge. The inadequacy of those ways is demonstrable, it can be shown that the actor's constructions are degenerate by comparison with those engendered by properly constructed, scientifically conducted operations. Such demonstrations are overwhelmingly of a logical sort, demonstrations that the actor's constructs *must be* inadequate, the necessary consequence of the fact that the actor's methods are not coherently worked out or consistently applied.

The actor, then, must be encouraged to put his/her house in order by reorganising those affairs to accommodate the requirements of adequate knowledge. However, *by definition* these requirements involve the implementation of a thoroughly coherent conception, so their implementation requires a *complete* reorganisation of affairs, a reorganisation effectively designed to *put the acquisition of knowledge first*. If our earlier argument about the 'specialised' character of the theoretical standpoint comes close to being correct, then the proper development of the actor's potential as theorist requires the single-minded pursuit of knowledge, not its subordination to the requirements of practicality. This is not merely a matter of substituting one thing for another in the actor's orientation, but rather one of calling for a fundamental restructuring of his/her priorities. Recall, though, that the initial assumption was that the orientation of 'rationality' was one which would engender greater *practical* efficacy, but it transpires that this efficacy will only be manifest if one takes a very *restricted* conception of practicality, namely, one which assumes that action is primarily, even exclusively, directed toward 'knowing' social reality.

The actor who is subjected to this remonstration might well be totally bewildered as to how such singular devotion to knowing might be implemented in actual life and may justifiably fear that the theoretical 'conception of social reality' turns out to be a cuckoo in the nest of practical conduct. It is a notable feature of the remonstrations about rationality that the actor is routinely advised that because of the inadequacy of his/her knowledge base, his/her practical projects are destined to fail. If this were so, then it is surely profoundly surprising that the members of society have not noticed the fact that their projects consistently fail. Perhaps this is because their projects do not consistently fail. Sometimes they do quite visibly fail of course: everybody knows that things often turn out badly. Whether these failures can be attributed to the 'irrationality' of the actors' conduct, however, surely raises the question as to whether projects based on 'objective scientific knowledge' invariably succeed? Those of doctors and engineers might instance the latter sorts of projects, and those certainly are not invariably successful. We suppose the argument might go into how the failures of doctors, engineers, corporate managers and others employing 'rational constructions' are to be understood, whether their failures reveal inherent limitations in the practical efficacy of supposed 'rational constructions', whether their failures are any fewer than those of allegedly 'irrational' actors and so forth. But we point to these lines of development only to stress that the topic of 'rationality', though much talked about, has actually only been very poorly considered.

Cautious as ever, we refrain from saying it is certain these tensions could not be resolved, but that we do not think they have been seriously addressed by the general run of sociological arguments, let alone effectively cleared up. The views we have developed effect a respecification of the problem. We reject the view of the social actor as theorist – at least as theorist of the kind the sociologist typically aspires to be. (It is perhaps worth drawing attention to the fact that insofar as the social actor is conceived as theorist it is as *practical* theorist, and that the conditions, occasions, procedures, and topics of his/her theorising are *socially sanctioned and socially furnished*, are constituted within and through the ways of their social setting – we mean by this nothing more controversial than that, say, findings of 'guilt' issue from the deliberations of juries on the matter of courtroom hearings, that educational abilities are determined through classroom testing, that the sales potential of products is estimated by market research teams, departments and organisations etc. Of course, we do not naïvely suppose that these ways are either ubiquitous or immutable – only the most wayward reading in of suppositions would treat our mention of these as other than to illustrate the presence of them as socially furnished, socially sanctioned ways to hand of 'finding facts' in our society, and to emphasise the *specificity* of, for random examples, reviewing the evidence presented by advocates when sequestered in a jury room, of administering written and oral tests in classroom time to children, and of conducting and computer-analysing surveys of consumer preferences to their various settings. The *mere* fact that things would be otherwise, that indeed, they *are* otherwise elsewhere, lacks the compelling fascination for ethnomethodology that it possesses for other sociologies. The latter are, of course, utterly engrossed with the purely, the sheerly *theoretical* possible, with 'actual' circumstances of interest 'merely' as a subset of the range of theoretically conceivable possibilities. Ethnomethodology's distinctive concern inevitably notes that from the point of practical action 'actual' circumstances are certainly not 'merely' such a subset, the domain of the actual being distinct from the conceivable, especially from that which is *in any practical sense* merely conceivable. This should not, however, provoke those dedicated to establishing that 'science' is a socially organised activity into thinking that we are supposing that inquiries under the natural attitude are socially furnished and sanctioned and that, by contrast, those of theoretical inquiry are not. Of course the latter are socially sanctioned and furnished! The point made in these parenthetical remarks about the *specificity* of methods of theorising and investigating to their settings should be borne centrally in mind. The method of science is (allegedly, but not we think, actually) *general* to science, but any such generality is precisely because of the institutionalised conditions for theoretical inquiry provided within the sciences: the mistake is to suppose that the method of science can be generally applied outside of science, which is not, of course, to say that scientists cannot appear as witnesses before juries, for example.)

So we dispose of the conventional problem of the relationship between 'social reality according to the sociological theorist' and 'social reality according to the member of society'. 'Social reality' is indeed a 'theoretical entity' for the sociological theorist, but assuredly is nothing of that sort for the member. Consequently, the idea that 'social reality the theoretical entity' might be substituted for 'the world of daily life' as the environment of social action is meaningless, simply presenting to anyone who would propose such a possibility the immense problem: explain/demonstrate how such a substitution would systematically *and practically* take place. Of course, this is not to deny to those theorists who want to construct and manipulate such theoretic entities their right to do so, it merely highlights the fact that the relevances through which social action will then be viewed will be (at least, should be!) strictly those of theory construction, and as such it is not logically possible for them to be treated as the relevances under which mundane affairs are conducted.[31]

One of the major faultlines separating sociological theories is their supposed willingness to recognise 'constraint'. Much supposed sociological reasoning is conducted pretty much at the level of a 'two legs good, four legs bad' mentality, and there are many circles in which the recognition of 'constraint' is automatically a major virtue. Naturally, ethnomethodology is excluded from the virtuous circle as being incapable of recognising 'constraint'. However, our argument is that the division is not between those who can acknowledge the existence of constraint and those who cannot, but in the *kind* of 'constraint' that is involved. The word 'constraint' has become rather like a piece of Conservative Party code-speak, meaning something significantly different from what it explicitly says. 'Constraint' in the vocabulary of the dominant factions of sociology tends actually to mean 'the limitations on action presented by "structurally given properties" of the social system', and since ethnomethodology finds no use for conventional theoretical constructs such as 'the social system' or 'the structure of the social system', it assuredly cannot undertake explanations of social action in these terms.[32] To that extent, and *only* to that extent, i.e. in terms of this utterly *partisan* conception of 'constraint', is it 'guilty' of 'failing to acknowledge constraint'.

The 'carry over' terms of the debate about an excess of 'voluntarism' in sociological theorising are not the context for ethnomethodology's manoeuvres, for the choice is not between an actor who is subject to constraint in this distinctive, one might even say quirky, sense, and an actor who is not subject to *any kind* of constraint. Of course, suggesting that this *is* the choice we have to make serves the purposes of those who wish to persuade us of the inevitability of their 'determinist' conception of action. Given that we have to choose between conceptions of the actor as one who is overwhelmingly, if not totally, constrained by 'structural conditions', and one who is utterly unconstrained by any such constraints, is in a state of extreme existential freedom, we will, on grounds of its reality, surely be compelled to opt for the former. Who would wish to deny that persons are products of their biography, that they are now the way they are because of their social origins, and that what they can conceivably do is restricted by the kind of person they are, their place in society, etc.? No reasonable person, surely? However, an affirmative answer carries no implication of the acceptance of 'determinist' views of social action, no acceptance of the appropriation of an uncontroversial truism on behalf of a tendentious theoretical position. Such notions as that persons are 'products of their biography', 'social place' and so forth are, if anything, *common sense* conceptions and are simply neutral with respect to the contentions of sociological theorists.

To suppose that ethnomethodology conceives the actor as existentially undetermined, results from reading its writings as though they perpetuated the conventionally construed dilemmas of sociological theory, thus overlooking the fact that it surely allows that the social actor is constrained: the social actor is a *practical* actor, and merely to offer that characterisation is to highlight that the actor will be *practically* constrained. The very notion of 'practical action' is, after all, of action under conditions which are not all of one's choosing, are unlikely to be all of one's preference, which are perhaps intractable to one's manipulations, of action 'coming to terms' with its circumstances in all their multiplicity and density. There is a temptation to emphasise the 'constraint' of practical circumstance, to suggest that it is pervasive and overwhelming, but this is the wrong move, for of course ethnomethodology is not attempting a distinctive conception of the nature or intensity of 'constraint' on the actor, but is simply pointing to what 'anyone can find'. The aim of structuralist/determinist conceptions is to make out that the social actor is *more* determined than he/she is made out to be, that he/she is subject to constraints of which he/she is unaware and that, typically, those constraints are at work even when the actor believes that his/her actions are free.

Engaging the debate on the structuralist's level and terms, existential conceptions will inevitably tend to shift the emphasis and make out that the actor is vastly less determined than he/she is made out to be – the very notion of 'bad faith' is, of course, that of the actor's own attempt to present as determined and decided matters which are necessarily open to the actor's choice. Ethnomethodology does not play either of their games, for it does not seek portrayals of 'social actors' as other than they are usually made out to be. It does not, therefore, seek to counter the structuralist preoccupation, one might say, 'obsession', with constraint by a rejection of the notion of all constraint, but substitutes inquiry into the working of everyday practical constraint that anyone can find for the investigation of constraints imposed by theoretically conceived requirements and theoretically postulated entities.

4   Actions in context

Unfortunately, even if the argument just given is accepted, it may still be thought that the problem of 'constraint' has not, thereby, been disposed of. We have previously noted that there are superficial reasons for taking ethnomethodological arguments as comparable to those of 'subjectivists', and the simplest response to our case might seem that subjectivists cannot seriously talk of 'constraint'. Two features of our own discussion – (1) its reliance upon Schutz's ideas and (2) its central emphasis upon the social actor's viewpoint – reinforce the view that ethnomethodology is not merely subjectivist, but thoroughly and radically so.

Taking the two points in reverse order, the preoccupation with the 'social actor's' standpoint betrays the fact that ethnomethodology supposes that society is merely a composite of individual viewpoints; the derivation from Schutz confirms this, since it was his objective to show how the fundamental forms of intersubjectivity were rooted in pure consciousness. Therefore, ethnomethodology is a radical subjectivism which postulates social reality as a matter of consciousness, an object which is constituted in and by the actor's consciousness. Social reality which comes into being entirely through postulation by individual consciousness can scarcely be considered constraining, for it can presumably be utterly transformed by another act of consciousness.

Unfortunately these conclusions only follow from a very partial consideration of the role of 'the actor's point of view' and of the nature of our dependence on Schutz's argument. Though ethnomethodology may have taken much inspiration from Schutz's idea, and of phenomenological ideas more generally, it has always reserved the right to treat these ideas selectively, and does not by any means slavishly adhere to Schutz's approach. Ethnomethodology does not follow Schutz in the attempt to derive the fundamental properties of the actor's experience from those of pure consciousness. Such an exercise is at least irrelevant to ethnomethodology in its character as a *sociological* venture, and in the light of many of its other arguments, such an exercise would be futile.

It would be futile just because it is hard, probably impossible, to see sense in the idea that social action can be conceived independently of a social order. From the social actor's point of view, social order is, as the saying goes, always already there. Schutz is by no means the only theorist who has sought to understand social order by 'wishing it away' for analytical purposes,[33] who has attempted to derive social order from something outside social order. But this whole *genre* of attempts will, as far as ethnomethodology can see, prove unsuccessful, for it will at least tacitly invoke the presence of the very social order that it is purportedly dispensing with. The 'primacy' which the 'actor's point of view' has so far been given is not the result of a reductionist commitment, an insistence that 'social reality' can be decomposed into an ensemble of individual points of view.

The usual individualist notion (supreme examples being Weber, cf. Weber, 1947b and 1949; and Popper, 1945 and 1957) is that the society consists only of the actions of individuals. These actions are to be understood in terms of the intentions and motives of their perpetrators as attempts to realise the ends that those individuals have. Any pattern to their activities is the *entirely exigent* outcome of actions which are independently motivated. At best, collective concepts figure as theoretical contrivances which individuals employ to explain and predict the behaviour of other individuals. The aim must, therefore, be to describe individual actions in ways which dispense with all collective concepts, save those which the actors themselves employ to carry out their affairs. Once again, ethnomethodology's overwhelmingly *methodological* orientation leads it to thoroughly recast such arguments, for they overlook at least these two issues: (1) that the primary identification of social actions is necessarily of them as actions-in-a-social-order, and (2) that the procedures for describing those actions are themselves integral to the organisation of the social setting within which those actions occur.

One of the most distinctive and neglected features of ethnomethodology is that ethnomethodology declines to conceive of the problem of social order as an *inductive one*. The relationship between 'social action' and 'social structure' – or between the phenomena those terms are designed to capture, at least – is not an inductive one. This is a critical difference but it is not a substantive one. It is made with respect to the most fundamental conception of the framework within which substantive matters are developed.

When we say that other theorists conceive the problem as an inductive one, we do not of course imply that sociological theorists disregard, for example, Popper's case that *bona fide* scientific inquiry is deductive for, assuredly, there are many theorists who advocate the deductive approach. Our notion of an 'inductive approach', though, is one which also applies to those who follow Popper's advice and proceed according to the hypothetico-deductive method. Our characterisation of the 'inductive approach' covers work governed by the underlying idea that the theorist is attempting to identify (to induce) a set of generalities which will optimally cover a collection of observed instances. The theorist observes the members of society going about some set of social activities and hypothesises that these activities exhibit regular properties because they embody or manifest the working of some general principles. It is the theorist's task to work out some set of generalisations which specify those regularities and which state those principles. In doing so, the theorist is appropriately governed by the rules of scientific evidence and inference and the notion of 'optimal cover', for any collection of observed inferences will therefore be substantially comprised of such requirements as maximal generality, parsimony of concepts and so forth.

The fundamental methodological problem, therefore, is that of generalising from instances, which is why the dominant methodological controversy in sociology has so often been between statistically based and case-study based inquiries. The issue between them is exactly that of the possibility, legitimacy and nature of generalisation, of how one can move from observed cases to 'covering laws'.[34]

It is not possible for ethnomethodology to take a comparable approach, since it does not acknowledge the separation of particular and generality that is its prerequisite, at least as far as the phenomena of sociology are concerned. Insofar as the subject matter of sociology is 'social action', then one cannot assemble a collection of observable occurrences without *already* having introduced a substantial element of generality, without already having subsumed the instance under a general pattern. This is not, however, a variant of the 'folk models' approach, which supposes that the generality figures as part of the actors' various attempts to explain each other's behaviour; it supposes that the appeal to generality is required to *identify* the action in the first place. Social actions are *irreducibly* events-in-a-social-order and they cannot therefore be adequately identified independently of the social order in which they are embedded. Neither, on the other hand, can the social order which is the site of those actions itself be identified independently of them. The particulars (the actions) and the pattern (the social setting/the social order) are inextricably connected, are mutually elaborative: but more on the documentary method shortly.

It is a regrettable feature that sociological arguments are often assessed relative to theorists' hopes, and that they can be set aside on the grounds that they apparently deny that some hoped for sociological future is possible. What we have said will certainly not appeal to those who envisage a general sociological theory which significantly (if not comprehensively) transcends the categories, conceptions and theories available to members of society, but there is a substantial and serious challenge here to anyone of that persuasion, which has not been seriously countered by any of ethnomethodology's critics. It is this: *show that you can collect a corpus of data which is comprised of instances of 'social action' without presupposing the organisation of a 'social structure' in the assembly of that very collection.*

Treating social order strictly inductively involves the kind of procedure which sociologists of all persuasions would, on reflection, find absurd. Imagine that we adopt a strictly behaviouralised mode of description on the supposition that this mode is the closest realisation of the ideal of identifying social phenomena independently of 'member's "theories"'. Thus, we describe a person as doing X, another person as doing Y, yet another person as doing Z. The problem now, is to theorise some adequate connection amongst them. We might theorise, for example, that the behaviour of these people is best explained by the concept of 'conjugal unit' and by the related ideas of 'social networks' of members of the conjugal unit having differential effects on their interpersonal behaviour. However, *for this same data* we could equally well theorise that it was as well explained by the concept of 'formal organisation' and the associated notions of 'formal' and 'informal' systems, of 'bureaucratic rules', 'hierarchies of expertise' and so on. Any one of a vast variety of explanatory schemes might be imagined which could bid, on the grounds of comprehensiveness and parsimony (amongst others), for the claim to be the best explanation of this data. Such a strategy would appear absurd to almost anyone because, of course, the cogency of the usual theoretical schemes of sociology depends upon the identifiability of the kind of commonplace social order to which the actions being theorised are attached: thus, notions of 'conjugal pair' and 'social network' have cogency if the people we are talking about are members of a family; those of bureaucratic rules and hierarchy of expertise, if we are discussing people who are part of a military, social-service or industrial organisation.

To press the point a little further, sociologists of education make studies to find out what goes on in classrooms, but they do not require explicit, specially developed methods to find relevant data. They certainly do not set out to study some activities and then *discover* that these events take place in classrooms (or that their taking place in classrooms is the 'best explanation' for them). They might discover, say, that teachers are more prejudiced against certain kinds of students than we had imagined, but they do not discover that these events are events-in-a-classroom, nor that the categories 'teacher' and 'pupil' are the best pair of categories for collecting together their observations. They start to collect their observations as events-within-a-classroom and they order them, furthermore, in terms of the relationship between 'teacher' and 'pupils' from the very beginning. They do not, that is, derive the categories 'classroom', 'teacher' and 'pupil' on the basis of a set of observations, but organise their observations and descriptions on the basis of those categories which are *in place from the very beginning*. They are, of course, in place from the very beginning because they are *institutionalised* (so to speak) in the social setting that is being described, because they are *socially sanctioned ways of describing* events which take place in that setting.

A notion of Sacks', which Jeff Coulter introduced in chapter 3 and which has a great appeal to many ethnomethodologists, though Sacks in fact dispensed with it in later work, is that of the 'category bound activity' (Sacks, 1972b). We are confident that much of its appeal is owing to the fact that it very forcibly points out that many actions are not *inductively* connected to social categories, though the procedures of sociological inquiry standardly operate on the assumption that the opposite is the case. The idea of 'category bound' actions is simply that some actions are normatively connected to certain categories of persons. Thus, in a notorious example which is more fully engaged in chapter 10, he considers the way that 'crying' is a thing which 'babies do'. The interest of methodologically committed sociologists may well turn to their favoured question: is this connection empirically sound: do babies cry? However, and here we pursue an idea that Doug Benson and John Hughes introduced in the previous chapter, should this happen they will have missed the point of Sacks' interest in the category bound pairing, which is not its *adequacy* as an empirical generality, but in a very different kind of *adequacy*, namely one which enables members of the society and sociological theorists to decide what is happening in a specific instance, a socially sanctioned adequacy. We decide that what is happening here, in this case, is happening just because these people are of this kind and this is the kind of thing that such people do. Thus, we determine *without further inquiry* that this woman is 'the mommy' of the baby and that the mommy is picking up the baby because the baby is crying, because that just is what mommies do, they pick up their babies, and they pick them up *because they are crying*. Thus, into the description of the specific occurrence there is built into it significant generality: these people are definitely doing these things on this occasion *because those are the sort of things that such people do*. Thus, the mundane occurrence of 'picking up a baby to stop it crying' will be observable as such only because the witnessing of it can be subordinated to a knowledge of the relevance of the organisation of families, of the positions which comprise such units, and of the motivations which *properly* govern transactions amongst inhabitants of those positions.

One other elegant way in which Sacks has tried to enforce the point, is in connection with 'doing being ordinary' (Sacks, 1984a). Here he tries to make nonsense of the idea of 'individual experience' which is widely deployed in sociology. The suggestion is that (in our culture, perhaps unlike others) people want to think of themselves as utterly distinctive, as though only they – as individuals – exist without any social order, and as though their experience was totally unique, quite unlike anyone else's. There might be places where people do indeed want to preserve a sense of the uniqueness of what happens to them, but a consideration of the ways people go about their ordinary lives suggests rather the opposite, that people want to conduct their lives substantially as 'ordinary people', that they want to have their experience to be much the same as anyone else's, to have happen to them the things that happen to 'anyone'.

In this respect, Sacks notes a feature of rounds of story telling, for example.[35] A first story's telling will occasion the telling of a round, and there will be (relatively) systematic relations between those stories. One such relation is that a second story will tell of the same sort of thing happening as in the first. Sacks invites us to consider how fundamental this kind of occurrence is to people's sense of *their individual experience*. He invites us to imagine how it would be if every time we told a story about something that happened to us, others told stories about how in comparable circumstances, utterly different things happened to them: if our experience were invariably at odds with other people we would think we were weird indeed. People frequently are, Sacks suggests, gratified to find out that what happens to them happens to 'anyone', and indeed are inclined to take what might otherwise be exotic experiences and 'turn them into' mundane things.

Yet one more of Sacks' reflections may be telling. It is notable, for example, that someone will on, say, seeing something in a shop window make a 'mental note' of this, go home and tell (say) their spouse that they have seen such a thing as the other has been looking to purchase. This is just one of the multifarious and mundane respects in which we look at the world through the eyes of others: we monitor events not only for our own interests in them, but for the interests that others would have in them, for things to tell them about and so on. The canonical idea of the individualisation of experience in our societies simply does not seem to apply to many (largely unnoticed by sociologists) aspects of actual experience.

Reading bits and pieces of Sacks' work solely with regard to their substantive content will invariably convey the impression that it is a much less significant body of writings than it is, underestimating the extent to which it is a carefully considered and thoroughly worked out alternative conception of basic sociological methodology to those which prevail in the textbooks and the overwhelming majority of studies. One or two examples from those writings cannot enable us to convey the cumulative force which the concerted development of a varied assortment of (otherwise) trivial instances are deployed by Sacks to make the point that social organisation is, so to speak, 'built in' to the very perceptions of the social actor, the extent to which their comprehension of events is fundamentally of events within a 'known' and regular social order. This theme is, of course, one which is prominently announced in Garfinkel's work, one which has already been introduced with respect to the topic 'reading clinic files' and which is, of course, the essence of the idea of 'the documental method'. Taking the concept from Mannheim, Garfinkel argues that it is the indispensable resource of members of society *and* of sociological theorists in enabling them to say definitely what is happening, what is being done, on some specific occasion of social action (Garfinkel, 1967: Ch. 3).

An implication of Garfinkel's application of the idea to the work of sociological theorists must be that the analyses as portrayed by those theorists will typically be at odds with their actual practice. The notion of 'documentary method' applies to their work because they conceive of 'social structure' as an 'identical homologous pattern underlying a vast variety of totally different realisations of meaning'. They thus, basically, conceive of 'social structure' as 'underlying pattern'. Explicitly, they are likely to suppose that such a pattern plays a 'generative' role, that the pattern produces, brings about, the events which it subsumes; the assumption being then, that pattern and instances will be independently identifiable such that (under conventional constraints of scientific method) it can be evidenced that the instances are covered by the pattern without that pattern already being 'built in' to the data which it subsumes.

It is here that the actual practice of inquiry will likely be at odds with its explicit methods for, whilst one may speak in the language of 'inductive' inquiry, the actual investigation will *have* to presume the presence of a specific pattern within the phenomenon from the start. In order to arrive at definite conclusions with respect to what people are doing, what they mean by what they say, what their writings assert, and so forth, it will be inevitable that one appeals to those things which are conceivable, realistic etc. *within a social setting such as this*.[36] The relationship between 'instance' and 'pattern' is not *in the practice of sociological theorising* typically generative, but is, rather, mutually elaborative: the pattern and the collection of instances are 'worked up' together, the theorist having to explicate the instance in order to show how it can be conceived as a case of the kind of thing the theory talks about, and, at the same time, the nature of the theory is clarified by showing how it re-describes ordinarily recognisable events and activities. Further, to achieve the definite identification of those 'ordinarily recognisable events' it will be necessary to appeal to the presupposed patterns of mundane social order which are not, themselves, explicitly included in the theorising.

Finding social order is not, then, fundamentally an inductive exercise, for it is not in fact even a *theoretical* exercise at all. It is, rather, a *practically and socially organised* one (in the sense of being one which is done *within the society itself* and which, insofar as it is done by sociological theorists, is done by virtue of their own membership, their own socially provided competencies). Ethnomethodology does not, therefore, confront the methodological problem of generalisation at all in the way that sociologies construing their inquiries as inductive must do: the generalisability of social actions is not in need of solution through logico-empirical methods, for it is already (so to speak) resolved in the phenomena themselves, resolved through the social organisation's own procedures, and the ethnomethodologist's own capability to make generalised description depends entirely upon his/her own competence in the management of everyday affairs.

The idea that ethnomethodology could conceive of social order as a composite of individual actions or, more radically, of individual consciousness, should now be shown up as ludicrous, for it is plain that one cannot conceive of social actions independently of a social order. Someone's asking a question, for example, is only adequately identified as (say) a teacher asking a lesson-relevant question of a pupil against the 'known in common' background of 'life in schools', where events are conceived as 'events in lessons' and where relations are to be subsumed under the categories 'teacher' and 'pupils'.

When we say 'known in common' we mean, of course, that these mundane facts of 'social structure' are 'known' in common to the participants *and* the researcher. To reinforce our rejection of the inductive conception of sociological theorising, let us note that the relationship between theorist *qua* investigator, and those whose activities the theorist may investigate, is thoroughly conceived. In the standard model, the theorist is an observer, who witnesses

the activities of members and then seeks to cover them with a suitable generalisation, but in ethnomethodology's understanding the term 'observation'
actually covers *courses of instruction*, with the theorist being instructed in
how to *adequately, competently* describe the social actions which take place
before his/her eyes. Conventional formats of inquiry will, then, from ethnomethodology's point of view, massively obscure the very methods by which
the investigator was instructed by those inhabiting the social setting(s) being
studied just how to identify, to observe and describe events which 'really' take
place within such (a) setting(s). The extent to which the study is the *joint*
product of the theorist and those being investigated will be thus 'suppressed'
as well as the extent to which the study has been produced in and through
reliance upon the features of the social order that it describes.

Those who allege that ethnomethodology, dispensing with the conventional notion of 'social structure', is thereby compelled toward complete
naïveté concerning the way in which actions are embedded in a 'wider social
environment' have an Hegelian capacity for standing things on their heads,
for one thing is certain: ethnomethodology insists that the business of sociological theorising (including the making of investigative inquiries) presupposes, and pervasively depends upon, a grasp of 'social structure'. We have
not, though, gone back on the statement that there is no work for the notion
of 'social structure' to do in ethnomethodology, for this is not *ethnomethodology's own notion* of 'social structure', and thus is utterly unlike the one that
finds employment in other kinds of sociological theorising, for there the
notion is a theorist's construction which is meant to provide a summary
characterisation of the environment of social action, viewed *sub specie
aeternitatis*. Hence, the concern with 'social structure' as a causal force which
might pre-empt agency and, in consequence, the (mis)reading of ethnomethodology's dissociation from the usual objectives of theory building and
explanation as a rejection of the realities that the notion of 'social structure' is
meant to capture. The notion of 'social structure' that gets attention from
ethnomethodology is that which is *indigenous* to the activities under study,
that which is found within the society itself, where 'social structure' figures as
a *thematic presence*. The connection that members of the society find between
'social structure' and 'social action' is unlike that between a general law and
an empirical occurrence. Rather, much more like that between a theme, its
elements and variations.

The citation from Mannheim on the documentary method formulates just
this point, that one is dealing with a problem of finding (often far from
apparent) unity amidst endless diversity, rather than of attempting to find
law-like regularities. To put it another way, we might say that ethnomethodology is much more concerned with *coherence* than *causality*, so naturally its
efforts will seem pathetic if they are understood as an attempt at the task of
'causally explaining social action'. Ethnomethodology's studies make vastly
more sense when understood as inspections of the ways social scenes have

visible coherence to even the most casual of witnesses, the ways in which the presence of social order can be readily detected within them; with the ways social order is exposed to even the most passing of glances (Sudnow, 1972b) and, reciprocally, the ways in which within such scenes the activities of individuals can be given a definite sense, trajectory and motivation relative to the 'transparently' organised properties of the scene.

Thus, on entering (say) an airport terminal building where large numbers of people are milling about one is *already* seeing people as (*inter alia*) categorised amongst those who are 'flight crew', 'groundstaff', 'passengers', 'people booking tickets', 'those meeting someone coming in from a flight' and so on. Indeed, the very identification of them as types has to some extent also picked out their motivations: they are e.g. waiting to meet someone, and it has anticipated their future course of action – all this, of course, being done utterly unreflectively. The multiplicity of comings and goings 'hang together' as organised occurrences, doings which are intricately and elaborately relatable together, unifiable by the omni-relevant theme of meeting-and-taking-plane-flights.

It is this kind of stark, staring you in the face, overwhelming *connectedness* that we try to emphasise by the word 'coherence'. Which is not, either, another form of *naïveté*, which says that *everything* reveals itself so unproblematically, for within any scene there will be possibilities of puzzlement, things that are not adequately apprehended by the passing glance, which call for further inquiry. However, these opacities are present against backgrounds which are, for any ordinary, wide-awake person, *overwhelmingly obvious*. Equally overwhelmingly, ethnomethodology attends to the ways in which social organisation is a *findable* phenomenon, placing at its very centre and taking uniquely seriously a notion which is not in fact distinctive to it.

All kinds of sociologists recognise that social order is ' "known" from within', that social order is encountered as a familiar fact of life within the environment of everyday affairs. Even Durkheim, after all, appeals to us to recognise the reality of social facts by way of the familiar example of the regard we have for the law as an imaginable, utterly familiar pattern of prohibition and enforcement. However, though theorists of all stripes acknowledge this fact, they pass over it rapidly, leaving it subsequently unconsidered: they do not ask themselves the question that ethnomethodology takes as its distinctive and exclusive province: how does a social organisation organise itself so that it can be 'known from within', such that an 'overall structure' or 'pervasive pattern' can be picked out amidst the flow of its routine affairs? Indeed, and reciprocally, how is it that the affairs of the social organisation themselves are available in the first instance *as* routine affairs.

Far from carrying us to the conclusion that ethnomethodology thereby proposes that social actions are inexplicable (say) that 'causes' cannot be identified, we note that ethnomethodology says pretty much the opposite.

Namely, that persons' actions are all too readily explicable and that causes often can be found, but that such explanation and cause finding is, itself, part and parcel of the self-same social scene in which the actions occur. These issues reproduce *for ethnomethodology* its recurrent question: and how, within a social scene, are explanations of persons' actions found?

We could say, then, that 'social structure' is conceived as a 'scheme of interpretation' save that we run the risk of playing into the hands of those determined to make out that we are naïve about the 'independence of social reality'. If we say ' "social structure" is a title for schemes of interpretation', those dedicated opponents will say: aha! We have said all along that social reality is in members' heads, that ethnomethodology is an idealist conceit. The truth is now apparent, social structure is a mental device, a mere construct in members' heads – perhaps a fancy version of the folk model! This is, alas, only the result of jumping to conclusions on the basis of part of an argument. Insofar as we do say that 'social structure' is a scheme of interpretation (and it is sometimes useful to say this, albeit always cautiously) we also say, first, that social structure is a *socially sanctioned* scheme of interpretation, and, second, that such schemes are *embedded* in social settings.

We cannot 'reduce' social structure to a scheme of interpretation in the actors' heads for the reason that we cannot identify either the scheme of interpretation nor the setting that the scheme interprets *independently of each other*. The point about 'mutual elaboration' is to be taken fully seriously, for, of course, it is every field researcher's experience that their sense of the definite character of the organisation of the 'field', and their sense of the activities they witness within it, *develop together over the course of their involvement* in it. Starting out with only vague notions of how 'such places' conduct themselves, and in the sure knowledge that there are many things going on before them now which they cannot adequately comprehend, they develop, over the time of their inquiries, a considerably fuller sense of what the ways of the setting are and of the character of occasions that they witness, the two going of course, hand-in-hand. One can more fully document 'the ways' of the setting, for one can recite instances which exhibit the working of those ways, what such ways prove to be in witnessable occasions, but, of course, one's capacity to specify the detailed character of such instances consists significantly in being able to relate them to the very ways whose reality they testify to and whose character they elucidate.

A main reason for difficulty in placing ethnomethodology in terms of dichotomies between 'social reality as objective' and 'social reality as subjective' is now perhaps apparent, and it is its disinclination to seek for a 'first term' for its sociological theorising, to seek to *begin* either 'the actor's point of view' or 'the social whole', and to derive everything from either one or the other: after all, this supposes that finding either 'subjectivity' or 'objectivity' is primarily a theorist's task when it is, to ethnomethodology at least, visible that both of these are readily findable within the affairs of daily life. Indeed, it is just one more near inversion of the actual facts that ethnomethodology has been condemned as 'subjectivist' when, in truth, it has persistently followed out Schutz's initiative in making the availability of 'the other' problematic. This is not, of course, a matter of maintaining that the other's point of view is too problematic to determine, for in that respect it is surely the case that other sociologies than ethnomethodology would treat that point of view as vastly more problematical, would treat it as elusive and perhaps ultimately indeterminate. Schutz's initiative presumes, instead, that the other's point of view is (often) very readily available, that one can determine unreflectively and fluently what the other is thinking, means etc. It makes the mutual availability of points of view problematic in the sense of reflecting upon that possibility, and gives tremendous emphasis to the way that availability is assured because it is embedded in the social distribution of knowledge, particularly the complex apparatus of social types, motivational characteristics and so forth, which is circulated as part of that distribution.

The following out of the broad lines of this initiative can be found in, for example, the invariably overlooked studies of Schwartz which have been extensively concerned with the identification of social conditions for 'subjectivity', for the way in which methods for finding states of mind (such as those of mental derangement, for example) are socially organised (Schwartz, 1976, 1978 and Schwartz and Jacobs, 1979). In addition to Schwartz's work one may also mention Schegloff's early and elegant treatment of the way in which the methods of the psychotherapeutic interview are designed to achieve the demonstrability of 'transference', the way the therapist is trained to talk in such ways that, when the patient proclaims their attachment to the therapist, the therapist will be capable of evidencing that this is 'merely subjective', that the entire history of the therapist's prior conduct is such as to give no defensible basis for the patient's claim (Schegloff, 1963). These are but two of innumerable instances in which studies of the routinely findable character of 'subjectivity' have been made, to which we might add a mention of the better known work of Pollner (1975) and Coulter (1975). These studies might even entitle us to say that the charge that ethnomethodology is irremediably subjectivist is a 'complete inversion' of the truth, but we prefer to go only so far as to say it is a 'near inversion' because we are chary of perpetuating unnecessary separations and consequently superfluous oppositions which are the stuff of life for so many inconclusive controversies.

5   Conclusion: explication

We have just tried to do once more the thing that we have been trying to do throughout, which is to evidence that ethnomethodology is engaged in a distinctive venture which puts it firmly outside the framework of dilemmas that typically demarcate the area of sociological disputation. Its disposition to remove itself from the substantive disagreements which are treated as the crucial basis for sociological controversy, is motivated by its conviction that it holds a fundamentally different conception of the business of sociological theorising than that which permeates the rest of the discipline, and which effectively imposes a specific – and from ethnomethodology's point of view – excessively restricted methodological decision upon it. The respects in which ethnomethodology sets itself apart are apparent enough in its writings, and the features we have emphasised are no doubt seen by its readers, but often go largely unnoticed by them. Denials that ethnomethodology is engaging in the sort of theorising that others assiduously pursue are very forcibly stressed when those otherwise various styles of theorising are collectively designated as 'constructivist'. The stark implication is that the alternative to this is a determinedly 'non-constructivist' approach. This is, however, apparently very widely disregarded, so that ethnomethodology's arguments and studies may be directly absorbed into the very controversies it has disavowed.

If, though, ethnomethodology eschews the fundamental commitment to explanatory theorising, what alternative is available? The substantial burden of its work is, we maintain, *explicatory*.

Explication, though, surely means the spelling out of that which is already known, so is ethnomethodology only in the business of telling people what they already 'know', repeating back to them their common-sense under-standings? Such a trivialising characterisation suggests that ethnomethod-ology is designed to compile an inventory of common-sense understandings, but this was never the point. The determination to identify 'common-sense understandings' is not meant to result in reiteration of those understandings for their own sake, but in a context which gives a *more perspicuous view* of their part in everyday activities and, also cogently, in the work of sociological theorists themselves. Of course such theorists 'know' all kinds of things that anyone might know, and it would therefore be entirely pointless to recite to those theorists a litany of things already known to them, especially if done as though this were a delivery of news.

The point is, of course, to try to get 'common-sense understandings' into a *rather different perspective*, it being that theorists have crucially lost sight of the pervasive and persistent dependence of their own theorising upon such 'common-sense understandings', of their *essential* reliance upon these to get their theories and studies to 'work out'. Their underestimation of their own *in practice* dependence upon common-sense understandings stands in recurrent tension with their *official, in principle* independence of these, and goes together with an impoverished characterisation of the part of such under-standings in daily life itself.

At its simplest level, this means that there is serious difference between ethnomethodology and sociology-at-large over the latter's frequent assump-tion that the rebuttal of some specific 'common-sense understanding' stands as a rebuttal *of the corpus of common-sense knowledge as a whole*. The former supposes that the rebuttal of one common-sense understanding typically presupposes, and crucially counts upon, other 'common-sense' understandings; that the retraction of one does not represent a beginning in the eradication of all; that the subtraction of one does not signify the first step in the totality of 'common-sense understandings'. The claim is, then, that at the least the relationship of standard sociological theorising to 'common sense' is erratic and ambiguous. The point should be strongly reinforced: ethnomethodology does not replace the sceptical standpoint (supposedly a constitutional requirement of the scientific approach) toward pre-given understandings with a credulous faith in the understandings that are inherent and incorrigibly common sense. Overlooked is the fact that it has refused to buy into the wholesale counter-position of 'common sense' and 'science' to begin with.

In substantive terms the divergence is most manifest in ethnomethodology's treatment of sociology as a natural language venture: with its eyes on, as examined by Jeff Coulter in chapter 3, logico-mathematical notations as the ideals of expression, sociological method will frequently disparate 'ordinary language', but will, *pending* the (perpetually postponed) systematic adoption of technically adequate symbolisms, itself speak of social life in the 'ordinary' language the theorist shares with other members of society. The extensive and unselfconscious employment of natural language to state the substance of sociological thought contrasts with the marginalised status of reflective examination of the natural language expression of social order.[37] This, further, relates to divergence between the view that ordinary language is the provisional, but inessential, vehicle for sociological discourse, and one of social phenomena as substantially constituted in natural language.

Failure to appreciate this does not help understand the origins and motivation of inquiries into the organisation of conversation. Though those inquiries may turn out to describe conversation as an 'interactional enterprise', it would be an impoverished assessment of them which would suppose that the demonstration of this was 'all' that those studies amounted to. One can, we suppose, give such a reductionist reading to those studies, interpreting them as showing that social phenomena consist 'only' in conversational interaction, but such a reading is not necessary and certainly less than compelling when set against (say) Harvey Sacks' *Sociological Description* (Sacks, 1963) where the issue is explicitly posed of sociology as a natural-language inquiry typically conducted without further, certainly without *systematic*, examination of natural language itself. Sacks' work extensively explores the topic of the natural language describability of social order as (primarily) evidenced within commonplace conversational exchanges, with that work carrying a strong sub-text about the situated, socio-culturally regulated character of inference.

The characterisation of social actions is, in an expression of Ryle's, a matter of 'thick description'.[38] Ryle coins the expression to make the relatively familiar point about the difference between behaviouralising formulations of an action which formulate those features of it that can be captured by some mechanical recording device such as a camera – these are 'thin' descriptions – and those characterisations which identify the action with reference to the intentions, purposes, circumstances, past history and future prospects of it, all features which cannot be captured by the camera in the same way as the behaviour involved in the action can – these are the 'thick' descriptions.[39] Ryle does not say that thin descriptions do not correctly characterise actions, but that they do so only thinly, omitting much that contributes to making the action the action that it is. His example is the movement of an eyelid, which though correctly described as its expansion and contraction, simply does not identify the action as the 'wink' that, in fact, it is. Ryle's terminology is not invoked solely to restate the familiar point about the difference between 'behaviour' and 'action', though, of course, that point is important to ethno-methodology, but serves a slightly different, less well appreciated one, which is that the description of action is then, relative to the description of *social* action. Whilst sociologists very generally and, nowadays at least, readily accept the point about the description of action, they nonetheless may be inclined to prefer 'thin' descriptions of *social* action.

This is perhaps why it could be thought that ethnomethodology (along with other 'social action' approaches) treats the identification of social action as something which hinges solely upon the actor's intention. Taking ethno-methodology as a mere reproduction of the standard point about the role of 'intentionality' in distinguishing action from behaviour, it is possible to over-look the fact that Ryle's own coinage makes thin/thick a *relative* contrast. If some sociologists (mainly in the Weberian tradition) are satisfied that attend-ing to the 'intentional' aspect of conduct provides for an adequate sociologi-cal treatment of social action, then ethnomethodology does not agree with them, for from its point of view the description of social action is thick not only with intentionality, but with *social-organisational* matters.

A good many 'social action' approaches are 'conventional' in the sense that they suppose that it is the sociologist's job to show the relevance of the social setting to the action. Sure enough, an action acquires its character, as the action that it is, from within its social setting, but the sociologist is required to work out the relationship between the action and the setting. Thus, it is a stan-dard objective of sociologists, including those of the 'social action' inclination, to establish that actions *are* social, their analytical apparatus being specifically designed for delivering the (nowadays) routine sociological surprise, that matters – such as illness, death, sex, entertainment, knowledge – which (allegedly) *no one supposed were social* are, in fact and after all, social! Such demonstrations designedly contrast 'the individualistic' conceptions available to social actors with 'the sociological' conception possessed by the pro-fessional theorist.

We do not want to defend the individualistic conception of the social actor, certainly not to project that as the cornerstone of social reality, for we need to contest *the attribution* of such individualistic conceptions to begin with. Such attributions result from the employment of procedures which are only 'thinly' descriptive of social action from the actor's point of view, which – since they orient to the study of action – acknowledge the role of the agent's intentionality but significantly underplay the extent to which, in the actor's own conceptions, the adequate description of them is as *social* action. It does not require the sociological theorist's special efforts to make actions out to be social since – at least for ethnomethodology – their social character is *built into* them from the start.

It is the 'thickness' of descriptions of social action which gives ethnomethodology its principal explicatory job, that of spelling out the extent to which even the most routine and otherwise unremarkable description of someone's action is permeated with social–organisational elements, or drawing out how far an attentiveness to the social character of conduct is built into even the most initial, pre-theoretical characterisations of it, how adequate recognition of ordinary actions, identification of them as the actions that they are, indispensably draws upon an awareness of the social setting within which they are found and which they reciprocally comprise. The priority which is given to the inspection of 'materials' is itself an outgrowth of just this concern, rather than of any empiricist or reductionist commitments which it is perhaps more usually seen to manifest. It certainly is not the supposition that social order 'reduces' to what can be caught on audio or video tape and subsequently transformed into transcripts. This would, indeed, be to substitute thin descriptions for the necessary thick ones, and it is ethnomethodology's own prominent theme that social phenomena will resist capture in such records.

The more one seeks to 'objectify' the phenomena, to capture them in so called 'hard data', then the more one will find, as Garfinkel alleges sociology recurrently does, that the phenomena evaporate, that the researcher shifts from studying the organisation of social action, which is the intentioned object of inquiry, to studying something else. But if *this* is true, why the insistence upon 'studies', and upon the focal inspection of materials such as audio and video tapes, written records and the rest? This reliance upon 'hard data' simply contradicts the acceptance of the inherent 'softness' of social phenomena.

The contradiction appears, however, only if one reads ethnomethodology in terms of someone else's dichotomy, that conventional one between 'hard' and 'soft' data. However, the audio and video recordings are not conceived as data in the usual sense: Schwartz has put the question directly in that sense: 'Data, who needs it?' he rhetorically titled one of his papers (Schwartz, 1978). It's tricky to get this point just right. To say (with Ryle) that the tape recording or camera cannot adequately capture the social activities they purportedly portray, is not quite right, because in important ways they precisely do record such occasions. This is to take an unduly 'thin' view of what the camera captures. The point is, rather, that the tape recording and video *on their own* cannot adequately capture the nature of the very activities they record, that it is only because they are employed *in conjunction* with people's everyday attentiveness to the socially situated character of their own and each other's doings that the audio and video record stand as recognisable portrayals of identifiable social occasions. The point of reviewing such materials is, therefore, first to spell out the fact that persons (including sociological theorists) do find recognisable, commonplace social activities within such records, that awareness of their socially sited character is thoroughly implicated in their very *identification as actions in the first place*. Secondly, it is to exhibit the intricate relationship between what, in a relevantly 'thin' sense, can be heard or seen in the record, and the socially provided competence which is required to view that same record and find in it the 'thickly' describable social actions that are, for those with appropriate competence, unreflectively heard or seen there.

If others find a distinction between 'individual action' and 'social order' the adequate base on which to found their project of theorising, then they will indeed have a tough task, which is that of relating individual action to the social order, one which requires that the theorist provide the solution, but they cannot necessarily expect that everyone should install that distinction at the very foundation of their discourse. Ethnomethodologists decline to put that separation in place just because it seems to them an artifact, resulting from pulling apart those things which need never have been dissociated, for appropriately thick descriptions of social actions will, *inevitably*, identify them as actions-conducting-the-affairs-of-a-social-order. The separation of individual action and the social order gives the theorist the job of finding ways of relating action and social order. The refusal to make that separation gives the theorist a rather different one, that of portraying the way in which individual action and social order are already related *not merely within, but by*, the social order itself and, reciprocally, the way the social order is assembled in, and made visible through, those self-same social actions.

NOTES

1 That some theories operate without a conception of the actor, or leave the conception implicit, is legitimate enough if the tasks the theorists have set themselves are ones which do not need such a conception or require its explication. Since we look on theories as purpose-built devices which are primarily to be understood and evaluated relative to a problematic, we cannot share the idea which apparently guides much sociological theorising (examples being Gouldner's, Habermas' and Giddens' global theorising) that a theory must cover *everything*.

2 The 'social action' and 'interactionist' traditions are, of course, leading examples, and ethnomethodology does *in some ways* continue along the line they project.

3 Both 'the subject' and the ambition for 'the grand narrative' are together the victims of the 'post-modernist' critique.

4 This is, of course, usually understood as an argument against the position that social actors are solely and entirely self-determining, as though the idea of working 'from the actor's point of view' stood on such an assumption. For us, though, the difference which people attempt to put in these terms is actually located in the wrong place. Both sides typically agree that the members of society are less than fully self-determining, but disagree on whether people are less self-determining than they believe themselves to be. Since we have doubts about the *estimates* that sociologists make of how 'self-determining' people believe themselves to be, we have real difficulty in a yes-or-no answer to that question. The problem itself is, in any case, less a matter of establishing that people are not entirely self-determining, but of the way to handle this, in truth, banal fact.

5 The 'symbolic interactionist' tradition has been most notable in arguing that many sociological conceptions significantly understate the active nature of social being. The *locus classicus* is Blumer (1969).

6 In fact, of explaining one in terms of the other which, ironically, can mean explaining one or other away.

7 Ethnomethodology might 'explain' in the sense of 'make clear' or 'make more intelligible', but the capacity to do this does not depend upon accepting the narrow and premature identification of 'explain' with 'derive from a generalised theory', which has such a strong influence on our intellectual culture generally and sociology specifically.

8 For an attempt to focus on this division with ethnomethodology, see Boden and Zimmerman (forthcoming).

9 For example, the 'symbolic interactionists' who are, from a 'philosophy of science' point of view far removed from the positivist end of the spectrum are nonetheless critically concerned with the standard evidence-and-inference problem that Doug Benson and John Hughes discussed in chapter 6, a preoccupation which shows their commitment to constructing explanatory generalities. See, for example, the discussion of the problem of 'analytic induction' (McCall and Simmonds, 1969).

10 And not just on our say so. The fact that some people profess to find one or other of these contentions not merely plausible but correct, can only be matched up against the fact that another substantial grouping find that same contention completely incredible.

11 For notable example, Althusser's (1971, 1976, and 1979) determined 'structuralist' standpoint, as resolutely anti-individualist as one can find, comes around to the admission that the individual is an indispensable and irreducible feature of our experience though, of course, he seeks to mute the extent of his concession – we almost said, concession to reality – by derogating it as an 'ideological' construction.

12 In the sense, at least, in which participants in the structure/agency debate understand these.

13 Thus, the questioning is of the utility of certain concepts, not the 'reality' of any specific phenomena. A given set of technical concepts are not perhaps the *only* way of handling certain phenomena.

14 The inclusion of 'from its point of view' here is critical. It should dispose of the problems that Goffman's work always encountered, of being treated as a proto-

ontological case about the unreality of the self. In Garfinkel's *Studies in Ethno-methodology* good *methodological* reasons are extensively given for declining to conceive the social actor as a determinate set of understandings, skills etc. This is not denying actor's possession of skills, understandings etc. but, rather, highlighting the problem of treating these as determinate *under the aegis of notions of determinacy supposedly taken from empirical science*. Garfinkel repeatedly tries to show the self-frustrating character of attempts to spell out and codify the supposed constituents of the actor's 'competence'.

15 Which is a very, very, long way from saying that ethnomethodology simply cannot talk about some phenomena that other sociologies have free and ready access to. It is a way of saying that – so far as we can see – ethnomethodology can as readily and freely talk of any pre-theoretically identified phenomena as any other sociology can, though it likely won't talk about them in remotely comparable terms. The best expositions of the idea of self-explicating settings remain Pollner's 'Explicative Transactions' (Pollner, 1979), and Weider's *Language and Social Reality* (Weider, 1974).

16 Though some individual sociologists – too many of them – show prejudice in the derogatory sense of being unreasonably dogmatic in their views, the term used here is not intended in this derogatory way but is intended to refer to the ways in which things have, from certain points of view, already been decided and settled.

17 One of the most sustained attempts to highlight the presence of these 'seen but unnoticed' matters to sociological inquiries is Cicourel's wrongfully neglected *The Social Organisation of Juvenile Justice* (Cicourel, 1976).

18 And who would want to support absurdities, who would want to deny that people make mistakes? Being in a position *as a sociologist* to say that certain people have made a mistake is, however, a quite different matter. Sociologists, *as sociologists*, simply have neither relevant competence nor standing in matters outside their own professional expertise viz, mainly in the history, sayings, and arguments of sociology, to say whether a mistake has been made.

19 In Kuhn's most central sense of the word, that is, which is meant to pick out a discipline-wide scheme of theory, not merely as an alternative word for 'framework'. See instance, Kuhn (1962).

20 Hence, no sociological scheme can *legitimately* take its own conception of 'mind independent reality' as a yardstick for evaluating the 'realism' of anyone else's conception. Indeed, some 'objectivist' positions are inclined to the view that this external reality will eternally evade our efforts to know it, which makes its invocation as any standard or evaluation even more problematic. Popper's philosophy of science (Popper, 1959 and 1972), is of this kind. We do not raise the issue of the horrendously paradoxical character of Popper's claims that science is approximating to a knowledge of that reality relative to his parallel insistence that science does not succeed in establishing its nature. A miss is as good as a mile, perhaps?

21 It is not that ethnomethodologists suppose that the gap between how social reality is, and how members of society represent it to themselves (which gap is the basis for the adoption of a supposedly systematic concept of 'ideology') does not exist, and therefore that persons in society do accurately comprehend 'objective social reality'. Rather, it is that ethnomethodology does not suppose that members of society are seeking to 'understand objective social reality' *in the sense, in which*

sociological theorists conceive of that. So it makes no sense to ask whether they represent this incorrectly or not.

22 Put another way, the theorist's point of view is not 'privileged' but 'specialised'.

23 Ethnomethodology assiduously pays attention to matters which the members of society overwhelmingly disattend.

24 Also of interest is Sacks' strategy which has now had to be invoked on two previous occasions in this volume, once in chapter 3, and once in chapter 6 (and which incidentally will again be invoked in chapters 9 and 10) of getting away from the fixation on 'correspondence' by treating the 'correctness' of many matter-of-course assertions as an analytically trivial matter, moving the focus of investigation from whether descriptions are correct to how they are possible and intelligible: a description standing as a 'possible description' is logically and analytically prior to its standing as a 'correct description'. See, *inter alia*, Sacks (1963 and 1972b).

25 See Garfinkel's presentation and reworking of Schutz's ideas on this, Garfinkel (1967: Ch. 8).

26 This point is made in another way in Sharrock and Anderson (1981).

27 'The reader' as a literary device is, of course, another matter, though not one for consideration now – but see Anderson (1978).

28 This, like other formulations we have used previously in this paper, is a provisional way of stating a problem, one whose developed treatment might well require abandonment of this way of talking about it. In other words, 'knowing' would be considered as a form of 'doing', which is fully consistent with our previous Schutz inspired treatment of scientific theorising as a matter of 'doing theorising'.

29 Classically, of course, these contortions may be construed in opposite ways, as manifestations of the depth, sophistication and penetration of sociological conceptions, or, on the other hand, as confused elaborations of fundamental muddle. The tendency of sociological theories which are one minute heralded as wondrous new insights and scarcely a moment later cited as instances of self-defeating, self-unravelling schemes convinces us that the latter assessment is far the more likely.

30 Insofar as the notion of 'rationality' is designedly a resource for a strictly empirical science it is, of course, a good and unresolved question as to how this normative element can legitimately enter in.

31 Harold Garfinkel (informally) remarked that the procedures of functional analysis resembled those of a teacher who sets students the task of writing an essay but does not give them a title for it. Once the essays have been written the teacher will decide what the title is and decide whether the essays are adequate responses to it. This point may have wider applicability than to functional analysis alone.

32 As it is not attempting a conventional theoretical task it assuredly does not require a conventional conceptual and theoretical apparatus.

33 This is, to use Garfinkel's delectable expression, a matter of taking away the walls the better to see what keeps the roof up.

34 We insert quotes around the phrase because some theorists do not adopt the covering law view of procedure, so the expression here applies to covering laws and *their functional equivalents*.

35 See chapter 1 of Sacks' unpublished book (Sacks, unpublished).

36 We might see many of the contemporary manifestations of scepticism that were discussed in chapter 4, those which seek to show the self-unravelling nature of

meanings not as a step beyond Garfinkel but as outstanding confirmation of his point: if one approaches issues of meaning (including within those the identification of social action, for, of course, the issue of 'meaning in texts' is really only a sub-variant of the generic topic 'the identification of social actions') from a rigorously theoretical point of view, fastidiously disdaining any reliance upon any presuppositions external to that point of view, then one simply cannot choose between possible meanings of a given text – indeed, there is something problematic about speaking of a 'given text' at all, here.

37 See Rose (1960).

38 Ryle develops the idea in 'The Thinking of Thoughts' (Ryle, 1971).

39 These remarks should not be confused as applying to the attempts made to capture aspects of social action for repeated scrutiny on video or tape recorders. In as much as analyses of these materials address *social action* they are oriented to the production of thick descriptions. We return to this issue shortly.

8

Cognition: 'cognition' in an ethnomethodological mode

Jeff Coulter

1 Introduction

This chapter is concerned with the exploration of the problem of analysing human cognition. Focussing upon the theoretical dimensions of this complex issue, I shall deal with some of the contemporary perspectives within which it has been conceptualised and studied. My chief aim will be to show to what extent a commitment to the exploitation of *computational* concepts in the field has precluded a properly sociological understanding of those properties, attributes, and capacities of people typically construed as 'mental' phenomena.[1] It thus elaborates upon one of the specifications of 'the actor' in the human sciences that was introduced in the previous chapter. Subsequent to this demonstration, I shall seek to illustrate in what ways a specifically ethnomethodological respecification of this field is defensible, intellectually productive, and constitutes a coherent and genuinely alternative approach to a range of problems traditionally subsumed under the cognitivist rubric.

I will begin by sketching some salient aspects of the historical background to the current 'cognitive revolution' in the human sciences. In particular, I shall try to show on this basis how, although many proponents of cognitivism claim that it has transcended its Cartesian roots by invoking essentially 'materialist' understandings of the mind–brain–behaviour relationship, there still remains an undissolved Cartesian core to their ways of thinking. The alternative to this is not, contrary to some critics of cognitivism, to embrace more fully a 'materialist' metaphysics of the mental, but will be argued to consist in a richer appreciation of the *praxiological* character of cognition.

2 Cartesian and materialist precursors to cognitive science

For Descartes, the human mind is a *res cogitans* (a 'thinking thing'). However, not only does the mind think, but 'willing, understanding, imagining and feeling are simply different ways of thinking, which all belong to the soul (mind)'.[2] The human body can walk, speak, hit, run, jump and engage in all manner of observable behaviour, but it is the *res cogitans* alone which thinks, understands, imagines and feels. This component of the human being is unobservable to all; its operations, however, such as thinking, are observable only to its possessor. Animals – the lower forms of life – were for Descartes 'thoughtless brutes' inasmuch as they were not endowed by the Creator with a soul. This doctrine survived relatively unchallenged among men of letters as a philosophical and theological orthodoxy for two hundred years, and it was to haunt Darwin's attempt to establish a naturalistic evolutionary biology of man. In the mid-nineteenth century, Emil Du Bois-Reymond, along with Brucke, Ludwig and Helmholtz, the great physiologist of perception, attacked this vitalist conception of the human being in claiming that 'no other forces than the common physico-chemical ones are active within the organism'.[3] However, Du Bois-Reymond came to differ with his fellow 'scientific materialists' in refusing to accept a simple reduction of 'thought processes' to 'brain processes'; for him, the correct answer to the enigma of how the brain gives rise to thought had to remain: 'IGNORABIMUS' (Lelland, 1958).

In the mid-twentieth century, after much labour had been spent establishing and developing an essentially materialist science of human psychology in which the Cartesian *res cogitans* played no part, but in which the role of the neurophysiological system in the human being had also been (deliberately) neglected – behaviourism – a fresh attempt was made to re-establish a reductionist understanding of the nature of mind. The Place–Smart–Feigl–Armstrong 'identity thesis' was propounded (initially by Place (1956)),[4] although Bertrand Russell had earlier argued for a neo-Spinozan 'double-aspect' theory of mind and matter (Russell, 1956). According to the 'identity' theorists, any characteristically 'mental' event, such as a sudden thought occurring to a person, simply *is* nothing more than a sudden neuronal firing or other describable event in the brain, by strict analogy to the scientifically established identity between a flash of lightning and electrical discharge. Although some neo-Cartesians (notably Eccles (1953) and Beloff (1964)) attempted to reinstate 'mind' as a full-fledged entity of a non-physical kind, a move later to be more fully adumbrated by Eccles and Popper (1977) in their 'mind–brain interactionist' account, this 'materialist' account of the relationship between the 'mental' and the 'physical' became very influential, and in various ways formed a foundation for what was to emerge as the 'computationalist theory of mind, brain and behavior'.[5] As Palmer has recently argued in a paper on computationalist versions of the nature of human mental phenomena:

The computational approach is dependent upon the assumption that philosophical problems about mind and body have been solved in advance. If minds are just brains, i.e., if some sort of thesis of contingent identity is correct, then we no longer have Hume's problem. For the thesis of contingent identity is just the thesis that there are no logical problems with regard to the postulation of that identity . . . Hume's problem might be stated by saying that we cannot dispense with intentionality. The identity thesis might well be stated by saying that ultimately there are no logical problems which stand in the way of dispensing with intentionality, even though it may empirically be the case that we cannot. (Palmer, 1987: 62)

The problem of 'intentionality' alluded to here is not about intentions in the ordinary sense of, for example, commitments to behave in a certain way, but concerns the essentially *relational* character of our concepts of thought, thinking, understanding, imagining, remembering, and the like. If, as the contingent identity thesis supposes, a thought were nothing other than an event in the brain, we have the problem of connecting what the 'thought' is/was *about*, *of*, *in* or *that* (etc.), given that nothing can be a thought *simpliciter*: a thought is necessarily a thought *about* something/someone, *of* something/someone, in some form or another (e.g., in English, in some image), or *that* something is the case, and so on through the array of possible object-complements. Brain events, such as neuronal firings, are not grammatically connectable to *any* object-complements: one cannot have a neuronal firing that, of, or about anything! Even if one were to back up and propose that the *expression* of the (silent) thought to oneself (e.g., the silent soliloquistic expression of the word 'Four') were identical to a brain event, it is clear that such an expression can express many *different* thoughts depending upon the context and purpose informing its deployment. It may, for instance, be a selection of 'any numeral from one to ten' in response to a command to think of such a numeral, or it may specify the thought of how many parking tickets one still hasn't paid, or how old one's daughter turned yesterday, or the product of two and two, and so on. Taking the expression itself as constant, there remains the problem of how a neuronal firing (or any other plausible neurophysiological candidate for correlation with it) could be *identical* to the expression, as distinct from causally implicated in its production. We do not know how to individuate the expression in such a way that it could begin to make sense to map its components onto brain events, however conceived. For, unlike the written or spoken 'Four', which has parts (e.g., letters) or acoustic properties that can be (variously) analysed, an instance of an *un*written and *un*spoken 'Four' leaves us bereft of criteria for such an analysis. It is obvious that orthographic conventions and acoustic processing devices for measuring waveforms are both profoundly extraneous, historical, human constructions. What is the warrant for supposing that the human *brain's* operations work on the basis of such componentialising constructions? Moreover, if one were to suppose that some individuating criteria actually operate, how can one make the transition from a claim for neural correlation or causation to neural *identity* for such an expression? One can, after all, obey an order to say 'Four' to oneself, but one can scarcely obey an order to fire one's neurons in such-and-such a configuration. One can forget some expression, but one cannot forget (if one ever knew) a neuronal firing. If one were to *look at* a neuron firing (or any comparable brain event) via some appropriate neurological probe, would one thereby be looking at the expression 'Four'? Or, if one were to *listen to* a neuronal firing (or any comparable brain event) would one thereby *hear* the *silent* articulation (sic!) of this number? How *could* one hear something which makes no sound? And note that, in all this, we are no longer speaking about (silent) 'thoughts' but about natural-language or numerical expressions, any single one of which may, contextually, express *different* thoughts.

I took the example of 'thought' here primarily because it is in relation to the problem of the nature of thought and thinking that both Cartesian and materialist schemata have been considered solutions. Let us pursue this further by exploring the Turing-machine account of thoughts and thinking.

3   Turing's computationalist account of human thought/thinking

In October 1950, the great mathematician, cryptanalyst and founder of computer science in Europe, Alan Turing, published a paper in the philosophical journal, *Mind*. In this paper, entitled 'Computing Machinery and Intelligence', inspired by an earlier (1949) disagreement with the chemist-turned-philosopher, Michael Polanyi, who had argued for the uniqueness and formal 'unspecifiability' of the human mind, Turing introduced an operational definition of 'thinking' and 'intelligence' in the service of an argument in favour of the claim that a machine could think. If a computer could be programmed such that its responses to interrogations from a human being could not be distinguished from those of another human being, where its identity *as* a computer was kept concealed, then ' "fair play" would oblige one to say that it must be "thinking" ' (Hodges, 1984: 415). This 'imitation principle' was advanced by Turing as a criterion for thinking by virtue of his implicit acceptance of the argument from analogy for 'other minds' (Turing, 1950). It also resonated in behaviourist circles for its studied unconcern for the 'inner processes' of either man or machine, in adjudicating a claim about whether or not someone or something can be credited with 'thinking'. Recall that for the behaviourists only publicly – externally – observable behaviour was to be admitted into the domain of scientifically respectable psychological data. It promised, in fact, to re-connect Psychology to its long-neglected phenomena of the mental, and on purely materialist premises, too. After all, we *know* that computers cannot have souls, because *we* made them, not God (should God, perchance, exist at all)!

Wittgenstein had appeared to set his face against any such argument. He had written:

But a machine surely cannot think! Is that an empirical statement? No. We only say of a human being and what is like one that it thinks. We also say it of dolls and no doubt of spirits too. Look at the word 'think' as a tool. (Wittgenstein, 1953: para. 360, 1968 edn)

Is a computer sufficiently 'like' a human being to justify this extension of the predicate 'thinking' to it? In what respects would it have to be 'like' a human being to justify such an extension of use? Why wouldn't a successful Turing Imitation Game supply sufficient justification? We may be able to program computers to simulate – even to execute – complex human activities, but does this constitute endowing the machine with the capacity to think? The core of Wittgenstein's point here will have been missed if we pursue the argument in this way.[6]

When Wittgenstein denies that what is at issue here is an empirical question, he is (characteristically) proposing that an essentially *grammatical* (conceptual, logical) remark is being made. If my clock tells the time and my infant tells the time, has my infant learned to do what the clock could do already? Isn't the question: 'Can a machine think?' really comparable to one such as: 'Can a child in England marry?' and not to one such as: 'Can a pelican fly?' We do not need to inquire into the biological make-up and physical capacities of English children and compare our findings with those from inquiries into the biological make-up of children in small African tribes where they *can* marry, in order to answer this question; nor do we require to identify the subtle 'power to marry' with African children as we might feel obliged to study what about its inner workings gives a machine the 'power to propel a vehicle'. If a child on some occasion does exactly what an adult does during a wedding ceremony (cf. Turing's Imitation Game), could such a child genuinely be said to have married someone? No: the reason why no child can marry (in England) has nothing to do with his or her investigable biological capacities nor range of behavioural possibilities (after all, a child might be as large as a small adult and might go through a marriage ceremony word-perfect). The reason is simply: he or she *is a child*. As Sharrock and Anderson (1986b) point out, Turing clearly considered the fact that a computer is a machine as so *consequential* for the question of what can be accorded the capacity for thought/thinking that he sought to have that fact about it *concealed* in his test for the attributability of those predicates! Thus, Turing has incorporated into his test the very thing which, as Wittgenstein emphasised, was the centrally disputed matter – the relationship between the attributability of thinking to the possession of a human or human-like physiognomy. It is not that possessing the capacity for thought is being *reduced to* the having of hands, eyes, feet and other physiological manifestations of humanness, but rather that having a humanoid form is one of our principal criteria for being acknowledged as capable of having thoughts, for being able to think. Another is being embedded in *a human weave of life* such that one's thoughts can be intelligibly related to topics which are comprehensibly so derived and so connected. Sharrock and Anderson put the point starkly when they paraphrase Turing's Game in the following way: 'Overlooking the fact that it is a machine, can a machine think?' (Sharrock and Anderson, 1986b).

Similar arguments can be advanced in respect of the claim that a machine can be termed 'intelligent' if, say, it could print out (or generate speech simulations of) a simple conversation in the English (or any other natural) language. We surely do *not* appeal to a capacity to engage in a simple conversation itself as a sign of 'intelligence'; many idiots can converse at great and boring length, and many kids can converse about Batman and Robin without our yet feeling confident that they are capable of 'intelligent conversation'! A computational machine that could simulate such conversing might strike us as marvellous, a brilliant feat of engineering, programming and so forth, but not necessarily as a sign of intelligence. After all, 'artificial intelligence' need no more be counted as a kind of human intelligence than artificial flowers are types of flowers.[7]

4   Rule-governance in man and machine

A further issue which arises from the analysis of computation in relation to the study of cognition in human beings is that of 'rule-following'. Can cognition be 'built up out of a mastery of the "syntactical instructions" that man and machine both follow' according to the precepts of computationalist cognitive science (Shanker, 1987a: 634)?

It appeared that Turing had demonstrated that the algorithms by which any computational system proceeds could be described as 'complex systems of meaningless subrules each of which can as such be applied purely mechanically' (Shanker, 1987a). If a digital computer implements programs consisting of meaningless subrules in a mechanical fashion, then, given that the human brain seems to digitise sensory 'input' from the external world (its neurons firing either ON or OFF), both man and machine may be construed as species of syntactical-rule-governed, information-processing automata whose operations on information facilitate their 'behaviour'.[8] The important point here, as Stich (1983) has argued at length, is the *syntactical* character of the information-processing rules based upon the (model of the) Turing machine. A syntactical operation involves purely formal manipulations of physically realisable symbols: in the case of Turing machines, the symbols are 0 and 1, which can be realised as OFF (no electrical pulse/no nerve discharge) or ON (electrical pulse/nerve discharge) respectively. Alphanumerically expressible informational content of any kind may be represented in strings of zeros and ones, or *binary* strings, and transformations of such codified information can be effected by altering the (physical realisations of) arrays of zeros and ones. Referring to this as the *formality condition*, which any representational and information-processing model of cognition must satisfy to count as a materialist theory, Fodor argues that when we speak, for example, of someone's thinking of or about one thing rather than another, we are to translate this into statements about 'formally distinct internal representations (via the formality condition) . . . (which) can be functionally different – can differ in their causal role'[9] (Fodor, 1981: 240).

Shanker, in a brilliant article, has recently argued against the view that Turing succeeded in analysing, *inter alia*, a human calculative act or operation into a set of simple operations, mechanical in nature.[10] Drawing upon several themes from Wittgenstein's work on the foundations of mathematics, he notes that there are three different points 'to be considered in the premise that an algorithm breaks down the act of following a rule into a set of noncognitive instructions such that they could be followed by a machine' (Shanker, 1987a: 636–42). He notes, first, that there is a tendency to think that any algorithm decomposes complex rule-governed operations into a series of utterly simple, syntactically implementable, hence mechanisable tasks. 'But', he remarks, 'an algorithm is not a *precise formulation* of a pre-existing rule; rather, it is a *different* set of rules from the original which it is intended to supplant' (Shanker, 1987a: 637). The outcome of, say, Davis' Doubling Program, is 'completely different from squaring inasmuch as it employs addition and subtraction to bypass the need for multiplication' (Shanker, 1987a: 637).

To be sure, the outcome of the program corresponds to the results yielded by the rules for squaring; but what matters here is how we learn and apply the two systems of rules ... The correct answer to 'How did you calculate that the square of 125 is 15,625?' is 'I multiplied 125 × 125'; not 'I (or my brain, or my unconscious mind) added 125 to itself one hundred and twenty-five times'. What is really involved here is simply the fact that one set of rules can prove to be far more efficient than another for different contexts/purposes. (Shanker, 1987a: 637)

A second problem faced by the view that Turing analysed human rule-following into mechanisable algorithms (*as distinct from* the view that he formulated algorithms to be implemented in machines which could then perform what *for humans* would be rule-following operations) is this: it fails to preserve the distinction between 'following a rule mechanically' and 'following a mechanical rule' (Shanker, 1987a: 636).

Certainly when we calculate, many of the familiar rules are performed (sic) unreflectingly; but it is our ability to articulate these rules if called upon to do so which warrants our calling such behavior calculation ... For the fact that we might follow such rules unreflectingly in no way licenses the inference that they are noncognitive and *a fortiori* such that a machine could *follow* them. (Shanker, 1987a: 640–1)

Related to this is the third problem: Wittgenstein stressed the distinction between *normativity* and *causality* in relation to calculation: ' ... if calculation reveals a causal connection to you, then you are not calculating ... What I am saying comes to this, that mathematics is *normative*.' (Wittgenstein, 1978, VII, para. 61.) (The same is argued to hold for any 'rule-following', or 'rule governed', activity carried on by human beings.) For example:

Does a calculating machine calculate? Imagine that a calculating machine had come into existence by accident; now someone accidentally presses its knobs (or an animal walks over it) and it calculates the product 25 × 20.
I want to say: it is essential to mathematics that its signs are also employed in *mufti*. It is the use outside mathematics, and so the *meaning* of the signs, that makes the sign-

game into mathematics. Just as it is not logical inference either, for me to make a change from one formation to another (say from one arrangement of chairs to another) if these arrangements have not a linguistic function apart from this transformation. (Wittgenstein, 1978, V, para. 2)

Being able to generate correct answers is, Wittgenstein shows, necessary but not itself sufficient for us to predicate of that generator the practice of 'calculating', just as regularity in behaviour is in itself insufficient for the predication of 'rule-following'. To follow a rule is to be capable of appealing to it in justifications, corrections, explanations, instructions, etc. A computer does not have *reasons* for behaving as it does, and cannot justify nor explain its conduct as human agents can. A machine (including a Turing machine), then, does *not* 'follow rules' at all. Nor does it *calculate*: it *simulates* the human practice of calculation, just as the animals who accidentally press the knobs and generate the product of 25 times 20 have not multiplied 25 and 20 but may perhaps be said to simulate (i.e., give the appearance or effect of) the human achievement of 'multiplying 25 by 20'. Shanker concludes from this that

. . . the reason Wittgenstein laid such emphasis on the normativity of calculation *à propos* Turing's thesis was to clarify that the relation between a computation and the results which conform with it is *internal*, whereas in Turing's mechanical example the relation between input and output is strictly *external*, not conceptual; an account of the program can only explicate why the machine produced its results: not whether or not these were correct. For only the rules of calculation can establish this, and it is for this reason that they are *antecedent* to the machine's operations. (Shanker, 1987a: 639)

The signs of mathematics are also employed in mufti – in civilian, non-specialised circles and activities; so also the rules of computation and calculation are anterior to the construction of any machine whose operations simulate their being followed. Indeed, it is our human, *machine-independent* (capacity to) appeal to such normative rules which enables us to judge whether or not any given machine (Turing-machine, computer) is functioning *properly* or *mal*functioning. In Shanker's beautiful formulation, 'to mechanise rule-governed actions is to substitute, not subsume' (Shanker, 1987a: 639).

Computational artefacts were originally called 'electronic brains', and the idea has persisted, in both lay and some scientific/philosophical circles, that computers can be programmed to do at least some of the things which human brains can do, viz., calculate, handle information, store information, make inferences, work out chess moves, etc. The problem here is that such ascriptions of activities to the *brain* make no sense; it is not my brain which does these things, but me as a *person*. The analogy, therefore, if taken seriously, at best begs the issue of the correctness of a mind/brain identity theory and at worst thoroughly anthropomorphises or personifies the brain. In fact, the computer can do some of the things which *people* can do, not their brains, even though they naturally need their brains to enable them do to these things. Computers are better thought of as simulating persons. However, there are still serious difficulties which inhibit the appeal to computational processes as embodied *gedankenexperiments* for human 'cognitive' phenomena. I shall consider two of these in some detail: the treatment of 'understanding' in terms of 'processing', and the treatment of 'memory' and 'remembering' in terms of 'storage'.

5   Understanding language as mental/neural processing

Although certain details may differ among proponents of computationalist cognitive science, most treat 'understanding a sentence' in a natural language as involving a computational process in the brain.[11] Whereas for the Cartesian, understanding is an operation of the 'mind', materialist theories conceive of understanding as an operation of the cortex. Computationalist cognitivism sustains this version, and seeks to depict the nature of this putatively cortical operation.

On this view, what happens when a person understands a sentence must be a translation process basically analogous to what happens when a machine 'understands' (viz., compiles) a sentence in its programming language. (Fodor, 1975: 67)

The basic idea is that people are able to understand each other's sentences/ utterances by virtue of an internal process involving a 'mapping from wave forms onto messages' (Fodor, 1975: 108): sounds register on the cochlea and are transduced into impulses which travel via nerves to the relevant sector of the cortex where they are 'interpreted', enabling the person to 'understand' what has been said to him/her. Naturally, this picture accords very well with the way in which a computer may be designed to accomplish the processing of spoken utterances: an artificial cochlea digitises the wave forms and then a complex sequence of operations is set in motion whereby the stored phonological, lexical, syntactic, logical, and, more problematically, contextual information is brought to bear on the 'input', resulting in a print-out or equivalent display of what the sentence 'meant', or perhaps simply connecting to a system for generating a suitable) 'response'.

What this picture distorts is the asymmetry between man and machine with respect to the ascribability of the predicate 'hearing', along with the range of object-complements which this predicate can take. Whereas human beings can hear 'sounds', they never hear 'wave forms'. Computers cannot 'hear' anything – not even 'sounds' – but their artificial cochleae may be capable of detecting wave forms. Further, it is never the case that when humans ordinarily converse in a natural language they are simply hearing 'sounds'; what we normally hear are *words* and/or *utterances*, along with what speakers are doing when they talk to us. We can hear someone complaining to us, asking us a question, and so on. When it is appropriate to say of us that we are hearing only 'sounds', the circumstances are such as normally to *preclude* saying of us that we are hearing someone speaking to us in our language. For Fodor, and many other computationalists, we are thought *always* to be hearing mere 'sounds', which await the subsequent phase of our 'understanding' of them, a phase consigned to the workings of our central nervous system which is presumed to involve (unconsciously!) finding the 'meaning(s)' of the sounds. (The left-over question begged by this formulation remains: how do we understand the explanation of the meanings of the sounds provided by the putative computational process? Must we posit a *further* computational process to enable us to accomplish this? And so on, *ad infinitum*. And, *a fortiori*, how could we begin to understand such meaning-explanations if they are never – or only rarely – 'present to consciousness'?) If, however, we realise that we are able, directly, to hear what someone is saying to us, then there is no problem to be solved concerning the transition from mere 'sounds' to coherent, meaningful 'utterances'. Note, moreover, that 'understanding' what someone has said is treated as an invariantly necessary *supplement* to having heard what they said. This supplementary 'process' is projected by the computational theory into the CNS. However, 'understanding', despite its pseudo-present-continuous-tense appearance, is not a 'process' verb at all. Distinguishable from a genuine process-expression like 'trying to understand', actually 'understanding' (which is not always the upshot of a process of trying to understand) is akin to an achievement, as Ryle long ago pointed out (Ryle, 1949). One can think that one understood, but determine that one did not: one can try to understand unsuccessfully, and one can misunderstand, to list but a few of the ways in which this predicate can be conceptually combined. One's understanding is shown by what one can do, in how one behaves (whether one can successfully paraphrase the utterance, respond to it appropriately, etc.), in the public satisfaction of circumstantially relevant criteria, not by indicating anything like an internal process.[12] If 'understanding' is not a process verb denoting a spate of mental or neural activity, then it cannot be theoretically treated as a 'computational process'.[13] Understanding is a predicate usable for *persons*, not for their 'minds' (in the Cartesian sense) nor their brains.

The cognitivist account of natural-language comprehension in human beings is conceptually flawed. It arose in large measure because of a fundamental allegiance on the part of its proponents to a behaviouristic impoverishment in the description given to the objects of acoustic perception: for 'stimulus' read 'wave form'. This illicit transposition is nourished in turn by assigning a (possibly correct) characterisation of how a computer may be designed to carry out simulations of natural-language understanding to human beings whose conduct forms the target of the simulation in the first place. The remaining question to be answered, then, is: can a computer genuinely understand *anything*? If internal processes are not criteria for comprehension, then surely what a computer could be programmed to do with natural-language expressions fed to it via artificial cochleae or other sensors may (one day) qualify for the ascription of this predicate? If understanding an utterance is not a process, but akin to an achievement involving the satisfaction of behavioural, discursive kinds of criteria, then perhaps a computer could (at least in principle, notwithstanding reservations about current computational capacities) be credited (some day) with understanding a sentence in English?

One does not need to be a species-chauvinist to reject this contention. If someone can only produce a proper or appropriate response to someone's utterance or action *if he/she is fed instructions as to what to say or do*, then we may well wonder if he/she has the capacity to understand what is being said or done. We often *contrast* someone's being 'programmed' to say something (e.g., to come up with a bit of behaviour) and his/her being able to exhibit his/her understanding in what he/she independently says or does. A key issue in deciding whether or not someone really understood something said or done is *on what basis* did he/she produce his/her own conduct in relation to what was said or done. Merely producing a 'correct answer', or a 'well-formed sentence fitted to the occasion', cannot *in isolation* be counted as a criterion for having understood whatever was to have been understood. This is because we can readily envisage people requiring explicit guidance as to how to shape their behaviour in some circumstance, where they would otherwise be incapable of doing what they did. Such a situation could be counted as one in which the person did *not* himself/herself understand something, but needed help to *appear to* understand it. If I do not understand algebraic equations, but I am given some simple instructions as to how to put the symbols together in solving an equation by someone who *does* understand such matters, I may well deliver a response which appears to show that I have understood how to solve such equations. The central equivocality will remain, however: can I do this *on my own*, spontaneously, without guidance, assistance or explicit instruction from any other source? Only when I can show that I can solve equations without outside support will I ordinarily be credited with 'understanding algebraic equations'. No computer can produce anything without a program and the pre-wired circuitry which facilitates the running of its program. It is *this* which would make of even its most life-like performance only a simulation of comprehension, rather than the actual achievement of understanding.

6   Memory as stored representations

We may speak, quite properly, of computers storing and retrieving information from its 'memory banks' or, in contemporary parlance, its 'buffers'. According to the Cartesian picture, human beings remember things by virtue of bringing to consciousness the impressions left in (stored in) their minds by past events and situations. Roediger writes:

The conception of the mind as a mental space in which memories are stored and then retrieved by a search process has served as a general and powerful explanation of the phenomena of human memory. There is currently no other general conception of the mind or memory that rivals this view. (Roediger, 1980: 239)

According to the materialist turn in philosophy, especially the 'contingent mind–brain identity theory', it is not our 'minds' which store, retrieve or remember, but our brains. Once again, computationalist theory aims to concretise this claim by giving us a working thought-model for how a material entity (such as a brain) might operate so as to retrieve (in discursive or imagistic form) stored data.

Since the Platonic conception of memories as akin to the impressions left in a wax tablet, we have entertained in various forms the idea that what we recollect is somehow something within us, a trace or stored representation of the actual experience itself. 'Engram' theorising in neuropsychology is based entirely upon such a general postulate. In recent years, again largely due to the influence of Wittgenstein's later anti-Cartesian arguments, such a conception has been subjected to rigorous critical scrutiny and found wanting.[14] There are several points of attack and, in what follows, I shall outline these with brief accompanying arguments.

'Remembering' is, first and foremost, not a state or process; nor is it a discrete 'event': it is, rather, a defeasible-achievement verb. (In this sense, its grammar may be compared to that of 'understanding'.) We (claim to) remember, recall, recollect *p*, that *q* occurred, how to *r*, to do *s*, why *t* happened, and so on. Dispositional remembering may be distinguished from occurrent remembering: the former is (roughly) having learned and not forgotten (e.g., 'He remembers his high-school French', said of someone currently lying asleep in bed), the latter is a situatedly displayed or claimed reference to some witnessed past state of affairs. Apart from remembering *to* do, or *how* to do, something, occurrent rememberings are analysable as accounts of past states of affairs personally witnessed or encountered by the one claiming the recollection. Further, for any such claim to be (in principle) ratifiable intersubjectively, the past states of affairs must actually have transpired: 'to remember (recall; recollect, etc.)', in the occurrent sense, is factive in that what distinguishes actually remembering from *seeming to* have remembered or *thinking that* one remembered, is the truth of the object-complement. A *memory*, therefore, is (schematically) a *correct* account of any personally witnessed past state of affairs; a *memory-image* (as distinct from a daydream, for instance) is a visualisation of what was actually witnessed. Restricting our focus to discursive and occurrent 'remembering(s) *that X*' (as distinct from *non*-discursive 'remembering(s) *how to Y*', analysable as abilities or capacities: one cannot 'store' an ability or a capacity), the question arises: what could it mean to 'store' correct accounts of personally witnessed past events or visualisations of such events?

An 'account' can typically feature as a component of the illocutionary activity of 'telling'. What we tell someone is subject to the purposes of the telling, the audience for the telling, and other contextually variable contingencies. Storage models of discursive recollection must necessarily both decontextualise and reify elements of what is manifested in an account of some witnessed past state of affairs, treating such elements as enduring properties of persons' brains rather than as contextually variable features of a telling's construction.[15] Literal decontextualisation is not an intelligible option; reification is a logical fallacy. There is, then, no generic solution available for the individuation of 'what has been stored':

Individuations of events, experiences, scenes and occasions, as well as actions, utterances and other 'intelligibilia', are routinely accomplished by practical speakers for specific occasions, audiences and purposes. There are no decontextualisable standards or criteria for otherwise individuating 'what happened', 'what was said', 'who did what', 'when it occurred' and the rest of the possible object-complements for expressions such as: 'I (just) remembered ---'. (Coulter, 1983b: 86)

Turning to the phenomena of memory-*images*, we still cannot escape from the consequences of the individuation problem. No image in itself specifies what it is an image *of*.[16] Conceptual, discursive resources are required to enable a person to treat any given image as expressing some witnessed, past state of affairs. *Which* witnessed, past state of affairs? How is it to be characterised? Once again, we are driven to employing *some* accounting scheme, and, given the possibility of describing something in a indefinite range of *alternative* but equally correct/reasonable ways; once again we cannot escape from the constraints of context and purpose in framing whatever account we may give. Alter the context and purpose, and the particulars of the account can vary considerably. What, then, one may again ask, is *the* memory such that one could develop a theory about *its* location in the brain?

Rather than construe memories as *themselves* neurally-encoded phenomena, we should instead think of neural structures, states or events as enabling, facilitating *the situated production of memory-claims* (to oneself or others) in all their variety. Furthermore, by thinking of remembering this way, the presumed 'gap' between a 'memory' and its 'retrieval' can be seen to be an *artifact* of storage theorising, rather than a genuine puzzle for it to solve.

7   The praxiological approach to cognitive phenomena

To this point, my arguments have been directed against the idea that human 'cognitive' phenomena can be illuminated by appealing to the concepts and achievements of computational theorising. The conceptual apparatus of this way of thinking, however, reflects and preserves many of the assumptions, metaphors and preconceptions which together inform both the Cartesian and the materialist prejudices of some of our 'quasi-theoretic' ways of speaking generally about the mind. Beguiled by superficial characterisations of our mental language, we are apt to think that, for example, when we say something like: 'A thought (or an image, or a recollection) popped into my head', we are alluding to some event involving the sudden appearance of a mental phenomenon (e.g., 'a thought') in a spatial medium (the 'mind' or the 'brain').

We may casually say such things as: 'He doesn't "process" what you tell him very quickly', or: 'She erased the event from her memory'. It is the task of the scientist (cognitive psychologist, neurophysiologist) to tell us how this actually happens.

A broader and deeper inspection of the grammars of our concepts of the mental (having a thought, understanding, remembering, etc.) reveals that they all have ineliminable connections with what we say and do in various sorts of circumstances in the social world. The reification and interior projection of the putative 'referents' of these concepts, a practice which is in turn nourished by the kind of theorising which is erected upon a deep misunderstanding of their grammars, involves *severing* these constitutive connections with public circumstances and criteria. Wittgenstein, in his later writings, spent many paragraphs attempting to dissuade us from the notion that such concepts should properly be analysed on the model of names and their bearers, or labels and 'referents', and he showed clearly how our practices of language acquisition and use could scarcely be what they are if such concepts are labelled purely *inner* 'phenomena' or 'processes'. In his terms, the so-called 'inner' stands in need of 'outward criteria' (Wittgenstein, 1968: para. 580). Following such an insight leads us directly into *sociological* territory. In particular, we are lead to realise that every category of the 'mental life' is, without exception, available for members' use within situated practical actions, interactions and the circumstances they inhabit. What conjoins neo-Wittgensteinian with ethnomethodological inquiries in this domain is the claim that the meaning or intelligibility of our 'mental' language is to be determined by the elucidation of its practical, engaged use-in-context by competent (acculturated) users of the language and by its implication in courses of practical conduct.[17] In this sense, a distinctively ethnomethodological focus upon topics in the study of cognitive phenomena follows the 'praxiological rule'[18] and treats all cognitive properties of persons as embedded within, and thereby available from, their situated communicative and other forms of activities. The central issue becomes: *how* can members tell, and *how* do they make tellable, *inter alia*, their beliefs, memories, forgettings, dreams, understandings, thoughts, 'states of mind', the rules they are following, and the knowledge they possess?

Ethnomethodological studies relevant to this domain have been directed formally to specifying, with empirical materials gathered from the recording of actual instances of social episodes and interaction processes, how members can discern the beliefs of others (Coulter, 1979b), how members formulate claims to knowledge (Pomerantz, 1984a, and Sharrock, 1974), how members assign credibility to others' assertions (Brannigan and Lynch, 1987) how members make sense of novel settings (Pollner, 1979), how members display their comprehension of utterances (Moerman and Sacks, 1988), how members determine the 'thought(s)' another is having (Sharrock and Katz, 1978, and Sacks, 1980), how members assign psychopathological status (Smith, 1978, Coulter, 1973b, and Lynch, 1984), how members attribute motives to one another (Schwartz, 1976, and Watson, 1983), how members display that and what they have forgotten (Goodwin, 1987), how members deploy 'recollection accounts' (Bogen and Lynch, 1989) and a variety of social phenomena involving the attribution of, avowal of, inference from and orientation to other putatively 'mental' properties or attributes of persons.

It is beyond the scope of this chapter fully to articulate the details of these studies. They are richly detailed analytical contributions which resist summary abbreviation and paraphrase. Instead, in order to specify the kind of inquiry which is involved in following the praxiological rule in analysing the mental, I shall concentrate exclusively upon some aspects of an ethnomethodological treatment of the central topic for cognitive studies in general: *intelligence*. When considered as a practical, social construction, much of its apparent obscurity as a feature of human beings evaporates.

8 'Intelligence' in action

Both sides of the long-standing 'nature–nurture' dispute about human intelligence have assumed that intelligence is a measurable property of human beings. We have various tests for warranting claims about 'amounts' of this property ('I.Q.' scores) for humans, on the basis of which differences between people's scores are argued to be functions of differences in their genetic endowment and environmental conditions in some (contested) proportion, and we have as well the Turing test (see above) for checking its presence or absence in artefacts. A praxiological approach to the study of intelligence reveals the conceptual confusion inherent in such notions. We have already discussed aspects of the Turing test; in what follows, human-intelligence determinations become our focus.

It has long appeared to sociologists that their only role in the 'nature–nurture' debate about intelligence was to furnish data which could help decide the contribution of an environment's specifically sociological 'variables' to an individual's operationalised 'level of intelligence'.[19] Such 'variables' were characteristically 'gross' features of 'social structure' (e.g., poverty level, educational attainment of parents, degree of parental involvement in home-based 'education-related' tasks, etc.), formulated in quantifiable terms, and correlated with various test-performance outcomes. However, the details of actual testing operations as forms of practical action and interaction were not subjected to analytical scrutiny until their ethnomethodological study was initiated by David Roth (1974). Concentrating upon the administration of the Peabody Picture Vocabulary Test,[20] Roth produced transcribed segments of the communicative interactions between testers and children for analysis. His primary contention was that both testers and children must find locally, thus circumstantially variable, ways of enacting the testing rules, and the methods whereby the necessary 'standardisation' of test administration is achieved for practical purposes involve forms of judgement, background knowledge, reasoning and communicative abilities which the testing format must *suppress from consideration* in the interest of generating codifiably standardised data.

Analysis of the recordings [of test administration] brings the context-bound negotiation of the performances into clear view. It shows us how the children receive the instructions from the tester and establish with the assistance of the tester whether the situations that emerge are the ones they anticipated. The recordings show us how the children discover in the course of the test that the meanings of the test rules and the test items are not what they first thought. We see how the tester and child adapt to unanticipated events, such as intruders, bells ringing, and the need to go to the bathroom, etc. In some cases we also find the children recognise the test as one they have taken before, and the testers emphasise children's previous experience with tests in explaining what they are to do. (Roth, 1974: 156)

By analysing recordings of testing sessions, Roth determined that 'important information about the children's organising and conceptual abilities was lost when the only record of the testing interaction was the test score sheet' (Roth, 1974: 157). The Peabody test involved matching words to pictures: Roth quickly saw that both the words and pictures given 'tapped and indexed varied experiences in the children's backgrounds. They recognised the words and pictures as signs representing other things in their experiences . . . One signification might be presumed correct by the test and the other taken as incorrect even though it was equally complex and abstract' (Roth, 1974: 175). Instead of treating the test as indicating the extent of a child's verbal abilities, it could instead be argued that '*the Peabody test is insufficiently verbal because it limits the child's verbal performance to matching picture and word. When the child is encouraged to verbalise about the pictures and words, we find that he knows much more than the test score indicates*' (Roth, 1974: 203, original emphasis). The sheer arbitrariness of standardised tests such as the Stanford–Binet and the Peabody consists in the strict pre-specification of the units of knowledge to be determined, and of the restrictions upon either the possibility of, or the recording of, situated inquiries or elaborations on the part of the child. Mackay reports an especially relevant instance of this restrictiveness in flight:

After completing a state-wide reading test designed to measure reading and inference skills, children were asked by researchers how they had decided on answers. The children often linked the stimulus sentence and the answer in ways which the test constructor had not 'meant' but which demonstrated their inference/interpretive skills in providing reasonable accounts of the world. For example, the stimulus sentence of one test item was about an animal that had been out in the rain. The 'correct answer' was a picture of a room with dotted wallpaper walls and a floor imprinted with a trail of animal tracks. When the child was asked what the picture was about, she replied, 'It's snowing'. When questioned about the design on the wallpaper – 'Do you know what these are?' – she replied, 'sprinkles'. The child had perceived the picture to be the exterior of a house with snow falling rather than the interior of a house covered with dotted wallpaper. Because of this 'misperception' she had chosen an answer which while it was reasonable within the frame of reference was the wrong answer. While the child demonstrated the inference/interpretive skills that were claimed to be 'measured by the test', no credit was given for this item. (Mackay, 1974a: 183–4)[21]

Happening to know some array of 'X's' (words, pictures) is not in itself, and in abstraction, a sufficient condition for our predicating 'intelligence' or 'verbal skill' of *anyone* in routine contexts of living. Test situations themselves are a particular species of social life, and are not somehow exempt from their own pragmatic contingencies such that they could be treated as transcendental vantage-points on any other communicative contexts. They cannot be considered as especially privileged modes of discernment; they are akin to games, and children assimilate them in this way. They are not encounters from within which supposedly pristine, trans-contextual attributes of *personae* may be revealed.[22] Although convenient as glosses, intelligence-test scores are useless as generic substitutions for situated attributions of intelligence. There need be no contradiction between someone's 'having a high I.Q.' and his behaving in a manner clearly appraisable on occasion as 'unintelligent'. Theorising about intelligence in the abstract too readily engenders its reification; it is forgotten that 'intelligence' is, first and foremost, *a nominalisation of an adverbial qualifier of (courses of) action*[23] (Coulter, 1989: 110). It has nonetheless been the practice of many proponents on *both* sides of the 'nature–nurture' issues in respect of 'intelligence' to predicate their studies upon test-outcomes. Criticisms of any such tests as 'culturally biassed' in relation to ethnic, class or other dimensions of possibly 'contaminating' differentiation are nonetheless still founded upon the argument that *some* such test can be constructed so as to 'reveal' persons' 'real' level or amount of 'intelligence' in some context-transcendent fashion. Researches such as those by Roth and Mackay indicate in fine detail how such tests, in their real-time character as administered schedules, structure and constrain the accountability of the very specific environments they are used to create. Rather than reflecting competences across contexts, they simply abbreviate and index such abbreviations of their own system of (locally managed) relevances. In this sense, they have in common with other pre-coded schemata for generating 'standardised' data sets the property of deleting and disguising the 'lived work' of their implementation. However, aside from the spuriousness of 'scientific' claims based upon their invocation as *explananda*, the 'official' recording of, and consultation of, intelligence quotients so generated may be consequential in a variety of ways in future determinations of a person's (scholastic and other occupational) prospects.[24] As putatively 'objective' substitutions (e.g., 'low I.Q.') for the 'subjective' appraisals of teachers and others (e.g., 'dull', 'dim-witted', etc.), they simply give the (challengeable) impression of the determinate quantification of a property, instead of the contestable specification of an opinion.

9   Concluding remarks: cognitive predicates in human action

Discussing Wittgenstein's account of 'thinking', Malcolm remarked: 'Thinking in one's mind (silent thinking, pausing to think) is not the most fundamental form of thinking, but instead presupposes thinking in play, work, or words' (Malcolm, 1978: 415). With the obvious exception of 'thinking aloud' in words, these latter forms of thinking in action are not necessarily themselves *discursively* manifested. One may attribute a 'thought' to someone which has a relatively 'complex' discursive content (such as: 'if two magnitudes are equal to a third, they are equal to one another') without thereby assigning such discursive content to the 'mind' or the talk of the subject of the attribution: a carpenter's wordless measurement and matching operations may entitle him to such an attribution (Malcolm, 1978: 414).[25] In *Zettel*, Wittgenstein develops this point by having us imagine a scenario in which someone is constructing something out of pieces of material. He selects some pieces, rejects others, selects and compares others, all the while making natural expressions of annoyance, puzzlement and eventually of triumph. He is then shown a film of himself doing these things: as he watches, he remarks: 'Then I thought: No, that won't do, I must try it another way', and so on. He had not, however, while originally at work, either spoken nor imagined these very words. Neither had he been operating 'mechanically' or 'thoughtlessly', however. Wittgenstein proposes that there is nothing in our concept of 'thinking', nor of 'having a thought', which precludes the worker properly saying of himself later, when watching his filmed behaviour, that he *thought* those things while he was at work even though he did not articulate them explicitly either in verbal remarks or 'in his head'. Thinking, even of fairly complex sorts, is not manifested solely in *discursive* conduct (Wittgenstein, 1968: 413):[26] neither is it a purely 'mental' phenomenon.

Similarly, 'intelligence' is not manifested solely through I.Q. results, nor is it manifested in *any* genuinely quantifiable manner. Is this merely a conceptual prejudice? Eysenck argued that it is, in the following passage:

The term intelligence originated, as we have seen, in departments of psychology and philosophy; it is by no means clear why we should give up using it because it is suggested that the man in the street uses it in rather a different sense. (Eysenck, 1973: 69)

As Block and Dworkin observe, Eysenck's philology is suspect. They note that the *OED* lists 'many uses of "intelligence" and "intelligent" in their present senses from the fifteenth century onward' (Block and Dworkin, 1976b: 431). Their main point, however, is that we cannot have it both ways:

One cannot use 'intelligence' to refer to what people ordinarily refer to when they use words like 'smart', and then also use it as a technical term stipulated to refer to whatever it may be that IQ tests test. The current social role of IQ tests is based on the presupposition that these two usages of 'intelligence' have the same reference. *But this presupposition is insistently ignored by too many of those whose intellectual responsibility is to either justify or reject it.* (Block and Dworkin, 1976b: 431, emphasis added)

For those who seek to transpose a conception of 'thinking' whereby a machine could be said to 'think', we might enter a parallel objection: all such efforts have been founded upon a very narrow and sometimes utterly inadequate appreciation of the socially occasioned role of this predicate in the weave of living, human affairs within which it has its primary home. In part because of the simple dichotomy of Cartesian *vis-à-vis* 'materialist' ontologising, both of which preserve an essentially unidimensional conception of what 'thinking' is, of how the concept actually functions in our lives, and in part because of a neglect of the fundamentally sociological – praxiological – character of concept-use, the human sciences have been operating with chimera in the domain of cognition. A major step toward a richer and more sophisticated appreciation of the phenomena of analytical interest to students of cognition will be taken once the lessons of Wittgensteinian and ethnomethodological inquiry are digested.

NOTES

1 A consequence of this argument is developed in the following chapter by John Lee when he takes up the issue of cognitivism in human science specifications of the relationship between language and culture.

2 Descartes, to Mersenne, 1637, in *Oeuvres de Descartes* (ed. C. Adam and P. Tannery, Vol. I, Paris, 1897), cited in Kenny (1970). Descartes, in ascribing such capacities to the 'soul', was one of the first to effect a link between the immortal soul and the material body of man, even though he is often correctly credited for codifying a 'mind–body dualism'. For, in treating the soul in this way, he could later propose a link between the corporeal brain of man and his transcendental soul via the operation of the pineal gland.

3 See R. Virchow, *The Mechanistic Concept of Life* (1850), trans. in Lelland (1958), and Shanker (forthcoming).

4 See also Place (1988). Place writes of the impact of materialist–reductionist analyses on the treatment of the mind–body problem as follows: 'Truly a remarkable transformation [has taken place] from the situation that existed thirty years ago, when every philosopher you met was quite convinced that whatever answer to the mind–body problem, if there is one, is true, materialism must be false' (Place, 1988: 208). For J. J. C. Smart's position, see Smart (1959), for Herbert Feigl's position, see Feigl (1958), and for D. M. Armstrong's position, see Armstrong (1968).

5 One of the most comprehensive arguments for the theoretical potency of computationalist cognitive science remains that of Dennett (1978).

6 In the ensuing paragraph, I am indebted to some arguments in Sharrock and Anderson (1986a).

7 Daniel Dennett once claimed in a lecture to the Boston Colloquium for the Philosophy of Science (1987) that we should no more hesitate to conceive of artificial intelligence as a type of intelligence than we should hesitate to conceive of artificial colouring as a type of colouring. This strikes me as an artifact of a one-sided diet of examples. I owe the 'flowers' example to Wes Sharrock.

8 For the classic source of this model and its elaboration in psychology, see Newell and Simon (1972).

9 An interesting Wittgensteinian critique of the views of both Stich and Fodor is furnished by Williams (1985).

10 For a defence of this interpretation of Turing's achievement, see Wang (1974).

11 This way of construing 'understanding' is also found in linguistics and anthropology. In the following chapter John Lee specifically takes this matter up with respect to linguistic and anthropological treatments of language and culture.

12 For a lengthy discussion and critique of cognitivist versions of 'understanding' language-use, see Baker and Hacker, 'The Generative Theory of Understanding' in Baker and Hacker (1984). See also their fuller treatment of the logical grammar of 'understanding' in 'Understanding and Ability' in Baker and Hacker (1980: 595–620).

13 For a more comprehensive treatment of this topic, see Coulter (1984).

14 For a superb review of theories of memory from antiquity to the present from a late-Wittgensteinian point of view, see Malcolm (1977).

15 For more detailed discussion of the 'individuation problem' for storage models of memory, see Coulter (1983b). Shanker (1987a), however, has drawn critical attention to a source of ambiguity in the conclusion to my earlier account of storage in this work.

16 See for instance Wittgenstein (1968: 185).

17 For elaborations of this claim, see Coulter (1979a, 1983b, and 1989).

18 For discussion of this rule and its implications for analysis, see Anderson, Hughes and Sharrock (1985).

19 See the contributions of Kamin, Bane and Jencks, and Carl Bereiter in Block and Dworkin (1976a).

20 Arthur Jensen, in his famous (or notorious) paper, 'How Much Can We Boost I.Q. and Scholastic Achievement?' (Jensen, 1969), cites the Peabody, the Raven and the Stanford–Binet as tests of abstract problem-solving, the latter construed by him as a significant 'component' of 'conceptual intelligence'.

21 Also see Mackay (1974b).

22 For some critical discussion of 'Intelligence as a Natural Kind', see this section of Coulter (1983b).

23 This is true also for many other categories of 'personality'.

24 The pragmatics of determinations such as these are more fully explored in Cicourel and Kitsuse (1963).

25 See Wittgenstein (1968: para. 330).

26 See Wittgenstein (1967: para. 100).

9

Language and culture: the linguistic analysis of culture[a]

John R. E. Lee

1 Introduction

There is a traditional puzzle about the relationship between the linguistic and the socio-cultural.[1] In this chapter I want to suggest that it involves a question about the relationship between linguistics and sociology. Specifically, the question concerns the relationship between their methodological and theoretical frameworks. There is a certain amount of comfortable correspondence between linguistics and sociology which is not surprising given that there are parallels and even direct connections between Durkheim and Saussure, for example. This chapter examines some basic aspects of this complex relationship. A main theme will be the identification of inadequacies in the models constructed by linguists in order to account for the relationship between language and culture. Notable are those inadequacies which accrue from the excessively 'cognitive' emphasis of linguistic models.[2] Such cognitive models give, at most, residual status to the *social* character of language – its *social organisation*. Indeed, it will be suggested that this cognitive emphasis is a conceptual outgrowth of linguistic treatments which have an in-built philosophical prejudice against the contemplation of action and the social dimension.

The argument will develop two strands. The first will consider the way in which attempts are made to accommodate the social aspects of language within the largely unmodified principles and suppositions of conventional linguistic theorising. Language is conceived in terms of linguistic theory, and the social is accommodated by showing how social variables determine, or are otherwise related to, linguistic ones. The second strand concerns the nature of the social. If the notion of language remains problematic, the notion of 'the social' is much more considerably so. There is less of a consensus about the fundamentals in sociology than in linguistics, so the attempt to interconnect social phenomena with linguistic ones is often no more than a witting, or unwitting, attempt to utilise linguistic resources to provide secure or well-

[a] I would like to thank two friends for their assistance in writing this chapter. Wes Sharrock, as always, gave generously of his time and capacity to make more sense of what I say than I do. Rod Watson has discussed these ideas with me.

196

founded theoretical and describable objects. In fact, there is no comparably well-entrenched conception of the social.

Generally, the problem of the relationship of language to culture has been conceived in terms of *abstract* specification. For example, saying whether one (culture) includes the other (language), or whether language causes cultural effects or vice versa. The idea or concept of the social within the specification does not, however, match the concern that linguists have manifested for the systematic description of their phenomena-in-hand. There is in fact no systematic scheme for the description of culture's organisation.

This kind of equation that is manifest in the relationship between linguistics and the social is common in sociology. Both of the terms are unknown and the connecting signs of uncertain character. However, the fact that such equations cannot really be resolved without a great deal of specification does nothing to discourage attempts to generate statements about language and culture. For instance, whatever their failings, cognitive anthropologists put the description of culture to the forefront as a foundational problematic. If, however, the legitimacy of cognitive anthropology's concern is for the need – under a programme of systematic, integrated analytic description – to develop some systematic treatment of the organisation of empirically found cultures, then the same need is very fundamentally present in Harvey Sacks' concerns. Sacks likewise finds unsatisfactory the attempt to articulate relations amongst social phenomena in entirely abstract ways, dissociated from the construction of an organised method of description. He argues that those who talk about 'social organisation', 'culture' and so forth, literally do not know what they are talking about (Sacks, 1963).

However, in proposing to take up 'language' as a topic of sociological investigation, Sacks demands a *respecification* of that phenomena as a topic of enquiry. He cannot leave in place the conventional apparatus of linguistic theory, for this apparatus is not designed for the analysis of *talk*. From Sacks' point of view, the attempts which have been made to recognise the fundamental presence of 'the social' in language, because language is found in talk and consequently, in social relations, by partially backtracking or diluting fundamental assumptions of existing linguistics, do not work. They are unable to provide for the comprehensive, thorough and systematically worked out description of the very organisation of talk. The attempt to relate the analysis of talk to the analysis of sentences or propositions will produce analytic muddle by mixing together incompatible frameworks. Sacks therefore provides a completely fresh start, one which seeks to develop ways of discovering and describing phenomena that are subsumed under the headings of 'language' and 'culture'.

The comfortable but unprincipled alliance between 'the linguistic' and 'the social', often accompanied by 'cognitivism', makes its appearance in the classic roots of both sociology and linguistics. An examination of this will form the first part of this chapter and serve to illustrate that fact, and the nature of the problems it produces. The second part will examine more contemporary attempts to use 'language' as the basis of the analysis of culture. It will be suggested that they are not free of some of the classic conceptual presuppositions which serve to make their work problematic. Thirdly, I will review certain attempts to resolve the problem of the relationship by the production of socio-linguistic theory. It will then be possible to demonstrate the revolutionary alternative that Sacks provides. This will be done by contrasting his work with the seminal and influential studies that will have been seen to have historically influenced contemporary thinking, and which may be used to draw out the problems which beset the traditional ways in which the question of the relationship between language and the social has been conceived.

2 Sociology and cognitivism: the traditional analysis of language form

One way to observe the mutually incompatible schemes of relevance of the traditional linguist (whose products are often adopted as resources by sociologists) and the analytic organisation required for the analysis of talk as natural action, is to start with De Saussure's (1916) distinction between 'langue' and 'parole'. With 'la langue' he focussed upon what he considered to be the proper province of linguistics: the construction of theoretically pure synchronic systems or codes of grammatical, logical, and phonological reality. Chomsky's generative grammar could, in some respects, be taken as the modern equivalent of this, and the distinction he makes between 'competence' and 'performance' is foreshadowed by the Saussurean distinction.

By 'parole' Saussure was referring to 'performance', to the activity of talk as contingently produced. Whilst this represents a base from which linguistic rules and categories are abstracted, it nevertheless reveals these in a degenerated form. The task of the linguist is purification, which means the elimination of individual differences, and of the irregularity marked by individual choice in contingent situations. The goal of analysis is to provide general systematic organisation, a goal which would necessarily be frustrated by consideration of local or contingently produced organisational relevances.

There is an obvious parallel here with De Saussure's intellectual mentor, Durkheim. Durkheim thought of 'social facts' as statistical regularities, as opposed to irregular and psychologically motivated individual activities. In this way 'social facts' could be conceived of as theoretically general (Durkheim, 1895, 1964 edn). At the level of 'method' the parallel continues. Following Durkheim, Saussure and many subsequent linguists and sociologists have sought to describe their materials in terms of pre-formed theoretical categories. They do this by treating them as representations, or as samples, arrived at by abstracting away contingent organisation in favour of requirements dictated by the logic of comparative analysis. Linguistic and logical categories of 'the language' appear, then, as both general and objectively given resources for facilitating de-contextualising schemes to describe and compare data.

Durkheim (1903, 1963 edn) himself treated language as furnishing formal classifications of the social. He saw these as reflecting and emanating from social organisation. However, because he deals with language in what is a very abstracted form, and not with occasioned language activities, he is free to seek a relationship between action and language categories by treating the latter as cognitively encoded thought structures. To Durkheim, language is the gateway to the 'Group Mind'. However, it should be noted that to accept this argument is to accept without question the argument, *contra* Wittgenstein, that language is, or can be, represented as a cognitive system. It might also be noted that Durkheim did not question this assumption, though given that he had abstracted language from its role in social practice and situated activity this is not surprising.

The loss created by sociology's treatment of language as a phenomena out-of-context may be revealed in the work of Durkheim and Saussure's protégé, Lévi-Strauss (1963). Lévi-Strauss, like Durkheim, understands language to be an underlying cognitive system for distinguishing meanings or symbols which relate to, or engage with, other logically ordered cognitive systems. Language is seen as furnishing context-free contrastive symbolic concepts or binary oppositional categories. These constitute our understanding of the empirical world by providing organising frameworks that allow human societies to structure their culture in ways that are broadly similar. In many respects his central thesis, that language, or logic categories, organise our knowledge and culture, is similar to the Whorf–Sapir hypothesis, though he emphasises cultural similarities whereas they emphasise relativity and difference.

Though Lévi-Strauss has an interest in comparative detail, his synthesising concepts, abstracted from natural language, are structured to facilitate general comparison. Consequently, it is not possible to see how his constructed formal categories engage with, or relate to, the *in situ* orientations of natural language users, and therefore to the organisation of language activity. His work reveals the central deficit of this approach to language in sociology. Language is conceived outside an organisational context. Even his so-called binary oppositional categories, such as 'left' and 'right', or 'black' and 'white', cannot be said to be 'opposites' outside an organisational context in which they are produced and provided for as opposites. By taking his categories for granted, Lévi-Strauss rejects any interest in the question of how societies' members organise those categories as a practical accomplishment.

3   The linguistic analysis of culture

The tradition jointly launched by Durkheim and Saussure, which was carried forward by Lévi-Strauss and, in a different way, by Whorf–Sapir and cognitive anthropology, has involved treating natural language, or language in general, as though it were *fact-stating*. That is, language is seen as making reference to, or corresponding with, reality; as expressing meanings, mental entities or ideas. It follows, therefore, that through an examination of language, its propositions and formal expressions, we should be able to arrive at the society's corresponding ideas or thought objects. Language can thus provide for the investigator access to a society's ways of thinking or its cultural 'reality'.

Given this orientation (or, rather, set of pre-suppositions) then it becomes possible to ask the question: 'what do differences and similarities in language amount to?' Taking on board the view that language expresses a cognitive system then a further question may be asked: 'do the phonetic, morphological, and semantic discriminations tell us that individuals are caught up in discrete cognitive systems that reciprocally organise different cultures?' This view is expressed in the Whorf–Sapir hypothesis, and the opinion that cultures can be extracted from language represents the position of cognitive anthropology. Because these versions are the most systematic expositions of these general theses, I shall examine them later on in some detail by contrasting their approaches to language and culture with that of Harvey Sacks.

Before doing so, however, I wish to pose the possibility that the conception of language as 'fact-stating' and, relatedly, as expressing cultural reality in a cognitive system, is highly problematic. For a start, if we consider *natural language* instead of formalised, de-contextualised, or abstracted language samples, it is not at all apparent that we can un-problematically identify instances of fact-stating or referencing. If we follow Sacks and look at instances of natural language use, we might be able to see how those instances can be consequential. But it is by no means apparent that specific utterances are *ever* notably useful and *validly* identified as 'fact-stating' or expressing cultural knowledge.

This being the case then, it is hard to know what to make of the arguments of contemporary analysts who either uphold or attack versions of the Whorf–Sapir language relativity claim on empirical grounds. The claim is that the variability of language expresses, or is matched by, variability in the cultural knowledge that language expresses. However the in-principle question of whether 'language' *per se* says anything at all about the way people think may not be resolvable empirically, but may involve a conceptual analysis of the ways in which we understand 'language'.

Yet much modern work sets out to show how attempts to relate world views to the possession, or lack, of linguistic structures have been based on faulted empirical linguistics, particularly faults of omission.[3] Kearney's (1984) sociological argument, that the prevalence of surface pronouns in capitalist countries reflects the world view of capitalist individualism, is seen as standing or falling on the question of whether, in terms decided by technical linguistics, the correlation is a good one or not (see Hill, 1988). Whilst theoretical development in functional linguistics might quite properly decide whether, in their own terms, a given linguistic form exists or not, it has no means to describe or analyse a people's thought and activities without the referential and cognitive assumptions previously alluded to. It is interesting to compare a linguistic referential version of pronoun function with much more multi-faceted interactional versions produced by Sacks (see Watson, 1985).

Consider the following:

The pro-drop variable appears to all human language; in some language, *the choice can become meaningful and express a view of the world.* The mere presence of one or another kind of form, however does not allow the inference of a particular concept of the self. (Hill, 1988, emphasis added)

Whilst this is produced as a cautionary example from someone upholding a 'moderate version of the language relativity claim', it fails to provide any constraints as to what would allow the inference from a regularity of grammatical form to cultural meanings and the expression of a way of life.

Recognising situational variation and the complexity of cultural difference, certain functional grammarians have argued that less emphasis should be placed on either uniqueness of form or linguistic variation. By contrast it is suggested that linguistic universals might be identified by asking if these relate to universal human capability. If one could construct linguistic universals, then it might be possible to see variations in the way in which they are culturally integrated. In this spirit questions are asked as to whether or not 'animal hierarchies', as expressed by, or in, 'grammar' are, or might be, considered to be 'universals' (Silverstein, 1976a). Against Tyler's (1984) claim that the visual sense of 'see' has a grammatical preference in relation to knowledge acquisition in Western language is Viberg's (1983) argument that many non-Western languages reveal the same preferences if subjected to deeper analysis, thereby providing ammunition against relativity, and suggesting the possibility of universal structure.

However, the underlying problem of all such studies is the lack of a principled way of relating linguistic form to cultural reality, and to ways of thinking or acting that these forms are presumed to manifest.

Modern investigations of 'form' do, of course, give recognition to questions of situational variation and context. For example, Silverstein (1976a and 1976b), Atkinson (1979) and Ochs and Schieffelin (1979), recognise the fact that language-in-use is not just fact-stating, but is multi-functional in a way that, for instance, Whorf–Sapir and cognitive anthropology did not. Focus has therefore to *some extent* shifted from questions of synchronic form towards a concern with speech, speech acts and diachronic language comprehension. The impossibility of separating language comprehension from background cultural knowledge which informs its production has also received different kinds of emphasis from many. For instance McLendon (1977) and Kempson (1975) are concerned with 'presupposition' and 'assertion' in relation to given cultural contexts. However, their work immediately raises the issue of the use of such theoretically established comparative classificatory categories. These classificatory categories for the description of utterances or utterance parts are not obviously invocations of natural language categories.[4] The question is whether such classificatory categories can unequivocally identify, or whether they are a function of an analytical collection composed to meet largely unknown constraints. A second problem concerns how they are related to what is done in speech. Categories like 'presuppositions' or 'propositions' present an analytic problem in that they gain their sense from their status as categories in logic rather than as recognisable human *activities* produced in speech.

A focus upon speech as activity is explicit in the work of Silverstein (1979), who insists on the necessity of recognising *classification systems* other than those designed to reflect referential uses of language. His work, together with that of Atkinson (Atkinson, 1982) and the work sponsored by Ochs and Schieffelin (1979), into language acquisition, attempts to show that both language and cultural acquisition is related to the stage-by-stage acquisition of different (language) functions.

Atkinson (1979) proposes that the ability to refer (in speech) 'presupposes' attention drawing, and he argues that the latter must, therefore, be a temporarily prior occurrence. This he suggests, explains the existence of 'attention manipulators' common in early years, where children learn to 'attend to' such objects as 'doggie', rather than to make statements. Apparent questions raised by children could be similarly interpreted as 'attention attractors', as children seem to ask questions only to answer them.

Ochs and Schieffelin (1979), and Schieffelin and Ochs (1987) likewise argue that it is the communicative process underlying conversation that guides the emergence and development of syntactic structures on language. They argue with Platt (Ochs and Schieffelin, 1979: Ch. 2) that, via participation in speech events, the child may learn how to encode 'propositions' by participating in a sequence which contributes a component of a proposition. Hence, they argue that one must analyse interactions' sequential construction rather than, for example, linguistic 'sentences', in order to understand the acquisition of, and the nature of, 'fundamental logical and pragmatic functions of utterance constraints'. However, as in this example, despite the fact that they see themselves as language pragmatists, they have no reservation about the use of categories derived from linguistics and logic to classify speech phenomena. They are unconcerned to provide constraints that might enable us to recognise the description 'proposition' as an object oriented to by speakers in the context of production.

The problem with multi-functionality as recognised by Silverstein and Atkinson is that they seem to require the replacement of the 'fact-stating model' of language with a set of models or a multi-dimensional model, which provide for a multiplicity of broad functions that relate to, or provide for, basic speech activities. The aim would seem to be a meta-linguistic list of language functions, and the theoretical discovery of how these are accomplished by, or in, linguistic forms or structures. This would necessitate the investigation of language from the theoretical base of identifying phenomena by their broad function. This contrasts with Sacks' orientation to speech as a field in which we might recognise a vast variety of different activities and where we must take care *not* to overgeneralise the language's own categories and expressions.,

Sacks' method of looking at conversational materials is designed to get around all attempts to impose theoretically given, poorly defined, and empirically problematical, categories onto utterances. Instead, a start is made by attempting to identify intuitively occasioned categories which could *unequivocally* identify *specific* utterances. To Sacks, the analyst should be able to say of an utterance, for example, *whatever else it does*, at least it (say) asks a question or makes a joke. The initial strategy is to *invoke the language's own categories* for the description of utterances, not to develop an analytical collection of them. Such a latter set of categories may be composed to meet heterogeneous and perhaps largely unknown constraints. They are not introduced out of a knowledge of the empirically findable properties of speech. Of course *given* that one is proposing to use the language to find out how its own categories are applied, then one immediately appreciates that the methods for the application of those categories cannot be those developed by linguistics or sociology, but must be the languages' own methods.

4   Linguistics and sociology: the search for connections

Many divisions and differences exist in the general field of socio-linguistics associated with such names as Fishman, Labov, Hymes, Gumperz and Erving-Tripp. However, all of them have generally been concerned with the study of language in its socio-cultural context, and also to a greater or lesser extent, with a concern to establish theory that seeks to relate language structure and function to culture and context. At the macro-linguistic level are correlatory Durkheimian studies that attempt to examine the relationships between language choice and social organisational contexts. These merge with studies that have attempted to relate language choice and code switching to institutional contexts. Fishman (1964, 1965 and 1972) suggested that there are different domains which constrain the use of one language variety over another. Thus for example, 'family' may constitute a context or a domain in which everyday topics, location, and the nature of roles of participants may provide for the use of 'low' rather than 'high' language. As with Greenfield's (1972) Fishman's studies were not, however, naturalistically based.

Such studies did, though, direct attention to the situational influences on language regularities, and they served to generate an interest in the question of how talk is organised and competently used in a context. Above all they raised the question as to whether 'parole' itself can be seen as involving normative cultural rules or structures which control 'competent' speech performances in a regular fashion. Erving-Tripp's (1972) analysis of rules of consistency and competence in the use of address terms, resting on the application of logic as much as the discovery of natural language organisation, can be seen as an analysis oriented towards the description of linguistic competence.

Hymes (1974) points to the influence of context. He points out that speech organisation itself is used as part of the background relevancies by which persons interpret messages. The performance of an utterance is regulated by its being part of, for instance, a joke, a narrative, an interview, a sermon or a lecture. Blom and Gumperz (1972) writing on code switching in a Norwegian village concluded that choice of code (for example dialect against formal language) in the course of conversation may affect the interpretation of a speaker's intentions, and thereby bring about differences in speakers' perceptions of each other and, therefore, influence the style of talk and the choice and nature of topics.

Hymes (1972 and 1974) searches for a theory of 'communicative competence' in an attempt to develop a theory of language which extends Chomsky's notion of linguistic competence into the socio-cultural domain. His aim is the formulation of abstract rules for specifying the competencies underlying the use of language functions. The socio-linguist's goal is seen as the provision *of a theory* which accounts for the production of orderly competent, meaningful talk within a normative framework.

Central to Gumperz's (1982) similar ambition is his view that talk ongoingly provides 'cues' and 'clues' for interlocutors as to a framework from which, or by which, participants make situated interpretations of each other's speech. He sees speakers as proceeding by way of 'conversational inferences' (context-bound processes of interpretation) which provide for their responses. Thus talk occurs in relation to furnished background assumptions about context, interactive goals, and interpersonal relations. The talkers derive 'frames' from out of expectations provided by the above, which they can use to interpret utterances. Included amongst these are, or can be, expectations about physical setting, participants' background knowledge and attitudes to each other, socio-cultural values concerning role relationships and social values etc.

These conversational strategies are not, however, just determined by external social constraints, but also by normative frameworks established from within the situation and its development. Contextualising cues are creative of contexts that allow speakers' interpretations to be inferred. Overall, Gumperz argues that we need to construct a theory as to how cultural background knowledge informs the establishment of these normative frameworks in the production of talk.

So, for both Gumperz and Hymes, the organisation of talk has some relation to the problem of how it is that social actors solve the problem of order, and how they co-ordinate their activities in meaningful ways. Their solution is much like Goffman's (1974 and 1981) for they posit that in the course of talk actors project a definition or frame that provides for appropriate interpretation, and hence appropriate normative conduct.

However, somewhat surprisingly, despite the fact that Gumperz recognises the import of the fact that 'we cannot assume that the linguist's notion of a grammatical system is equivalent to the folk notions of language' (Gumperz, 1982: 21), he, like other socio-linguists, is still concerned with objects as defined by linguists, and seeks to accommodate them to the social:

Interpretation at the level of conversation is a function of an inferential process that has as its input syntactical, lexical and prosadic knowledge. (Gumperz, 1982: 117)

He does not see that this way of putting the matter involves him in having to resolve the relationship between linguistic knowledge, as this is represented by linguists, and the social. Perhaps this problem of resolution leads him, despite the fact that he has called for a revolution in linguistic thinking, to sustain an interest in the correlation of lexical items with socio-cultural variables. His objective remains a traditional one. This is further registered by his complaint that 'we are still far from a theory of verbal communication which integrates what we know about grammar, culture and interactive conventions in a single overall framework' (Gumperz, 1982: 4).

His interest in interpretation and cognitive processing exhibits the traditional methodological device of turning talk into a mental entity. In effect he is asking: 'how do speakers interpret the phenomena recognised by linguists in order to make conversation?' The problem with this question is that the phenomena of linguistics have been articulated without reference to how real-time phenomena are oriented to in particular situations in social interaction. Consequently, not only is there an absence of any systematic account of such relationships, there just cannot be one at all while linguistic phenomena are constituted by being purified of context.

Generally, the problem for those socio-linguists such as Gumperz, who are seriously concerned to examine discourse as a social phenomenon, is that they tend to 'add together' two incompatible frameworks that are related to very different objectives. On the one hand there is the desire to see how talk is controlled by 'external' social variables (the classic sociological model), and on the other, the desire to weld this concern with an interest in talk or natural language as self-organising 'achievement'. It is this latter interest which leads both Gumperz and Hymes to try to incorporate Sacks' notions of sequencing into their models.

However, they reveal no analytical concern with the question of whether or not, in principle, that form of wielding is viable. They do not examine the feasibility of simply adding together the theoretical objects of different disciplines, or the concepts which are related to different organisational relevancies.

Whilst their concern is the study of talk in context, the notion of context remains problematic because its possible ingredients appear limitless. This is necessarily so because the focus of analysis shifts from production phenomena, to interpretations, to the meanings of linguistic forms. Thus, rather than developing a theory or a set of rules for conversational organisation, what emerges is a list of possible relevancies for the analyst to take account of when studying any given conversational extract.

Gumperz and Hymes, following the linguist Firth, have been powerful influences in directing attention away from language as 'la langue' and focussing upon 'parole' as a basis for the study of social activities. However, what they fail to do is rid themselves of the methodological framework of correlation, with its allied notions of 'causal variable' and 'internal' and 'external' constraints. They have not extracted themselves from the conventional desire to produce a sociological theory of talk, and in consequence they have been willing to adopt pre-formed linguistic and sociological categories without ever asking how, or whether, such categories can be related to the organisation of talk as activities. These facts have militated against the production, in socio-linguistics, of hard, replicable, and general findings about how talk is organisationally produced.

5   Harvey Sacks and the study of language

Harvey Sacks' studies of conversation, which were mainly worked out in a series of lectures from 1964 to 1972 provide a respecification of the topic of enquiry that is involved in the study of language, culture and the relationship that holds between them. In the previous section, some of the problematic features of this relationship have been introduced. It is possible to show that the way in which the relationship has been made problematic in traditional socio-linguistic studies stems from at least three conceptual assumptions that Sacks' work seriously questions.

These assumptions run throughout linguistic and socio-linguistic concerns with culture, but they are particularly apparent in some important schools or fields of enquiry. The intention here is to show how Sacks' work may be used to reveal the nature of the problems underlying these fields, and at the same time to suggest how the problems may have been avoided had certain conceptual assumptions not been made.

Firstly the Whorf–Sapir hypothesis will be investigated to show how a formal and philosophical orientation to language may give rise to conceptual confusion, leading, in this case, to the adoption of cultural and epistemological relativism. Secondly, cognitive anthropology will be considered to show the problems which emerge should one use a linguistic version of language and language categories to try to specify the content and organisation of culture. Thirdly, the problematic assumptions involved in trying to produce a systematic theoretical model of the relationship between activity/talk and linguistic form will be discussed in relationship to discourse analysis.

It is *not* my intention to *review* these three developments, but simply to sketch out how they most fervently display the assumptions that pervade attempts to correlate the linguistic and the social. From a critical consideration of these assumptions it will be possible to describe how Sacks avoids them, and how by doing so he respecified the topic of inquiry. Before explicitly turning to these three areas, however, a few general remarks about Sacks' work are in order.

Sacks' explorations into the social organisation of talk represents part of his concern to show how sociologists might make warrantable findings about the organisation of social activities of whatever kind. To do this he sought to develop a sociology that oriented to the social activities revealed in natural materials. He argued that it was crucial that the way such materials exert control over any findings should be available for replicable inspection.

To Sacks, many of sociology's troubles, such as its seemingly endemic incapacity to conduct properly replicable enquiry and, relatedly, its inability to furnish unequivocal findings, are the inevitable consequence of the way in which a variety of scholars have conceived of language as a resource to build pictures of how societies work. Usually, in the case of sociology and anthropology, this task has been shaped and formulated by the desire to depict a society or culture as a unit within which stable and regular patterns of behaviour occur.

From the start, Sacks' observations provide a basis for questioning the authenticity of this general direction. His work reveals that natural language is, itself, a socially organised activity which takes its character, and furnishes its order, from the 'context'[5] in which it occurs and which it illuminates. This being the case it is by no means obvious how, or even if, we might use samples of de-contextualised talk as illustrative of the nature of culture and social regularity in general.

Whilst students of culture use natural language, the question is whether their research strategies preserve its natural order within, and as, a topic of their studies. The concern of this discussion restricts itself to the ways in which study policies and methodological convictions have led scholars to adopt a picture of language that does not correspond to the role which language plays in our practical affairs. The adoption of that picture, together with its latent pre-conceptions or implicit philosophical positions, can be shown to be standing in the way of the development of a rigorous empirical investigation of language and culture.

(1) Whorf–Sapir and the philosophical presuppositions underlying cognitivism in the linguistic analysis of culture

No one illustrates the problems of taking on board implicit philosophical presuppositions about language better than Whorf–Sapir. Their thesis argues that a given society's language comprises a conceptual scheme by which it parcels up and organises 'reality'.[6]

We dissect nature along lines laid down by nature's languages . . .

The world is organised by our minds . . . and this means largely by the linguistic systems of our minds. (Whorf–Sapir, Sapir, 1949: 150)

Thus Whorf–Sapir argue that we need to study language patterns – grammar, lexical and syntactical structures – in order to provide the basis of a people's understanding of social reality. Defenders of this thesis provide numerous examples which demonstrate linguistic differences between cultures and which are, or were, used to support the validity of their ontological hypothesis about perception of reality. For example, the Navaho were found to have no colour terms corresponding directly to English speakers' 'black' and 'grey', 'brown' or 'blue'. It is thus suggested that the cognitive organisation of their reality does not contain these colour objects, consequently the possibility of making such distinctions does not exist. From this kind of evidence Whorf–Sapir conclude that ideas or cultural objects cannot be the product of sense experiences, for otherwise the different languages would have the same form. Therefore, they argue, if thinking is not a product of sense experiences it must be a product of language or the logic that underlies it.

Ideas about the world are determined by language structure. Nouns or noun classes refer to objects or object classes, the latter providing for the meaning of particular nouns (nouns name things). Verbs as a class (doing words) provide for the meaning of particular given verbs. The way tenses are organised correspond to, and therefore control, ideas about, for example, time. Sentences of a language, essentially propositional and referential, are composed of logical relations between word categories conveying meanings or ideas about the world. Thus, it would seem to follow that if different languages display different categories or different relationships between them, they must express different ideas or a different ontology. If it can be then shown that different languages have different structures, the relativistic conclusion that there are different realities can be drawn.

At the outset it is noticeable that Whorf–Sapir never attempted to ground their claim that different linguistic or grammatical structures necessarily involve differences in meaning, even though such a view is crucial to their thesis. Their whole argument rests on the assumption that a sentence's grammatico-logical structure must control its meaning – what else could? However, if the sentence 'I went for a walk' is compared with 'I went driving', then despite the fact that the two sentences have a different structure, it is not apparent that they have different meanings or function in different ways. This fact has consequences for the often quoted language comparisons between Europeans, and Eskimos who have twelve words for snow. Whorf–Sapir suggest that because Eskimos have twelve words and Europeans only one, the latter must be comparatively restricted in their conceptions of snow. Yet if the way in which language functions is examined, it can be found that Europeans are in no way restricted by the lack of nouns. There are infinitely many combinations of words which Europeans use to describe or think of snow. Formal grammar does not, as Whorf–Sapir suggest, operate as a grid limiting conceptual possibilities.

From Whorf–Sapir's point of view, translation is highly problematic because, given that language structure determines meaning, a translation requirement would be the provision of an equivalent word in English for every Eskimo word. What they fail to see is that the objective of translation, like the objective of the hearer listening to the utterances of another, is to understand the 'point' or the 'purpose' or what is being said and done in words. Of course this need not be done by one to one translation.

Sacks' argument is that what talk is doing is accomplished by reference to an analysis of its 'point' or 'purpose'.[7] In natural language, speakers/hearers do not organise their activities and constitute the activities of others by reference to grammatical or abstract models, but by reference to 'point' and 'purpose' as displayed in such local organisational matters as the placement of utterances *vis-à-vis* other utterances.

In this respect consider the following material:

A: That was a good suggestion you made to come here.
B: You made it.
A: I did?
(Sacks, lecture, 29 May 1968)

The question of the intelligibility of the utterance 'you made it' resides in the activity it accomplishes. In this example, as Sacks explains, the answer to the question hinges upon the observation that B saw that A was making a compliment, and that he gave an answer that turned on his seeing what action was being done, and seeing that the action was not done to its proper recipient. Sacks regards the question of characterising the object 'You made it' not as an issue of what the language means, nor as an issue of how we might classify its linguistic form. Instead, he is concerned with what does it do in the sequence *as* activity. The advantage of posing the question that way, as a production phenomenon, is that it limits and specifies the scheme of analytic relevances required to analyse the materials provided.

Consider two teenagers talking:

A: Let's face it Ken you're a little rich kid.
B: Yes mommy.
(Sacks, Lecture 5, 1966 and 14 April 1967)

To Whorf–Sapir, 'Yes mommy' would be rendered into something like: affirmation directed to a noun class referring to the culturally and cognitively ensconced idea of female parent. However, it is highly questionable that the utterance is a *reference* to anything. What the utterances do is insult and counter-insult. They do so by the membershipping and co-membershipping of speakers, and possibly by a finding of 'deliberate' misidentification in relation to a normative version of appropriate identity.

So Sacks is showing that the production of what is *done* in a culture cannot be understood by reference to what Whorf–Sapir see as language or the inherent topic of language structure. Rather, cultural objects can be understood by reference to how natural language organisation achieves such activities as 'insults', 'greetings', 'invitations', 'offers' and so on. Sacks' concentration upon production phenomena allows the analyst to see how natural language is organised so as to enable cultural objects – activities – to be produced in utterly familiar ways. Such organisations can only be analysed for how they work *in situ*.

Sacks' analysis raises the question of what the analyst perceives the analytic object to be. The term 'language' seems to indicate a single clearly defined phenomena and object of study. However, this is illusory. Language can be understood to be the organisation of sound, or the organisation of grammatical rules, or a structural organisation. But, these uses implicate quite different ranges of phenomena, each with their own different problematics which require different schemes of analytic relevance.

In general terms, Whorf–Sapir invoke the 'fact-stating' model of language. They conceive of examples of language as providing certain facts about the nature of the language user's world. The facts, stated, referred to, or represented in the language, represent 'reality'. It is seen as crucial that one obtains this knowledge because of the roles that it must have in shaping the conduct of those persons studied. Conduct is seen as responding to the 'reality' that is expressed in language. Hence the tendency is to view language, not for how it is employed to produce activity, but for what it might tell us about the natives' 'reality'. Ironically, conceiving of language in this way precludes a consideration of the sense in which natural language is doing and organising activities themselves. This encourages the social scientist to conceive of language as an entity divorced from social praxis.

Whorf–Sapir's argument takes the following direction: a sample of the language, for example, a given sentence, is taken and the question posed 'what does it mean?' As a cultural object, an English sentence *must* mean something and its meaning *must* be conveyed by its structure, be it sentential, propositional or whatever. So, *given the removal of the sentence, phrase, word or utterance from a context, and therefore from whatever role it might have been playing,* then its meaning must reside in the correspondence between the structure and what it mirrors, represents, or stands for. Its verbs represent activities or ideas and so on. Given that one has now ontologised a realm of ideas or cultural objects, it becomes necessary to find a conceptual receptacle for them, and, as Ryle (1949) points out, the notion of 'mind' fills the role admirably. It only remains to suggest that language can be investigated for the principles of storage and organisation, and cognitive theories and systems of language are established. The role of language as activity is consequently buried. Whorf–Sapir continue the argument by declaring that if language represents reality, then how can reality exist independently of the particular language it is represented in. The door is opened not only to cognitive theory, but also to relativism. From beginning to end this kind of theorising is based upon the idea that there is no alternative to this way of thinking about language and about language and reality. Sacks, in the tradition of Wittgenstein, is showing otherwise.

The philosophy of Wittgenstein (1968) is dedicated to the eradication of this correspondence version of language, which he sees as coming about as a necessary consequence of considering language removed from the role that it has in our activities and practices. Instead of viewing words or combinations of words, or obtaining meaning by their correspondence in relation to those ideas they are said to represent, he regards them as tools for the performance of activities. As such they are bound up with social practices and the social rules and maxims that govern them. Above all he argues that it does not make sense to look for the meaning of words outside of the contexts from which they take their sense. His notion of a language game refers to such rules of practice underlying the use of words and expressions.

Wittgenstein argued that the question of how language represents reality is a false question. It rests on a mistaken view of how language works, and an extrapolative view of 'reality'. Not only do words only sometimes name things, but whether they do or not depends on the role they are playing in our activities – of their role in a language game. In Sacks' insistence that we look to the 'point' or 'purpose' that words and utterances have in our activities, we can see that Sacks exhibits what Wittgenstein may, in significant part, have been talking about with that utterly gnomic expression 'language games'.

The danger in the human sciences, including linguistics, is to treat language as though it had an existence independently of real people who say things and by saying them *do* things, at particular times and places. Whorf's example of language, like most of the grammatically constituted objects of linguistics, say or represent nothing. They have no 'point' or 'purpose' because they have no context. As Cook says of Whorf–Sapir, they are:

> treating mere sentences as though they could say something as though they could speak from the pages of a grammar book, where no one, no flesh and blood being in some context, is giving a warning, reporting an accident, explaining how something works, or anything of the sort. (Cook, 1978: 26)

In contrast to Whorf–Sapir, Sacks is unconcerned with 'language' as furnishing objects of study. His first concern is to see what activities are being performed. The cultural question is, how does the culture work to furnish organisation available in speech so that societies' members can recognise and produce activities which involve their seeing the point of the talk, and what it implies for them, in the 'here and now'?

The fact that any sensitive account of language must be constrained by how that language figures in people's lives is now accepted by some philosophers (Cook, 1978) and some linguists (Harris, 1981). The lesson that should be taught by Whorf–Sapir's failures is that without such constraints 'language' tends to be reified into a theoretical object, such as a conceptual scheme, on the basis of which bizarre and counter-intuitive claims may be made and go unchecked.

The work of Sacks has suggested to us that it is of no use to try and accept, even partially, an existent linguistic theoretical framework from which to view spoken language. Such frameworks, like Whorf–Sapir's, start with their objects of analysis constructed without reference to the 'point' and 'purpose' of talk in specific circumstances and, therefore, without reference to how, through talk, we act and interact in the world.

One linguist who seems at least to partially recognise this is Harris, who writes:

Any theoretical account which abstracts from the phenomena of communication in such a way as to ignore these facts (communicational purposes) can have no serious claim to be a theory of human activities and capacities . . . There is no question of simply 'adding on' some appendix to the apparatus of modern linguistics to deal with the phenomena of language. (Harris, 1981: 66)

It should be made clear, however, that Sacks is not concerned with the phenomena of language as such. On the other hand Sacks' work accepts the spirit of Harris' argument and starts with communicational purpose. He does, however, take an even more radical direction. He rejects the notion of theory altogether, making it his business to *describe* how talk does activities *in situ*. This concentration on the question of how people understand one another involves him in the refusal to theoretically categorise, insisting that you cannot take language out of context. His message is that if you are going to see how people act, then you must start with the reality they act in. As we shall see cognitive anthropology suffers the consequence of trying to take the other direction.

(2) Cognitive anthropology: language and the production of cultural order

Goodenough (1967), drawing on the works of Durkheim, Boas and Malinowski, seeks to show how language contributes to the production of social and cultural order. He declares that a culture can be considered to be the totality of a society's concepts or classificatory categories, together with the principles according to which they are used. Samples of such uses should be investigated to discover the conceptual models with which a society operates.

Goodenough's intention is that natural materials displaying such uses should form a control over the construction of such analytical representations of the natural mind. His argument is that a culture consists of essentially standard ways of deploying cultural categories. These regular ways of deployment must be theoretically organised by the native speaker to achieve competence (acceptable regularity). It ought, therefore, to be possible to discover categories and the rules for their deployment in order to locate what native speakers regard as competence, and therefore to find, at a factual level, the roles for the production of regularity.

Goodenough writes:

Whatever it is to know or believe in order to operate in a manner acceptable to its members, and to do so in any role that they accept for anyone or themselves. It is the forms of things that people have in mind, their models for perceiving, relating and otherwise perceiving them. Ethnographic description, then, requires methods of processing observed phenomena such that we can inductively construct a theory of how informants have organised the same phenomena. It is the theory not the phenomena alone which ethnographic description aims to present. (Goodenough, 1967: 167–8)

The aim is to develop formal analysis which is in principle generalising, and which avoids the production of *ad hoc* interpretations of culture. Cognitive anthropologists such as Goodenough, thus take seriously the requirement to produce a rigorous description of culture based on the empirically revealed orientations of its members.

Cultural regularity and stability is sought in the ways in which a society's members deploy sets of labels as classifications relating to the external world of cultural objects. So, again, language is oriented to as displaying, clarifying, referring or describing. Its referents are the culture's objects and its organisation portrays the formal principles of competent classification. The theory of how culture in language secures regularity and order depends upon that. Given situation 'A', then principles 'A' dictate the choice of words and the cultural understanding (see Eglin, 1980 and Wieder, 1971). 'Here comes an elephant' is a proper cultural description and understanding given that it is a valid reference to a cultural object. Given the same situation again, then these principles of valid reference dictate the choice of the same words (and therefore the understanding). Competence and the production of situational regularity (order) lies in the correct application of categories and descriptions.

As is the case with Whorf–Sapir, cognitive anthropology's proper aim of situating its description of culture in the vernacular language fails because it examines language samples ripped from context as though speakers were orienting to their talk as fact-stating, and as though correct reference were the sole criterion of competent talk. That this is a mistake is demonstrated in Sacks' 'Everyone Has to Lie' (1975), where 'everyone' is shown to have quite other than nominal or referencing uses. Also, as with Whorf–Sapir, cognitive anthropology is forced to adopt a version of culture wherein the use of language and talk to do action is treated as a residual feature. They treat speech activity as a matter of ongoing cultural description and look for the principles according to which it must work as such.

Their version of social order is that interactants, in the course of interaction, make correct recognitions of objects or activities to bring them under some appropriate norm. They are seen as doing so 'transituationally'. Consequently, it seems that there must be some shared set of general rules for category application so as to achieve 'transituational' regularity. Such rules must be applied to a setting from without. They are seen as being cognitively stored, and as having the kind of ontological status that they have in most social theories of order and regularity.

As Garfinkel (1967) has shown, the problem of such models of social order is that they take for granted the very basis of what they propose to explain. According to cognitive anthropology, the cultural object of 'suicide' dictates our choice of the word or description. However, the social order question is properly concerned with the issue of how people arrive at the version 'suicide' in the first place.

Sacks (1963) is also arguing that 'suicide' or 'suicide again' cannot be achieved as description by the application of logico-semantic correspondence rules. In this Sacks (and Garfinkel) are in the Wittgensteinian tradition, for Wittgenstein specifically warned that such rules work only in the context of a variety of tacit social agreements. This is why he pointedly remarks that there can be no fixed rules to interpret the rules, and asks the question when is 'the same', 'the same'? (Wittgenstein, 1968).[8]

For Sacks the issue of rigorous description is fundamental to the human sciences. His own sociology commences with the observation that sociological theorising regularly topicalises phenomena which it cannot describe, and that whilst sociologists can, and do, talk of social life as culturally ordered phenomena, they cannot actually identify the constituents of any specific culture, nor detail the ways in which it organises observable phenomena (Sacks, 1963).

The problem is that correct description has been taken as a task for the human sciences in their work of categorising persons, objects, and activities. Much of the methodological mileage of sociology has been built upon the quest for principles, for a formula to produce correct and proper description. For example, Durkheim's famous definition of suicide is intended as a proper description and an operationalising procedure, invoking the primacy of technical language. The problem with such languages which seek to redefine common-sense terminology is that the conceptual language which is produced, and the findings expressed in it, cannot be translated back into, nor understood in terms of, the vernacular language. The problem with this is that it is what we ordinarily understand in the vernacular by 'suicide' that the sociologist seeks to study. Consequently any findings expressed and conceived in terms of the technical language gain an indeterminate significance.

Sacks' examination of the phenomena of description, itself, makes it clear that it is an activity in the world like any other. As such it is always subject to local organisational constraints. Sociological descriptions are as subject to local constraints as any others and cannot, therefore, independently specify the details and conditions of their application. This has great consequence for the practice, adopted across the range of the human sciences, of specifying correct and valid description, and for their attempts to base generalisation upon it. *If it is the case that description is always locally organised, then this makes the quest for formula, which might determine correct descriptions, frivolous.* Sacks is not promising to solve the problem of correct description, he is seeking to show that the problem itself can be made trivial.

Most frequently ethnographers have relied upon native formulations for their description of activities. Thus to use one of Sacks' examples (Sacks, 1979), they might take a person who can be described, amongst other things, by native American youth as a 'hot-rodder', and use that as a basis for describing his driving in the streets as 'dragging'. If on the other hand he is not so easily describable as a 'hot-rodder', then his driving might be described as 'driving' as opposed to 'dragging'. Certainly describing both persons and activities involves selections from a range of possibly correct descriptions, and the describing of activities and the perpetrators of those activities, have a possibly mutually constitutive local relationship. The methods governing such relationships are investigable and proper topics of analysis into *in situ*-social organisation (Sacks, 1966 lectures, see particularly Spring 1966, Lecture 18).

Sociologists, however, are motivated to assume correspondence-correct criteria for deciding how to describe both actor and activity. Should, for example, they follow a theory that provides for an ethnic socio-cultural attitude to religion, then they are motivated to interview someone who *could* be described as ethnic, and assume that any attitude to religion discussed *is* the religious attitude of an ethnic. However, because that person *can* be described as an ethnic, does not mean that there is any scientifically warrantable basis for treating any one of his or her activities as *ethnic activities*. As a person *may* be described as an ethnic, so too may they be described in numerous other ways. There is no principled legitimation for attributing so called religious attitudes to the person's ethnic status.

This has serious implications for general sociological practice. Sociologists proceed by inducing a descriptive cultural category which formulates membership (or co-membership) of some collectivity. They then seek attributes or characteristics of 'co-membership' which they take to be the characteristics of the collectivity. This, as Doug Benson and John Hughes have argued in chapter 6, involves treating these attributes or characteristics as additive, making it possible to refer to, for example, the opinions of 'teachers', or the religious view or views of 'the ethnic', or the 'power bids' of the 'working class'. However, Sacks is arguing that the characterisation of persons and attributes, and the linking of them together, is situationally achieved out of contingent circumstances on each and every separate occasion. No formal rules of description exist (as in chemistry) to provide a basis according to which we might properly treat descriptions as furnishing numerically comparable or additive phenomena.

Following Sacks, Moerman (1974) was forced to question the principles involved in anthropologists' customary procedure of describing tribal or societal culture by accumulating traits and characteristics, and attributing these to a given collection of persons. Like Sacks, he argues that such phenomena are not properly additives for the sociologist, because each description or categorisation is situationally achieved. In so doing they both undercut the whole process by which anthropology (including of course cognitive anthropology) construes culture as a unique system of ideas and practices that may be regarded as the property or characteristics of some set of people.

> The set of ethnic labels are *possible* identifications for human objects which can also be properly given labels from other identification sets. (Moerman, 1974: 65)

Even the term 'Lue' (the name of the tribe studied by Moerman) is only one of a set of possible sets of identifications, and, though it may have high priority in the talk of certain persons and in certain practices, it is a circumstantially, socially organised priority. The use of the term 'Lue', as a resource for constructing a theoretical account of a society's or a culture's general organisation, departs in uncontrolled ways from its use as part of vernacular language activities.

Thus, forgetting the sense in which description is an organised language activity in its own right, sociologists have used their versions of it to construct theoretical accounts of society's or culture's general organisation. On the one hand this has led to an extrapolative view of cultural organisation itself, and on the other to an indifference to the nature of language activities. Sociology has thereby forsaken the question of how language activities are co-ordinated into, and constitutive of, social activities, and are thereby productive of order.

The investigation of how this is so involves the necessary suspension of a preconceived theory as to how culture is organised by language. It also involves relinquishing the typical ways in which discovered materials are classified or described in pre-conceived theoretical designs or grammatical categories. This necessity is emphasised by Garfinkel's (1967) discovery that sociology's phenomena – embodied activities – are self-organising, rather than the product of externally articulated rules.

In this regard consider the following:

Passenger: Do you have a cigarette?
Stewardess: No we don't provide them any more.
(Sacks, lecture, 8 May 1968)

The stewardess could have been addressed in a variety of ways. Clearly, the question of how she *is* being addressed is relevant for how we or she, might describe what the passenger was doing when he addressed her. She treats it as an address which is oriented to her status as the air-line representative. In her response she displays that she has conducted such an analysis – note her use of 'we' – and used it to formulate her reply. In this respect, consider how the analyst was able to evoke the descriptions 'passenger' and 'stewardess' when transcribing this exchange – on the basis of the analyst's sense of the inter-actants' own visible analysis of the interaction.

The point is that in such interaction, co-participants make available and visible the nature of their activities in the very course of their production. They achieve an understanding of action from the very scenes in which they are engaged. They display their understandings in the 'recipient design' (Sacks, Schegloff and Jefferson, 1974) of their utterances. It is for this reason that it is possible to discover organisations in natural talk that co-ordinate activities into scenes and settings, and organise the talk into conversations, stories, speeches etc.

Rather than accepting sampling as a basis for the discovery of generality with its implied requirement of theoretical abstraction and pre-formed research categories, linguistic or otherwise, Sacks is urging both the possi-bility and necessity of undertaking single event sociology.[9] In the course of interaction in such single events the general possibility of multiple description is not a problem for participants in the way it is for the sociologist. This is because participants furnish each other with instructions for discovering the sense and interactive implications of their talk.

However, Sacks is not saying that such a single event sociology is without generative features. The discovery of the social organisations by which societies' members analyse the sense and implications of their actions, is the discovery of the organisations that children learn when they learn culture through their participation in single contexted events. Children do not learn general rules as some sociologists and linguists seem to imply, and, yet, such is the power of cultural machinery 'that every infant comes out pretty much the same' (Sacks, lecture 33, 1966).

(3) Discourse analysis and the drive for integration

The earlier discussion of sociolinguistics concluded that linguistically based studies of social conduct have suffered from the fact that the language resources were, by and large, un-examined with respect to their integrat-ability with the analytic relevancies required for the study of the social. This contention is probably best examined in relation to the tradition of 'discourse analysis' founded by Sinclair. Discourse analysis is arguably the most system-atic attempt to integrate 'language' and 'the social'. It is further significant in that it has attempted to incorporate some of the findings of Sacks *et al.* into its analytic scheme.

As with the sociolinguistics of Gumperz and Hymes, discourse analysis is influenced by the work of Firth in its attempts to operate with a conceptual apparatus that includes: speakers' roles, the (social) situation, and speakers' intentions. Sinclair and Coulthard (1975) quote with approval Firth's argument about the necessity of studying:

The functions of complete location in the context of the situation or typical context of situations, the province of semantics. (Firth, 1957)

Nevertheless, their exercise of 'discussing the relationship between linguistic form and the interactive functions proposed' is characterisable as linguistic, or at least as having a foundation in linguistic thinking. That there may be some equivocality as to whether the framework is linguistic or sociological, may be seen by comparing the following two concerns. On the one hand they are concerned to see:

What function does a given utterance have – is it a statement, question, command or response – and how do the participants know, what type of utterance can appropriately follow what, how and by whom are topics introduced and how are they developed. (Sinclair and Coulthard, 1975: 1)

However, on the other hand, they formulate their overall project as:

One stage in a continuing investigation of language function and the organisation of linguistic units above the rank of clause. (Sinclair and Coulthard, 1975: 1)

Generally, the objective of discourse analysis is to find out how utterances containing what is described as 'moves' (actions) fit together to produce discourse. To facilitate this it is argued that a higher level of analytic classification than grammar is required. This is because *in situ* 'part of the meaning of sentences' (Sinclair and Coulthard, 1975) or grammatical units are determined by situationally organised rules or maxims, so that performatory function must take account of a higher level of situational relevancies.

Sinclair and Coulthard attempt to describe the structure of typical multi-sentential sequences up to the level of 'transactions'. Performances/sentences are seen as obtaining their 'meaning' or character *partly* in relation to the situation. This includes a speaker's tactics within a situation so that typical transactional sequences between individuals are expected to occur embedded in situations such as pupil–teacher classroom situations.

Sinclair and Coulthard propose an overlapping hierarchical rank ordering of different levels that organises talk such as 'pupil–teacher talk'. At the non-linguistic organisational level, and at the highest rank, is found, for pupil–teacher talk: 'course', 'period', and 'topic'. At the next level down, 'the discourse' level (though overlapping with the above) is found: 'lesson', 'transaction', 'exchange', 'move' and 'act'. At the lowest level, but again overlapping, there is the level of grammatical organisation. Discourse analysis is concerned with how such levels of organisation relate. It assumes that they do, or that they must do, in some kind of systematic way.

Sinclair and Coulthard commence with the linguist's problem of the lack of fit between grammatical categories and performance categories. For example, what they describe as the interrogative 'what are you laughing at' is interpretable either as a question, or, in some circumstances, as a command. They assert (without evidence) that in the classroom it is *usually* heard as the latter.

This suggests that the situation has transformed the interrogative and that it should, therefore, be possible to spell out a series of (transforming) rules or maxims which determine how what may have the grammatical force of a question, can, or should, be interpreted as something else: as for example a command.

How *one* particular context guides *the interpretation of grammatical structure.*
(Sinclair and Coulthard, 1975, my emphasis)

The rules or maxims are seen as being bound up with the context or the organisational features of the situation. Thus an interrogative, for example, 'can you play the piano John?' becomes a command if the following conditions hold:

(1)   If it contains one of the modes: 'can', 'could', 'would' (and sometimes) 'going to'.
(2)   If the subject of the clause is also the addressee.
(3)   If the predicate describes an action which is physically possible.

On the basis of such rules both speakers and the linguist uses knowledge of the non-linguistic environment to 're-classify' items.

At the level of discourse a teacher who provides for a pupil to speak next can be seen as *initiating* action or talk from that pupil with the discourse value of eliciting information. However, all sorts of moves might be built into initiation which have, or appear to have, a controlling effect upon the response. Thus any initiating utterance could contain directive, information or elicitive acts which regularly beget response acts of (acknowledgement) react, acknowledge and reply respectively. The idea is to classify relationships between sentences and utterances in terms of these functional classifications so as to build upon transaction or exchange types. thus:

Teacher – Elicitation – Do you know what we really mean by accent?
Pupil   – Reply   – It's the way we talk.
Teacher – Accept   – The way we talk.
         – Evaluator   – This is a very broad comment.

The goal is, thereby, to describe ranges of typical exchange structure and to explain how their form relates to, and is controlled, not just by linguistic form, but also by different situationally organised rules of interpretation.

Having considered Sacks' concern for the problems of classification and description in sociology and the human sciences, we might properly commence an examination of discourse analysis with the question as to why we should accept *these* functional or action categories as analytic givens. Sacks exhorts the analyst to use natural language itself to describe what is being done in natural language, not corral what is done into a restricted range of analytically defined and specified classification. However, discourse analysis starts the other way around. It takes pre-formulated classifications such as 'informing', 'directing' and 'eliciting', and then seems to apportion these descriptions to what the analyst finds. In fact their classifications derived, and developed from, Bellack *et al.*'s (1966) linguistic theory, and as such, they became instructions for analysing natural talk into the kind of formally relatable general categories required by the comparative dictates of the theoretical model. They thus, necessarily, deflect attention from the contingent accomplishment of the talk, from what *particular action* it performs, and is found to have performed by relevant hearers. This means that the 'point' or 'purpose' that is achieved and displayed for particular instances of talk is obscured. Given Sacks' argument above, that any given conversational utterance organises a co-conversationalist's version of the next appropriate activity, the basis according to which speakers achieve co-ordinated talk or interaction is lost to discourse analysis.

There is a sense in which Sinclair's classification scheme has pre-directed the range of possible purposes and activities we might find, and which conversationalists might orient to. It has substituted for them a theoretically furnished set of functions or properties. These functions, or operationalising categories, are not articulated from speaker–hearer's sense of 'point' and 'purpose' in their talk, and they, thus, have an uncertain relationship to the vernacular language. It is as though conversationalists formed their talk 'to initiate', or 'to react', instead of to do such things as 'greeting', 'promising', 'doubting' etc. – these being genuinely interactive categories as oriented to, and used by, members. This means that the connectedness of utterances or parts of talk is not so much the achievement of the speaker–hearer's demonstrable understanding of the import of the talk, but is furnished by the abstract model which links together the categories.

Sinclair and Coulthard imply that the categories or descriptions they furnish are oriented to by interactants, and are provided for by general rules or maxims which link situations to the interpretation of the talk. These categories are, however, made problematical by Garfinkel and Sacks' revelation that talk is locally organised, and is not a function of some general rule system. If local or self-organisation does provide for the interactional sense of utterances, then one would not expect general rules for relating situation to utterance performance to be discriminative, predictive, or to account for the talker's production of orderly co-ordinated interaction.

Take, for example, Sinclair's stipulation that 'can you play the piano John' is a command where conditions one, two, and three above pertain. Consider, however, the following imaginary conversation in a classroom with a piano in it.

1 Teacher: Kathy do you know how to play the piano
2 Kathy: Yes teacher
3 Teacher: Can you play the piano John
4 John: Yes teacher I can as well

Contra Sinclair, it is not counter-intuitive to hear line 3 as a question, and not a command. We should, however, note that Sinclair does envisage the possibility of exceptions to the rules he formulates when he says that such a rule is predictive *in most cases*. However, this raises the question of how many exceptions are allowed, and how are they to be related to the model.

Discourse analysis faces the fact that such rules or maxims do not provide prediction in a manner similar to Grice's confrontation of the same problem. They treat some circumstances as exceptions and provide another rule or maxim to provide for the problematic exception. The problem with such a procedure, however, is that it is potentially limitless given that 'contextual variation' seems to be limitless. This would mean that they provide what seems to be an unclosed rule set. In itself this might not matter. However it does for discourse analysis, because these maxims are implicated in the discourse analysis classification procedures themselves. This raises questions as to the status of the model itself.

Also leading to questions about the status of the model is Sinclair's treatment of the meaning of utterances and 'the interpretation of utterances', both of which appear to be central to the endeavour. Indeed, the application of the discourse analysts' categorisation scheme is reliant upon having already established the meaning of sentences or utterances. The issue of whether grammatical organisation or situationally furnished rule, or both, provide for the function, turns out to be an issue of what accounts for the meaning. Sinclair and Coulthard assert that 'part of the meaning of a sentence must always be determined by the context in which it is uttered' (Sinclair and Coulthard, 1975: 12). They further argue that misinterpretation can occur when a pupil relies on the grammatical sense of an expression and misapplies the situational rules. Apart from the question of whether it is sensible to talk of the grammatical sense or meaning of expressions or utterances, this raises the question of how the meaning, or what the analyst might divine as the real meaning, of utterances or sentences can be established independently of the role particular utterances play in people's understanding of them. The issue of meaning is one over which conversationalists themselves might dispute, and about which there seems to be no valid superior court of appeal.

Sacks does not have to confront the question of meaning in this way. He is exclusively concerned with the activities that are observably performed by utterances, and with the way those activities are demonstrably oriented to in the production of subsequent activity. Thus, unlike discourse analysis, conversation analysts are not forced into the role of detectives or legislators, with a primary task of deciding the meaning or 'real meaning' of utterances.

So too does Sacks avoid the conceptual problems of searching for a systematic connection between the linguistic and the social or environmental, and having 'meaning' playing the role of mediator. As a basis for solving the relationship, discourse analysis suggests that they use information about the linguistic environment to 're-classify' the (meaning) 'function' from that provided by the linguistic. They suggest that they are doing so on the basis of the methods used by speakers/hearers. But the question of what is being reclassified from what to what is unclear. Presumably, the first hearing or interpretation based on grammatical grounds is an incorrect one. That is, the hearer, depending upon linguistic organisation, will have 'misinterpreted' the meaning. In other circumstances it is suggested that, providing that the situation does not gain-say it, one may rely upon the grammatical organisation to supply the meaning or function. However, if a 'part of the meaning is determined by context', then presumably a part is not. We thus come to a version that conceives, in principle, of meaningful language with no context or utterances related to the purposes of particular speakers.

I am not exposing these problems to be critical of the ingenuity which discourse analysis displays in their attempts to model the social world, but to illustrate the kinds of problems that are experienced by operating with an inherently problematic concept such as 'meaning' or 'function' – *where they are used as equivalents*. Neither discourse analysis nor Gumperz's sociolinguistics heed Wittgenstein's warning of the analytic problems associated with the search for the meaning of language. Whilst his concern was a philosopher's concern with the problem of the meaning of words, his argument as to the need to concentrate upon 'use' still applies (Wittgenstein, 1968).

An examination of discourse analysis' non-linguistic concerns reveals, as in Gumperz's work, a concatenation of sociological familiars: roles, situations, power relations etc. Whilst discourse analysts state that they have no intention of treating such matters in the manner by which socio-linguists use them as variables or social correlates or activities, they do, however, use them as a contextual basis for describing the talk, and for establishing the rules or maxims for producing the description. The problem here is that they use an analytically ungrounded description of the talkers, to establish the nature of the talk. This is at the heart of what I have indicated to be Sacks' problem of description. Because it is possible to describe the speaker as 'a teacher', does not licence or justify the analytic description of the talk as 'teacher's talk', or as organised by reference to the fact that the person is a teacher. There may be many other correct descriptions. The analyst is not entitled to treat these categories as omni-relevant or omniscient. Sacks' example of the 'stewardess/passenger talk', displays the way in which the roles of 'steward' and 'passenger' are constitutively and commonsensically established as relevances in the course of the talk. The question of how these categories arise and are constituted by the participants in the course of their talk is of primary analytic interest, and it has consequences for the question of what the talk is doing, and for how it is organisationally produced.

Discourse analysis has sacrificed an enquiry into the natural organisation of talk because it has set up the problem to be addressed, the relationship between talk as action and grammar, under the assumption that there *must* be some systematic relationship. To address the relationship discourse analysts have moved away from descriptions or versions of the talk and its situational relevances as based upon interlocutors' demonstrable orientations.

It is not just their solution that is conceptually problematic, it is their version of the problem. The desire to link linguistic concepts with the social organisation of talk and the conceptual apparatus of sociology should be moderated by the question of whether it is logically feasible to do so, and, at the same time, hold the phenomena within, relevant to, and inseparable from, their conceptual and analytic frameworks.

Ever since Auguste Comte, sociologists have attempted to solve problems of compatibility by describing phenomena in a hierarchy, and then describing how the different tiers of the hierarchy *must* be related. However, it is the sociologists who established the hierarchy in the first place in order to make their frameworks look systematic. The question of whether it is systematic or not, hinges upon the validity of certain assumptions about the so-called levels. Whilst discourse analysis starts with the interesting idea that language must be looked at in context, and must be treated as a social institution, discourse analysts do not consider what this might involve conceptually. Consequentially, it becomes unclear what they mean by the term 'language'. The notion of grammar, or 'language form', represents one kind of conceptual orientation to language. 'Talk' is quite another, having quite different conceptual and organisational relevances relating as they do to institutional practices and to forms of social organisation, the nature of which they have not examined analytically. It is with both the nature and detail of such organisation that Garfinkel and Sacks have been concerned.

6   Conclusion

It is clear from Sacks' 'Sociological Descriptions' (Sacks, 1963) that much of his work may be understood to be a thematic development of Harold Garfinkel's ethnomethodology, and as this chapter has suggested, Sacks' studies can be read as a demonstration of what the idea of 'language game' might stand for. Consequently, it can be suggested that Sacks' studies also exhibit Garfinkel's study policy of treating social phenomena as 'achieved'. Thus the drive of Sacks' analysis is to locate 'conversational structures' as organising natural conversation. However, these conversational structures, for example, 'adjacency pairs' (Schegloff and Sacks, 1973), and their analysis and description, are treated as end-products viewed for how they are constructed and oriented to by conversationalists in real time. Crucial to Sacks' enterprise is that these natural phenomena be formally described in their own right for how they relate to conversationalists' achievements, whatever these may be. As such they are not, and cannot be, dislocated and made into analytic or descriptive resources to accomplish other tasks, without forsaking the primacy of this analytic task, and without dislocating them from the natural materials in which they are embodied and which they organise. This fact accounts for the resistance which ethnomethodologists show to the attempts made by sociolinguists, or discourse analysts, to embody such conversational structures and observations made upon them into theoretical and analytical schemes which are essentially alien.

Throughout this chapter, and in order to emphasise the revolutionary character of Sacks' work, it has been necessary to be highly critical of other studies of language and culture without reference to the many achievements and positive interests these studies have generated. The reason for the critical emphasis has been to try and make it clear that Sacks re-specifies the phenomena involved. His methodology, with its related conceptual apparatus, represents a major departure from traditional forms of sociological and linguistic study.

Together, Garfinkel and Sacks strive to reverse the standard understanding of the relationship between activity and structure, never denying that structures can be found, but always maintaining that it is not possible to know what naturally organised structure is like until it has been located and examined *in situ*, and formally described. To do this, and therefore to depart from the traditional practice of taking natural structures for granted, or from using *ad hoc* versions of them, requires a major methodological respecification.

This respecification involves:

(1)   Suspending general questions, such as the question of the relationship between 'culture' and 'language' until these have been described with respect to the question of how they translate into the witnessable understandings and activities of social interactants.

(2)   Treating social activities, such as talk, strictly in terms of the production of witnessable events, rather than as a product of adopting the philosophical and conceptual assumptions involved in treating language as cognitively generated.

(3)   Dissolving the conceptually un-analysed notion of 'language' and language form into the question of how social actors co-ordinate their activities in and through talk, seeking to locate structures by which they do so without preconceived notions of what these structures look like.

(4)   Taking it that the ways persons co-ordinate their talk/activities in fine detail necessarily reveal how co-conversationalists ongoingly achieve order in their collective behaviour. Thus the drive to solve sociology's problem of order is relocated in terms of the ways in which culture is furnished and produced.

(5)   Neither treating culture as 'external' to, and constraining upon, language, nor treating language as 'external' to, or constraining upon, culture. But

treating culture as an embedded phenomenon in language-in-use, on the grounds that culture is encountered that way by society's members.

(6) This involves the total rejection of the traditional view of culture as an abstract, transcendental object or system to be related, in favour of treating its organisation as a recoverable, reproducible stock of knowledge and skills available in daily, routine, mundane ways of talking and acting.

NOTES

1 This focus means that I will not discuss the work of so-called 'post-structuralists' such as Foucault (1972), and Derrida (1976 and 1978), nor the related work of Barthes (1975). My excuse is lack of space. The question of language and culture in the human sciences is so broad that I have necessarily had to restrict the issues I take up in order to provide the sense of an ethnomethodological respecification of the relationship between language and culture. The fact that I am unable to discuss 'post-structuralism' will no doubt be a loss for some. However, an ethnomethodological respecification remains the same irrespective of the ways in which I have chosen to lead up to it, and I therefore hope that those interested in 'post-structuralist' writers will still find these arguments worth their contemplation.

2 Jeff Coulter's discussion of 'cognition' in the previous chapter provides a general backdrop, in the front of which this argument is developed.

3 For example, see Voeglin, Voeglin and Jeanne (1979) and Malotki (1983).

4 It is important to note that Kempson moves towards a recognition of this problem.

5 When I refer to the necessity of analysing talk in *context* I am not endorsing a sociological or philosophical view that context is a fixed background of organisational and organising features. Examples of this sort of use of context are to be found in studies that invoke the idea of speakers' 'roles' or the idea that a 'context', such as the talk occurring in an 'interview', is, in principle, omni-relevant, for the organisation of the talk. Indeed, following Wittgenstein and Sacks, the argument is that this is not the case. Rather, the argument is that the way in which talk is organised is in relation to its placement *vis-à-vis* other talk and activities. That can be seen to be a *context* that speakers, in the construction of their activities, orient to as relevant for doing those activities. Thus context is an important issue for analysts because it is displayed by interactants to be important for the organisation of their talk, and what context consists of is also provided by interactants in the ordering of their actions-in-interaction. See Schegloff (1987 and forthcoming) for a discussion of these matters which draws upon Sacks' work on categorisation activities.

6 A long literature and heated controversy exists as to what precisely, Whorf–Sapir had to say about the relationship of language to culture. As Hill (1988) and Rosch (1974) make clear, it is possible to hold the 'strong view' suggesting that language is an epistemology, or the 'weak view' suggesting that language difficulties in some ways represent a guide to cultural differences, the latter being upheld by the distinguished Whorf scholar, H. Hoijer (see Hoijer, 1953). The intention here is to

analyse the strong version, on the grounds that it is more theoretically interesting and better illustrates themes that are attended to throughout the chapter. The weak version is possibly even more problematic in that it seems to indicate little more than that there are differences in grammar and culture which might have some sort of relationship with one another.

7 Cognitive theorists might recognise that talk has 'point' and 'purpose'. They generally consider this as evidence for the existence of internal cognitive states and have thus sought to locate intentionality as relating to a hidden realm from which talk and action gains its meaning. In line with the related arguments in the previous chapter, by contrast the emphasis here is away from ontological psychology and towards witnessable activities accomplished in and through talk. 'Point' and 'purpose' is thus found and displayed in the talk by interactants who thereby display the methods through which 'point' and 'purpose' can be found.

8 In this respect see Sacks Lectures 1966 particularly lecture 32.

9 See Doug Benson and John Hughes' discussion in chapter 6, for a detailed consideration of what is involved here, and the related discussion by Wes Sharrock and Graham Button in chapter 7.

10

Values and moral judgement: communicative praxis as a moral order

Lena Jayyusi

1 Introduction

The question of 'values' and moral judgement has pervaded the human sciences and philosophy since their inception. This chapter will deal with the way this question has been formulated and pursued in sociology and moral philosophy, the problems that arose with the different formulations, and the ethnomethodological respecification of the *base* problematic.[1] It was within sociology (as distinct from economics, political science, or psychology) that the issue of 'values' in social science was most significantly topicalised, and it was from within sociology that the ethnomethodological respecification of the domain of human scientific inquiry originated. At the same time, it was moral philosophy that made the sustained and systematic exploration of moral and ethical matters an object for attention, developing on, and addressing, some of the same philosophical antecedents that informed modern social science.

The question of 'values' has classically had two prongs to it. On the one hand there is the conceptualisation and study of the relationship of 'values' to human conduct; on the other hand there is the conceptualisation and study of the relationship of 'value' to human inquiry. For sociology (until the ethnomethodological turn) the latter problematic has been paramount; for moral philosophy, the former problematic has been the central one, leaving the latter to other sub-branches of philosophy. Throughout both these domains of inquiry, however, the problematics have been articulated around a central set of axes (distinct but interdependent) which shall provide the pivot for this discussion: (1) the distinction between 'fact' and 'value'; (2) the is/ought dichotomy; (3) the problem of 'relativism' versus 'objectivity', and (4) the related issue of 'moral diversity'.

2 Sociology and the problem of value

(a) The distinction between 'fact' and 'value'

Perhaps the clearest distinction between 'fact' and 'value', between the realm of description and that of valuation, is to be found in the work of Durkheim and the 'positivists'. Durkheim's methodological principles, and his injunction to 'treat social facts as things' (Durkheim, 1964) hold two implications. First, that the values of the investigator are not relevant. The objects of social scientific inquiry are as independent of investigation and investigator as are the objects of natural scientific inquiry. Second, that the values of the actors (for example, suicide agents) are also irrelevant. 'Social facts' are subject to law-like explanations that need not take into account the reasons and explanations of the actors.[2] The objects of social scientific inquiry are thus constituted without recourse to any notion of values (and one might add perceptions, understandings, interests) at all. We have here a radical banishment of 'values' into the domain of the irrelevant, the inconsequential – at best 'values' would be seen as *contaminants*. Broadly speaking, this same stance characterises the view of the logical positivists on the relationship between 'value' and 'inquiry', and can be traced back to Kant.

In the tradition of Dilthey, Weber was concerned with making a distinction between the 'natural sciences' and the 'cultural sciences'. They are distinct by virtue of the fact that the latter's domain of inquiry includes actors who themselves attach meanings and understandings to their actions and their consequences. To achieve an understanding in the cultural sciences therefore, one must take such meanings into account – there must be empathetic understanding. Here, then, the 'values' of the actors can be part of the object of investigation. The 'values' of the scientist, however, are still construed by Weber in the Kantian mode, presupposing a dichotomy between 'fact' and 'value'. Inquiry needs to be, and indeed can be, 'value-free' (Weber, 1946). The values of the investigator enter only in the selection and determination of what phenomena to study. Here the cultural values and interests of the social scientist do operate to fix the inquiry onto matters deemed of significance, but in the actual conduct of the inquiry the 'values' need not and, indeed, must not, intervene. One can have an 'objective' social science even though the selection of topics can be culturally relative. Here again, the conception of 'values' as potential contaminants of social scientific inquiry is evident, but is modified by the conception of 'values' as 'regulative' (and regulatable).

In contradistinction to this, Marx's conception of the relation between 'fact' and 'value' was grounded in German historicism. 'Turning Hegel on his head', Marx saw material interests as primary, and therefore as 'determinants' of the sphere of 'culture' which includes 'values'. The material base, and the relationships of production, of superordinate and subordinate classes, determined the realm of ideas, the superstructure. Consequently, the 'ruling ideas of any age are the ideas of the ruling class', and ideas and values are relative to a socio-historic configuration (Marx, 1965). In turn then, the work of inquiry and theorising, and the results of such inquiry, are determined by the values of the investigator, values generated by particular socio-historic locations and interests.[3] Thus, a 'value-free', or 'value-neutral', science of human affairs is impossible. 'Values' are *determinant* of the character of inquiry, even if they are themselves already determined by material conditions. In this version, the in-principle first-order distinction between the world of fact and the world of value is maintained. But the two are seen as intimately bound up together.

In the Marxian conception, the concept of 'interests' interfaces closely with the notion of 'values', leaving room for confusion. Indeed, in both Marxist and Weberian accounts one encounters an overworking of the notion of 'value', and a blurring of relevant concepts (moral beliefs, values, evaluations, interests, moral judgements, moral standards, criteria, etc.) which philosophy after the linguistic turn (most notably with the work of Wittgenstein) was to begin to discriminate finely, opening up the way for the detailed ethno-methodological elucidation of communcative praxis.

(b) The is/ought dichotomy: in search of justification

Weber maintained the dichotomy between 'is' and 'ought' inherited from Kant. The ideal of a 'value-free' (if culturally significant) social science in pursuit of generalised *causal explanation* was one way of articulating the fact/value distinction consistent with the view that one cannot move from the level of the 'is' to the level of the 'ought' scientifically. For the social scientist this was not only a methodological ideal, but also an ethical ideal, in keeping with a particular conception of scientific responsibility (Weber, 1946).

Marx's conception on the other hand went in a different direction. 'Values' (in their interface with 'interests'), as determined by the material base, were determinant of ideas and perceptions. 'Value-commitment' is inevitable, and as such it must be pursued clearly and explicitly. This position, advocated by later Marxists, approaches the 'regulative' conception of 'values'. The social scientist is ultimately either committed to promulgating the ideas and interests of the ruling class (and the dominant relations of production) or in dereifying them and combating them. One indeed does, and must necessarily, move from the realm of the 'is' to the realm of the 'ought'. Given the first-order and in-principle dichotomy between 'fact' and 'value' underlying Marxian conceptions however, Marx, and later Marxists, became involved in the project of justifying that move ontologically. Marx, Lukacs (1971) and Goldman (1969) were to locate that in the universalisability of the emancipatory interest of the proletariat – their emancipated condition would be a universal emancipation, therefore their interests were the interests of the species as a whole. This was itself, of course, a normative, indeed morally articulated premiss.

(c) Relativism and objectivity: the problem of diversity

Both Marx's and Weber's historicist conceptions (in the former thorough-going, in the latter constrained and modified) provide a picture of socio-historic and moral–cultural diversity. This diversity inevitably raises the issue

of relativism and the question of objectivity. Marx's response was twofold –
on the one hand he gives a normative–ontological argument, and on the other
hand he provides a praxiological answer. Both were to be picked up by later
Marxist writers, albeit differently. On the one hand, as we have seen, he
locates universality in the emancipatory interest (and therefore value-stance)
of the proletariat, and it is the adoption of this stance that, therefore, can produce objective thought and knowledge (by which he meant universally valid
and significant). Here begins the debate over the issue of 'ideology', to which
Mannheim's work (Mannheim, 1936) and the project of a sociology of
knowledge can be traced back.

On the other hand, Marx was to say that philosophers have so far
'interpreted the world' but the task 'is to change it' (1965: 667). And in the
second thesis on Feuerbach he constituted the question of 'objectivity' as a
praxiological one. He writes:

> The question whether objective truth can be attributed to human thinking is not a ques-
> tion of theory but is a *practical* question. Man must prove the truth, that is, the reality
> and power, the this-sidedness of his thinking in practice. The dispute over the reality
> or non-reality of thinking which is isolated from practice is a purely *scholastic*
> question. (Marx, 1965: 665)

If there is any connection between the two positions, it is that praxis ultimately
brings about proletarian emancipation, the end of pre-history, and the beginning of human history, and thus makes possible the end of ideology and the
beginning of genuine human inquiry. The relationship then is a means–end
one: the former answer to the problem of objectivity is relevant to the conception of history itself, to the conception and determination of human goals,
to the long term emancipatory project; the latter to the means by which such
ends are ultimately attained.

Weber's formulation of the problem of objectivity was that this could be
attained by providing ('value-free') causal explanations, based on observation, of actors' meanings and value-commitments, that related them to the
total value system. Given the diversity of 'meanings' and value-commitments,
however, Weber's work inevitably raised two sorts of issue, round which two
debates within the human sciences developed. The first one was this: given the
causal explanation of conduct that was Weber's project, where was priority
to be placed in the social scientist's description? On the actors' own meanings
(and inherent value stances)? Or on alternative formulations of them? And
does this not involve the social scientist in 'taking sides', or making her or his
own value assessments? (Becker, 1967; Gouldner, 1968). The second debate
that is of significance here is the debate on understanding and inquiry (Winch,
1958 and 1970; MacIntyre, 1970a and b, 1978). Although this debate is not
explicitly about 'values', it is of deep relevance to the subject, if one is to treat
values as in any way 'part' of ordinary persons' conceptions of their actions
and their world. The question is this: given that an actor's understandings are

embedded in a total cultural system of concepts and ideas, how is the social scientist to be said to 'understand' and give 'objective' rendition to the actions/ beliefs of subjects under scrutiny, if she/he does not share them? The question of the *nature* of social scientific description is at issue here, a question which was also taken up by Louch (1966) who went so far as to insist that all descriptions of action are 'moral descriptions'.

It is in these debates, and their relevance to the problem of 'values', that a new conception of the relationship of 'values' to inquiry and to conduct (a new conception of the 'moral') begins to surface, one in which they are not contaminant, regulative or determinant, but *constitutive*. This emerges out of developments within philosophy, particularly the work of Wittgenstein, and begins to locate the intimate ('internal' in Winch's terms (1958)) connections between the 'normative' and the 'conceptual' on the one hand, and between concepts and action on the other.

3   Moral philosophy and the linguistic turn

Since Plato and Socrates, philosophy has been concerned with the place of ethics in human life, and with the nature of morals and the good society. With *The Republic*, the logical elucidation of moral concepts decisively entered into the realm of philosophical discussion. Both Plato and Aristotle were concerned with the inculcation of values as an essential function of public discourse and political life. With the development of modern conceptions of science, however, beginning in the seventeenth century, 'values' and ethical commitments began to be viewed as matters that could be eliminated from 'factual' discourse. Kant's work in the eighteenth century firmly established the distinction between 'fact' and 'value' and the is/ought dichotomy. Nevertheless, he was still concerned seriously with the investigation of the character of our moral concepts and precepts, and specifically what it was about them that made them *moral*. Placing duty at the heart of morality, he propounded his notion of the moral imperative (which he called the categorical imperative) and argued that the test of a genuine moral imperative was that it could be universalised by the agent. In a sense, then, one can say that after Kant the site of many of the central issues raised in modern moral philosophy was already established.

With the advent of logical positivism, language becomes the site for the distinction between 'fact' and 'value'. All meaningful propositions are either formal or factual, whereas evaluative talk is treated as mere self-reports, not subject to truth-value assignation. Emotivism, most significantly expounded by Stevenson (1945) held that all evaluative (especially moral) judgements were simply expressions of preference on the part of the speaker. An expression such as 'This is good' meant 'I approve of this; do so as well'. It was neither true nor false, but simply displayed the speaker's attitude and attempted to produce a similar attitude in others. Although, to a limited extent, the pragmatic feature of such utterances is implicitly noted here, the doctrine misses the performative character of such expressions (Austin, 1955) given as moral judgements. 'This is good' could be said, for instance, to commend, contrast, agree, and the like. Language here is still treated in the pre-Wittgensteinian (and pre-Austinian) mode, as either reports on the world outside, or on the feelings and preferences of the speaker. For the emotivist then, moral judgements cannot be rationally justified. But what are preferences based on? And how can one make them intelligible, let alone reproduce them in others, if they are not grounded in some common order of conventional agreement?

In contrast, analytical moral philosophy insists that there can be logical moral argument, that moral expressions and judgements are not merely the expressions of individual preference, but that, rather, there is a rational basis for moral judgement.[4] This basis is located in principles that can be universalised – albeit, once you get to that point, you can find no further extrinsic justification. However, the distinction between fact and value is maintained here as the distinction between the 'language of fact' and the 'language of value', the study of the nature of moral concepts was now to be, unremittingly, the study of the logic of moral language (as distinct from factual), and the is/ought dichotomy is discussed in terms of the possibility of moving from statements of 'is' (factual premises) to statements of 'ought' (evaluative conclusions).

Modern moral philosophy is, of course, also concerned with the relationship between 'action' and moral beliefs, and with the nature of moral judgement, as well as a number of related issues. Yet while its domain of inquiry has elaborated the kinds of concepts under discussion (instead of just the 'hold-all' of 'values', we now have beliefs, judgements, standards, commendations, etc.) the arguments, with their opposing positions, still revolve around some of the same basic issues and distinctions. Hare (1952, 1963), for example, maintains the is/ought dichotomy and the fact/value distinction. This overlooks the practical conduct of ordinary persons, and the actual ways and contexts in which they make moral judgements or decisions. It also misconstrues, in the first place, the nature of that rational basis of moral judgement and of the logical linkage that exists between various moral judgements. For if there were some such set of common agreements (principles, procedures, judgements), as indeed one has to admit there are, then it is hard to see why a moral judgement would not be treated, in the real world, *as a matter of fact*. And why a set of factual circumstances, could not, in particular contexts, be generative of specifically moral judgements. At the same time that Hare maintains this distinction, he argues for a universalisability criterion for all genuinely 'moral' stances (Hare, 1963), a position that, being itself a normative one, tends to rule out moral diversity on certain matters as somewhat irrational. Foot (1958), on the other hand, attempts to show that there can indeed be a move from 'is' to 'ought' statements, from factual premises to moral conclusions, but her formulation of some of these moves as logically *entailed* also runs into the problem of actual moral diversity.[5]

The problem of diversity and relativism has maintained its importance in the work of the moral philosophers, yet they seem ill-equipped to deal adequately with it. As Louch (1966) aptly puts it:

Moral philosophers have come to deal with their subject in isolation from actual human performances because of their addiction to univocal conceptions of truth, argument and evidence, supposing that it is their business to exhibit these conceptions in or foist them upon moral language and argument. (Louch, 1966: 235)

The distinction between evaluation and description begins to be challenged in the work of contemporary philosophers after Wittgenstein. Yet Wittgenstein's contribution was only to be partially taken up by philosophers distinctly concerned with the issue of morality and moral discourse (for example Pitkin, 1972; Kovesi, 1967). The fundamental problem here was twofold: the reformulation of the fact/value distinction into a dichotomy operating at a different level, namely that between 'moral discourse' and various other forms of *discourse*, albeit judgement and description were seen to be intertwined *within* each form of discourse. The second problem, closely linked to this, was that moral philosophers continued to neglect the detail of actual social practices, and actual social conduct, for the understanding of the logic of moral matters (values-in-use, beliefs-in-context, judgements-in-practical-settings etc.). Wittgenstein's emphasis (1968, 1974) on practices and conventions of practice as the embedding network for concepts, standards and criteria, his elucidation of how the logical grammar of particular concepts was deeply entwined with the practices within which they make sense, his insistence on the conventional and intersubjective foundations of sense and nonsense, and his discussion of the notion of 'language games', clearly bring together the logical, the normative, and the practical into the *same circle of intelligibility*. Thus, once we start looking at the *practices* in which our moral concepts come to life – once we abandon the commitment to an in-principle dichotomy between language and activity, and between language and the world (following Wittgenstein, on the one hand, as well as Austin and other ordinary language philosophers on the other), then we can see in detail, that, and how it is that, description and appraisal are, in fact, deeply intertwined.

Louch (1966) points out that 'describing' and 'appraising' are not opposing ways of examining the world, but that rather, *appraisal*, is a form of description itself, a way of seeing the world – in other words, a way of constituting reality. Descriptive categories are themselves, often and unproblematically, *moral* or *aesthetic* categories.[6] Louch pursues the notion of *action as performance* which necessitates that the investigation of action should be sensitive to appraisal as a constitutive feature of that action, and should indeed necessitate, conversely, that the study of ethics be founded in, and pursuant of, 'the detail of particular human actions providing the contexts in which moral puzzles and conflicts arise' (Louch, 1966: 235). Indeed, this is the lesson of Wittgenstein's analysis of the logical-grammar of our concepts and the practical contexts in which they are intelligibly used. Louch states:

But the inappropriateness of the covering law theory of explanation to the understanding of human action can only be brought out by indicating what sort of paradigms govern our observation and description of human behavior and thus the kind of queries we have about it. The paradigm which I have tried to uncover in various contexts is rooted in the concept of an action itself, *viewed as a performance*. Performances, in turn, are actions which can only be identified as appropriate, felicitous or successful . . . so the puzzles that occur to us . . . are . . . in a broad sense, moral puzzles, requiring . . . justification, warrant or excuse to make them clear . . . *an epistemological query joins with a moral inquiry.* (Louch, 1966: 233–4, emphasis added)

If any intellectual tradition was to pick up this gauntlet and to take up Louch's 'promissory note' (Louch, 1966: 235), and more radically, Wittgenstein's regrounding of philosophical inquiry, it was ethnomethodology, as founded in the first place by Harold Garfinkel, and pursued by Harvey Sacks and later ethnomethodologists.

4   Ethnomethodology and the socio-logical turn

Ethnomethodology's interest in practical action and practical reasoning includes the explication of the ways by which the rationality, intelligibility, objectivity, accountability, and reproducibility, etc. of actions and their settings is organised and made visible. One particular trajectory or variant of ethnomethodological inquiry, which has explicitly incorporated the Wittgensteinian turn in philosophy, concerns itself with the investigation of the *socio-logic* of members' practices in naturally occurring communicative settings. Rather than giving accounts and explanations of members' conduct, values, beliefs and judgements, it analytically examines the ways that conduct, belief and judgement are organised, produced and made intelligible in members' own accounts and descriptions, and how these are embedded in various other practices. The accounts are treated as features of those practices, the descriptions as constituents of conduct.

On one level, ethnomethodological inquiry (pertinent to the question of 'values') would seek to elucidate in detail, within actual settings: for example, the normative construction of features of those settings; the normative construction of facticity; the practical intelligibility of moral standards; the interactional logic of moral ascriptions etc. More specifically, some of the phenomena for analytic investigation might be: the ways agreements and disagreements are organised, generated, displayed and managed, and the activities they are constituents of; what counts as a reasonable warrant for certain sorts of action ascription; how particular action ascriptions are tied into responsibility ascriptions, and to the activities of blaming or praising; how factual disagreements are productive of different moral accountings (different verdicts, outcomes, interactional upshots); how different descriptions of an action can provide for different interactional tasks; how moral standards themselves can be interactionally assessed in consequential ways etc. The normative, logical and practical is always *conjointly in focus* within such inquiry, since these come 'laminated' in actual real worldly contexts of action and discourse. This is what the notion of a 'socio-logic' seeks to capture, elucidate and pursue. Moral concepts and beliefs turn out not to inhabit a high ground that overlooks the terrain of action, or 'fact' – rather they are *constituents* of these, and practical reasoning turns out to be morally organised.

Ethnomethodological inquiry thus *relocates* the site of the classical problematics of value and inquiry, and value and conduct (neutrality and commitment; the fact/value distinction; the is/ought dichotomy; the issue of relativism and objectivity, universalisability and specificity) – these are matters of practical and ongoing relevance for members in the conduct of their everyday life. As such, ethnomethodology reconstitutes them as *topics* for sustained analytic elucidation, by which their logic-in-use can be uncovered. The discussions and debates over 'values' in human affairs are transformed into an investigation of the socio-logic of the moral order, that same order within which both inquiry and conduct are conjointly embedded. Let us, then, turn in greater detail to the ethnomethodological regrounding of the inquiry into 'moral order'.

5 Ethnomethodology's groundwork: the moral foundations of social order

Garfinkel's distinct achievement, *from this point of view* (and his achievement manifestly resists encapsulation into a single set of issues or parameters) was to elucidate *the normative grounding of social order*, and to elucidate it *not* as a general theoretic viewpoint or formal principle, but in and through the details of the ongoing, irremediably situated production of order in particular settings – the *in situ* local organisation of intelligibility, and its normative embeddedness in 'background expectancies' (Garfinkel, 1967).

Specifically taking off from Parsons on the one hand,[7] and Schutz on the other, Garfinkel's work constitutes a re-direction of the way the problem of 'social order' is addressed. 'How is social order possible?' is a question which in Garfinkel's work can be seen to be reconstituted via (i) a focus on the produced detail that is a proper answer to the puzzle of the 'how', and (ii) a deconstruction of the generic notion of 'social order' into the notion of particular practical 'orders' of various occasioned settings in everyday life. It is these 'orders' which, when examined, turn out to be the generative constituents of the 'macro' social order, as it is encountered and oriented to by both actors and investigators.

In his essay on 'The Routine Grounds of Everyday Practical Actions'

(Garfinkel, 1967), he uncovers, through his 'breaching experiments', the irremediably normative foundations of intersubjectivity and of the very possibility of concerted action and intelligible accountable discourse. Here he begins to locate the moral foundations within which 'social order' is *praxiologically generated* and which, in turn, are thus reconstituted and reestablished as 'grounds' for accountable, rational, intelligible actions, inference and judgement within discourse. What he locates is the reflexive order of practical action. Thus, these 'background expectancies' embed the production of interactive episodes, and of local understandings of the sense, reference, relevance and significance of utterances and actions, and are thus made intelligible, accountable, and visible by just that. In his opening paragraph Garfinkel says:

A society's members encounter and know the moral order as perceivedly normal courses of action – familiar scenes of everyday affairs, the world of daily life known in common with others and with others taken for granted. (Garfinkel, 1967: 35)

In this context, the orientation to a 'reciprocity of perspectives', stressed by Schutz (1962), finds its place – Garfinkel's studies show how it is a normative requirement of concerted action, a formative assumption of the course of mutual understanding as it unfolds in an interactive episode. It is a *matter of trust* between participants that certain orientations and tacit understandings are taken to be mutually oriented to, so that:

Many matters that the partners understood were understood on the basis not only of what was actually said but what was left unspoken. (Garfinkel, 1967: 39)

In this context, the notion of 'trust' is:

used there to refer to a person's compliance with the expectancies of the attitude of daily life *as a morality*. (Garfinkel, 1967: 50)[8]

In his 'breaching experiments', which were perceived by the subjects involved as posing a 'threat to the normative order of events', it becomes clear that intelligibility, as a practical matter, is, and *is taken to be* by participants in their local settings, a matter located in a normative/moral weave of background understandings. Reciprocity of perspectives, relevance, the sincerity of the communicative/interactive stance (which is distinct from the sincerity or truthfulness of particular claims that are locally advanced), consistency, are clearly moral presumptions and foundational stays for the production of any interactive order and an *intersubjectively knowable social world*. But we are not here talking of internalised norms that govern actions (*à la* Parsons). Nor merely of presupposed norms that inform actions. Rather, and to reiterate a fundamental point, we are talking of criteria, presuppositions, and understandings that operate as the constituents of action, but which reflexively, in the very conduct of social life, in the very particulars by which actions and settings are produced, are themselves reconstituted, reaffirmed, played out and made relevant. What is being located here is not a determination or a causal nexus. It is, rather, the reflexive nexus of social praxis – and this reflexive nexus is a *creative*, not a merely replicative one, constituting the workings of an ongoing and *ramifying* social order. Garfinkel's experiments, therefore, demonstrate one level, a *foundational* one, at which moral order is constitutive of the intelligibility of human action and human understanding. The domain of 'value', 'morality', the 'normative' now clearly comes into view, not simply as regulative of conduct and inquiry, but as constitutive of it. The insights developed in the work of Wittgenstein are now being equally generated in the domain of sociological inquiry – demonstrated as evidentially operative in the details of social organisation and interaction. Just as sociology, in the work of the ethnomethodologists, took off from the 'linguistic turn', so now philosophy, in the work of the ethnomethodologists, encounters the *'socio-logical turn'* in the inquiry into intelligibility and morality.

Harvey Sacks further develops the explication of this tie between the moral and the intelligible along a number of dimensions. In his work, Louch's points on the nature of the study of human action as performance come to life. Both in his explication of the logic and organisation of membership categorisation devices (Sacks, 1967, 1972a, 1972b) and in his work together with Schegloff and Jefferson on the sequential organisation of conversational order and the turn-taking system (1974), Sacks uncovers the moral foundations of sense, interactive order and the known-in-common social world – of intersubjectivity as practically evidenced and ongoingly reconstituted by members of the social world.

Perhaps the most fundamental point about Sacks' work on membership categorisation practices, and one that seamlessly joins with Louch's concerns, is, as Jeff Coulter noted in chapter 3, and John Lee elaborated in chapter 9, the distinction that he made between appropriate and correct description. It is this distinction, clearly a matter of programmatic importance in the understanding of members' practices of sense-production and understanding, that marks out, more than anything, the moral weave, and the moral groundings of ordinary discourse. If the same person can be correctly described as a mother, a daughter, an American, a Catholic, a university professor, a wife, a socialist, a scientist, a pro-choicer, etc. then what are the criteria by which a selection from among this range of possibilities is made in practice, and on particular occasions? The fact that all these may be correct descriptions of the same person does not, in itself, settle for us, the *in situ* intelligibility of particular descriptions as produced within the course of practical action. What are the conventional implications of particular selections, what are their inferential consequences? *How* is their intelligibility produced and made visible?

To locate some answers to these concerns we can develop issues that were introduced by Jeff Coulter in chapter 3, and discussed, in part by Wes Sharrock and Graham Button in chapter 7, with respect to Sacks' (1972b) analyses of the 'story', told by a three-year-old:

The baby cried. The Mommy picked it up.

As Jeff Coulter has already mentioned, both the notions of membership categorisation *devices* (collections of categories that members treat as 'naturally' going together), and also of category bound activities, are explicated as constituents of the intelligibility of such a story – that is, that the person who picked up the baby was not any woman who happened to be also someone's mother, but the baby's *own mother*. The story is hearable as being about, and produced to be about, normal familial relations.[9] Out of this story, Sacks formulates what in chapter 3 he was seen to call 'the consistency rule' – a hearer's version being that if some category from a given device is used locally to characterise a member of a population, and a second category is then used in close proximity to characterise another member, then if that second category can be heard as coming from the same device, we hear it that way. In combination with the notion of category-boundedness, whereby certain activities and properties are seen as conventionally tied to some category (crying is tied to baby, and the obligation of picking up a crying baby is tied to 'mother'), we hear the 'mother' in the story as being the baby's *own* mother. It is a routine, un-problematic, 'natural' hearing – rooted, that is, in the 'natural attitude of everyday life'. It would be *unfounded*, from within the stance of daily life, the 'natural attitude', to hear the 'mother' in the story as being, for example, the baby's neighbour, who, in addition to being the neighbour, was also the mother of some children. This would, in fact, be an argumentative or non-cooperative hearing.

Now imagine that the story had gone like this: 'The baby cried. The scientist picked it up.' Here, contrary to the first story, the second categorisation cannot be seen as coming from the same device as the first one, and indeed the activity of 'picking up a baby' cannot be seen as bound to that second category of 'scientist'. In this case, to hear the scientist as being the mother of the baby is, again, to engage in a hearing based on the suspension, or questioning, of mundane understandings – an 'argumentative' or 'non-cooperative' hearing. Rather, a routine way of hearing this might be to constitute for it a setting in which the categorisation 'scientist', as a chosen category for the story, would be relevant – a laboratory setting for example.[10] Underlying this, as indeed the hearing of the first story and the very operation of a consistency rule there, is an orientation to the 'relevance' of category selections, and of descriptions, an orientation that is taken to be simultaneously and mutually engaged in, and attended to, by speakers and hearers. The presumption is that the selections and descriptions used are relevant to the point of the story, or the action, which is constituted by any local utterance/discourse, relevant that is to the task at hand, and also relevant for the *hearer's understanding* of the discourse and task at hand. This assumption of relevantly produced/designed utterance and activity underlies the very assignment of intelligibility to an utterance/action, and the constitution, *in situ*, of its sense and reference. And underlying this assumption, an assumption that is taken to be reciprocally shared by interactants, is therefore the assumption of the sincerity of the interactional/communicative stance, that there is no radical or hidden *disjuncture* between description and purpose at hand, between the category selection and the relevances that inform the *occasion* for which that selection was made – no radical 'bad faith' in the organisation and production of communicative action.

This presumption that the relevance is mutually oriented to and 'respected' is an instantiation of Garfinkel's idea of 'trust' in the routine operation of background expectancies that participants to a setting hold, and is clearly a foundation for any local constitution of sense. Otherwise we would, as ordinary members, be in the eternal position of the detective, going out with an array of tools to hunt for clues and discover the answers to the mystery she/he was initially presented with. But a member, operating from within the natural attitude, and enmeshed in the practical flow of ordinary everyday life experiences, is *not* presumptively and programmatically such a detective. Members are rather, *mundane* actors/reasoners (Pollner, 1987). We can see here that the foundations of mundaneity are irredeemably moral.

Where members engage in lies, deception, and fraud in their communications, they do so by relying on precisely the presumption of a mutual orientation to relevance and sincerity. And when members 'uncover' lies, deception or fraud, or suspect them, look out for them etc., they do not thereby suspend their programmatic and normative expectancy of sincerity and relevance and the reciprocity of perspectives – they indeed manifestly reconstitute them and use them, draw and rely on them, and *make them visible*. As Heritage (1984: 100) points out, deviations from a norm are treatable routinely as *departures* from it – in other words it is the norm-in-use that makes them visible and accountable in just the way that they are. And conversely, it is such marked, noted 'deviations', as just *these* deviations, that reconstitute and make the 'norm', the 'ordinary', visible *as just that*.

Even when hearers later find that their understanding say, of the speaker's task at hand, and their ascription to him of particular relevances as 'read' from some description or stretch of talk, was 'mistaken'; that, in other words the speaker turned out to have a 'hidden agenda', a hidden set of relevances, they will take it that the selection of descriptive items nevertheless was meant and fitted to providing for the sense and relevance of the talk *as it was meant to be taken by participants*. The 'lie' then, the 'deception' turns precisely on this moral grounding of the communicative/interactional encounter, this reliance on a 'reciprocity of perspectives'.

What emerges from both Garfinkel's and Sacks' work is the understanding that all communicative praxis presupposes, and is founded in, a 'natural' ethic – an ethic, that is, which is constitutive of, and reflexively constituted by, the *natural attitude of everyday life*.

In this context, Grice's co-operative principle (1975, 1978), with its attendant maxims, is, as formulated by him, operative at best at the surface grammar of communicative order. The 'ethic' revealed through Garfinkel and Sacks' work is locatable at the deep grammar of communicative practice. It is that which enables us to say 'morality presupposes community, as community presupposes morality' (Jayyusi, 1984). Or as Peter Winch says 'the social conditions of a language and rationality must also carry with them certain fundamental *moral* conceptions' (Winch, 1972: 61) so that 'the existence of a norm of truth-telling is a *moral* condition of language' (Winch, 1972: 63). On the other hand, Habermas' four validity claims (1979) – one of which replicates Winch's truth-telling norm – do not advance our understanding of communicative praxis in much depth. They are provided as abstract principles which are universalisable to all communicative encounters, thereby missing the more interesting phenomena – the very *how* by which they are oriented to, and made operative in, actual communicative settings to provide for a range of different sorts of interactive possibilities, and for the detailed ways in which a mundane social order is constructed by members to a particular setting. For it is, after all, reflexively through such practices of 'reality construction' that such principles are made visible as oriented-to 'principles' of proper talk and interaction, and reproduced as grounds for that. It is this in part, that is the distinctly ethnomethodological contribution.

6   The moral constitution of praxis

The above is one level at which Sacks' work elucidates the way that description and appraisal are intertwined. What description is usable and intelligible in context is embedded in an appraisal of relevance, point, task at hand, recipient etc. – the description here is co-fitted to the appraisal, a feature of it, and is taken to be produced in this way by co-participants.

In Sacks' work on membership categorisations however, another dimension of the mutually constitutive character of appraisal and description in social life emerges. It is in the very *character* of these category concepts and, therefore, of the uses made of them, the social practices they constitute and make possible. Sacks' notion of category bound actions, rights, and obligations not only points out the moral features of our category concepts, but also provides thus for the very moral accountability of certain actions or omissions. His elucidation of the notion of certain categories as standardised relational pairs (Sacks, 1972a) not only uncovers features of the organisation of members' conventional knowledge of the social world, but clearly demonstrates, via his detailed empirical analysis, how that knowledge is both morally constituted and constitutive of moral praxis – it provides for a variety of ascriptions, discoveries, imputations, conclusions, judgements, etc. on the part of mundane reasoners. It shows how our knowledge is constitutive of, and provides for, a *moral inferential logic* – a logic of moral inference that is at the same time a moral grounding of practical inference.[11] I have elsewhere, building on Sacks' work, tried to show in some detail how moral reasoning is practically organised, and how, at the same time, and perhaps more significantly, practical reasoning is morally organised (Jayyusi, 1984). Very clearly, the use of even mundanely descriptive categories, such as 'mother', 'doctor', 'policeman', for example, makes available a variety of possible inferential trajectories *in situ*, that are grounded in the various 'features' bound up with, or constitutive of, these categories as organisations of practical mundane social knowledge. These features might be 'moral' features in the first place (such as the kinds of 'rights' and 'obligations' that are bound up with one's being a 'mother', or a 'doctor' or 'policeman'), or they might be otherwise – such as the 'knowledge' that is for example, taken to be bound up with a category such as 'doctor', or the kind of 'work' that is taken to be constitutive of, or tied to, a category such as policeman. But even in the latter case, it turns out that as evidenced in our actual practices, for example, 'knowledge' has its responsibilities[12] – even *these* features provide grounds for the attribution of all kinds of moral properties, for finding that certain kinds of events or actions may or may not have taken place, for determining culpability, even for defeating the applicability of the category or description in the first place. The practices, in which our category concepts are embedded and used, and the knowledge contexts bound up with them, are ones in which description and appraisal, the conceptual, moral, and practical are reflexively and irremediably bound up with, and embedded in, each other. Intelligibility is constituted in practico-moral terms. And that, after all, is what Wittgenstein's later work so insistently revealed. It was left to ethnomethodology, however, to give that work (and indeed philosophical inquiry generally) the socio-logical turn which would demonstrate how that is the case in detail, and in the course of that, explicate in great depth and cumulativity, a variety of the features of members' practico-moral activities and discourse.

A brief catalogue of particular investigations might include the following: the constitution of moral 'profiles' (Watson, 1978), the use of, and orientation to, a religious geography (Drew, 1978), the moral order of cognition (Coulter, 1973b, 1979a), the ascription and construction of mental illness (Smith, 1978, Coulter, 1973b), the constitution of hierarchies and dilemmas (Jayyusi, 1984), blamings (Pomerantz, 1978a), the relationship between the scenic intelligibility of the social world, and thus the logic of visual transition in film, and members' category knowledge (Jayyusi, 1988), the relationship between a corpus of knowledge and a collectivity (Sharrock, 1974), the presentation of victim and offender in police interrogations (Watson, 1983).

All the phenomena addressed by these investigations (and the many others besides), exhibit the reflexive embeddedness of the moral, the conceptual, and the practical in each other. From within this reflexive nexus it becomes evident that the constitution of persons, actions, events, facticity, objectivity, predictability, consequentiality, and the like is irredeemably *moral*, whether these moral features are explicitly topicalised and made a focus *in situ* (as in the domain of 'ethics') or whether they remain resources, present but unnoticed organising properties of talk and action. It is here that Louch's remarks on the project of understanding human action comes home: 'an epistemological query joins with a moral inquiry' (1966: 234).

One other domain of ethnomethodological inquiry wherein one might see, in more concrete detail, how the conceptual, the moral and the practical are intertwined, is that of the sequential organisation of ordinary conversation. As Sacks, Schegloff and Jefferson (1974),[13] followed later by Pomerantz (1978b, 1984a), Drew (1984), Button (1987a and b) and others have shown, conversational activities are organised sequentially, and what kind of activity is being performed in and through an utterance is given by its sequential location, its context within a just prior utterance and a just subsequent one. Indeed, Schegloff and Sacks (1973) showed that certain sorts of utterances/ activities come in pairs – they called them adjacency pairs. Thus answers have questions as a next pair part, greetings have greetings, invitations have acceptances or rejections, etc. Here the notion of 'preference' is made operative by the analyst (see, for example, Sacks, 1987; Sacks and Schegloff, 1979; Schegloff, Jefferson and Sacks, 1977; Pomerantz, 1984b) – questions prefer answers is the formulation given; invitations prefer acceptances. This notion of 'preference' is clearly a normative one, grounded in our understanding of the contingencies of practical actions *and* their embeddedness in a moral context. If we look at the pair greeting/greeting, for instance, we can see that it is not the case that a greeting will in actuality always elicit a greeting. The formulation here is not one of empirical regularity. Rather, it is that a greeting is expected in return, as a matter of routine practico-moral order. What does it mean to say that a greeting is expected in return? – it means that there is a normative orientation to the propriety of a return greeting, in order to accomplish an encounter as routine, 'normal', 'ordinary', 'as usual'. 'unproblematic', etc. And for that to be the case, one has to have a knowledge of the concept of 'greeting' – what it is, what it accomplishes, how it enters our life, as Wittgenstein would put it. It is through this, that when a greeting is not returned, the occasion can be characterised by a member as one of a *noticeable absence* (Sacks lectures, 1964–72). That absence is accountable – and it is an occasion for some inference as to what the actual or hidden circumstances are behind that absence, as well as for some directly moral judgement. Thus, one can see that one is being snubbed, that a person does not want to recognise you because he does not want, for example, to acknowledge some past shared history together (Turner, 1970); that someone is haughty, rude, hard of hearing, etc., depending on other contextual detail. But manifestly, we see that the practical, the conceptual, and the moral are laminated together in the organisation of situated action and discourse, and in their very intelligibility.

Coulter (1983a) has argued that the sequential structures described by conversation analysis are essentially apriori in character, rather than purely empirical discoveries, and that the data analysed serves as 'reminders', or a way of facilitating observations on the finer points of discourse organisation. One has to agree with Coulter, yet at the same time, note that what conversation analysis is doing is revealing the practical organisation, the inter-actional character, of specific discourse moves/actions. That, in itself, is not at odds with the apriori character of the sequential structures and adjacency pairs – *rather it takes off from it*. What is further the case, is that these practical/interactional possibilities, grounded as they are in our knowledge of the concepts that animate them, *are also and at the same time* grounded in, and constitutive of, a moral order bound up with those self-same concepts and the practices they enable. We can see this clearly when we look closely at the notion of adjacency pairs, at the notion of preferences, and at the way the relevant interactional moves get situatedly produced. Questions expect answers – that is part of our understanding of the notion of question, and of our knowledge of how it enters into our practices; what role it plays in our forms of life. But this means that, when a question is not answered, the 'silence', the 'walking off', the *'non sequiter'*, etc., all get assessed in terms of the question that is asked – they will count as 'responses' to that question, whatever one might try to do about it. There is no time out from that. The fact that questions expect answers is not taken, by members, to be simply a float-ing generalisation of some kind that one can take or leave – rather it is taken to be a matter of *moral and practical consequence*.

All the above means, of course, the erasure of the programmatic distinctions between fact and value and between 'is' and 'ought' as we have known them to date within the human sciences and philosophy. These dichotomies never-theless surface as members' issues in occasioned ways that are investigable for their particulars, and for what further features of the moral order they display and constitute.

7   The praxiology of moral order

The ethnomethodological relocation of the site of inquiry into moral order, and its respecification of both the methods and phenomena of our investi-gation, has critical ramifications for our understanding of what, in various of our practices, mundane and theoretical, we call 'morality'.

(1) *Moral values are publicly available* – they are not locked into the heads of persons, not secreted in a hidden space in the actor's subjectivity, to be made available only at the decision of that actor. Rather, they are given, rendered, displayed, and made visible and ascribable on the basis of the actors' actions and discourse, in much the same way as mental predicates: intentions (Louch, 1966; Coulter, 1979b), beliefs (Coulter, 1979a and b), understanding (Coulter, 1979b) , etc., and in the same breath. The very organisation of the details of a person's discourse, her/his descriptions, judgements and inferences

make available the 'values', 'relevances', 'concerns' of that person. Thus, one's being seen to elide, for example, the description of some action with its consequences, thereby not providing for the mechanics of that action which brought about such consequences, is hearable as indicative of a particular 'moral' stance, a particular set of values and significances – I have described this in terms of a member's use of a 'moral ascription rule' (Jayyusi, 1984). It is of course in this that the attributions and readings of 'ideology' from certain textual practices, whether by practical actors or social scientists, are themselves grounded in the routine grounds of everyday activities, and are thus unavoidably available in the course of members' practico-moral engagements in, and constructions of, the everyday world.[14]

(2) *Morality has a modal logic* – inasmuch as descriptions/actions are *situated* and occasioned accomplishments, that are normatively constituted; inasmuch as the details of their organisation are sensitive to and productive of, various contexts and accomplishments, then the 'moral' itself, as a set of intelligible, visible, accountable, and displayable particulars, is tied to setting's order, occasion, task, history, etc. – it is *modal in its logic* (Jayyusi, 1984). Even though we might have 'general principles', conventions, rules, these don't provide for their *own* application in the intersubjective and *ongoing production of activity conjunctures* – that, which in other words, constitutes the complex and intricate flow of human life. The cross-cutting multiplicity of conventions and understandings, relevances and practical circumstances means that even that which is 'conventionally given' has to be explicated in terms of its situated production, display, constitution, and even modification. This is as much so for members as it is for analysts. That is to say, conventionality, even though it is what makes possible the production of a shared and known in common social order in the first place, is nevertheless *praxiologically given to members*. It is that which is so deeply missed by so many moral philosophers who attempt to locate specified principles that underlie conduct and reasoning in decontextualised ways (for example the universalisability principle advanced by Hare, 1963), or to explicate the workings of moral discourse and moral reasoning as though there were some kinds of notions that are already 'closed' (Kovesi, 1967; see also Jayyusi's critique, 1984).

(3) *Moral diversity and difference are given in the logic of conventionality* – the conventions which underpin our practices, and ground our communicative activity, including the 'logical grammar' or our concepts, do not rigidly designate what it is we can do, or how it is we can talk about some action, experience or event. Our concepts, as Wittgenstein has shown, have a multiplicity of criteria for their use and application, they are *open-textured* in Waismann's (1965) words. They also have a multiplicity of features 'bound up with them' – part of their logical grammar (Sacks, 1967, 1972a and b; Jayyusi, 1984), and can therefore serve as *conduits* to other categories, concepts, and therefore stances in context (Jayyusi, 1989). What this means is that conventionality has an essentially *metamorphic logic* (Jayyusi, 1989). Differ-

ence, diversity and change are thus *inherent in*, and emergent from *within*, the weave of conventionality.

This is where MacIntyre's central thesis in his book *After Virtue* is so wrong. His claim is that the contemporary language of morals is in grave disorder, moral concepts having lost the original historical contexts from which they derive their significance, so we now 'possess indeed the simulacra of morality, we continue to use many of the key expressions. But we have – very largely, if not entirely – lost our comprehension, both theoretical and practical of morality' (MacIntyre, 1981: 2). He acknowledges a persistence to the language and 'appearance of morality', but asserts that the 'integral substance of morality has to a large degree been fragmented and then in part destroyed' (MacIntyre, 1981: 5). MacIntyre reiterates this claim later in a way that is pertinent to one of the central issues of the inquiry into the 'moral' – the distinction between 'fact' and 'value':

> Up to the present in everyday discourse the habit of speaking of moral judgments as true or false persists; but the question of what it is in virtue of which a particular moral judgment is true or false has come to lack any clear answer. That this should be so is perfectly intelligible if the historical hypothesis which I have sketched is true: that moral judgments are linguistic survivals from the practices of classical theism which have lost the context provided by these practices . . . Thus, in the contemporary world: . . . moral judgments lose any clear status and the sentences which express them in a parallel way lose any undebatable meaning. Such sentences become available as forms of expression of an emotivist self which lacking the guidance of the context in which they were originally at home has lost its linguistic as well as its practical way in the world. (MacIntyre, 1981: 57)

If anything, the ethnomethodological relocation and respecification of the 'moral' serves to undercut precisely this kind of position. MacIntyre's stance, for all its claims and qualifications to the contrary (1981: 10) fails to look at the substance of *moral praxis* in the real world, substituting for that, in large part, the analysis of intellectual and philosophical debates and arguments. Indeed to talk of moral judgements as expressions of an 'emotivist self' that has 'lost its linguistic and practical way in the world' is to constitute mundane practical actors as cultural dopes (Garfinkel, 1967: 66–8). What MacIntyre radically misses is that change, difference, and diversity (the interminable moral arguments of our age against which he rails) are not a 'disorder', but are rather emergent from a specific practical order of (reflexively available) optionalities that are ongoingly realised, constructed, defeated, played out, worked up, and otherwise made relevant and oriented to, in the conduct of practical life.

(4) *Objectivity is praxiologically constituted* – ethnomethodological analysis points to a different route by which the 'objective', the 'true' can be understood. It is not, as Wes Sharrock and Bob Anderson argue in chapter 4, that these notions are to be *discarded* in favour of a thorough-going relativism. Rather, for social actors/reasoners, 'objectivity', and 'truth' are real and

fundamental features of the world, to be oriented to, sought, established, and asserted, taken as self-evident, pointed to, relied on etc., within the conduct of everyday practical actions (whatever these may be). For members, there is a known-in-common objective social world – one that is intersubjectively constituted. And it is in their practices, by which they take this for granted, rely on it, and by which they establish, assert, point to, etc. the 'objectively true', that this 'objective world' is reconstituted and made visible. To assume, orient to, and rely on an 'objective world' (even though it is in and through this that it is established and maintained), and yet at the same time to be enmeshed in a radical relativism of stance and outlook, one that is completely incommensurate with as many other different stances as there are, would not yield the possibility of any communicative/interactive order (and would, correspondingly, not be a reasonable analytic view of the organisation of mundane practice). Rather, it is clear, that the conventional foundations of our practices, and the conventions of logical grammar that are constituents of these, provide for a shared world in which *commonality* is both assumed and discovered, and 'objectivity' can be, therefore, displayed, attested to, accomplished or challenged (in a member's sense – viz. an accounting of some event) and 'recognised'. That our conventions provide for the possibility of change and difference, as indicated above, does not contradict this – for difference is that only from within the frame of some agreements. The diversity of morals or understandings is not a free-standing one, not an arbitrary one, but one *given* as a procedural possibility in our conventions – so that even in difference, one can still recognise the *grounds* for the other position, even if one did not share it. What ethnomethodology points to, therefore, is that 'truth', 'objectivity' etc. is praxiologically organised, yet it is a systematically oriented to, and recognisable, matter for members in the everyday world, in actual occasions of conduct and discourse. It is a matter that members can decide on, point to, debate, defeat, acknowledge or recognise in situated ways, grounded in our conventionality, logical grammar, and the particular assumptions about, and knowledge of, an objective social world. One might say, then, that the ethnomethodological enterprise here is to elucidate, in detail, a new sociologic of objectivity – where 'objectivity' is taken to be the practices which secure and underpin agreement. The work of Pollner (1987), Smith (1974, 1978), Eglin (1979), Bittner (1973) and Zimmerman (1974), come to mind here.

(5) *There is no exit from the moral order* – it becomes clear from the foregoing that the 'moral' does not stand in relation to social praxis as the 'poetic', for example, or the 'scientific'. It is, rather, a pervasive and constituent feature of it, irremediably available as both resource and topic, foundation and project. It is not a distinct and specific domain of discourse and practice, as moral philosophers have tended to treat it, although it may appear to be, as when it is topicalised in the domain of the 'ethical'. Heritage puts it well when he says:

The 'chess-board' of meaning is revealed to be self-righting. The normative account-ability of action is a seamless web, an endless metric in terms of which conduct is unavoidably intelligible, describable and assessable. (Heritage, 1984: 100)

Just as one cannot get out of language to talk about language (Pears, 1971), so one cannot get out of the moral order in order to talk about the moral order. What does this mean for the analyst? It means that she/he uses her/his moral membership, her/his knowledge of the mundane organisation of the practico-moral order as a *resource*, even as she/he turns it into a *topic*.[15] To describe an action-in-context, for example, as one that can be oriented to as a 'breach' by members to a setting, or to find that certain kinds of category-organised knowledge provide routinely for certain kinds of moral judgement and, thus, to account analytically for certain textual readings, or court-room moves, or interactional upshots, etc. is to use the resources of her/his ordinary member-ship, but *to lay them out for view* and pursue them analytically.

It seems necessary at this point then to address (albeit too briefly) a debate that has recently and inevitably surfaced among ethnomethodologists – and that is the issue of the possible supplementation of analysis with critique, or the *extension* of description into criticism. Perhaps the most salient example of this debate lies in some recent articles by McHoul (1988) and Bogen and Lynch (in press). While McHoul (specifically focussing on Jeff Coulter's work), proposes that Wittgensteinian inspired ethnomethodology can be read 'as a crucial starting point' for a political pragmatics, Bogen and Lynch argue that that kind of work serves less as a starting point than as a 'crucial terminus' for that impulse to 'critical social theory'. They reject the possibility of using detailed investigations of praxis (descriptions of ordinary language use in mundane settings, for instance) in the service of social critique. But it is not really clear on what they base *this* conclusion (which is distinct from arguing against *particular* uses of such investigations). And in what analytic/theoretic capacity is it made?

A central part of the argument turns on the character of the 'descriptivist' stance, and the notion of ethnomethodological indifference.[16] Here we have a new version of the old problematic (Weberian versus Marxist approaches; the position exemplified by Foot in modern moral philosophy versus the position exemplified by Hare). The point that is immediately relevant to our concerns is one that Mike Lynch introduced in chapter 5: ethnomethodological indifference (Garfinkel and Sacks, 1970) is *just that* – that the ethnomethod-ological analyst is indifferent, in her/his analysis, to the contingencies and relevances of practical theory or action *either way*. It means that from *within* the analytic descriptivist 'moment',[17] the analyst will not collude with one set of descriptions or characterisations over against others that may be equally available to members as *in situ* options (or worse, of course, unavailable *in situ*). She/he will not, in her/his analysis, privilege one over the other. But she/he can, and indeed must, lay out the various optionalities available *in situ* (at least as appropriate for her/his analytic purposes). In practical contexts, there are routinely more than one set of characterisations (or categorisations/ descriptions) that are relevantly available to members – sometimes taking off each other, sometimes contrastive (often constituted as morally or politically significant).

As I have tried to show elsewhere, in an analysis addressing Letters to the Editor on the issues of capital punishment and abortion (Jayyusi, 1989; see also Jayyusi, 1984), members work with, and orient to, a *relevant category environment* in making judgements, or proffering descriptions, and they routinely maintain and display a visible orientation to two different kinds of category or description at the same time. There is a pervasive and systematic optionality that characterises our human practices and the organisation of our conventional knowledge, where the different relevant options, 'reflexively constitute each other and are played off each other, *in situ*, in ways that exhibit a particular socio-logic' (Jayyusi, 1989). Members may privilege one set of categories, for example, 'as the *agenda-providing ones* in context' (Jayyusi, 1989) yet they will recognise the 'relevant category environment as the ground for the other position, that which accountably provides warrant for the other, even though they may want to undercut or even negate its actual or local relevance, or its moral power for whatever issue at hand' (Jayyusi, 1989).

Further, as Coulter himself commented in a recent work:

In conceptualizing the activities and objects of the world, members may proffer accounts, reports, descriptions, etc., which, while in significant respects *true*, can none the less disguise their own perspectivality and mislead us into assuming that *the assessment of their truth*, or even its relevance, is shared where it may not be. (Coulter, 1989: 48)

He concludes:

For the monitored co-existence of 'parallel' truths about phenomena may be subtly informative as to the basis of the particular 'true' designation of the perceived object, scene or setting. (Coulter, 1989: 49)

Thus, alternative characterisations or assessments, that may have morally or 'politically' contrastive or disjunctive implications, are routine features of certain kinds of mundane settings, occasions and practices (Jayyusi, 1984: Chs. 4 and 5). Indeed such alternative characterisations may remain *present* for members but *unmentioned*. Given that members routinely topicalise moral features of action and discourse (indeed 'politicise' them), and given the more general point that the conceptual, the practical, and the moral are mutually embedded in each other, as we have attempted to elucidate, then descriptions of just these practices and occasions, in the ways that they are constituted, implicated, organised, made 'present', assumed, addressed or otherwise oriented to can, indeed need to be, phenomena for investigation.

In this context it becomes difficult to sustain the kind of position taken by Bogen and Lynch without paradox, for being unable to exit from the moral order in order to describe it or talk about it means, for the analyst, the follow-ing: that in exhibiting and laying out the resources by which she/he makes her/his analysis of the optionalities of action and description available *in situ*, and in offering detailed descriptions of the ways that practices get constituted locally as politically or morally relevant, she/he is involved, minimally and unavoidably in *laying bare the moral significance of these practices as these are made available in our culture*.[18]

Not only may that, *in itself*, be treated as morally or politically significant,[19] but such Wittgensteinian inspired ethnomethodological analyses may cer-tainly provide a base and a set of resources for a political pragmatics. How can one rule that out except by fiat? For the analyst, working from within the rubric of the descriptivist 'moment', to deny the relevance of a 'thick' analysis of locally available optionalities where some of these can be treated as 'partisan' or 'political', and to do so *across the board* and for all analytic purposes, or to reject the usability of such analyses, once made, for the (admittedly distinct) project of critique, is, in either case, paradoxically to 'defend' the descriptivist stance in the process of *abandoning it*. The intract-able reflexivities of social praxis, that are emergent from, and present within, what Garfinkel in chapter 2 describes as the 'haecceity of immortal ordinary society', can offer up no pristine and established *pathway* of cultural dis-engagement, only the 'descriptivist moment' (given both to members as well as analysts), that is nevertheless irretrievably grounded in the stream of mundane practical 'order'.

NOTES

1 It is, of course, not possible, within the scope of a chapter such as this, to deal com-prehensively with the question of 'value', and its various ramifications and articu-lations in the human sciences and philosophy. Clearly, such an undertaking would demand, at the very least, a book-length treatment. For this reason, I focus on a delimited set of problematics that have been significant, and attempt to delineate some of their major features, so as to lay out what I deem to be significant about the ethnomethodological approach. Unhappily, even here much has to be left out or treated too succinctly. The reader is invited then to treat this chapter as a simplified topical 'map', designed to show selected routes from some origins to our presently assigned destination: the ethnomethodological respecification.

2 One should note here the recent work by Gane (1988) which proposes a major reappraisal of Durkheim's method, arguing that fundamental errors, some trace-able to mistranslations of the original texts, have been made in the interpretation of Durkheim. I shall not take up Gane's position here, since I am more concerned with a tradition of work and thinking that originated in Durkhiem *as he was made available*.

3 I am not here in any way suggesting that Marx offered a crude or reductionist 'determinism'. Indeed, the understanding of what 'determines' (and by extension, 'determinant') means or signifies in Marx has been (and still is) an ongoing matter of debate. Is the determination operative on the *specifics*, or the limits of the sphere of culture, for example; is the material base therefore reflected in, or merely refracted through, the ideational sphere, a causal agent or merely a structuring one? Given the strong praxiological dimension of Marx's work, and his emphasis on the 'dialectic' between ideas, action, and material conditions (modes of production), I take the relationship between base and superstructure in Marx to be operative in the *latter* sense, and not in the reductionist or mechanistic sense that some writers have taken it. Nevertheless, the conception is still one of *determination*, rather than 'constitution' (as in later language–philosophic or ethnomethodological approaches), specifically because the two domains are still treated as essentially *extrinsic* to one another. This is where the difference hinges.

4 See, *inter-alia*, the work of Hare (1952, 1963); Foot (1958–9); Gert (1970); Warnock (1971); Donagan (1977) and Gewirth (1978).

5 A related disagreement here, one that is to a point already pre-figured in Weber, is whether philosophical inquiry is to be neutral between evaluations, rather than partisan. This is Hare's position, and accords with his distinction between 'fact' and 'value', 'is' and 'ought'. Foot's position would suggest that to understand our moral concepts is to be bound by the criteria informing their proper application. Philosophical inquiry which reveals this cannot be morally neutral. This same debate resurfaces within the ranks of ethnomethodologists, and will be taken up in that form in more detail towards the end of this chapter.

6 Note here, for instance, the way Kovesi (1967) treated this. Whilst suggesting that evaluation and description are intertwined, he makes a distinction between the world of description and the world of evaluation, so that the former is evaluated by descriptive notions, the latter described by moral notions. He therefore simply shifts the line of divide between the moral and other kinds of discourse, but preserves it albeit in a reconstituted fashion. See Jayyusi (1984) on Kovesi.

7 For a detailed discussion of their relationship, see Heritage (1984).

8 See also Garfinkel (1963).

9 This is, of course, also the kind of story that one reads as being of particular concern and interest to a three-year-old, so that the sense of the story is also provided by the perceived tie between teller's category membership and the particulars of the story told. Thus, the property of category-boundedness is reflexively ramifiable in any local production and understanding of sense.

10 Indeed, when I presented this 'story' in class, on various occasions, students invariably read it as taking place within a laboratory setting.

11 Refer to Jeff Coulter's discussion of 'logic' in chapter 3 for a detailed consideration of complementary concerns with logic.

12 For example, I use this mundane property of practical knowledge as a way of analysing the produced equivocality of a textual reading, in 'The Equivocal Text and the Objective World: An Ethnomethodological Analysis of a Media Text', paper read at the Eastern Communication Annual Convention, Baltimore, Maryland, April 1988.

13 See also Schegloff (1968); Jefferson (1972, 1978, 1988b).

14 By 'everyday world' here I include both that which constitutes the *uneventfully*

mundane, as well as the *mundanely eventful* (such as, for instance, muggings, accidents, elections, strikes, earthquakes, epidemics, falling in love, going mad, etc.).

15 On this see McHoul's discussion in *Telling How Texts Talk* (1982). See also Pollner (1987), especially pp. 147–50.

16 The discussion on this is advanced with reference to the analysis of a particular interaction between a prospective mental patient/mental-welfare officer in Coulter's work. See Coulter (1979b: 26); McHoul (1988: 376–80).

17 The term 'moment' is here used advisedly – for 'disinterested' description is a very specific and irremediably *embedded* activity. It is one engaged in by members, however, as much as analysts – but it takes its force precisely from its relationship to the context in which it is engaged. Description, as we have seen, always involves appraisal of purpose and setting (as well as of the individual constituents of that setting) – it is embedded in a practico-moral context. For the *analyst* then, its 'point' resides in the attempt to uncover *fully* members' own practices and relevances within the locally produced phenomena of interest, rather than substituting one's own. But of course, the analyst is drawing on one's own membership to identify and describe such relevances in the first place. And once that 'full' description is given, the descriptive 'moment' is over – its point done. The insistence on 'disinterested' description cannot then be extended beyond this moment of 'uncovering' without erasing the 'boundaries' which provided its context and point in the first place.

18 For the ethnomethodologist to deny this is to engage in undercutting some of the fundamental premises of the ethnomethodological project (see also McHoul, 1982 and Pollner, 1987). It is to retain a residue of the classical fact/value dichotomy. Foot's position, on the other hand, does *not let go* of the fundamental premise; that the criteria for the application of moral judgements are routinely factual and intersubjectively given – *therefore* once elucidated, or found to be applicable, they have *some purchase* on us. Her position, however, runs into another problem: it fails to see that in any situation there may be a multiplicity of locally relevant criteria and a cross-cutting set of relevances, the systematic optionalities conventionally given that make possible diverse local characterisations of, and stances towards, specific matters. She therefore treats the is/ought move as one of logical necessity, rather than one which is praxiologically given, and conventionally grounded.

19 Consider how the practices (and ideas) of 'deconstruction' and 'dereification' have routinely been treated as 'subversive' and/or 'revolutionary', both in the history of ideas as well as in civic and political praxis. Consider also how notions of 'uncovering', 'exposing', 'digging up', 'revealing' etc. are part and parcel of the language of mundane moral and political practice.

References

Alexander, J. (1988). *Action and Its Environments*. Columbia, New York: University Press.

Althusser, L. (1971). *Lenin and Philosophy And Other Essays*. London: New Left Books.

(1976). *Essays in Self-Criticism*. Trans. G. Locke. London: New Left Books.

(1979). *For Marx*. London: Verso.

Anderson, D. (1978). Some Organisational Features in the Local Production of a Plausible Text. *Philosophy of the Social Sciences*, 8, pp. 113–35.

Anderson, R. J., Hughes, J. A. and Sharrock W. W. (1985). The Relationship between Ethnomethodology and Phenomenology. *Journal of the British Society for Phenomenology*, 16 (1), pp. 221–35.

(1988). The Methodology of Cartesian Economics: Some Thoughts on the Nature of Economic Theorising. *Journal of Interdisciplinary Economics*, 2, pp. 307–20.

(1989). *Working for Profit: The Social Organisation of Calculation in an Entrepreneurial Firm*. Aldershot: Avebury.

Anderson, R. J. and Sharrock, W. W. (1986). *The Ethnomethodologists*. London: Tavistock.

Anderson, R. J., Sharrock, W. W. and Hughes, J. A. (1987), The Division of Labour. Paper presented at the converence on *Action Analysis and Conversation Analysis*, Maison des Sciences de L'Homme, Paris, September.

Armstrong, D. M. (1968). *A Materialist Theory of the Mind*. London: Routledge and Kegan Paul.

Atkinson, J. M. and Heritage, J. C. (eds.) (1984). *Structures of Social Action: Studies in Conversation Analysis*. Cambridge: Cambridge University Press.

Atkinson, M. (1979). Prerequisites for Reference. In E. Ochs and E. Schieffelin (eds.), *Development Pragmatics*. Cambridge: Cambridge University Press.

(1982). *Explanations in the Study of Child Language Development*. Cambridge: Cambridge University Press.

Austin, J. L. A. (1955). *How To Do Things With Words*. The William James Lectures, Harvard; J. O. Urmston and M. Sbisa (eds.). Harvard University Press; 1981 edn, Oxford: Clarendon Press.

Baccus, H. D. (1986). Sociological Indication and the Visibility Criterion of Real World Social Theorising. In H. Garfinkel (ed.), *Ethnomethodological Studies of Work*. London: Routledge and Kegan Paul.

Baker, G. P. and Hacker, P. M. S. (1980). *Wittgenstein. Understanding and Meaning. An analytical Commentary on the 'Philosophical Investigations'*, Vol. 1. Oxford: Basil Blackwell.

(1984). *Language, Sense and Nonsense*. Oxford: Basil Blackwell.

Baldamus, W. (1976). *The Structure of Sociological Inference*. London: Martin Robertson.

Bar-Hillel, Y. (1954). Indexical Expressions. *Mind*, Vol. 63.

(1970). *Aspects of Language*. Jerusalem: Magnes Press, Hebrew University of Jerusalem.

Barnes, B. (1974). *Scientific Knowledge and Sociological Theory*. London: Routledge and Kegan Paul.

Barthes, R. (1975). *The Pleasure of the Text*. New York: Hill and Wang.

Barton, A. H. (1955). The Concept of Property Space in Social Research. In P. F. Lazarsfeld and M. Rosenberg (eds.), *The Language of Social Research*. New York: The Free Press, pp. 50–7.

Becker, H. S. (1963). *Outsiders*. New York: The Free Press.

(1967). Whose Side Are We On? *Social Problems*, 14 (3), pp. 239–47.

Bellack, A. A., Kliebard, H. M., Hyman, R. T. and Smith, S. C. (1966). *The Language of the Classroom*. New York: Teacher's College Press.

Bellman, B. (1975). *Village of Curers and Assassins: On the Production of Fala Kpelle Cosmological Categories*. The Hague: Mouton.

(1981). *The Language of Secrecy*. Unpublished monograph, Department of Sociology, University of California, San Diego.

Beloff, J. (1964). *The Existence of Mind*. New York: Citadel Press.

Benney, M. and Hughes, E. C. (1956). Of Sociology and the Interview. *American Journal of Sociology*, 62, pp. 137–42.

Benson, D. and Drew, P. (1978). Was There Firing on Sandy Row That Night?: Some Features of the Organisation of Disputes About Recorded Facts. *Sociological Inquiry*, 48, pp. 89–100.

Benson, D. and Hughes, J. (1983). *The Perspective of Ethnomethodology*. Harlow: Longman.

Bittner, E. (1973). Objectivity and Realism in Sociology. In G. Psathas (ed.), *Phenomenological Sociology*. New York: John Wiley, pp. 109–25.

(1977). Must We Say What We Mean? In P. F. Ostwald (ed.), *Communication and Social Interaction*. New York: Grube and Stratton.

Bjelic, D. and Lynch, M. (1991). The Work of a [Scientific] Demonstration: Respecifying Newton's and Goethe's Theories of Prismatic Color. In G. Watson and R. Seiler (eds.), *Not Everything is in the Text, Yet there is Nothing but the Text*. London: Sage.

Blackwell, K. (1981). The Early Wittgenstein and the Middle Russell. In I. Block (ed.), *Perspectives on the Philosophy of Wittgenstein*. Oxford: Basil Blackwell.

Blalock, H. (1982). *Conceptualization and Measurement in Social Science*. London: Sage.

(1984). *Basic Dilemmas in the Social Sciences*. London: Sage.

Block, N. J. and Dworkin, G. (eds.) (1976a). *The I.Q. Controversy*. New York: Pantheon Books, Random House.

(1976b). IQ, Heritability, and Inequality. In N. J. Block and G. Dworkin (eds.), *The I.Q. Controversy*. New York: Pantheon Books, Random House.

Blom, J. and Gumperz, J. J. (1972). Social Meaning in Linguistic Structures: Code-switching in Norway. In J. J. Gumperz and D. Hymes (eds.), *Directions in Sociolinguistics*. New York: Holt, Rinehart and Winston.

Bloor, D. (1976). *Knowledge and Social Imagery*. London: Routledge Direct Editions (forthcoming). Left- and Right-Wittgensteinians. In A. Pickering (ed.), *Science as Culture*. Chicago: University of Chicago Press.

Blum, A. and McHugh, P. (1986). *Self-Reflection in the Arts and Sciences*. Atlantic Highlands, New Jersey: Humanities Press.

Blumer, H. (1956). Sociological Analysis and the Variable. *American Sociological Review*, 21, pp. 683–90.

(1969). *Symbolic Interactionism: Perspective and Method*. Englewood Cliffs, New Jersey: Prentice-Hall, Inc.

Boden, D. and Zimmerman, D. H. (eds.) (forthcoming). *Talk and Social Structure*. Oxford: Polity.

Bogen, D. E. and Lynch, M. (1989). Taking Account of the Hostile Native: Plausible Deniability and the Production of Conventional History in the Iran-Contra Hearings. *Social Problems*, 36, pp. 197–224.

(in press). Social Critique and the Logic of Description: A Response to McHoul. *Journal of Pragmatics*.

Boole, G. (1948). *Mathematical Analysis of Logic*. (Originally Cambridge, 1847.) 1948 edn, Oxford: Oxford University Press.

Brannigan, A. and Lynch, M. (1987). On Bearing False Witness: Perjury and Credibility as Interactional Accomplishments. *Journal of Contemporary Ethnography*, Vol. 16, No. 2, pp. 115–46.

Brown, J. S., Collins, A. and Duguid, P. (1989). Situated Cognition and the Culture of Learning. *Educational Researcher*, 18 (1), 32–42 (January–February).

Burns, S. (1986). *An Ethnomethodological Case Study of Law Pedagogy in Civil Procedure*. Unpublished monograph, University of California, Los Angeles.

Button, G. (1987a). Answers as Interactional Products: Two Sequential Practices Used in Interviews. *Social Psychology Quarterly*, 50 (2), 160–71.

(1987b). Moving Out of Closings. In G. Button and J. R. E. Lee (eds.), *Talk and Social Organization*. Clevedon: Multilingual Matters, pp. 101–51.

Button, G. and Lee, J. R. E. (eds.) (1987). *Talk and Social Organization*. Clevedon: Multilingual Matters.

Callinicos, A. (1990). *Against Post-Modernism: A Marxist Critique*. Oxford: Polity.

Callon, M. (1986). Some Elements of a Sociology of Translation: Domestication of the Scallops and the Fishermen of St Brieuc Bay. In J. Law (ed.), *Power, Action, and Belief: A New Sociology of Knowledge?* London: Routledge and Kegan Paul, pp. 196–223.

Campbell, D. T. (1969). Prospective: Artifact and Control. In R. Rosenthal and R. Rosnow (eds.), *Artifact in Behavioural Research*. New York: Academic Press.

Cartwright, N. (1984). *How the Laws of Physics Lie*. Oxford: Oxford University Press.

Cavell, S. (1971). Must We Mean What We Say? In C. Lyas (ed.), *Philosophy and Linguistics*. New York: Macmillan.

Chomsky, N. (1957). *Syntactic Structures*. The Hague: Mouton.

(1964). *Aspects of the Theory of Syntax*. Cambridge, MA: MIT Press.

Churchill, L. (1966). Notes on Everyday Quantitative Practices. Paper delivered at Annual Meetings of the American Sociological Association (August).

Cicourel, A. V. (1964). *Method and Measurement in Sociology*. New York: The Free Press.

(1973). *Theory and Method in a Study of Argentine Fertility*. New York: Wiley.

(1976). *The Social Organisation of Juvenile Justice*. London: Heinemann.

Cicourel, A. V. and Kitsuse, J. I. (1963). *The Educational Decision-Makers*. New York: Bobbs Merrill.

Collins, H. M. (1982). Special Relativism – The Natural Attitude. *Social Studies of Science*, 12, pp. 299–305.

(1983). An Empirical Relativist Programme in the Sociology of Scientific Knowledge. In K. Knorr-Cetina and M. Mulkay (eds.), *Science Observed: Perspectives on the Social Reality of Science*. London and Beverly Hills: Sage, pp. 85–113.

Collins, H. M. and Cox, G. (1976). Recovering Relativity: Did Prophecy Fail? *Social Studies of Science*, 6, pp. 423–44.

(1977). Relativity Revisited: Mrs Keech, a Suitable Case for Special Treatment? *Social Studies of Science*, 7, pp. 372–80.

Cook, J. (1978). Whorf's Linguistic Relativism. *Philosophical Investigations*. Illinois: Decatur.

Costner, H. (1972). Theory, Deduction and Rules of Correspondence. In H. M. Blalock and A. Blalock (eds.), *Methodology in Social Research*. New York: McGraw-Hill.

Coulter, J. (1973a). Language and the Conceptualization of Meaning. *Sociology*, Vol. 7.

(1973b). *Approaches to Insanity: A Philosophical and Sociological Study*. London: Martin Robertson. New York: John Wiley.

(1974). Decontextualized Meanings: Current Approaches to Verstehende Investigations, revised and expanded version of Decontextualized Meanings: Current Approaches to Verstehende Investigations, *The Sociological Review*, 19 (3), 1971. In A. Truzzi (ed.), *Verstehen: Subjective Understanding in the Social Sciences*. New York: Addison-Wesley.

(1975). Perceptual Accounts and Interpretive Asymmetries. *Sociology*, Vol. 9.

(1979a). *The Social Construction of Mind: Studies in Ethnomethodology and Linguistic Philosophy*. London: Rowman and Littlefield.

(1979b). Beliefs and Practical Understanding. In G. Psathas (ed.), *Everyday Language*. New York: Irvington Press.

(1983a). Contingent and *A Priori* Structures in Sequential Analysis. *Human Studies*, 6 (4), pp. 361–76.

(1983b). *Rethinking Cognitive Theory*. London: Macmillan.

(1984). On Comprehension and 'Mental Representation'. In N. Gilbert and C. Heath (eds.), *Social Action and Artificial Intelligence*. Nottingham: Gower Press.

(1989). *Mind in Action*. Oxford: Polity Press.

(1990). Elementary Properties of Argument Sequences. In G. Psathas (ed.), *Interaction Competence*. Washington DC: University Press of America.

Craib, I. (1984). *Modern Social Theory Today: From Parsons to Habermas*. Brighton: Wheatsheaf Books.

Davis, J. A. (1971). *Elementary Survey Analysis*. Englewood Cliffs: Prentice-Hall.

Deleuze, G. and Guattari, F. (1987). *A Thousand Plateaus: Capitalism and Schizophrenia*. Minneapolis: University of Minnesota Press.

Dennett, D. (1978). *Brainstorms*. Vermont: Bradford Books.

Derrida, J. (1976). *Of Grammatology*. Trans. G. Spivak. Baltimore: Johns Hopkins University.

(1978). *Writing and Difference*. Trans. A. Bass. London: Routledge and Kegan Paul.

Dilman, I. (1984). *Quine on Ontology, Necessity and Experience: A Philosophical Critique*. Albany: SUNY Press.

Donagan, A. (1977). *The Theory of Morality*. Chicago/London: University of Chicago Press.

Donnellan, K. (1971). Reference and Definite Description. In D. Steinberg and L. A. Jakobovits (eds.), *Semantics*. Cambridge: Cambridge University Press.

Drew, P. (1978). Accusations: The Occasioned Use of Members' Knowledge of 'Religious Geography' in Describing Events. *Sociology*, 12, pp. 1–22.

(1984). Speakers' 'Reportings' in Invitation Sequences. In J. M. Atkinson and J. C. Heritage (eds.), *Structures of Social Action: Studies in Conversation Analysis*. Cambridge: Cambridge University Press, pp. 129–51.

Duncan, O. D. (1984). *Notes on Social Measurement: Historical and Critical*. New York: Russell Sage Foundation.

Durkheim, E. (1952). *Suicide*. Trans. J. Spaulding and G. Simpson. London: Routledge and Kegan Paul.

(1963). *Primitive Classification*. Trans. P. R. Needham. London: Cohen and West; Chicago: University of Chicago Press.

(1964). *The Rules of Sociological Method*. New York: Free Press.

Eccles, J. C. (1953). *The Neurophysiological Basis of Mind*. Oxford: Oxford University Press.

Eccles, J. C. and Popper, K. R. (1977). *The Self and Its Brain*. New York: Springer International.

Edgerton, S. Y. (1975). *The Renaissance Rediscovery of Linear Perspective*. New York: Harper and Row.

Edie, J. (1987). *Edmund Husserl's Phenomenology*. Indiana University Press.

Eglin, P. (1979). Resolving Reality Disjunctures on Telegraph Avenue: A Study of Practical Reasoning. *Canadian Journal of Sociology*, 4, pp. 359–77.

(1980). Talk and Taxonomy. *Pragmatics and Beyond Monograph*, No. 8.

Eglin, T. (1974). Introduction to a Hermeneutics of the Occult: Alchemy. In E. Tiryakian (ed.), *On the Margin of the Visible: Sociology, the Esoteric, and the Occult*. New York: Wiley.

Ervin-Tripp, S. (1972). On Sociolinguistic Rules: Alternation and Co-occurrence. In J. J. Gumperz and D. Hymes (eds.), *Directions in Sociolinguistics*. New York: Holt, Rinehart and Winston.

Eysenck, H. J. (1973). *The Inequality of Man*. London: Maurice Temple-Smith.

Feigl, M. (1958). The 'Mental' and the 'Physical'. In H. Feigl, M. Scriven and G. Maxwell (eds.), *Minnesota Studies in the Philosophy of Science, Vol. 2*. Minneapolis: University of Minnesota Press, pp. 370–497.

Feyerabend, P. (1975). *Against Method: Outline of an Anarchistic Theory of Knowledge*. London: New Left Books.

(1988). Knowledge and the Role of Theories. *Philosophy of the Social Sciences*, 18, pp. 157–78.

(1987). *Farewell to Reason*. London: Verso.

Firth, J. R. (1957). The Techniques of Semantics. In *Papers in Linguistics 1934–1951*. Oxford: Oxford University Press.

Fishman, J. A. (1964). Language Maintenance and Language Shifts as Fields of Inquiry. *Linguistics*, 9, pp. 32–70.

(1965). Who Speaks What Language to Whom and When. *La Linguistique*, 2, pp. 67–88.

(1972). Domains and the Relationship Between Micro- and Macro-Sociolinguistics. In J. J. Gumperz and D. Hymes (eds.), *Directions in Sociolinguistics*. New York: Holt, Rinehart and Winston.

Fodor, J. A. (1975). *The Language of Thought*. New York: Thomas Cromwell.

(1981). Methodological Solipsism Considered as a Research Strategy in Cognitive Psychology. In J. A. Fodor, *Representations*. Cambridge, MA: M.I.T. Press.

Fodor, J. A. and Katz, J. J. (1963). The Structure of a Semantic Theory. *Language*, 39.

Foot, P. (1958). Moral Arguments. *Mind*, 67, pp. 502–13.

(1958–9). Moral Beliefs. *Proceedings of the Aristotelian Society*, 59, pp. 83–104.

Foucault, M. (1972). *The Archaeology of Knowledge*. Trans. A. M. Sheridan-Smith. New York: Harper Colophon.

(1979). *Discipline and Punishment: The Birth of the Prison*. Trans. A. M. Sheridan-Smith. New York: Vintage/Random House.

Gane, M. (1988). *On Durkheim's Rules of Sociological Method*. London: Routledge.

Garfinkel, H. (1962). Thoughts on How Members Count Members. Unpublished research note, Department of Sociology, University of California, Los Angeles.

(1963). A Conception of, and Experiments with, 'Trust' as a Condition of Stable Concerted Actions. In O. J. Harvey (ed.), *Motivation and Social Interaction*. New York: Ronald Press, pp. 187–238.

(1967). *Studies in Ethnomethodology*. Englewood Cliffs: Prentice-Hall.

Garfinkel, H., Livingston, E., Lynch, M., MacBeth, D. and Robillard, A. B. (1989). Respecifying the Natural Sciences as Discovering Sciences of Practical Action, I & II: doing so ethnographically by administering a schedule of contingencies in discussions with laboratory scientists and by hanging around their laboratories. Unpublished paper, Department of Sociology, University of California, Los Angeles.

Garfinkel, H., Lynch, M. and Livingston, E. (1981). The Work of a Discovering Science Construed With Materials From the Optically Discovered Pulsar. *Philosophy of the Social Sciences*, 11, pp. 131–58.

Garfinkel, H. and Sacks, H. (1970). On Formal Structures of Practical Actions. In J. C. McKinney and E. A. Tiryakian (eds.), *Theoretical Sociology: Perspectives and Developments*. New York: Appleton-Century-Crofts, pp. 337–66.

Geertz, C. (1973). *The Interpretation of Cultures*. New York: Basic Books.

Gellner, E. (1975). Ethnomethodology: the Re-enchantment Industry or the Californian Way of Subjectivity. *Philosophy of the Social Sciences*, 5, pp. 431–50.

(1985). *Relativism and the Social Sciences*. Cambridge: Cambridge University Press.

Gert, B. (1970). *The Moral Rules: A New Rational Foundation for Morality*. New York: Harper and Row Press.

Gewirth, A. (1978). *Reason and Morality*. Chicago: University of Chicago Press.

Giddens, A. (1976). *New Rules of Sociological Method: A Positive Critique of Interpretive Sociologies*. London: Hutchinson.

Giddens, A. and Turner, J. (eds.) (1987) *Social Theory Today*. Oxford: Polity.

Gilbert, G. N. and Mulkay, M. (1984). *Opening Pandora's Box: A Sociological Analysis of Scientists' Discourse*. Cambridge: Cambridge University Press.

Goffman, E. (1974). *Frame Analysis: An Essay on the Organisation of Experience*. New York: Harper and Row.

(1981). *Forms of Talk*. Oxford: Basil Blackwell.

Goldman, L. (1969). *The Human Sciences and Philosophy*. London: Cape.

Goldthorpe, J. (1983). Women and Class Analysis: In Defence of the Conventional View. *Sociology*, 17 (4), pp. 465–88.

(1984). Women and Class Analysis: A Reply to the Replies. *Sociology*, 18 (2), pp. 491–9.

Goodenough, W. H. (1967). Cultural Anthropology and Linguistics. *Georgetown University Monograph Series on Language and Linguistics*, 9, pp. 167–73.

Goodwin, C. (1987). Forgetfulness as an Interactive Resource. *Social Psychology Quarterly*, 50 (2), pp. 115–31.

Gouldner, A. (1968). The Sociologist as Partisan: Sociology and the Welfare State. *The American Sociologist*, May issue, pp. 103–16.

(1970). *The Coming Crisis of Western Society*. London: Heinemann.

Greenfield, L. (1972). Situational Measures of Normative Language Views in Relation To Person, Place and Topic among Puerto Rican Bilinguals. In J. Fishman (ed.), *Advances in the Sociology of Language, Vol. 2*. The Hague: Mouton.

Grice, H. P. (1975). Logic and Conversation. In P. Cole and J. L. Morgan (eds.), *Syntax and Semantics 3: Speech Acts*. New York: Academic Press, pp. 41–58.

(1978). Further Notes on Logic and Conversation. In P. Cole (ed.), *Syntax and Semantics 9: Pragmatics*. New York: Academic Press, pp. 113–28.

Gumperz, J. J. (1982). *Discourse Strategies*. Cambridge: Cambridge University Press.

Gurwitsch, A. (1964). *The Field of Consciousness*. Pittsburgh: Duquesne University Press.

Habermas, J. (1979). *Communication and the Evolution of Society*. Boston: Beacon Press.

Hacker, P. M. S. (1987). *Appearance and Reality*. Oxford: Basil Blackwell.

Hacking, I. (1983). *Representing and Intervening*. Cambridge: Cambridge University Press.

Halfpenny, P. (1982). *Positivism and Sociology: Explaining Social Life*. London: George Allen and Unwin.

Hannan, M. T. (1971). *Aggregation and Disaggregation in Sociology*. Lexington: D. C. Heath.

Hare, R. M. (1952). *The Language of Morals*. Oxford: Oxford University Press.

(1963). *Freedom and Reason*. Oxford: Oxford University Press.

Harré, R. (1972). *The Philosophies of Science*. Oxford: Oxford University Press.

Harris, R. (1981). *The Language Myth*. London: Duckworth.

Heap. J. L. (1986a). *Sociality and Cognition in Collaborative Computer Writings*. Unpublished paper prepared for discussion at the University of Michigan School of Education Conference on Literacy and Culture in Educational Settings, 7–9 March, February.

(1986b). *Collaborative Practices During Computer Writing in a First Grade Classroom*. Unpublished paper prepared for presentation at the annual meetings of the American Educational Research Association, San Francisco, March.

Heidegger, M. (1967). *What is a Thing?* Chicago: Henry Regnery.

(1977). *The Question Concerning Technology and Other Essays*. Trans. W. Lovitt. New York: Harper and Row.

Helling, I. K. (1984). A. Schutz and F. Kaufmann: Sociology Between Science and Interpretation. *Human Studies*, 7, p. 141–61.

Heritage, J. C. (1984). *Garfinkel and Ethnomethodology*. Cambridge: Polity Press.

Hill, J. H. (1988). Language, Culture and World Views. *Linguistics: The Cambridge Survey Vol. IV*. Cambridge: Cambridge University Press.

Hill, R. J. and Crittenden, K. S. (eds.) (1968). *Proceedings of the Purdue Symposium on Ethnomethodology*. Institute Monograph Series, Number 1, Purdue, IN: Institute for the Study of Social Change, Department of Sociology, Purdue University.

Hodges, A. (1984). *Alan Turing: The Enigma*. New York: Touchstone, Simon and Schuster.

Hoijer, H. (1953). The Relation of Language to Culture. In *Anthropology Today*, Chicago: University of Chicago Press.

Hollis, M. and Lukes, S. (eds.) (1982). *Rationality and Relativism*. Oxford: Basil Blackwell.

Husserl, E. (1970a). *Logical Investigations*, Vol. I. Trans, J. N. Findlay. London: Routledge and Kegan Paul.

(1970b). *Logical Investigations*, Vol. II. Trans. J. N. Findlay. London: Routledge and Kegan Paul.

(1970c). *The Crisis of European Sciences and Transcendental Phenomenology*. Trans. D. Carr. Evanston: Northwestern University Press.

Hymes, D. (1972). On Communicative Competence. In J. B. Pride and J. Holmes (eds.), *Sociolinguistics*. Harmondsworth: Penguin Books.

(1974). *Foundations in Sociolinguistics*. University of Pennsylvania Press.

James, S. (1984). *The Content of Social Explanation*. Cambridge: Cambridge University Press.

Jayyusi, L. (1984). *Categorization and the Moral Order*. London: Routledge and Kegan Paul.

(1988). Toward a Socio-Logic of the Film Text. *Semiotica*, 68 (3/4), pp. 271–96.

(1989). Conventionality and Difference. Paper presented to the 1st D.A.R.G. Conference on Understanding Language Use in Everyday Life, 23–6 August, Calgary, Canada.

Jefferson, G. (1972). Side Sequences. In D. N. Sudnow (ed.), *Studies in Social Interaction*. New York: Free Press, pp. 294–338.

(1978). Sequential Aspects of Storytelling in Conversation. In J. Schenkein (ed.), *Studies in the Organization of Conversational Interaction*. New York: Academic Press, pp. 219–48.

(1979). A Technique For Inviting Laughter and Its Subsequent Acceptance/Declination. In G. Psathas (ed.), *Everyday Language: Studies in Ethnomethodology*. New York: Irvington.

(1988a). Notes on a Possible Metric which Provides for a 'Standard Maxim' Silence of Approximately One Second in Conversation. In D. Roger and P. Bull (eds.), *Conversation: An Interdisciplinary Perspective*. Clevedon: Multilingual Matters.

(1988b). On the Sequential Organization of Troubles Talk in Ordinary Conversation. *Social Problems*, 35 (4), pp. 418–42.

(1990). List Construction As a Task and Interactional Resource. In G. Psathas (ed.), *Interactional Competence*. Washington, DC: University Press of America.

Jensen, A. (1969). How Much Can We Boost I.Q. and Scholastic Achievement? *Harvard Educational Review*, 39, pp. 1–123.

Kahn, R. L. and Cannell, C. F. (1952). *The Dynamics of Interviewing: Theory, Techniques and Cases*. New York: Wiley, Chapman and Hall.

Kaufmann, F. (1944). *The Methodology of the Social Sciences*. New Jersey: Humanities Press.

Kearney, M. (1984). *World View*. Novato: Chandler and Sharp.

Kempson, R. (1975). *Presuppositions and Delimitation of Semantics*. Cambridge: Cambridge University Press.

Kenny, A. (1970). Cartesian Privacy. In G. Pitcher (ed.), *Wittgenstein: The Philosophical Investigations*. London: Macmillan.

Kneale, W. and Kneale, M. (1962). *The Development of Logic*. Oxford: Oxford University Press.

Knorr-Cetina, K. and Mulkay, M. (eds.) (1983). *Science Observed: Perspectives on the Social Reality of Science*. London: Sage.

Kovesi, J. (1967). *Moral Notions*. London: Routledge and Kegan Paul.

Koyre, A. (1986). *Metaphysics and Measurement*. London: Chapman Hall.

Krenz, C. and Sax, G. (1986). What Quantitative Research is and Why it Doesn't Work. *American Behavioral Scientist*, 30, pp. 58–69.

Kuhn, T. S. (1962). *The Structure of Scientific Revolutions*. Chicago: Chicago University Press.

  (1977). The Function of Measurement in Modern Physical Science. In T. S. Kuhn (ed.), *The Essential Tension: Selected Studies in Scientific Tradition and Change*, pp. 178–224. Originally published in *Isis*, 52 (1961), 161–93.

Kyburg, H. E. (1984). *Theory and Measurement*. Cambridge: Cambridge University Press.

Langmuir, I. (1968). Pathological Science. Transcriber and editor R. N. Hall. Report No. 68-C-035, General Electric Research and Development Centre.

Lash, S. (1990). *Sociology of Postmodernism*. London and New York: Routledge.

Latour, B. (1987). *Science in Action*. Cambridge, MA: Harvard University Press.

  (1988). *The Pastuerization of France*. Trans. A. Sheridan and J. Law. Cambridge, MA: Harvard University Press.

Lave, J. (1988). *Cognition in Practice*. Cambridge: Cambridge University Press.

Lazarsfeld, P. F. (1955). Interpretation of Statistical Relations as a Research Operation. In P. F. Lazarsfeld and M. Rosenberg (eds.), *The Language of Social Research*. New York: The Free Press.

  (1958). Evidence and Inference in Social Research. *Daedalus*, Fall.

Lazarsfeld, P. F. and Barton, A. H. (1951). Qualitative Measurement in the Social Sciences. In D. Lerner and H. Lasswell (eds.), *The Policy Sciences: Recent Developments in Scope and Method*. Stanford: Stanford University Press.

  (1955). Some Relevant Principles of Questionnaire Classification. In P. Lazarsfeld and M. Rosenberg (eds.), *The Language of Social Research*. New York: The Free Press.

Lazarsfeld, P. F. and Menzel, H. (1969). On the Relation Between Individual and Collective Properties. In A. Etzioni (ed.), *Complex Organizations: A Sociological Reader*, 2nd edn, New York: Holt, Rinehart and Winston.

Lazarsfeld, P. F. and Rosenberg, M. (eds.) (1955). *The Language of Social Research*. New York: The Free Press.

Lee, J. R. E. (1987). Prologue: Talking Organisation. In G. Button and J. R. E. Lee (eds.), *Talk and Social Organisation*. Clevedon: Multilingual Matters.

Lelland, J. K. (ed.) (1958). *Disease, Life and Man*. Stanford: Stanford University Press.

Levinson, S. C. (1983). *Pragmatics*. Cambridge: Cambridge University Press.

Lévi-Strauss, C. (1963). *Structural Anthropology*. New York: Basic Books.

Liberman, K. (1986). *Understanding Interaction in Central Australia: An Ethnomethodological Study of Australian Aboriginal People*. London and New York: Routledge and Kegan Paul.

Lieberson, S. (1985). *Making it Count: The Improvement of Social Research and Theory*. Berkeley: University of California Press.

Littlewood, B. (1983). Review of the Public and the Private, E. Gamarnito *et al.*, *Sociology*, 17 (4), pp. 587–9.

Livingston, E. (1986). *The Ethnomethodological Foundations of Mathematics*. London and New York: Routledge and Kegan Paul.

(1987). *Making Sense of Ethnomethodology*. London: Routledge and Kegan Paul.

Louch, A. R. (1966). *Explanation and Human Action*. Oxford: Basil Blackwell.

Lukacs, G. (1971). *History and Class Consciousness: Studies in Marxist Dialectics*. London: Merlin.

Lynch, M. (1984). Turning Up Signs in Neurobehavioral Diagnosis. *Symbolic Interaction*, 7 (1), pp. 67–86.

(1985). *Art and Artifact in Laboratory Science: A Study of Shop Work and Shop Talk in a Laboratory*. London: Routledge and Kegan Paul.

(1988a). Alfred Schutz and the Sociology of Science. In L. Embree (ed.), *Worldly Phenomenology: The Influence of Alfred Schutz on Human Science*. Washington, DC: Centre for Advanced Research in Phenomenology and University Press of America.

(1988b). Sacrifice and the Transformation of the Animal Body into a Scientific Object: Laboratory Culture and Ritual Practice in the Neurosciences. *Social Studies of Science*, 18, pp. 265–89.

(1988c). The Externalized Retina: Selection and Mathematization in the Visual Documentation of Objects in the Life Sciences. *Human Studies*, 11, pp. 201–34. Reprinted in *Representation in Scientific Practice*, M. Lynch and S. Woolgar (eds.), Cambridge, MA: The MIT Press, 1990.

Lynch, M., Livingston, E. and Garfinkel, H. (1983). Temporal Order in Laboratory Work. In K. Knorr-Cetina and M. Mulkay (eds.), *Science Observed: Perspectives on the Social Study of Science*. London and Beverly Hills: Sage.

Lyotard, J. F. (1979). *La Condition Postmoderne*. Paris: Minuit.

Macbeth, D. (1987). *Management's Work: The Social Organization of Order and Troubles in Secondary Classrooms*. Unpublished doctoral dissertation, School of Education, University of California, Berkeley.

MacIntyre, A. (1970a). Is Understanding Religion Compatible with Believing in it? In B. R. Wilson (ed.), *Rationality*. Oxford: Basil Blackwell, pp. 62–78.

(1970b). The Idea of Social Science. In B. R. Wilson (ed.), *Rationality*. Oxford: Basil Blackwell, pp. 112–30.

(1978). *Against the Self-Images of the Age: Essays on Ideology and Philosophy*. Notre Dame: University of Notre Dame Press.

(1981). *After Virtue: A Study in Moral Theory*. London: Gerald Duckworth and Co.; Notre Dame: University of Notre Dame Press.

Mackay, R. W. (1974a). Conceptions of Children and Models of Socialization. In R. Turner (ed.), *Ethnomethodology*. Harmondsworth: Penguin, pp. 180–93.

(1974b). Standardized Tests: Objective/Objectified Measures of 'Competence'. In A. V. Cicourel *et al.*, *Language Use and School Performance*. New York: Academic Press, pp. 218–47.

Malcolm, N. (1977). *Memory and Mind*. Ithaca, New York: Cornell University Press.

(1978). Thinking. In E. Leinfellner *et al.* (eds.), *Wittgenstein and His Impact on Contemporary Thought*. (Proceedings of the Second International Wittgenstein Symposium), Vienna: Holder-Pichler-Tempsky.

Malotki, E. (1983). *Hopi Time*. Berlin: Mouton.

Mannheim, K. (1936). *Ideology and Utopia*. New York: Harcourt, Brace and World.

Margolis, J. (1986). *Pragmatism Without Foundations*. Oxford: Blackwell.

Marx, K. (1965). *The German Ideology*. London: Lawrence Wishart.

McCall, G. and Simmonds, J. L. (1969). *Issues in Participant Observation*. Reading, MS: Addison–Wesley.

McCawley, J. D. (1981). *Everything that Linguistics Have Always Wanted to Know about Logic*. Chicago: University of Chicago Press.

McHoul, A. W. (1982). *Telling How Texts Talk: Essays on Reading and Ethnomethodology*. London: Routledge and Kegan Paul.

(1988). Language and the Sociology of Mind: A Critical Introduction to the Work of Jeff Coulter. *Journal of Pragmatics*, 12, pp. 229–86.

McHugh, P., Raffel, S., Foss, D. C. and Blum, A. F. (1974). *On the Beginning of Social Inquiry*. London: Routledge and Kegan Paul.

McLendon, S. (1977). Cultural Presupposition and Assertion of Information in Eastern Pomo and Russian Narrative. In M. Saville-Troike (ed.), *Linguistics and Anthropology*. Washington: Georgetown University Press.

Merleau-Ponty, M. (1962). *Phenomenology of Perception*. Trans. C. Smith. London: Routledge and Kegan Paul.

Meyer, L. (1985). *Making a Scene: Probing the Structure of Understanding in Sibling Interaction*. Unpublished manuscript, University of California, Berkeley.

(1988). 'It Was No Trouble': Achieving Communicative Competence in a Second Language. In R. Scarcella, E. Anderson and S. Krashin (eds.), *Development of Competence in a Second Language*. Newbury House.

Moerman, M. (1974). Achieving Ethnicity. In R. Turner (ed.), *Ethnomethodology*. Harmondsworth: Penguin Books.

Moerman, M. and Sacks, H. (1988). On 'Understanding' in the Analysis of Natural Conversation. In M. Moerman, *Talking Culture: Ethnography and Conversation Analysis*. Philadelphia, PA: University of Pennsylvania Press, pp. 180–6.

Morrison, K. L. (1976). *Reader's Work: Devices for Achieving Pedagogic Events in Textual Materials for Readers as Novices to Sociology*. Doctoral dissertation, Department of Sociology, York University, Toronto.

(1981). Some Properties of 'Telling-Order Designs' in Didactic Inquiry. *Philosophy of the Social Sciences*, 11, pp. 245–62.

(1990). Some Researchable Recurrences in Disciplinary Scientific Inquiry. In D. Helm, W. T. Anderson, A. J. Meehan and A. W. Rawls (eds.), *The Interactional Order: New Directions in the Study of Social Order*. New York: Irvington.

Newell, A. and Simon, H. A. (1972). *Human Problem Solving*. New Jersey: Prentice-Hall.

Ochs, E. and Schieffelin, B. (eds.) (1979). *Developmental Pragmatics*. Cambridge: Cambridge University Press.

Palincsar, A. S. (1989). Less Charted Waters. *Educational Research*, 18 (4), 5–7, (May).

Palmer, A. (1987). Cognitivism and Computer Simulation. In A. Costall and A. Still (eds.), *Cognitive Psychology in Question*. New York: St Martin's Press.

Parsons, T. (1937). *The Structure of Social Action*. New York: McGraw-Hill.

(1951). *The Social System*. London: Tavistock.

Pawson, R. (1989). *Measure for Measure*. London: Routledge and Kegan Paul.

Pears, D. (1971). *Wittgenstein*. London: Fontana/Collins.

Pearson, K. (1911). *The Grammar of Science*, 3rd rev. edn. London: Adam and Charles Black.

Phillips, D. (1971). *Knowledge from What?* Chicago: Rand McNally.

Pitkin, H. F. (1972). *Wittgenstein and Justice: On the Significance of Ludwig Wittgenstein for Social and Political Thought*. California: University of California Press.

Place, U. T. (1956). Is Consciousness a Brain Process? *British Journal of Psychology*, 47, pp. 44–51.

(1988). Thirty Years On – Is Consciousness Still a Brain Process? *Australasian Journal of Philosophy*, 66 (2).

Pollner, M. (1975). The Very Coinage of Your Brain: The Anatomy of Reality Disjunctures. *Philosophy of the Social Sciences*, Vol. 5.

(1979). Explicative Transactions: Making and Managing Meaning in a Traffic Court. In G. Psathas (ed.), *Everyday Language: Studies in Ethnomethodology*. New York: Irvington, pp. 227–55.

(1987). *Mundane Reason: Reality in Everyday and Sociological Discourse*. Cambridge: Cambridge University Press.

Pomerantz, A. M. (1978a). Attributions of Responsibility: Blamings. *Sociology*, 12, pp. 115–33.

(1978b). Compliment Responses: Notes on the Co-operation of Multiple Constraints. In J. Schenkein (ed.), *Studies in the Organization of Conversational Interaction*. New York: Academic Press, pp. 79–112.

(1984a). Giving a Source or Basis: The Practice in Conversation of Telling 'How I Know'. *Journal of Pragmatics*, Vol. 8, pp. 607–25.

(1984b). Agreeing and Disagreeing with Assessments: Some Features of Preferred/ Dispreferred Turn Shapes. In J. M. Atkinson and J. C. Heritage (eds.), *Structures of Social Action: Studies in Conversation Analysis*. Cambridge: Cambridge University Press, pp. 57–101.

(1987). Descriptions in Legal Settings. In G. Button and J. R. Lee (eds.), *Talk and Social Organization*. Clevedon: Multilingual Matters, pp. 226–43.

Popper, K. (1945). *The Open Society and Its Enemies*. London: Routledge and Kegan Paul.

(1957). *The Poverty of Historicism*. London: Routledge and Kegan Paul.

(1959). *The Logic of Scientific Discovery*. London: Hutchinson.

(1972). *Objective Knowledge*. Oxford: Clarendon Press.

Psathas, G. (ed.) (1979a). *Everyday Language: Studies in Ethnomethodology*. New York: Irvington.

(1979b). Organizational Features of Direction Maps. In G. Psathas (ed.), *Everyday Language: Studies in Ethnomethodology*. New York: Irvington.

(ed.) (1990). *Interaction Competence*. Washington, DC: University Press of America.

(forthcoming). In D. Boden and D. H. Zimmerman (eds.), *Talk and Social Structure*. Oxford: Polity Press.

Quine, W. van Orman. (1960). *Word and Object*. Cambridge, MA: MIT Press.

(1961). *From A Logical Point of View: Logico-Philosophical Essays*. New York: Harper and Row.

(1966). *The Ways of Paradox and Other Essays*. New York: Random House.

(1981). *Theories and Things*. Cambridge, MA: Harvard University Press.

(1990). *Pursuit of Truth*. Cambridge, MA: Harvard University Press.

Ramazanoglu, C. (1989). *Feminism and the Contradictions of Oppression*. London: Routledge.

Robillard, A. B. and Pack, C. (1976–82). Research and didactic video tapes, occasional papers, in-house memoranda, tape and video recorded rounds and medical and clinic conferences, and lectures. Department of Human Development, Michigan State University, East Lansing, Michigan.

Robillard, A. B. and colleagues. (1983). *Pacific Island Mental Health Counselor Training Program: A Final Program Narrative and Evaluation Report*. Honolulu: Department of Psychiatry.

(1984). *Pacific Islander Alternative Mental Health Services: A Project Summary Report*, Honolulu: Social Science Research Institute.

(1986a). Mental Health Services in Micronesia: A Case of Superficial Development. In C. E. Hill (ed.), *Current Health Policy Issues and Alternatives: An Applied Social Science Perspective*. Athens, Georgia: University of Georgia Press.

(1986b). Community-Based Primary Health Care: Reality of Mystification? In T. S. Osteria and J. Y. Okamura (eds.), *Participatory Approaches to Development: Experiences in the Phillipines*. Manilla, Phillipines: De La Salle University.

(1987). *Pacific Islander Mental Health Research Center*. Grant Application, Department of Mental and Human Services, Public Health Service.

Robinson, W. S. (1950). Ecological Correlations and the Behaviour of Individuals. *American Sociological Review*, 15, pp. 351–7.

Roediger, H. (1980). Memory Metaphors in Cognitive Psychology. *Memory and Cognition*, 8, p. 238.

Rosch, E. (1974). Linguistic Relativity. In A. Silverstein (ed.), *Human Communications*. New York: Wiley.

Rose, E. (1960). The English Record on Natural Sociology. *American Sociological Review*, 25, pp. 383–92.

Rosenberg, M. (1968). *The Logic of Survey Research*. New York: Basic Books.

Ross, W. D. (ed.) (1958). *Topica et Sophistici Elenchi by Aristotle*. Oxford: Oxford University Press.

Roth, D. R. (1974). Intelligence Testing as a Social Activity. In A. V. Cicourel *et al.* (eds.), *Language Use and School Performance*. New York: Academic Press, pp. 143–217.

Russell, B. (1956). *Portraits from Memory*. London: George Allen and Unwin.

(1959). *My Philosophical Development*. London: Allen and Unwin.

(1968). The Philosophy of Logical Atomism (1918). In *B. Russell, Logic and Knowledge, Essays 1901–1950*, ed. R. C. Marsh. London: Allen and Unwin.

Ryle, G. (1949). *The Concept of Mind*. Chicago: University of Chicago Press; 1984, Harmondsworth: Penguin.

(1954). *Dilemmas*. Cambridge: Cambridge University Press.

(1971). *Collected Papers*, Vol. 2. London: Hutchinson.

Sacks, H. (unpublished). *Aspects of the Sequential Organisation of Conversation*. Department of Sociology, University of California, Irvine.

(1963). Sociological Description. *Berkeley Journal of Science*. Vol. 1.

(1964–72). Unpublished transcribed lectures, University of California Los Angeles and Irvine. Transcribed by Gail Jefferson.

(1966). The Search for Help: No One to Turn to. Doctoral Dissertation, University of California, Berkeley (Department of Sociology).

(1967). The Search for Help: No One to Turn to. In E. Schneidman (ed.), *Essays in Self Destruction*. New York: Science House, pp. 203–33.

(1972a). An Initial Investigation of the Usability of Conversational Data for Doing Sociology. In D. N. Sudnow (ed.), *Studies in Social Interaction*. New York: Free Press, pp. 31–74.

(1972b). On the Analyzability of Stories by Children. In J. J. Gumperz and D. Hymes (eds.), *Directions in Sociolinguistics: The Ethnography of Communication*. New York: Holt, Rinehart and Winston, pp. 329–45.

(1975). Everyone Has to Lie. In B. Blount and M. Sanches (eds.), *Socio-Cultural Dimensions of Language Use*. New York: Academic Press.

(1979). Hotrodder: A Revolution Category. In G. Psathas (ed.), *Everyday Language*. New York: Irvington Press.

(1980). Button, Button, Who's Got the Button? *Sociological Inquiry*, 50 (3/4), pp. 318–27.

(1984a). On Doing 'Being Ordinary'. In J. M. Atkinson and J. Heritage (eds.), *Structures of Social Action: Studies in Conversation Analysis*. Cambridge: Cambridge University Press, pp. 413–39.

(1984b). Notes on Methodology. In J. Atkinson and J. Heritage (eds.), *Structures of Social Action: Studies in Conversation Analysis*. Cambridge: Cambridge University Press.

(1987). On the Preference for Agreement and Contiguity in Sequences in Conversation. In G. Button and J. R. E. Lee (eds.), *Talk and Social Organization*. Clevedon: Multilingual Matters, pp. 54–69.

(1988/89). On Members' Measurement Systems. *Research on Language and Social Interaction*, 22.

(1989). 1964–1965 Lectures. With a memoir by E. A. Schegloff. *Human Studies*, 12 (3–4).

Sacks, H. and Schegloff, E. A. (1979). Two Preferences in the Organization of Reference To Persons In Conversation and their Interaction. In G. Psathas (ed.), *Everyday Language: Studies in Ethnomethodology*. New York: Irvington Publishers, pp. 15–21.

Sacks, H., Schegloff, E. A. and Jefferson, G. (1974). A Simplest Systematics for the Organization of Turn-taking in Conversation. *Language*, 50 (4), pp. 696–735.

Sapir, E. (1949). The Status of Linguistics as a Science. In *The Selected Writings of Edward Sapir*. University of California Press.

Sartre, Jean-Paul. (1957). *The Transcendence of the Ego: An Existentialist Theory of*

Consciousness. Trans. F. Williams and R. Kirkpatrick. New York: Farrar, Straus and Giroux.

Saussure, F. de. (1916). *Course in General Linguistics*. Trans. W. Baskin (1966). Berkeley, California: McGraw-Hill.

Schegloff, E. A. (1963). Toward a Reading of Psychiatric Theory. *Berkeley Journal of Sociology*, Vol. 1.

(1968). Sequencing in Conversational Openings. *American Anthropologist*, 70, pp. 1075–1095.

(1972). Notes on a Conversational Practice: Formulating Place. In *Studies in Social Interaction*, D. Sudnow (ed.), New York: Free Press, pp. 75–119.

(1987). Between Macro and Micro: Contexts and Other Connections. In J. Alexander, B. Giesen, R. Munch, and N. Smelser (eds.), *The Micro–Macro Link*. Berkeley and Los Angeles: University of California Press, pp. 207–34.

(forthcoming). Reflections on Talk and Social Structure. In D. Boden and D. H. Zimmerman (eds.), *Talk and Social Structure*. Oxford: Polity.

Schegloff, E. A., Jefferson, G. and Sacks, H. (1977). The Preference for Self-correction in the Organization of Repair in Conversation. *Language*, 53 (2), pp. 361–82.

Schegloff, E. A. and Sacks, H. (1973). Opening Up Closings. *Semiotica*, 7, pp. 289–327.

(1979). Two Preferences for the Organization of Reference to Persons and their Interaction in G. Psathas (ed.), *Everyday Language*. New York: Irvington Press.

Scheiffelin, B. and Ochs, E. (eds.) (1987). *Language Socialisation Across Cultures*. Cambridge: Cambridge University Press.

Schenkein, J. (ed.) (1978). *Studies in the Organisation of Conversational Interaction*. New York: Academic Press.

Schlick, M. (1959). The Turning Point in Philosophy. In A. J. Ayer (ed.), *Logical Positivism*. Illinois: Free Press, 1959.

Schrecker, F. (in press). Doing a Chemical Experiment: The Practices of Chemistry Students in a Student Laboratory in Quantitative Analysis. In H. Garfinkel (ed.), *Ethnomethodological Studies of Work in the Discovering Sciences*. London: Routledge.

Schutz, A. (1943). The Problem of Rationality in the Social World. *Economica*, 10, 130–49. Reprinted in A. Schutz, *Collected Papers II*, pp. 64–90. The Hague: Martinus Nijhoff, 1964.

(1953). Common-Sense and Scientific Interpretation of Human action. *Philosophy and Phenomenological Research*, 14, pp. 1–38. Reprinted in A. Schutz, *Collected Papers I*, pp. 3–47. The Hague: Martinus Nijhoff, 1962.

(1962). *Collected Papers I*. The Hague: Martinus Nijhoff.

(1964). *Collected Papers II*. The Hague: Martinus Nijhoff.

(1966). *Collected Papers III*. The Hague: Martinus Nijhoff.

Schwartz, H. (1976). On Recognising Mistakes: A Case of Practical Reasoning in Psychotherapy. *Philosophy of the Social Sciences*, 6, pp. 55–73.

(1978). Data – Who Needs It? *Analytic Sociology*, 2 (1).

Schwartz, H. and Jacobs, J. (1979). *Qualitative Sociology: A Method to the Madness*. New York: The Free Press.

Scribner, S. (1984). Studying Working Intelligence. In B. Rogoff and J. Lave (eds.),

Everyday Cognition: Its Development in Social Context. Cambridge, MA: Harvard University Press, pp. 9–40.

Searle, J. (1969). *Speech Acts*. Cambridge: Cambridge University Press.

Shanker, S. G. (1987a). Wittgenstein versus Turing on the Nature of Church's Thesis. *Notre Dame Journal of Formal Logic*, 23 (4).

(1987b). Artificial Intelligence at the Crossroads. In B. Bloomfield (ed.), *Questions in Artificial Intelligence*. London: Croom Helm.

(forthcoming). Review of 'Mindwaves'. *Human Studies*.

Sharrock, W. W. (1974). On Owning Knowledge. In R. Turner (ed.), *Ethnomethodology*. Harmondsworth: Penguin.

Sharrock, W. W. and Anderson, R. J. (1981). The Demise of the Native. *Human Studies*, 15 (2).

(1986a). *The Ethnomethodologists*. Chichester: Ellis Harwood Ltd.

(1986b). But a Machine Surely Cannot Think. Unpublished paper, Department of Sociology, University of Manchester.

(1987). The Definition of Alternatives: Some Sources of Confusion in Interdisciplinary Discussion. In G. Button and J. R. E. Lee (eds.), *Talk and Social Organisation*. Clevedon: Multilingual Matters.

Sharrock, W. W. and Katz, B. A. (1978). Playing with Other Minds. *Analytic Sociology* 1 (2).

Silverman, D. and Torode, B. (1980). *The Material Word: Some Theories of Language and its Limits*. London: Routledge and Kegan Paul.

Silverstein, M. (1976a). Hierarchy of Features and Ergativity. In R. M. W. Dixon (ed.), *Grammatical Categories in Australian Languages*. New Jersey: Humanities Press.

(1976b). Shifters, Linguistic Categories and Cultural Description. In K. H. Basso and H. A. Selby (eds.), *Meaning in Anthropology*. Albuquerque: University of New Mexico Press.

(1979). The Functional Stratification of Language and Ontogenesis. In J. V. Wertsch (ed.), *Culture, Communication and Cognition: Vygotskian Perspectives*. Cambridge: Cambridge University Press.

Sinclair, J. H. and Coulthard, R. M. (1975). *Towards an Analysis of Discourse*. London: Oxford University Press.

Smart, J. J. C. (1959). Sensations and Brain Processes. *Philosophical Review*, 68, pp. 141–56.

Smith, D. E. (1974). The Social Construction of Documentary Reality. *Sociological Inquiry*, 44 (4), pp. 257–68.

(1978). K. is Mentally Ill: The Anatomy of a Factual Account. *Sociology*, 12, pp. 23–53.

(1987). *The Everyday World as Problematic*. Boston: Northeastern University Press.

Spector, M. and Kitsuse, J. I. (1977). *Constructing Social Problems*. Menlo Park, California: Cummings.

Stanworth, M. (1974). Women and Class Analysis: A Reply to John Goldthorpe. *Sociology*, 18 (2), pp. 159–70.

Steinberg, D. D. and Jakobovits, L. A. (eds.) (1971). *Semantics: An Interdisciplinary Reader*. Cambridge: Cambridge University Press.

Stevens, S. S. (1946). On the Theory of Scales. *Science*, 103, pp. 677–80.

Stevenson, C. L. (1945). *Ethics and Language*. New Haven: Yale University Press.

Stich, S. (1983). *From Folk Psychology to Cognitive Science: The Case Against Belief*. Cambridge, MA: MIT Press.

Styazhkin, N. I. (1969). *History of Mathematical Logic from Leibniz to Peano*. Cambridge, MA: MIT Press.

Suchman, L. A. (1987). *Plans and Situated Actions: The Problem of Human Machine Communication*. Cambridge: Cambridge University Press.

Sudnow, D. (ed.) (1972a). *Studies in Social Interaction*. New York: Free Press.

(1972b). Temporal Parameters of Interpersonal Observation. In D. Sudnow (ed.), *Studies in Social Interaction*. New York: The Free Press, pp. 259–79.

(1978). *Ways of the Hand*. Cambridge, MA: Harvard University Press.

(1979). *Talk's Body: A Meditation Between Two Keyboards*. Harmondsworth: Penguin.

Taylor, C. (1985). *Philosophy and the Human Sciences*. Cambridge: Cambridge University Press.

Torgerson, W. (1958). *Theory and Method of Scaling*. New York: Wiley.

Turing, A. (1950). Computing Machinery and Intelligence. *Mind*.

Turner, R. (1970). Words, Utterances and Activities. In J. D. Douglas (ed.), *Understanding Everyday Life: Toward the Reconstruction of Sociological Knowledge*. Chicago: Aldine Publishing Co., pp. 169–87.

(ed.) (1974). *Ethnomethodology*. Harmondsworth: Penguin.

Turner, S. P. (1986). *The Search for a Methodology of Social Science: Durkheim, Weber, and the Nineteenth-Century Problem of Cause, Probability, and Action*. Dordrecht: D. Reidel.

(1987). Underdetermination and the Problem of Statistical Sociology. *Sociological Theory*, 5.

Twer, S. (1972). Tactics for Determining Persons' Resources for Depicting, Contriving, and Describing Behavioral Episodes. In D. Sudnow (ed.), *Studies in Social Interaction*. New York: The Free Press, pp. 339–66.

Tyler, S. A. (ed.) (1969). *Cognitive Anthropology*. New York: Holt, Rinehart and Winston.

(1984). The Vision Quest in the West, or What the Mind's Eye Sees. *Journal of Anthropological Research*, 40, pp. 23–40.

Viberg, A. (1983). The Verbs of Perception: A Typological Study. *Linguistics*, 21, pp. 123–62.

Voeglin, C. G., Voeglin, F. M. and Jeanne, L. M. (1979). Hopi Semantics. In A. Ortig (ed.), *Handbook of North American Indians Vol. 9. Southwest*. Smithsonian Institute.

Waismann, F. (1965). Verifiability. In A. G. N. Flew (ed.), *Logic and Language*, 1st and 2nd series. New York: Doubleday.

Walby, S. (1989a). Theorising Patriarchy. *Sociology*, 23 (2), pp. 312–34.

(1989b). *Women, Theory and Society: From Private to Public Patriarchy*. Oxford: Blackwell.

Wang, H. (1974). *From Mathematics to Philosophy*. London: Routledge and Kegan Paul.

Warnock, G. J. (1971). *The Object of Morality*. London: Methuen.

Waters, M. (1989). Patriarchy and Viriarchy: An Exploration and Reconstruction of Concepts of Masculine Domination. *Sociology*, 23 (2), pp. 193–211.

Watson, D. R. (1975). The Interactional Uses of Pronouns. *Pragmatics Microfiche*. Fiche No. 3.

(1978). Categorization, Authorization and Blame-Negotiation in Conversation. *Sociology*, 12, pp. 105–13.

(1981). Conversational and Organizational Uses of Proper Names for Persons. In P. Atkinson and C. Heath (eds.), *Medical Work: Realities and Routines*. Aldershot: Gower Press.

(1983). The Presentation of Victim and Offender in Discourse: The Case of Police Interrogations and Interviews. *Victimology*, 8 (1/2), pp. 31–52.

Weber, M. (1946). Science as a Vocation. In H. Gerth and C. W. Mills (eds.), *From Max Weber: Essays in Sociology*. Oxford: Oxford University Press.

(1947). *The Theory of Social and Economic Organisations*. Trans. A. M. Henderson and T. Parsons. Oxford: Oxford University Press.

(1949). The Methodology of the Social Sciences. Trans. E. Shills and Finch. New York: The Free Press.

Whitehead, Alfred N. (1925). *Science and the Modern World*. New York: Macmillan.

Wieder, D. L. (1970). On Meaning By Rule. In J. D. Douglas (ed.), *Understanding Everyday Life: Towards the Reconstruction of Sociological Knowledge*. London: Routledge and Kegan Paul.

(1974). *Language and Social Reality*. The Hague: Mouton.

Wiles, P. (1971). Criminal Statistics and Sociological Explanations of Crime. In P. Wiles and W. G. Carson (eds.), *The Sociology of Crime and Delinquency in Britain*, Vol. I. London: Martin Robertson.

Willer, D. (1984). Analysis and composition as theoretic procedures. *Journal of Mathematical Sociology*, 10, pp. 241–69.

Williams, M. (1985). Wittgenstein's Rejection of Scientific Psychology. *Journal for the Theory of Social Behavior*, 15 (2).

Wilson, B. R. (ed.) (1970). *Rationality*. Oxford: Basil Blackwell.

Wilson, T. P. (1971). Normative and Interpretive Paradigms in Sociology. In J. D. Douglas (ed.), *Understanding Everyday Life: Towards the Reconstruction of Sociological Knowledge*. London: Routledge and Kegan Paul.

(1984). On the role of Mathematics in the Social Sciences. *Journal of Mathematical Sociology*, 10, pp. 221–39.

Winch, P. (1958). *The Idea of a Social Science and its Relation to Philosophy*. London: Routledge and Kegan Paul.

(1970). Understanding a Primitive Society. In B. R. Wilson (ed.), *Rationality*. Oxford: Basil Blackwell, pp. 78–111.

(1972). *Ethics and Action*. London: Routledge and Kegan Paul.

Wittgenstein, L. (1961). *Notebooks 1914–1915*. Eds. G. H. von Wright and G. E. M. Anscombe, trans. G. E. M. Anscombe. Oxford: Basil Blackwell.

(1967). *Zettel*. Eds. G. H. von Wright and G. E. M. Anscombe, trans. G. E. M. Anscombe. Oxford: Basil Blackwell.

(1968). *Philosophical Investigations*. Oxford: Basil Blackwell.

(1974). *On Certainty*. Oxford: Basil Blackwell.

(1978). *Remarks on the Foundations of Mathematics*. Eds. G. H. von Wright, R. Rhees and G. E. M. Anscombe, trans. G. E. M. Anscombe, 3rd edn Oxford: Basil Blackwell.

(1980). *Remarks on the Philosophy of Psychology, Volume I.* Oxford: Basil Blackwell.

Woolgar, S. (ed.) (1988). *Knowledge and Reflexivity: New Frontiers in the Sociology of Knowledge.* London: Sage.

Zerubavel, E. (1985). *The Seven Day Circle: The History and Meaning of the Week.* New York: The Free Press.

Zimmerman, D. H. (1974). Fact as a Practical Accomplishment. In R. Turner (ed.), *Ethnomethodology.* Harmondsworth: Penguin, pp. 128–43.

Zimmerman, D. and Pollner, M. (1973). The Everyday World as Phenomenon. In J. D. Douglas (ed.), *Understanding Everyday Life: Towards the Reconstruction of Sociological Knowledge.* London: Routledge and Kegan Paul.

Index of names

Adam, C., 194n
Alberti, 81
Alexander, J., 10, 11, 18n, 252, 266
Althusser, L., 58, 137, 172, 252
Anderson, D., 174n, 252
Anderson, E., 262
Anderson, R. J., 9n, 15, **51–76**, 125, 130,
    133n, 135n, 174, 180, 194n, 195n, 245,
    252, 267
Anderson, W. T., 262
Anscombe, G. E. M., 269
Aristotle, 20, 21, 38
Armstrong, D. M., 177, 194n, 252
Atkinson, J. M., 38, 252, 256, 263, 265
Atkinson, M., 201, 202, 252
Atkinson, P., 269
Aulus Gellius, 21
Austin, J. L. A., 30, 31, 32, 37, 38, 48, 232,
    233–4, 252
Ayer, A. J., 23, 24, 266

Baccus, H. D., 119, 120, 122, 123, 125, 126,
    252
Baker, G. P., 22, 29, 34, 195n, 252
Baldamus, W., 134n, 253
Bane, 195n
Barber, B., 18n
Bar-Hillel, Y., 34, 253
Barnes, B., 76n, 253
Barthes, R., 225n, 253
Barton, A. H., 113, 115, 120, 121, 253, 260
Baskin, W., 266
Bass, A., 256
Basso, K. H., 267
Becker, H. S., 138, 148, 230, 253
Bellack, A. A., 220, 253
Bellman, B., 15, 253
Beloff, J., 177, 253
Benney, M., 122, 253
Benson, D., 9n, 80, 95, **109–35**, 160, 172n,
    215, 226n, 253
Bereiter, C., 195n
Bittner, E., 36, 59, 67–8, 69, 70, 73, 246, 253

Bjelic, D., 15, 98, 108n, 253
Blackwell, K., 50n, 253
Blalock, A., 255
Blalock, H., 85, 114, 116, 120, 133n, 253,
    255
Block, N. J., 193–4, 195n, 253
Blom, J., 204, 253
Bloomfield, B., 267
Bloor, D., 76n, 79, 254
Blount, B., 265
Blum, A. F., 67, 254, 262
Blumer, H., 109, 172n, 254
Boas, F., 212
Boden, D., 172n, 254, 266
Bogen, D. E., 95, 190, 247, 248, 254
Boole, G., 22, 254
Brannigan, A., 189, 254
Brown, J. S., 91, 254
Brucke, 177
Brunelleschi, 81
Bull, P., 256
Burns, S., 15, 254
Button, G., **1–9**, 38, 135n, **137–75**, 226, 237,
    242, 254, 261, 263, 265, 267

Callinicos, A., 3–4, 254
Callon, M., 107n, 254
Campbell, D. T., 110, 254
Cannell, C. F., 122
Carnap, R., 23, 24
Carr, D., 259
Carson, W. G., 269
Cartwright, N., 133n, 254
Cavell, S., 26, 254
Cherry, C., 13
Chomsky, N., 25, 83, 126, 198, 204, 254
Churchill, L., 106n, 254
Cicourel, A. V., 83, 84, 85, 86, 120, 121, 122,
    133n, 135n, 173n, 195n, 254, 255, 262,
    264
Cole, P., 258
Collins, A., 254
Collins, H. M., 57, 255

271

Subject index

action(s), social, 5, 7, 8, 10, 11, 15, 33, 63, 137–75, 156–60; and language, 202, 211; and the natural attitude, 55, 56; and speech, 202; as endogenous logic, 38–9, 55, 97; concrete/analytic distinction, 12, 13, 14, 18n; intelligence in, 190–2; practical action, 11, 12, 14, 16, 18, 35; reflexively accountable, 6; studies of practical action, 14–15; The Structure of Social Action, 10, 11, 12, 14, 18; unit act, 12, 100

actor(s), 7, 8, 60, 84, 117, 123, 176, 228, 137–75; and social structure, 137–42, 154–5; as reader, 150, 174n; as theorist, 142–56; in context, 156–66; point of view of, 68, 69, 137, 138, 156, 165 204–5

ad hoc practices, 87, 88, 126

adjacency pairs, 37

agreement, 105n

Alberti's optical treatise, 81

American Sociological Association, 10, 80

anatomists, 136n

anthropology, 6, 91, 130; cognitive, 50n, 197, 200, 201, 212–17; *see also* language

artificial intelligence, 195n

biology, 110

Boolean Algebra, 22

breaching experiments, 109, 236

British Sociological Association, 2, 3

calculus ratiocinator, 22, 26; *see also* logic

Cartesianism, 30; *see also* epistemology and cognition

causal modelling, 116

coding practices, 86–8, 98–9, 121, 123

cognition, 7, 8, 176–95; Cartesian version of, 176–9, 184, 185, 186; cognitivism, 198–9; computational model of, 176–81, 194n; ethnomethodological studies of, 189–90; praxiological approach to, 188–90; *see also* rule-following; language, and intelligence

common sense, 54–61, 88, 120, 122, 123, 124, 126, 129; and science, 56, 57, 58–9, 60, 61; and common-sense reasoning, 85, 86, 129

communicative competence, 204

communicative praxis, 20, 23, 26–34, 35; *see also* logic, and language

constraint, 154–6

constructive analysis, 12, 13–14, 16

conversation analysis, 8, 11, 14, 16, 17, 35, 38, 132, 242–3

counting, 92, 101–4, 113–14, 127–8 *see also* measurement

culture, *see* language

description, 127, 131, 158–9, 174n, 175n, 214–16, 219, 222, 233, 237, 240, 250n, 251n; literal, 117

determinism, 250n

discourse, analysis of, 207, 217–23; practices of, 90; *see also* language

economics, 6, 133n

epistemology, 5, 6, 7, 18, 33, 51–76; Cartesian method of systematic doubt, 56, 57, 58–9, 60, 61; objectivism, 53–4; philosophical scepticism, 51, 52, 66, 67; sociological scepticism, 66, 67, 174n, 175n

etcetera problem, 127

ethnic origins survey, 118–19

ethnomethodology: and social reality, 52, 67; and the respecification of the human sciences, 1–9, *see also* respecification; as science, 139–42; ethnomethodological indifference, 16, 83, 86–91, 94–5, 97, 105, 247–8; evidence and inference in, 126–32; proto-ethnomethodology, 83–6; Purdue symposium on, 5, 88–90; rigour in, 132; the character of ethnomethodological studies, 16–17

evidence, 109–36

experiences, 65, 70, 71, 72, 73, 75, 160

276